BUSINESS SCHOOL ESSAYS

T. Nick Zinni

Cover designed by Cover Designer

Scenario names and characters either are products of the author's imagination or are used fictitiously. Any resemblance to actual persons, living or dead, events, or locales is entirely coincidental.

T. Nick Zinni
Visit my website at TNickZinni.WordPress.com

Printed in the United States of America

First Printing: December 2018
Kindle Direct Publishing

ISBN-13 978-1-7908236-2-8

Thanks to all the mentors who took the time to teach me their crafts.
And to my Lord, who granted me the ability to learn from them.

PREFACE

Business programs at the Master's and Doctorate levels require intensive reading, research, and writing. This book is a compendium of that work from fields in organizational psychology, statistics, human resources, and consultancy. Although names in scenarios have been changed, all statistical data, analysis, and applications are real findings.

The publishing of this material is in hopes that students looking for assistance in writing their own papers, as well as business professionals alike, each finding inspiration and direction towards their successes. Below are comments from doctorate-level reviewers for your validation.

Best wishes and good luck in your endeavors!

T. Nick Zinni

"It was a pleasure reading your papers. Your writing is excellent. Very Solid..."
Shanan Farmer, Ph.D., Harvard National Security Fellow

"Well-written and well-researched. You've done a good job!"
Jan Jones, Ph.D., Therapy Resource Associates

"Great work... overall."
Jimmy Brown, Ph.D., Lead Consultant, J. Brown Group

"Excellent work. You have captured the essence of this..."
Candi Karsjens, MBA, CAGS

CONTENTS

PART ONE:
BUSINESS ETHICS

1.1 FRIEDMAN V. DRUCKER

Milton Friedman and Peter Drucker reverently stood in opposition to one another in what the role of business is with concerns to ethical and social responsibilities. Although each provided convincing arguments for their time, Friedman could not foresee the impact that business actions would have on societal controls and the changes these controls would impose, in turn, upon business.

Drucker attempted prediction through historical analyses and began the framework for what today is the culmination of business as active members within society and the expected roles of behavior and the consequences of violating public trust. By reviewing the perspectives of these two schools of thought, we can then understand the evolution of training future leaders, the monitoring and control business actions, and the modern expectations of business within society.

MILTON FRIEDMAN

Milton Friedman was a traditionalist who argued that managers are subject to the expectations of his/her principals, which is to earn maximized profits for them. Philanthropic endeavors, such as giving money to the poor, and other social responsibilities could be donated from the individual's resources, but conflicts with principals' interests when allocated from business resources. Friedman believed that giving resources beyond those allocated through taxation was a form of socialism and burdened (empowered) managers beyond the scope of their purpose (Friedman, 1970).

Milton Friedman further argued this empowerment provides the manager with the same legislative authority to decide "tax rates", to impose and collect "taxes", and to decide expenditures and allocations of those collections in the form of price increases, contributory inflation, and other social controls. Friedman contemplated these practices directly oppose the manager's obligation to earn maximum profits for the owners/shareholders. Friedman concluded, "There are no 'social' responsibilities in any sense other than the shared values and responsibilities of the individuals... and the voluntary groups they form". However, he recognized that he was forced to acknowledge compliance with social controls upon the business (laws) is required for success in a free enterprise market system.

PETER DRUCKER

Peter Drucker was a learned historian and believed managers are limited by the scope of the culture their business is located. These limitations were rooted in historical religious contexts of Confucianism and Christianity, of recorded reasoning behind past events, and of the needs of society; particularly the business society. Accepting that ethics embrace conventions for behavior, Drucker initially rejected the concept that business could be subject to rules of ethical behavior because of its virtual existence. He reasoned, "There is only one ethics, one set of rules of morality, one code, that of individual behavior in which the same rules apply to every person alike" (Drucker, 1981, p. 19).

Continuing this line of thought Drucker claimed that since business is composed of individuals who cannot consent upon the singularity of the application of these rules, then business (as an entity) cannot be bound by ethical responsibilities.

This traditional point-of-view failed to answer questions of cultural differences in definitions of what constitutes the mores and offences for acceptable behaviors for Drucker. For instance, in Japan retired government employees are encouraged to become "counselors" for business whereas in the United States, the same practice is considered unethical. Do to this conflict, Drucker proposed to strike a balance between individual ethics and social responsibility to subordinates utilizing the casuistry method of requiring leaders to place the needs others before their own; however, he believed the outcomes gain political motivation rather than ethical consideration if used (Drucker, 1981).

Peter Drucker also considered the ethics of prudence, wherein leaders are not only held accountable for subordinates, but also lead by example in their business and personal lives. Under this aesthetic perception, the individual questions their own behaviors for wrongness, rather than goodness of action or legality. Prudence therefore fails to sustain ethical definition and congruence with social responsibility as "appearances may mean more than substance".

Scrutiny shifts then to interdependence which dictates that all parties (managers, employees, citizens, etc.) are obligated mutually through harmony and trust to reach goals by providing the needs of the other. For example, capitalists provide jobs to proletarians, who in turn, provide labor and services for the employer. From a business ethics analysis, violations occur when a manager fails to provide entitlements to the respective beneficiary. This contrasts the mutual relationship requirement by placing all burdens upon the business, even if the other party fails on their part.

To illustrate, if an employer fails to pay a worker, then an ethics violation has occurred; but if the employee performed poorly, no violation. Although interdependence serves as Drucker's strongest argument for today's definition of ethical and social responsibilities, he ascertained four key elements (learned by combining perspectives) be present:

1) a clear definition of relationships,
2) universal rules of conduct,
3) focus on correct behaviors rather than wrongdoing, and
4) ensure that behaviors compensate relationships equally.

COMPARATIVE ANALYSIS

Friedman and Drucker each acknowledged the fundamental responsibility of managers is to earn profits for their principals. The distinction is Friedman draws a defined line here to furthering social responsibilities (philanthropic) for business where Drucker continued upon an historical foundation for pluralism. This abruptness exposes weaknesses within Friedman's argument for other types of responsibilities, such as environmental effects caused by business operations, and ignoring the changing nature of the rules of conduct. Using Friedman's definition, an environmental catastrophe (such as an oil spill) reverts responsibility to the sitting administrator rather than the company as a whole if there were no laws dictating corrective action procedures.

Peter Drucker's holistic approach encompasses the reality of changing needs for business and societal expectations and recognizes "social responsibilities" are shared by business, managers, societies served, and continue to evolve based upon situational needs of the conglomerate. This perspective leaves room for entitlement mentalities to develop and acknowledges changes in definitions due to rights movements without limiting innovation.

CONCLUSIONS

According to Archie Carroll (2009), expectations of business through social responsibility has evolved similarly over the last few decades to the arguments of Peter Drucker, with less support in the communities for the traditionalist views of Milton Friedman. Most business courses now incorporate ethical discussions, typically referring to the millennial scandals that led to the Sarbanes-Oxley Act of 2002, in effort to train upcoming leaders to think in terms of "right" behaviors.

Rather than simply concentrate on maximizing profits for shareholders as Friedman would have us do, students are now taught to balance the triple bottom line concept of sustainability through economic, social, and environmental aspects (Carroll & Buchholtz, 2009). Clearly this is begun by acknowledging Drucker's four key elements of ethical and social responsibilities, although not a complete framework.

Carroll (and others since) continued this work by developing a component model of Corporate Social Responsibility containing economics, legal, ethical, and philanthropic considerations. Friedman's claim consisted of the first two components in that business should be profitable and obey all laws, but lacked by insistence that avoidance of questionable practices and giving back to society were individual requirements rather than corporate expectancies.

Given these perspectives and historical changes through events, we can now conclude that to be successful, business must willingly take on social responsibilities using ethical practices in order to achieve sustainability (long life), profitability, and reduce governmental interference. To be ethical is not simply to avoid wrongdoing as a child would do to avoid punishment, but to make well thought-out decisions of "rightness" and to act accordingly upon those decisions. Social responsibility then is best defined by Joseph McGuire (1963) as "The idea... that the corporation has not only economic and legal obligations, but also certain responsibilities to society which extend beyond these obligations".

* * *

1.2 COMMUNITY AND ENVIRONMENTAL IMPACT OF WAL-MART

In the world of consumerism Wal-Mart stands out as a favorite one-stop retailer for low and middle-income shoppers due to the value-added experience of Everyday Low Pricing (EDLP). On the flipside, smaller retailers cringe at the news that any one of the Wal-Mart holdings is moving into their domain and employ a variety of blocking tactics in the name of self-preservation.

On occasion, political maneuvers successfully discourage this expansion based upon current research for the time, but this trend may be changing as Wal-Mart leadership is learning to adapt for the sake of reaching growth goals. The sections that follow discuss this transition through internal and external impact analysis upon the environment and social boundaries then offer alternative suggestions for entrepreneurial survival.

COMMONALITIES AND DIFFERENCES

Commonly, the major opponents to Wal-Mart localization include claims that the retail giant forces smaller entrepreneurial ventures to close, that jobs are lost, that tax revenues dissipate, that the local economy will suffer, and that in the pursuit of growth Wal-Mart will demonstrate a lack of social responsibility by ignoring secondary stakeholders. The responsibilities of cultural integration (rather than acculturation or "*californication*" – the American Northwest term for 'forced ethnocentric change of a foreign culture to be more like one's own'); acts of philanthropy, such as support for children's athletic activities; and payment of living wages fill courtroom and chamber testimonies as lacking in benefit from Wal-Mart presence. Journals, newspapers, and business textbooks share this complainant theme with nearly as many methods for measuring the desired outcome, however several also overlook reasonable explanations when searching for causal implications.

Until 2007, Hicks (2007) disputed that analytic techniques had not matured well enough to accurately measure effects of a move by Wal-Mart into a new region. Citing absence of controls for underlying conditions and selection bias when making statistical comparisons during literature search reviews, Hicks argued most studies ignored regions without a Wal-Mart facility or failed to calculate probable effects of Wal-Mart not choosing the specific location. This is especially important when recognizing Wal-Mart does not enter areas in economic decline or with populations of less than 5,000 persons.

Amidst the myriad of statistical formulas proposed by some researchers (e.g., Gielens et.al., 2008) to measure Wal-Mart's acceptance, perhaps the easiest method is to observe market trends; specifically share pricing. Strategic management courses in business schools emphasize the assumption market prices accurately reflect what the market will bear. In other words, if Wal-Mart displeases investors with social irresponsibility, then this information will immediately be revealed in the form of lowered stock prices. This was the case when Arthur Anderson was indicted for accounting fraud during the Enron Scandal, causing the accounting firm to close its doors.

The major problem behind this theory is that Wal-Mart is so large and financially powerful that incidents affecting only singular stores may not have a notable effect upon the stock price of the entire corporation. For example, until a new site location is approved for construction by local authorities, this expansion information does not have to be made public by Wal-Mart (unless previously disclosed of course), so if the plan fails, stock investors may be unaware of the situation and market prices do not fluctuate in response.

Due to fears arising from American community 'experiences' with job losses in combination with Wal-Mart's inability to acculturate in Germany, residents in England became concerned with the announcement Wal-Mart had purchased the country's third largest grocery chain, Asda. Positive and negative effects were assessed (Gielens et.al., 2008) including increased channel productivity and adverse effects on performance for local retailers; however, some uncertainty into employment realities at the process level could not be legitimized due to lack of previous examples of the situation per the culture.

In Hicks (2007) study of county-level effects in Ohio on jobs and public assistance programs, he was able to determine (compensating for shortcomings discussed earlier) that Wal-Mart only has an initial effect on third-party retail jobs when it moves into a new community, but overall a negligible effect (-.02%) after five years. Kmart, Sears, and Home Depot experienced similar results (Basker, 2007).

A common complaint that Wal-Mart exploits property tax abatements, tax credits, and other discounts (Basker, 2007; Hicks, 2007) is justified in that these incentives are available to any business, albeit at lower dollar amounts due to volume. But these benefits are passed on to primary stakeholders in the form of lower prices.

Wal-Mart falls between a production and a managerial view of the firm in that it demonstrates through actions that its primary stakeholders are the owners and customers, with suppliers as secondary. The distinction is pivotal on the Everyday Low Price strategy. Essentially, the owners profit when the customers are enabled through volume purchasing and suppliers are required to conform their operations to meet this goal (Lai, Cheng, & Tang, 2010; Carroll & Buchholtz, 2009).

This prerequisite for doing business with Wal-Mart removes suppliers as primary social stakeholders in Wal-Mart and, in many cases, transforms Wal-Mart into a primary social stakeholder in the supplier's business. In other words, the dependency developed upon Wal-Mart for sustainability due to socialized controls by these businesses creates a direct stake by suppliers. Unfortunately for smaller mom-and-pop's retailers, this level of strategic stakeholding is not probable.

Buchholtz and Carroll (2009) emphasized preference for the stakeholder synthesis approach "because it holds that business does not have moral responsibilities to stakeholders but that they should not be seen as part of a fiduciary obligation". To simplify, this approach to ethical recognition implies that duty is owed to primary stakeholders first (traditional view) while performing ethically when interacting with others (modern view). This helps to explain, in part, why Wal-Mart chooses not to become involved with traditional community philanthropic activities, such as sponsoring little league baseball teams.

These kinds of expenditures violate the Everyday Low Price philosophy and cost-cutting strategy metaphorically given to every customer at every purchase. This break-under expectation more is not visually obvious given Wal-Mart is the largest retailer in the world and provides to everyone, rather than specific groups or individuals.

ENVIRONMENTAL ACTIVITIES

Wal-Mart engages with suppliers at the transactional level and forms partnerships through the current green initiative. Literature is disparate to claims against Wal-Mart for anti-environmental activity concerns, however, in contrast there is an abundance of research and activity results on behalf of the retailing monarch. According to Lai, Cheng, and Tang (2010), "Wal-Mart... estimates it could save around 3,800 trees and 1,000 barrels of oil with an economic [sic] savings of $2.4 million by reducing unnecessary packaging of its private-label toy products".

Environmentally, this statement exhibits social concerns for environmental preservation as well as reduction in manufacturing costs - in line with Wal-Mart's growth and cost reduction priorities. Other process developments include the purchase of diesel-electric trucks (rather than diesel only). This is the same technology used in General Electric built locomotives and has attributed to a 25% improvement in fuel economy, $75 million in fuel cost savings, and 400,000 tons of carbon dioxide emissions annually (Lai, Cheng, & Tang, 2010).

Other than transportation and packaging, green initiates implemented involve product design, procurement, and cooperating with non-government organizations (Plambeck, 2007) in a movement toward stakeholder symbiosis. For example, Wal-Mart partnered with Samsung Electronics of America by coordinating the "Samsung Recycling Direct" program that allows Wal-Mart to act as intermediary between Samsung and the public to recycle Samsung electronic devices free of charge, in addition to some Wal-Mart private-label brands.

Similarly, P&G adapted its manufacturing facilities on request of Wal-Mart to produce only concentrated detergents saving 430 million gallons of water, 80 million pounds of plastic, and 125 million pounds of cardboard between 2007 and 2010. Furthermore, more than 60,000 suppliers had been asked to take part in measuring their carbon footprint.

CONCLUSIONS

It is well known that Wal-Mart is the most sued corporation in the world, the most studied by academics, and probably the most misunderstood. Although isolated instances of unethical behavior occurred at various times in the company's history, it is not evident these events are practiced company-wide. Reviewing competitor prices is common and openly advertised by other dominant companies such as Sears (a K Mart subsidiary and Wal-Mart competitor) with in-store kiosks, Allstate Insurance, and Progressive Indemnity and Casualty displaying online rate comparisons.

Wal-Mart developed a renowned customer-focused culture and strategic operations methodology that like McDonalds, serves as a model for other retailers striving for efficiencies and cost-cutting (Plambeck, 2007; Basker, 2007). Unlike other types of retailing chains, Wal-Mart tends to meet fevering opposition when entering new geographic markets. Rarely is published a report claiming Home Depot was denied welcome when a local lumberyard and/or hardware store faces closure.

Claims of job losses remain unsubstantiated when smaller entrepreneurs close shop in response to inabilities to effectively compete with the price leader as do self-righteous exhortations that Wal-Mart fails to reinvest in the communities served. Lower prices are passed to every customer; environmental innovations reduce costs, waste, and damages; and savings acquired through tax cuts are equally available to all retailers wishing to consume them.

Gielens, Van de Gucht, Steenkamp, and Dekimpe (2008) offered incumbent small retailers the following proactive strategies for survival when a Wal-Mart store enters the local market:

1. If using a low price strategy, consider switching to a hi-lo strategy to render price comparisons with Wal-Mart more difficult.
2. Reduce overlap in product lines (Target and Home Depot use specialized, niche, etc.).
3. Offer depth in existing product lines as Wal-Mart prefers a variety of lines rather than choices in specific product models.

Although unconventional by traditional business standards, Wal-Mart understands who its stakeholders are and strives to maintain their positioning. According to Dependency Theory, Wal-Mart's exertion of power to force suppliers into compliance for sustainability may have ethical implications needing further study as indicative by the corporation's failure to acculturate into Germany. ✱✱✱

1.3 ETHICS OF INTERVIEWS

Little recent research has been conducted in terms of the types of acceptable personal questions that may be asked of applicants during the staffing processes of recruitment and selection from a global-ethical standpoint. The primary difficulty with establishment of standardized ethical norms lies in cultural differences not only between countries, but also across multicultural perimeters. For instance, in the United States, looking the person one is speaking to in the eye is an expected norm for verbal communication in the majority of the country, however many Native Americans find the behavior intrusive to personal space and a social taboo related to traditional cultural beliefs ("attempting to peer into one's soul").

Foregoing the lack of formalized studies, ethical issues still become codified at the federal and state levels; usually due to violations of privacy, fiduciary duties, negligence, and other civil claims. The reformative Sarbanes-Oxley Act of 2002 (SOX) resulted not from compilations of scholarship, but gross neglect by corporate administrators to conduct business ethically in the name of stakeholders.

The Pregnancy Discrimination Act (PDA), The Fair Labor Standards Act (FLSA), The Americans with Disabilities Act (ADA), and portions of The Civil Rights Act (particularly the amendments) each share the same origins in unethical behaviors by employers. Although laws may find creation because of unethical behavior, acting unethically within the law remains commonplace; hence the requirements for public corporations to develop and implement measurable codes-of-conduct and values for executive personnel within the SOX legislation (Walsh, 2010).

Along this line of reasoning, the discussion enters as to exactly which questions may be considered unethical during an employment interview and when after hire this relationship may change, if at all. By comparison of competing perspectives of legal issues, organizational culture fit, and global distinctions, weight can be leveraged either way depending upon the situation.

LEGAL ISSUES

Historically, interviews were conducted in an unstructured format. They were unplanned, informal, and quick in preparation in order to diagnose the suitability of the applicant. Questions were subjectively open-ended ("Tell me why you are the better applicant."), speculative ("Where do you see yourself in five years?"), or obtuse (If you could be a... tell me why."). This low-reliability format is still widely used and lacks validity for predicting success in future job performance (Heneman III & Judge, 2009).

Inconsistencies in interviewer evaluations, applicant levels of physical attractiveness, weights of negative information over positive information, timing of first impressions, similarities of applicant attributes to the interviewer, and poor recall by interviewers have led researchers to find methods to reduce error and bias in the selection process.

Structured interview formats, conversely, alleviate these problems utilizing a format that standardizes objective questions uniformly of applicants. Inquisitions reflect experiences with behaviors, leadership, conflict resolution, adaptability, flexibility, negotiation, and other Knowledge, Skills, and Abilities (KSAs) (Cadotte, et al., 2008) with an average high validity of 0.37 (Heneman III & Judge, 2009). Examples include:

1) "Describe a time when *you demonstrated leadership* skills."
2) "Tell me about a work situation when *you had to be adaptive*."
3) "What was *your role* in your previous team assignment?"

Of course, questions should be tailored to the specific job based upon a formal job evaluation, including the job description, to ensure that KSAs needed are actually measured during the interview.

Considering questions such as "Who are your personal heroes and why?" can lead to legal implications, especially if motivational purpose lacks KSA discovery related to the position. If the applicant is otherwise considered as a finalist, but denied employment based upon response to the unrelated question, the organization may be charged with liability under legislation. For illustration, disparate treatment under ADA *may* occur when the applicant is rejected for claiming a woman with many children as a hero when the interviewer wanted to hear about a person who is dedicated to the company with no plans of having children and makes this point known (Walsh, 2010). This means an offer of employment must have been tendered and rescinded based upon the information. After formal employment of the applicant, the rules change. The employer enjoys freedom to solicit various types of personal questions, including the target above, but still may not terminate given the same motivation.

ORGANIZATIONAL CULTURE FIT

Organizations maintain their own cultural systems and seek employees that can easily integrate. These "soft skills" are especially important to service oriented companies that center upon customers as primary stakeholders in terms of motivation, interpersonal communication abilities, and intrapersonal communications with suppliers as secondary stakeholders (Walsh, 2010). Generally, these "other characteristics" expand KSAs into KSAOs and are subjectively measured during the interview process through impressions upon the interviewer, determining if the applicant is a good "fit" for the organization.

Internally, this fit means the potential employee not only integrates easily into the specific job, but also within the cultural framework (values and norms) that includes other employees, processes, and atmosphere. Externally, the definition expands to secondary social stakeholders of the organization.

Heneman and Judge (2009) contend that personality testing, although continuously increasing in validity and reliability as predictors of job success cannot fully assess the full spectrum of differing cultural characteristics in the myriad of individual companies. Walsh (2010) added, "Assessing the... types of 'fit' is certainly trickier and more subjective than measuring job skills. Methods exist but are less developed and less studied for validity than tests of job skills or aptitude". The incident in Great Britain where the potential manager for The Body Shop was denied employment for not fitting into the corporate culture is common globally. Ethically the particular method of questioning about personal heroes to determine culture fit (Carroll & Buchholtz, 2009) may raise questions of authenticity and relativity; however, the existence of purpose remains.

GLOBAL DISTINCTIONS

In the United States, a person is theoretically innocent until proven guilty. Great Britain emphasizes the opposite approach in that defendants must prove their innocence when accused. This difference in standards helps to explain why The Body Shop aggressively took a stance when accused of unethical (and possibly illegal) behaviors. British defendants are accustomed to seeking defense mechanisms to prove innocence whereas their American counterparts can enjoy passivity in the reality of the burden of proof by accusers. Therein separation of ethical definition originates.

Similar divergences occur across other cultures due to religious backgrounds (the color green is inappropriate for product packaging in Taiwan), language syntax (slang expressions do not translate intention well), and other regional characteristics. Violation of expectations then leads to ethical dilemmas (Carroll & Buchholtz, 2009) across global cultural borders.

CONCLUSIONS

Differences in cultural norms and values preclude ethical variations in the practices of corporate business operations. Expectancies in one culture may be taboo or offensive in another. Historical experiences mature processes through legislative means, such as the dozens of federal employment laws in the United States. Business finds itself in constant conformance as these problems are addressed, not necessarily in the same direction and in further conflict with cross-cultural development. Although easier in the homeland, the increasing need for personal privacy initiatives and lack of concrete ethical definition hinders progression of commutable guidelines that business can utilize when crossing into new physical territory. Even at home, ethical definition is situational at best, particularly when applying to employment legality issues.

In closing, Kirkwood and Ralston (1999) and Heneman and Judge (2009) offer businesses seven tangible guidelines to assist protection from ethical dilemmas when selecting applicants:

1. Train recruiters and interviewers in ethical practices of human resource management.
2. Disclose the intent of questions and responses to applicants' answers (transparency).
3. Invite open discussion from applicants to discover personal insights (internal culture fit).
4. Only ask direct questions related to KSAOs needed to perform the job.
5. Utilize local interviewers when entering new markets to reduce ethical violations (external culture fit).
6. Avoid unrealistic questions (such as "personal heroes") unrelated to the intended topic.

Research legal constraints before developing recruitment and selection initiatives.

* * *

1.4 PRODUCTIVITY AND PUBLIC IMAGE

In light of the scandals of the early 2000s, many organizations have come to realize public image can influence the future well-being of future objectives. Nike discovered firsthand that once a company enters focal attention of external stakeholders, it is extremely difficult to defend reputation. Wal-Mart learned this lesson through the stigma of becoming the most sued corporation in the world. Martha Stewart demonstrated that by taking individual responsibility for unethical practices a company can be spared the internal degradation of values that leads to self-destruction, as in the case of Arthur Anderson.

These cases beg the question of whether productivity fluctuates in response to changes in the reputation of the organization. The following discussion dissects productivity at the internal and external levels and then assesses how management of issues/crises may direct desired responses beyond sustainability.

INTERNAL PRODUCTIVITY

Internally, we can simply define an organization's reputation as the "collective opinion of stakeholders toward [the] organization based upon its past record" (Nakra, 2000). More specifically as a process rather than an object, Kartalia (1999) explained that an organization's reflection is the "method of building and sustaining... good name [by] generating positive feedback from stakeholders that will result in meeting strategic and financial objectives". As managers succumb to pressures for leaner processes, increased performance, decreased costs, and higher quality products and services, strategic gains may be lost in favor of short-term solutions that frequently link to negative outcomes (Nakra, 2000).

Sometimes illegal and other times just unethical, these tactical actions may result in unhealthy competition, cheating, theft, decreased employee morale, fraud, misrepresentation, or negligence

(Carroll & Buchholtz, 2009; Nakra, 2000). If left unchecked, ethical values begin to erode within the organization, further damaging the micro-level reputation.

Although dated by today's academic standards, Michael Birnbaum attempted to discover in a 1973 study using an averaging statistical model how many moral actions were required by an individual to cancel the effects of one immoral deed among consensus of peers. He concluded that it depends upon the degree of severity of the bad deed as to wherein the answer lies. With most extreme negative actions, the offender never fully recovers, regardless of the number of commendable achievements performed either before or after; and forevermore these positives are individually weighed against the worst offending action.

Lesser offenses, conversely, seem to not follow any mathematical average (Birnbaum, 1973). In application of understanding, such as in the cases of Arthur Anderson and Enron, the bundle of negative actions throughout the company forbids recovery (and thus defunct) whereas the lesser offenses attributed to a specific individual had little lasting effect upon Martha Stewart's company survival.

Any manager of team-oriented directives knows that when membership morale suffers, so does productivity in terms of winning matches. The same is true of employees. Organizational psychologists recommend usage of intrinsic rewards (e.g. praise, positive recognition, and job satisfaction) in combination with extrinsic amenities (e.g. fair wages, humane work environment, and adequate tools) to increase and maintain employee morale, to reduce absenteeism, and to increase productivity (Cadotte, et al., 2008; Luthans, 2008). For example, the Hawthorne Studies revealed that productivity increased with environmental light levels (as long as workers did not know they were being studied).

EXTERNAL PRODUCTIVITY

Wal-Mart, Nike, Martha Stewart, and other retail/manufacturing companies (especially in the garment segment) that either operate their own manufacturing facilities or subcontract fabrication, constantly undergo public scrutiny for unethical practices, most frequently labor stratification issues. This external attention, like internal lingering, can permanently damage a company's reputation. As the speed of information and technological advances increase so too does the demand by consumers, investors, and global stakeholders for background information (Nakra, 2000).

John D. Rockefeller (Standard Oil) discovered firsthand what Michael Birnbaum correlated with philanthropy versus worst offensive action at the external level. Mr. Rockefeller enjoyed giving money to people on the streets, donating to schools, and other ways of giving back to his community; however, union strikes, environmental activists, and the federal government, respectively, plagued Standard Oil for changes to ways employees were treated, the unscrupulous damages caused to the land, and the first monopoly breakup in history (Online Highways, unk). Ninety years later, Standard merged with British Petroleum (BP) during the 1980s and today controls less than 23% of the market (Helman, 2010), thus validating Birnbaum's analysis.

Stock markets exist under the assumption that markets are intelligent, meaning as new information about a particular organization becomes available, the market will respond with stock exchanges accordingly. Measuring with ten-year return to investors, Economic Value Added and the price to earnings ratio, *Fortune Magazine* conducted a longitudinal study that indicated companies with better reputations maintain better financial performance (Saxton, 1998).

Although none of these measures conclusively demonstrate productivity, higher cost of goods sold (COGS) would lower these measures through fixed costs lost in lowered productivity. Additionally, Reputation Quotients (RQ) for the top 15 companies scored between 77.9 (Microsoft) and 83.4 (Johnson & Johnson). It would be notable to acknowledge that Carroll and Buchholtz (2009) describe Johnson & Johnson as one of the most socially responsible corporations in how it handled the Tylenol Tampering Scandal.

CONCLUSIONS

The definitions of "reputation" provided by Nakra and Kartalia lack the forward looking components necessary to successfully manage both the positive and negative aspects required to extend beyond sustainability when organizational issues and crises dominate public view. Nakra acknowledged that overall reputation extends beyond issues management to encompass the bigger picture and offers some insight to this reality, whereas Kartalia realized crisis management is a continual cycle; however, each limited input to past and present experiences. Combining their definitions of reputation with onward insight, the resulting view evolves into:

"Reputation is the combined methods of building and maintaining positive feedback from internal and external stakeholders that increases future positive opinions, while reducing past and present negative opinions toward the organization that further enable the organization to meet or exceed tactical, strategic, and financial objectives."

Positive correlations exist, although indefinite in magnitude due to the complexity of specific situations, between levels of productivity and micro/macro levels of an organization's overall reputation with various types of stakeholders. Internal stakeholders, such as employees and customers, can have immediate effects upon production levels consistent with measurable motivational factors, like turnover and absenteeism, while external stakeholders (community, stockholders, etc.) can affect productivity over the long-term through boycott, stock sales, government regulation, and other retaliatory actions as measured through financial ratios.

In closing, Carroll and Buchholtz (2009) recommend organizations be prepared for crises by formally identifying areas of vulnerability through bridging issues management, developing a plan for dealing with threats, forming crisis teams, drilling for these events, and learning from the experience through active communication... "When used in tandem, issues and crisis management can help managers fulfill their economic, legal, ethical, and philanthropic responsibilities to stakeholders".

* * *

1.5 MARTHA STEWART CASE REVIEW

In 2004, Martha Stewart was convicted in federal court on charges of obstruction of justice, conspiracy, and providing false statements. The original charge of securities fraud by the Securities Exchange Commission (SEC) was dropped, leaving variegated attitudes about justification. Supporters of the craft mogul contended she was railroaded by the government as a scapegoat in light of the then recent and ongoing headline business scandals. At the other extreme, some proponents of the verdict felt her sentencing was too lenient. For her multiple crimes, Martha endured only five months in prison and subsequent house arrest for an equal period.

In order to functionally evaluate these stances, an understanding of motivations underlying personal and business ethical principles when making decisions, the moral climate enveloping the individual facing dilemma, and tests for screening and implementing decisions are necessary prerequisites.

MOTIVATIONS UNDERLYING ETHICAL PRINCIPALS

The Martha Stuart case was exceptional in the selling of her shares in ImClone, based on insider information provided by Dr. Waksal, was not directly related to her stake in Martha Stuart Living Omnimedia. Her motivation to reduce financial losses within her personal portfolio as a shareholder (and her trust in Dr. Waksal as a friend and fellow CEO) lead to taking action based upon the news. It is doubtful that Martha had no knowledge her deeds were illegal given her position as a CEO in a publicly traded company post-Enron, but it is probable she believed she would not be caught due to her distal working relationship with ImClone. Following the Market Ethic of self-interest in combination with the Means-Ends Ethic of allowing immoral tactics to fulfill those interests would explain Martha's behavior in this context, especially the deceitful steps of denial taken to cover them up once confronted.

Indirectly, the convictions of Martha Stuart affected not only her personal reputation, but also Martha Stuart Living Omnimedia as an organization. Her mandated removal and banning from serving in any directorship forced the company(ies) to reorganize leadership positions to fill the void(s) fashioned by her absence. This violation of the Organizational Ethics principle ignored the duty to subordinate self-interests for the greater good of the organization. Furthermore, the Professional Ethic principle of doing "only that which can be explained before a committee of [one's] peers" (Carroll & Buchholtz, 2009) failed to materialize during the court trial.

From a shareholder point-of-view in Martha Stuart Living Omnimedia, Martha Stuart violated Conventional Ethics principles when her lying violated the law and Utilitarian Ethics by failure to act in the best interests of the stakeholders (shareholders and employees). Albeit, her personal belief in not getting caught may invalidate these principles to some degree, however her knowledge of the illegality of her actions, together with her official positions of CEO and directorships across multiple boards, override her personal conflict. As Michael Birnbaum (1973) predicted, Martha Stuart Living Omnimedia never fully recovered as stock prices initially dropped by 60% at indictment only to increase by 37% later; providing a total stock value loss of 45.2% from original value.

MORAL CLIMATE

During the scandals era, the Sarbanes-Oxley Act of 2002 (SOX) was created in response to demand for moral change among corporate administrators and to develop standardized accountability for immoral actions taken (primarily financial) in order to reduce harmful impacts upon stakeholders (shareholders, employees, communities, etc.) for those decisions. SOX provided a fundamental framework for ethical responsibility beyond financial implications by mandating development of Codes of Conduct, Values Statements, processes for resolution of conflicts, and initiatives for self-reporting (Luthans, 2008). In response, Martha Stewart Living Omnimedia posted the following statement on their corporate website (Martha Stuart Living Omnimedia, 2010):

"MSLO, its subsidiaries and affiliates, are committed to full compliance with the local laws and human rights and labor standards ("Standards") of those countries in which they conduct business and strive to conduct their businesses in an ethical manner."

Unfortunately, links to the Code of Conduct remain as placeholders at the time of this writing, but notice the emphasis on conducting business ethically rather than acknowledging ethical duties of employees.

Minority groups demonstrated the most support for Martha Stewart during the company's crisis period; such as women through comments like "This is all about the need to make an example of a powerful woman... Martha Stewart is not Enron" (Naughton & Gimbel, 2004), Rosie O'Donnell (female and homosexual), and Bill Cosby (African-American). By allowing personalization of the issues rather than concentrating on their justification as Lawrence Kohlberg suggested (Carroll & Buchholtz, 2009; Papalia, Olds, & Feldman, 2009), MSLO survived through political application of Carol Gilligan's Care Ethic perspective when it distanced itself from direct commentary during the trial period. MSLO strategically capitalized upon the emotions of supporters by incorporating this stance into the corporate climate. This forward-looking approach to the company's reputation strengthened probability of sustainment.

TESTS FOR SCREENING AND IMPLEMENTING DECISIONS

Several tests exist for leaders and organizations allowing for moral decision-making; 1) Common Sense, 2) One's Best Self, 3) Disclosure, 4) Ventilation, 5) Purified Idea, 6) Big Four (greed, speed, laziness, and haziness), and 7) the Gag Test, to name a few.

When Martha Stewart made the decisions to sell her stock in ImClone and to lie about doing it once she was caught, she failed the Common Sense test by not considering practical consequences for her behavior. The same result can be concluded under the One's Best Self inquisition as MSLO revolved around her personal reputation and again by not asking herself that if she was to volunteer the information about the behaviors to the public would she feel comfortable with the attention?

The Ventilation test could be viewed in two different ways. Using the first perspective that Martha followed the advice and actions of ImClone's CEO Dr. Waksal, a friend and business peer, one could argue she successfully disclosed her intent and arrived at the same conclusion to sell her personal holdings in ImClone; however, most would confront the decision as incorrect under this test in that Martha Stewart knew Dr. Waksal's actions were illegal and she should have conversed with administrators in MSLO before taking action.

The Purified Idea is the approach indirectly supported by MLSO only after the damage was done. Rallying on minority support and celebrity support, and defense consultation through her lawyer, Martha embellished her actions were correct. Ideally though, she failed this test by being held accountable and further sanctioned by the court.

The virtues of greed and speed tackled Martha Stewart when making the decision to sell her stock. In an effort to save $52,000, she ended up costing her company and stockholders millions of dollars, taxpayers hundreds of thousands of dollars for prosecution, and herself incalculable costs in reputation, fines, and lost income. Unfortunately, only Martha can know if the Gag Test applied to her personally.

Carroll and Buchholtz (2009) offered suggestions leadership can use in forming ethical decisions:

1. Articulate and embody the purpose and values of the organization.
2. Focus on organizational success rather than on personal ego.
3. Create a living conversation about ethics, values, and the creation of value for stakeholders.
4. Create mechanisms of dissent.
5. Know the limits of the values and ethical principles they live.
6. Frame actions in ethical terms.
7. Connect the basic value proposition to stakeholder support and societal legitimacy.

In the case of Martha Stewart and her company, the better advice is "the leader must infuse the organization's climate with values and ethical consciousness, not just run a one-person show".

CONCLUSIONS

Utilizing the ethical analysis tools provided, it is clear Martha Stewart failed every applicable test to analyze her behaviors before acting on conclusions. From Kohlberg's (and the legal system's) perspective of justice, Martha's convictions were justified, even if only to demonstrate an example to other executives. Stakeholders suffered far greater losses in the end giving retribution to the spirit of those who lost livelihoods and sparked creation of the Sarbanes-Oxley Act of 2002. To these stakeholders, the actual punishment received may seem delicate.

Carol Gilligan's Care Ethic perspective through public support of the individual provided sustainable recovery for Martha Stewart Living Omnimedia, but to a lesser degree than likely if she had not violated the law in the fashion and timing that she did. Today it is evident MSLO was more concerned with an ethics orientation than compliance by way of published comments on the corporate website and avoidance of discussion of previous events. For those employees and investors, Martha's punishment may seem exceptional, or at a maximum, appropriate.

* * *

1.6 GENETICALLY MODIFIED FOODS

The American public first became alarmed about the possible effects of Genetically Modified (GM) foods in 2007 after learning Taco Bell had used Starlink corn in taco shells. Well, not really, but the fear became real with homecoming to American consumers. A year earlier, Greenpeace discovered GM rice for sale in European stores for human consumption; an escapee from Bayer laboratory field tests that contaminated regular crops five years earlier and survived.

A few years earlier, meat from cloned animals was banned for human consumption after scientists repeatedly failed to produce any viable species that did not die prematurely from physical complications. The phobias acquired by consumers from eating GM products heightened after the mostly global ban on meats produced by genetic manipulation and the discoveries of corn and rice in open markets. It is important to note however, in the United States, GM agricultural products are legal as animal feeds that will later be consumed by humans (other recent exceptions noted later).

The types of genetic manipulation in agricultural and animal species are as diversified as the reasons scientists pursue them. Plants may be modified to produce their own pesticides, to be resistant to certain herbicides, or even to produce different colors of flowers. "Natural pesticides" means that farmers do not have to apply additional chemicals to crops to distract damaging pests (insect, fugal, and disease), therefore reducing production costs and possibilities of water source contamination. Not having to apply herbicides equates to virtually no tilling, less soil erosion, and lowered production costs. Other reasons commonly given by growers and producers include increased nutritional content, hardiness to climate changes, lowered mechanical processing costs (such as in seedless grapes or the difference between juice and meat tomatoes), naturally enhanced flavors (sweet lemons from Arizona), and many other characteristic enhancements.

Religious groups often cite affiliate scripture to support their perspectives and/or lack of understanding behind the issues, often without conclusive stances. For instance, Islamic leaders take the stance that employing GM technologies for food satisfies the Qur'anic and Biblical directives to "feed the people [or poor]" when used for that purpose, and is further allowable by verse 2:255, "[God] knows all that lies open before men and all that is hidden from them, whereas they cannot attain any knowledge except that which He wills [them to attain]". From this view exists no conflict between science and Islam

(Al-Hyani, 2007). However, engagement arises when the Muslim pillar of not profiting from charity finds violation when corporations create the foods not for the purpose of feeding the hungry, but in motivation towards profit gains. Fatima Al-Hyani provides convincing arguments in balance of these goals:

"The biotech industry must accept its share of responsibility to care for our ecosystem and our health, to ascertain that the drive for monetary gain does not eclipse wider benefits, to take care that the results of scientific gains via GM foods are not detrimental to the needy and at their expense."

It is unclear whether any consensus exists among farmers for adoption of GM crops and persuasion lies primarily within economic outcomes (Lawson et.al., 2009). U.S. commercial GM farming began in 1996 and had expanded to 87% of cotton crops, 73% of corn yields, and 91% of soybean production by 2007. A survey of Danish farmers indicated less than one-third of ag-producers demonstrate negative attitudes toward genetically modified crop production; of these, "a significant number... would revise their choice if the chemical plant protection inputs are reduced". Yield increases and lowered production costs peak the claims of the 45% of farmers who actively support GM farming. Only the 28% of neutrally biased producers expressed concerns about environment contamination, possible health risks created, and influences on biodiversity.

Rushing into new technologies without understanding consequential effects upon biodiversity that chain into environmental contamination and health risks is not new to global societies and can still be witnessed today. In Great Britain, once it was realized rats carried plague organisms, snakes and cats were imported to eat the rats, but then the cat population became overwhelming and bounties enforced to bring them under control. In the United States, similar events occurred in southern Illinois with the Japanese beetle from 2003 to 2005.

Today, it is estimated the Boa Constrictor population of the Florida Everglades exceeds the 100,000 mark due to the foreign species escaping captivity as pets. These phenomena are extensions of Newton's Laws of actions creating equal and opposite reactions and objects in motion tend to remain in motion – if not properly controlled and accounted for in the planning stage. By employing new GM technologies without understanding long-term consequences, opponents argue time/space correlations cannot be conclusive.

In 2007, the United Stated Department of Agriculture (USDA) financed a joint study to develop a method for valuing third-party information and to determine the willingness of the consumer market to pay for genetically modified foodstuffs (Rousu et.al., 2007). By employing simulated auctions for products, disseminating varied levels of private (proprietary) information about the products through labeling varieties to customers, and surveying feedback, researchers were able to determine "verifiable information in the GM food market has potentially large and statistically significant social value".

Fifteen to 21.5% of "bidders" switched to GM products labeled with verifiable information beyond those who received only biotech industry information. Interestingly, buyers were also willing to pay more for GM products given their reduced production costs. This one-in-six correlation, however, only demonstrates the ability of information to persuade consumers to purchase questionable products, not specifically the acceptance rate of consumers to purchase GM products.

In a separate USDA study, the same year that polled residents of France, U.K., and the U.S., it was determined consumers generally value the benefits over the risks of GM products in willingness to consume (Traill, et al., 2006). One can see this in action by watching drug commercials on television and paying attention to the disclaimers where the risks tend to be more severe than the condition treated, e.g. some birth control medications can cause stroke, heart problems, and so forth. Benefit perceptions ranged from two out three consumers viewing medium benefits over risks overall (40% in France) and more than half of sampled consumers were willing to ingest GM foods.

CONCLUSIONS

The real question of safety in genetically modified food products is not in their existence for human consumption, rather in the techniques utilized to create them. For thousands of years, both nature and humankind the world over have employed cross-pollination to generate plant products that are healthier, prettier, stronger, sweeter, resilient, hardier, and more resistant to pests. Gene manipulation picks up where nature concedes to limits and then forces biological changes to occur across species (Rousu et.al., 2007).

The equivalent is true with interspecies breeding among animals. For example, when a horse and a donkey copulate, a mule is conceived. A mule may be as intelligent as a horse and contain the resiliency of a donkey; however, nature limits future intermixing by making all mules infertile. The rule also applies to a zorse (zebra and horse mix). It is through gene manipulation the miniature horse market was formed. Influence outside of natural limitations begs the questions then of "Why does nature impose these maximums?" and "Are there any new dangers, perhaps unforeseen, perhaps uncontrollable, or perhaps latent spawned when these thresholds are exceeded?"

Stakeholder relationships can be as difficult to define (Carroll & Buchholtz, 2009) as the purposes, benefits, risks, and boundaries of genetic modification. Studies indicate societies are warming up to the idea of consuming GM agricultural products, but not GM animal products as banning legislation demonstrates. The sharing of private information beyond biotech propaganda seems to initiate higher acceptance rates beyond labeling alone, given historical events. Crop producers generally prefer to realize economic benefits from GM products regardless of environmental anomalies while religious groups remain divided toward acceptance depending upon the purpose behind the commercialization of the technologies.

Many GM products have been approved by the Food and Drug Administration (FDA) for human consumption, such as corn for cooking oils and sweeteners; although the public is generally unaware of their commercial use (this writer had no clue). Debates continue to flourish among the long-term effects and limited information provided to consumers while markets concurrently expand regardless, due to economic realities.

The primary stakeholders then seem to be the farmers, who through technological acceptance increasingly grow GM crops for transformation into consumable products. Consumers as stakeholders are less accepting of genetically modified foods when confronted with the lack of knowledge for potential risks, but incline to ignore risks when informed about benefits. It becomes imperative everyone be informed of both the risks and the benefits resulting from GM technologies and then to allow these stakeholders to decide acceptance (or rejection) for themselves.

* * *

1.7 LEGAL V. SOCIAL RESPONSIBILITIES

I t is no surprise Americans have a tendency to bring legal action suits against businesses based upon events of trivial pursuit, making the United States the most litigious country in the world. Even among the bureaucratic complications created through enactments of legislation in attempt to protect consumers and business from mistreatments by the other, occasionally seemingly absurd trials come into the public spotlight.

Sometimes the absurdity forms in the nature of the claim, and other times it heightens through the justification of the means. For example, asserting that a business is liable when a customer spills a hot beverage on themselves, foregoing obvious warning it is hot, and without due diligence in handling the package; then again, through compensatory awards of monies that greatly exceed amounts plaintiffs would earn if the particular incident had not occurred.

The attempt here is not to address the fairness of either the quality of claims or justice in any case, but to assess the questions of how far an organization must go with products and services to remain socially responsible toward consumers as well as what it means for customers to return like-in-kind relationships. By reviewing common legalities and social trends involved, the sometimes fine line between legal and social responsibility clears within an ethical context.

LEGAL ATTRIBUTES OF RESPONSIBILITY

Historically, the tradition of *caveat emptor* ("buyer beware") served as the legal norm in the United States in court decisions regarding product/service liability issues. This meant that consumers assumed most of the risks involved when purchasing and using business offerings (Jennings, 2006). If the purchaser decided to use an axe for a hammer and injured their leg, well, then "common sense" dictates the situation is just too bad for them – they should have used the axe correctly! Following this philosophy, those persons who spilled hot coffee on themselves in the McDonald's suits would not likely have been granted forum for their cases and the company's motions for summary judgment most likely would have been approved. However, as times, products, and needs change, legal standpoints and views also evolve. By the late 20th century *caveat vendor*, or "seller beware", reversed legal and communal mindsets as the dominant philosophy in the business/social stratification perspective (Carroll & Buchholtz, 2009).

Over the ten year period between 1976 and 1986, small airline companies reported a 775% increase in liability costs resulting from changes in legislation and court opinion. New general aviation aircraft sales declined by 90% during this phase of governmental deregulation while accident rates increased 25% to 35% between 1981 and 2000. The latter is blamed on the former by the industry as causing fleets to age without modernization through replacement (Nelson & Drews, 2008). In their study indicating a negative relationship between new plane sales and accident rates, Nelson and Drews estimated more than one-third of the accidents during the time in question could have been prevented if newer aircraft had been available at affordable prices.

Depending upon the industry, the Consumer Product Safety Commission is primarily charged with the responsibilities of issuing and enforcing mandatory standards, protecting the public from dangerous products, and conducting research on potential product hazards. The regulatory body cannot possibly cover every product in every industry due to budgetary constraints (Carroll & Buchholtz, 2009). Other agencies therefore take control of certain industries to help balance the gaps: The Food and Drug Administration (FDA) regulates its namesake; the Federal Aviation Administration (FAA) enforces aircraft construction and use; the Bureau of Alcohol, Tobacco, and Firearms (ATF) reigns confidently to control "sin" products from both industrial and consumer perspectives.

Although manufacturers and retailers are coming increasingly liable from a legal standpoint for how their products are utilized (foreseeable or sometimes not), some state courts reduce compensatory and punitive damage awards proportionately among the plaintiffs and defendants according to their percentage of responsibility for the misuse/abuse/neglect of the product (Jennings, 2006). "*Caveat vendor*" may be the rule in many cases, but retains relationship with its predecessor caveat emptor.

SOCIAL INFLUENCES OF RESPONSIBILITY

The Green Movement, like other social rallies for change, has witnessed an increased focus upon business to create and maintain products and services that are socially acceptable in a push for a cleaner environment. From automobiles that use less gasoline (or none at all) to production plants that emit virtually no carbon footprint from their smokestacks to conveying Kaizen principles in everyday consumption routines (recycling/waste reduction), industries are increasingly pressured to focus processes on the desires of end users rather than wholly upon bottom line intentions. Social cooperation in this manner is one aspect of the triple-bottom-line concept managers are relying upon for sustainability (Carroll & Buchholtz, 2009).

In the 1980s, medical professionals fluently began calling, individually and collectively, processes involving patients "care". The point was to stress an emotional appeal to patients that those workers involved in helping in healing and wellness initiatives came to work for more than a paycheck... they were honestly concerned about the health and well-being of their "customers". For doctors, nurses, and other healthcare workers the term "care" as a way of doing their respective jobs implied a commitment to the patient.

Three decades later, Congress still refuses to buy into the "care" exception and to initiate liability caps for medical professionals and institutions, despite unending lobbying. The Hospital Quality Alliance was formed as an independent collaboration of healthcare organizations that surveys patients to determine quality of care (collectively) rather than depend upon traditional business techniques (Isaac et.al., 2010). Although extremely limited in scope to scoring only three types of surgery and one illness, HQA is a step closer to closing the gap between self-inflicted social responsibility and business liability.

CONCLUSIONS

During the 1960s, the U.S. government imposed the national speed limit system contrary to social popularity. Following in the 1990s, control was given back to the states in exchange for implementing mandatory seat belt usage, but this time the details were left up to states' decisions as to the degrees of details for enforcement. Also, around this time, saw initiation of the mandatory child seat movement that became fully active as law in the early 2000s. Unfortunately, studies do not agree on the effectiveness of child seats compared to regular seatbelts (not lap belts), but all do find agreement that any kind of restraint is more effective in preventing injury than using no restraint device whatsoever (Doyle Jr. & Levitt, 2010). In response to the conflicts indicated, many states have adjusted the upper limits that require child seat usage.

The hot coffee spill case of McDonald's may contain absurdity in relation to its origin, but it has also helped to define trends in where social and legal transitions are headed. Organizations at all levels and scopes (business, government, and consumer) are realizing they share responsibilities to one another, individually and collectively, in terms of legal liability and social responsibility. Manufacturers and retailers increasingly fall prey to caveat vendor, consumers remain obligated under caveat emptor, and government continues obligation to listening to both sides rather than seizing total control when making legislation. Organizations may benefit most:

1) by not taking stakeholders for granted;
2) by not assuming that stakeholders provide sustainability through a sense of obligation;

3) by not assuming that liability is relieved by circumstances not yet foreseen;

4) by implementing feedback measures that enhance collaboration with stakeholders;

5) by realizing that even trivial characteristics of products and services can have detrimental effects that reflect social responsibility of the organization; and

6) by understanding that stakeholder requirements upon the organization undergo constant change.

* * *

1.8 HIRING ON THE BASIS OF LOOKS

Physical attractiveness is a subjective concept, or as the old adage proclaims, "Beauty is in the eye of the beholder". Beauty (or lack of) cannot foretell a person's personality, temperament, work ethic, past achievement, future accomplishment, family values, organizational values, (dis)honesty, occupational skill, or any other demonstrative attribute apparent to others. Nor has any study successfully offered any convincing correlation, positive or negative, in relating physical attractiveness as a measure for these qualities.

However, within certain industries physical attractiveness may be a determining factor for career entry or exit timing, such as commonly found within modeling agencies. Over the last decade though, models have grown older, shorter, and sometimes physically heavier than those of preceding generations. John J. Macionis (2010) attempted to provide an induced explanation by way of changes in societal norms brought about by litigation fears (age, disability, etc.), an aging population, diversity initiatives, and changes in family values and education. Albeit, even facially disfigured persons are employed to demonstrate cosmetic effects of makeup, acne, and scar removal products in advertising.

As of this writing, there are no federal laws that define using physical attractiveness of an applicant (employee) as prejudiced or discriminatory when utilized by hiring managers in making employment decisions. The topic still falls under at-will doctrine of private property at the federal and state levels, with exception only of the District of Columbia Human Rights Act (Carroll & Buchholtz, 2009; Heneman III & Judge, 2009) (Note: D.C. is not a state as Carroll and Buchholtz stated, but a sovereign entity designed to remove favoritism to any singular state by overlapping three states). The District of Columbia prohibits 13 kinds of discrimination and, as many states, places stricter enforcement mechanisms and penalties for noncompliance.

ATTRACTIVENESS AND HIRING STUDIES

In a study conducted by Shannon and Stark (2003), photographs were attached to applications for a fictitious management position. Evaluators were asked to assess the likelihood of employing each application based upon the amount of beardedness of the male applicants and perceived attractiveness. The evaluators were also told not to consider other job qualifications in the applicant files, as these were previously considered, so as to eliminate experimenter bias by not attempting to appear as though attractiveness influenced other qualifiers.

The result was that the amount of facial hair impacted the hiring decision even though it did not significantly affect the evaluations themselves. Of the 50 "applicants", clean shaven men were considered nearly twice as attractive as either full-bearded males or those with only a mustache whereas full-bearded men were 2.5 times more likely to be considered unattractive as those who were clean shaven (Shannon & Stark, 2003).

This study is significant in that it corroborates previous studies that signify the influence of physical attractiveness in hiring decisions and intellectual abilities are further degraded among evaluators when an applicant is considered unattractive. By controlling for the intellect of applicants as variables, direct comparisons can be made in distinguishing personal evaluator biases from perceived applicant ability. In Shannon and Stark's experiment, evaluators were told all applicants were qualified outside of the appearance category. Surprisingly, the ratio of male to female evaluator decisions was equal when deciding the attractiveness correlation of beardedness.

Toward the feminine side of attractiveness studies, the westernized stereotypical aspects of body mass (fatness) and physical body measurements (proportions) were taken on by Wilson, Tripp, and Boland in a 2005 experiment to determine if Body Mass Index (BMI) and Waist to Hip Ratio (WHR) affect perceptions of what others see as beauty. Using three levels of WHR (0.66 low, 0.72 average, 0.76 high) and three levels of BMI (17.0 underweight, 22.6 average weight, 28.2 overweight), thinner models were perceived to be more attractive and a low WHR was desirable only among women with low or average body weight.

In short, WHR seems to have less affect than BMI in western cultures when determining physical attractiveness in females. In simpler terms this means fatness plays a larger role than proportions (Wilson, Tripp, & Boland, 2005). "Western" is stressed here, as it is common in some island cultures for males to desire larger women when selecting companionship (Native Hawaiians, for example). This helps to explain why a majority of women who are employed in positions requiring public contact (administrative assistants, direct sales, etc.) may differ in proportions, but remain in the average to low weight ranges without regard to facial attractiveness.

CONCLUSIONS

Study after study demonstrate consistent conclusiveness that although hiring managers claim to ignore physical attractiveness as a variable in job-filling processes, personal biases still abound when other variables (intellect, job related skills, academic credentials, etc.) are controlled for. Elements of attractiveness can be finite as in the presence of facial hair in males or infinite to a dislike for certain body proportions at differing body masses in females. Generally, though, it seems women are more harshly judged on their appearances than their male counterparts (Macionis, 2010) and include stricter guidelines for conformance.

More studies are needed to determine why these iniquities exist beyond the realms of evolutionary theory and patriarchal lineages as excuses since humans change their perceptions by conscious choices made – not biological reprogramming. Compendiums of these results need to be comprised and adapted into workable solutions that human resource managers may implement into their hiring (yes, and promotion) systems to ensure the best-qualified, rather than best-looking, individuals are recruited, hired, and retained. From the information provided above, an obvious beginning is to refute the usage of photographs with applications and to reduce confrontation until the pool of candidates has been reduced to the best qualified candidates.

* * *

1.9 EMPLOYEE SAFETY OR DISCRIMINATION

Social conflicts arise when consensus cannot be readily determined in issues that affect community stakeholders including citizens, business organizations, legal systems, and surrounding environments. Each stakeholder must interact with every other in give-and-take (sometimes in cause-and-effect) relationships that determine harmonies related to those issues in question to arrive at solutions equitable, albeit sometimes unbalanced, for everyone involved. On occasion, consensus of particular issues exist as extraordinary feats beyond the capabilities of involved parties due to absences of information available, technologies for implementation, rationalization abilities within social contexts (Macionis, 2010), or just plain stubbornness of parties to empathize perspectives.

Other times, sufficient time and/or experiences with the myriad of situational possibilities on a social issue may not have come to pass to arrive at mature conclusions. The question of priority for employee safety or discrimination adequately falls within this realm of thinking by the situational nature of the issue, the differing perspectives of the stakeholders, the technologies employed as controls, and the experience levels of the stakeholders to arrive at a mature consensus.

SITUATIONAL NATURE OF THE ISSUE

Does the employer of pizza delivery drivers have a greater responsibility to the safety of those employees and can the business be held liable for disparate impact against *potential* customers by refusing service to particular geographical patronage areas that would endanger those employees? The Occupational Safety and Health Act of 1970 (OSHAct) declares that employees cannot be forced by employers to work in situations they personally believe their health or safety may be endangered (United States Department of Labor: Occupational Safety and Health Administration, 2010).

Under this provision the implication that organizations that offer pizza delivery services must allow drivers to make the decision themselves whether they will or will not enter neighborhoods considered by the employer unsafe for the occupation. In other words, the employer should first warn the driver of the known dangers and allow that driver to choose. This doctrine assists with decisions regarding potential impacts related to discrimination.

Doctrine concerning customer bases for organizations is limited at best. Business, through free-market enterprise, may target any group they desire as potential customers. For example, cosmetic companies seek female customers for makeup, tool manufacturers generally target males, and doll retailers utilize young girls for their market segment, depending upon traditional social roles. Philanthropic undertakings often limit services, just as plumbers and electricians, to certain geographic locations. Legislatively forcing organizations to expand customer segments due to geographic location is not common for restaurant establishments.

The Civil Rights Act of 1964 did force all industries to not discriminate customer bases by means of racial segregation. The amended Act of 1991 further allowed for claim against disparate impact under the Four-Fifths Rule in cases of employment, but lacks coverage in cases of customer focus that involve geographic selection.

STAKEHOLDER PERSPECTIVES

As discussed above, employees have the right to feel safe in their workplaces as well as the right to complain when forced to perform their work in environments that violate feelings of safety. Additionally, organizations are free to choose the location of their business and the market segments served so long as civil rights of those customers selected are not violated, or a protected group excluded because of a protected characteristic.

In the case of pizza delivery, excluding certain neighborhoods within a geographic location may demonstrate disparate impact if it can be shown the excluded community is within the advertised geographic service area of the business, the service area does not envelop the excluded neighborhood, and that proportional demographics of the excluded area do not resemble any other service location. However, unlike practices common prior to the Civil Rights Movement Era by businesses that refused service to certain races of residents in the principle location, these customers are being excluded by an unprotected demographic.

TECHNOLOGICAL LIMITATIONS AND EXPERIENCE

Currently, the pizza retailers limit their knowledge and conclusions for determining safety thresholds upon software development and data analysis by third parties (such as Dominoes in Michigan (Carroll & Buchholtz, 2009)). This limitation disallows personal experience of franchise owners, unknown statistical conclusions for new neighborhoods, and the trend for unreported crime levels in more affluent neighborhoods (Macionis, 2010).

Further compounding these data is the fact police officers tend "to retain the power to define which situations and incidents are deserving of policing action, for the most part selectively focusing their attention upon volume and major crime" (Herbert, 2006). Often this means that up to 90% of criminal acts go unreported/underreported (Macionis, 2010). Therefore, reliance upon outside resources can dramatically skew the reliability of technological measures utilized as controls by these organizations for safety determination of employees and the true characteristics of "dangerous neighborhoods".

It is recommended that store managers consider their own experiences when considering the viability of particular community segments in conjunction with technological availabilities.

CONCLUSIONS

Innes, Abbot, Lowe, and Roberts (2009) concluded that "By capturing intelligence data that more accurately and precisely articulates how individuals and groups are viewing their situated environments, the aspiration would be to achieve policing interventions that are more effective". From a managerial standpoint, this recommendation serves as a guideline when considering technological and historical data compiled by sources alien to the current business environment. Organizations should integrate experiences with questionable neighborhoods before excluding them from the customer base.

When questions arise about employee safety initiatives versus potential customer exclusion, employers are obligated to train employees about potential hazards and then to allow the employee to make decisions regarding pursuance. Managers should consider hiring employees that reside in "dangerous" neighborhoods to reduce feelings of coercion, rejection, fear, prejudice, and possibly discrimination by employees and customers alike. In any case, legislation that intrudes upon the rights and privileges of the free enterprise system should be avoided and considered as situational to the organization.

* * *

1.10 ENRON: AN ETHICAL ASSESSMENT

Enron was formed in 1985 as a result of merger between Houston Natural Gas and InterNorth under the leadership of then CEO Kenneth Lay. By 1992, Enron was the market leading seller of natural gas in North America with assets that included gas pipelines, electricity plants, pulp and paper plants, water plants, and broadband services. Stock prices climbed significantly faster than any other listing in the energy industry during the 1990s accounting for a six-fold book value through market capitalization (Healy & Palepu, 2003). During the year 2000 alone, this trend equated to an 87% increase of stock price in light of the 10% decrease for the industry within the S&P 500 index. Unfortunately, watchdog economists tended to ignore these financial trends as warnings for investors that possible accounting problems may exist and relied instead upon the vague financial statements to assess the company's health.

Between August 2001, when Jeff Skillings suddenly resigned as CEO after six months despite unprecedented earnings, and December when Enron filed for bankruptcy, the second largest (to date behind WorldCom) corporate financial scandal dominated the global news. New concerns about the safety of public market trading flourished, adding to complaints of extravagant executive pay levels, soaring healthcare costs among reduced coverage benefits, job insecurities after plant relocations under free trade agreements, increased terrorism activities and threat of war (pre-Afghanistan), and a plethora of other stressors.

Financial analyses, timelines, and business model considerations are beyond the scope of topic here as discussion will focus upon the ethical implications that led up to Enron's collapse, during proceedings of investigations and trials, and post-convictions with the affects endured by stakeholders. By definition, stakeholders include internal and external varieties such as employees, partnerships, communities, government, and shareholders. Analysis of executive profiles in terms of action during the scandal period and why they were hired precludes impact analyses for stakeholders, reputation management, comparative views, and social versus legal responsibilities.

EXECUTIVE PROFILES

Of the 18 convictions resulting from federal probes into Enron, 16 persons entered guilty pleas with only Kenneth Lay and Jeffery Skilling maintaining innocence. Five executives headlined news media as the primary architects and executioners of white collar crimes ranging from "aiding and abetting securities fraud" to making false statements to banks; eight convicts received leniency for testimonies against Lay and Skilling.

Kenneth Lay

Kenneth Lay was born the son of a poor Baptist minister and held a PhD degree in economics from the University of Houston. Lay began his private enterprise career in 1970 with ExxonMobil Corporation before assignment as an undersecretary for the Department of the Interior and later returning to work for Florida Gas Transmission. At the time he became CEO of Enron through the merger of InterNorth and Houston Natural Gas, Kenneth Lay also served on the board of Eli Lilly and Company. During 2000, he was further considered for the position of Treasury Secretary by President George W. Bush, a year before he started dumping $300 million worth of his personal Enron stock (mostly options) while encouraging common employees to purchase more stock (retirement funds) as the price fell (Superseding Indictment, 2004).

An overview of the criminal charges, according to the 65 page indictment against Mr. Lay, included engaging

"in a wide-ranging scheme to deceive the investing public, the SEC, and others (the 'Victims), about the true performance of Enron's businesses by: (a) manipulating Enron's publicly reported financial results; and (b) making public statements and representations about Enron's financial performance and results that were false and misleading in that they did not fairly and accurately reflect Enron's actual financial condition and performance, and [he] omitted to disclose facts necessary to make those statements and representations fair and accurate."

Lay was found guilty by jury trial on 10 of the 11 original charges but died of heart complications before sentencing could occur. He was expected to serve between 20 and 40 years in prison.

Jeffery Skilling

Jeffery Skilling graduated from Harvard Business School in 1979, earning his MBA before becoming a consultant (then partner) in McKinsey and Company. Later in Houston, Skilling resigned from First City Bancorporation of Texas (owned by Enron) when the bank suffered near failure. Kenneth Lay employed Jeffery Skilling in the course of 1990 as Chairman and CEO of Enron Finance Corporation, and then promoted him to Chairman of Enron Gas Services the following year. By way of various mergers and promotions, Skilling elevated to Chief Operating Officer of Enron in 1997 before being named as CEO on February 12, 2001.

Skilling implemented mark-to-market accounting methods within Enron that forced the creation of shell companies ("special purpose entities") that enabled forecasting of market prices through transactions. These transactions shared ownership of specific cash flows and risks among outside investors and lenders (Healy & Palepu, 2003), or more specifically, allowed for hiding of excessive debt from Enron accounting reports by placing them on the books of the shell companies. Jeffery Skilling was found guilty on 19 of the 35 indictment counts against him and was sentenced to 24 years and four months in federal prison, including $45 million in fines. As of this writing, the U.S. Supreme Court vacated part of the conviction on appeal and remanded the case back to trial court on June 24, 2010.

Andrew Fastow

Andrew Fastow earned his MBA from Northwestern University and worked for Continental National Bank and Trust Company in Chicago where he assisted in the development of asset-backed securities, which allow banks to "create" revenue while removing assets from the balance sheets. The bank suffered the second largest financial failure behind Washington Mutual in 2008. In 1990, Fastow was hired by Enron Finance Corporation, the same year Jeffery Skilling took over as Chairman and CEO of the Enron subsidiary. By 1998, Jeffery Fastow was appointed as Chief Financial Officer of Enron and assisted Skilling with the development of the shell companies that performed business solely with Enron. However, Fastow hid his own agenda of defrauding Enron through investing personal funds into these entities and threatening banks with losing Enron accounts if they did not also invest into these funds.

In return for his testimony against Lay and Skilling, Andrew Fastow plea bargained with federal prosecutors to plead guilty to two counts of wire and securities fraud and began serving his six year prison term on January 14, 2004 (now released).

Michael Kopper and Mark Koenig

Michael Kopper was the first Enron executive to plead guilty for his part in the scandal and received just over three years of home confinement and a $50,000 fine as punishment. His plea bargain agreement included guilty pleas to charges of money laundering and conspiracy to commit fraud. Kopper worked as a managing director of Enron Finance Group reporting directly to Andrew Fastow (Hays, 2006).

Mark Koenig served as the Vice President of Investor Relations for Enron and was "responsible for all activities related to Enron's investor constituencies and [was] a member of Enron's Management Committee", according to his company bio formerly posted on Enron's corporate website at http://www.enron.com/corp/pressroom/bios/markkoenig.html (American Patriot Friends Network, n.d.). Upon pleading guilty to aiding and abetting securities fraud in August 2004, Koenig surrendered $1.5 million over to the government and was the first prosecution witness to testify against Lay and Skilling. Unlike Michael Kopper and Andrew Fastow, Mark Koenig was never accused of self-dealing (Hays, 2006).

HIRING AND ORGANIZATIONAL/CULTURAL FIT

Kenneth Lay stacked-the-deck when he hired Jeffrey Skilling and Andrew Fastow constructed upon comparable characteristics:

1. Skilling and Fastow demonstrated abilities to disguise debt in a profitable manner through manipulation of cash flows and balance sheets.
2. Both executives enjoyed economics majors and earned MBA degrees.
3. Both men began their careers with the Enron Finance Group.
4. Each hire knew how to advantage special purpose companies.
5. Lay placed each into leveraged positions of authority.

These characteristics enabled Lay to develop an executive organizational culture of leadership with parallel goals as evidenced through the trickle down similarities with subordinate executives, such as Kopper and Koenig. Although Fastow later revealed separate agenda for fraud, he willingly participated in the managerial cover-up activities for reasons of personal financial gain.

ETHICAL TESTS OF THE MORAL CLIMATE

Several tests exist for leaders and organizations to exhibit moral decision-making; 1) Common Sense, 2) One's Best Self, 3) Disclosure, 4) Ventilation, 5) Purified Idea, 6) Big Four (greed, speed, laziness, and haziness), and 7) the Gag Test to name a few (Carroll & Buchholtz, 2009). Additionally, when faced with decisions involving moral conflict, Carroll and Buchholtz recommend three guidelines to assist managers:

1. When two or more moral obligations conflict, choose the stronger one.
2. When two or more ideals conflict, or when ideals conflict with obligations, honor the more important one.
3. When the effects are mixed, choose the action that produces the greatest good or least harm.

Common Sense

The test of Common Sense requires that individuals inquire within themselves if the action or decision under consideration makes sense in terms of the consequences of that action or decision. For example, if a deed may end with the granting of the decision-maker experiencing a prison term, then that option probably is not ethical. When utilizing this test, caution must be reserved when questioning the probability of getting caught where the self-reply should always be "yes". Kenneth Lay, Jeffery Skilling, and Andrew Fastow failed this check when they created the "specialized companies" by means of intentions of hiding corporate debts from investors. Andrew Fastow went astray when he invested personal funds into these shell companies to defraud Enron, and Michael Kopper when he laundered funds under direction of Andrew Fastow.

One's Best Self

The ethical test of One's Best Self requires an individual to question if the action about to be undertaken is compatible with their self-concept when he or she views themselves at their best. The downfall of this test is when a person's self-concept includes harming others, such as when a serial killer finds gratification from the tactics employed in their crimes or in not getting caught. Jeffery Skilling displayed this mentality when he applied to Harvard Business School and was asked by interviewers if he thought he was smart. His reply was, "I'm f***ing smart!" (McLean & Elkind, 2003). This behavior carried over into denial of wrongdoing even after his convictions. From a business career perspective, all of the executives miscarried the One's Best test when their convictions revealed each of them at their worst in the public's view.

Making Something Public

The Test of Making Something Public, or disclosure rule, also finds fault in itself when the examiner has an egocentric personality. Generally, an individual would ask themselves how they would feel if their actions were known by the public or broadcast public through media sources. Denial of allegations toward Enron executives may be construed as finding their actions unethical when applying the disclosure rule. But how does one apply this test when a serial criminal writes letters to the press praising their own actions (Lindbergh Baby Killer, Zodiac Killer, Bonny and Clyde, etc.)? This exemption can also be applied here as the conspiracy spanned several years of planning and execution by the team of executives.

Test of Ventilation

The Ventilation Test asks the decision maker to expose their options to an outsider before finalizing that decision. Quarrel can be made that Enron executives performed exposure by revealing conspiracy plans amongst themselves, but stronger arguments of leadership coercion upon more junior executives and the real intent of the test invalidate the claim. Intention is that an "outsider" definition includes persons unrelated to the organization, decision, or action under consideration. It should be evident that Enron executives failed the Ventilation Test, but the truth is inconclusive given that supporting organizations either participated in attempting to destroy evidence (Arthur Anderson) or succumbed to retaliatory power threats (banks).

Purified Idea

The Purified Idea claims an action may be ethical if a person holding authority states the action is appropriate, including supervisors or attorneys. This is the most common ethical error people make (Carroll & Buchholtz, 2009) as the decision-maker is ultimately held responsible if the action is not defensible. Excluding the five top executives targeted throughout this discussion, the remaining 13 employees convicted in the federal case may have attempted to excuse their roles with claims of orders by their supervisors to perform the acts. No matter how discovered, they were still accountable.

The Big Four

The four characteristics of greed, speed, laziness, and haziness are temptations that lead to unethical behavior. Greed is the personal drive to acquire more in self-interests. Kenneth Lay purchased a $200,000 boat for his wife while holding several millions of dollars in personal debts and attempted to explain the transaction by claiming it was difficult to change the lifestyle he had become accustomed to. Substantial bonuses, some exceeding base salary levels, may have been a driver that encouraged executives to devise the conspiracy to show increasing market values for Enron through unrealistic growth revenues.

Speed, or reacting to pressures of time, enhanced the scheme since performance indicators are related to time. Laziness became apparent through the building of the conspiracy to increase excessive revenues rather than continue traditional business models at slower, more realistic, paces.

Although not a valid claim for top executives, haziness (an unclear understanding of issues at hand) may have been a contributing factor for junior executives convicted, but not an excuse from professional expectations of knowledge and conduct.

Gag Test

The Gag Test is purely subjective in scope, entirely unpredictable in outcome, and completely unreliable across cultures or individuals. Actions found detestable by one person may seem expected, traditional, or neutral in terms of acceptability by any other. As a simple example, slurping soup from a bowl may be considered by many traditional Americans as bad manners requiring removal of the offender from the dining room table. At the same time, the same slurping is considered a sign of compliment to the Chinese-born chef who prepared the meal. Kenneth Lay sought out executives with the specific skills needed to design and execute the fraudulent plans within Enron while Jeffery Skilling's egocentric views clouded any chances for success in the Gag Test; therefore, the test cannot reliably be used in this case.

INTERNAL/EXTERNAL RELATIONSHIPS AND REPUTATION MANAGEMENT

Gibelman and Gelman (2004) reasoned the scandalous atmosphere initiated by Enron and succeeding non-government organizations further decreased public trust in regard to business credibility. The six primary categories of wrongdoing found include personal life style enhancement, parallel enterprises, resource expansion opportunities, theft, mismanagement of resources, and support of activities and groups outside of the organization's purview – all recorded charges among the Enron conspirators. The public response demanded heightened accountability measures for corporate officers, boards, and stronger compliance initiatives.

Nationally, the rash of scandals during such a short period of time concerned the Department of Justice that the public may lose faith in other industries, such as healthcare, causing irreparable harm to the economy. In response, the DOJ implemented a program that would seek pre-trial conviction agreements against questionable organizations in exchange for, essentially, non-disclosure:

"This approach may include a negotiated agreement to defer or not pursue prosecution in exchange for the company's admission of illegal behavior and a commitment to enumerated actions to prevent future occurrences; compulsory adoption or enhancement of the entity's corporate ethics and compliance program; corporate reorganization; and/or the appointment of a federal corporate monitor responsible for ensuring adherence to the agreement between the company and the DOJ, and making regular reports to the U.S. Attorney" (Boozang & Handler-Hutchinson, 2009).

At Enron and Arthur Anderson, thousands of people lost jobs, retirement funds, and career opportunities, placing additional stressors upon social programs and job markets. This particular subject has been "beat to death" by researchers and media and so will not be further discussed here. It should be noted however, these events precluded legislation (discussed later) to prevent current and future companies from entertaining similar deceitful practices and that in conjunction with the terrorist attacks of September 2011, contributed to the recession that followed.

Reputation has been previously defined as the combined methods needed to build and maintain positive feedback internally and externally from stakeholders to increase future positive opinions, while reducing negative opinions, of the organization enabling the organization to further meet or exceed tactical, strategic, and financial objectives.

Michael Birnbaum demonstrated that once an organization (or its members) has created a poor image for itself that it most likely may never fully recover regardless of the successive positive publicity it may receive (Birnbaum, 1973) and that the severity of the situation dictates if any recovery is possible. By example, Enron collapsed after revelation of scandals and ensuing bankruptcy, Arthur Anderson closed by accusation alone through indictment, and Martha Stuart Living Omnimedia stock initially decreased by 60% only to regain 37% of the value losses (45.2% end losses under original values).

FRIEDMAN V. DRUCKER MENTALITIES

Milton Friedman preached that leader's responsibilities center around profits and the financial bottom line. He believed that philanthropic and social activities should not burden business as these detract from the goals of maximum value for shareholders. Individuals may alternatively give from their personal incomes and time. Friedman concluded that providing resources beyond those necessary to sustain the organization constituted socialism and burdened, or empowered, managers beyond the scope of their purpose (Friedman, 1970). Kenneth Lay and his team of executives demonstrated this system of traditional mentalities through efforts to inflate stock prices by means of fraudulent deceptions.

Peter Drucker opposed Milton Friedman's point of view through reasoning that historically, cultures dictated acceptable mores that sustain business (Drucker, 1981). However, his analysis was incomplete in terms of the extent to which cultures influence sustainability. Exactly two decades later, public outrage in the United States demonstrated business is expected to treat employees fairly and with equity, to take responsibility for environmental impacts created by business operations, and to operate within the laws established for business. In other words, ethical performance is not only individualistic, but includes empathetic reasoning and action at the collective level. Joseph McGuire (1963) defined social responsibility as "The idea… that the corporation has not only economic and legal obligations, but also certain responsibilities to society which extend beyond these obligations".

Researchers continue to work at developing component models of corporate social responsibility that contain economics, legal, ethical, and philanthropic considerations (e.g. Archie Carroll). Additionally, many companies have adopted triple-bottom-line accounting methods that report social and environmental performance of the company alongside financial data (Carroll & Buchholtz, 2009).

LEGAL V. SOCIAL RESPONSIBILITY

Congress passed the Accounting Reform and Investor Protection Act, better known as the Sarbanes-Oxley Act of 2002 (SOX), in response to the epidemic of business scandals perpetuated by Enron. Much backlash resulted from public corporation leaders in terms of complaints of burdening through additional paperwork and compliance costs. Others have since withdrawn from public (stock) markets, returning to closed or private status to avoid these pitfalls, however the rate of scandals effectively calmed as a result of the legislation.

This legislation amended securities laws to provide better protections for investors in public companies. Protections include auditor independence (avoids Arthur Anderson type relationships with business CFOs), enhancements with financial disclosure requirements, prohibition of personal loans to executives and directors, and reporting of internal controls utilized. Personal responsibility is placed upon CEOs and CFOs for the accuracy of financial reports and protections enabled for whistleblowers with stiff penalties for noncompliance. To date, long-range studies on the impact of the SOX legislation are unfeasible due to its recency. It will be interesting to see how the law reforms ethical perspectives of business, adapts public perceptions of social responsibilities of business, and revisions to SOX over the long term.

CONCLUSIONS

Kenneth Lay and Jeffery Skilling argued their innocence based upon the traditional business ethics model described by Milton Friedman to no avail. Each of these men began their careers during the

Friedman Era of thinking and developed their fraudulent business model for Enron believing that bottom line financial results for stockholders overruled social responsibility to other internal stakeholders (employees and partners), and external stakeholders like economic contribution to the communities served and governmental intervention upon public corporations.

Through power plays, these individuals coerced energy markets, subordinate executives, employees, the banking system, and myriads of others into (sometimes unknowingly) conforming their own beliefs, practices, and systems for the purposes of achieving deception and fraud.

Positive outcomes were achieved in result of the fall of Enron beyond the more often written about negative outcomes. Scandalous corporations, rather leaders, were exposed for whom they really were, ultimately creating confidence in government protections for the public and investors alike, Direction was provided in the evolution of acceptable ethical business practices. Accounting questions found resolution; the art of business analysis through financial measures became more finite, and the concept of triple-bottom-line accounting gained basis as a norm for social and ethical responsibility in conjunction with cultural mores and norms. Although problems with unethical behaviors still exist, the DOJ has found ways to balance enforcement without severe communal and economic ill effects.

* * *

PART ONE REFERENCES

Al-Hyani, F. A. (2007, March). Biomedical Ethics: Muslim Perspectives on Genetic Modification. Zygon, 42(1), 153-162.

American Patriot Friends Network. (n.d.). ENRON'S Mark E. Koenig. Retrieved December 15, 2010, from American Patriot Friends Network: http://www.apfn.org/enron/koenig.htm.

Basker, E. (Summer 2007). The Causes and Consequences of Wal-Mart's Growth. Journal of Economic Perspectives, 21 (3), 177-198.

Birnbaum, M. H. (1973). Morality Judgment: Test of an Averaging Model with Differential Weights. Journal of Experimental Psychology, 99(3), 395-399.

Boozang, K. M., & Handler-Hutchinson, S. (2009). "Monitoring" Corporate Corruption: DOJ's Use of Deferred Prosecution Agreements in Health Care. (B. U. Law, Ed.) American Journal of Law & Medicine (35), 89-124.

Cadotte, E. R., Bruce, H. J., Gardial, S. F., Garval, D., Gilbert, K. C., Jacobs, J. D., et al. (2008). The Management of Strategy in the Marketplace. Knoxville, TN: Innovative Learning Solutions.

Carroll, A. B., & Buchholtz, A. K. (2009). Business & Society: Ethics and Stakeholder Management (7th ed.). Mason, OH: South-Western Cengage Learning.

Doyle Jr., J. J., & Levitt, S. D. (2010). Evaluating the Effectiveness of Child Safety Seats and Seat Belts in Protecting Children from Injury. Economic Inquiry, 48 (3), 521-536.

Drucker, P. F. (1981, Spring). What is "Business Ethics"? The Public Interest (63), pp. 18-36.

Friedman, M. (1970, September 13). The Social Responsibility of Business is to Increase its Profits. New York Times Magazine, pp. 32-33, 122-124, 126.

Gibelman, M., & Gelman, S. R. (2004, December). A Loss of Credibility: Patterns of Wrongdoing Among Nongovernmental Organizations. Voluntas: International Journal of Voluntary and Nonprofit Organizations, 15(4), 355-381.

Gielens, K., Van De Gucht, L. M., Steenkamp, J.-B. E., & Dekimpe, M. G. (2008). Dancing with a Giant: The Effect of Wal-Mart's Entry into the United Kingdom on the Performance of European Retailers. Journal of Marketing Research, XLV, 519-534.

Hays, K. (2006, November 17). 2 Former Enron Executives Receive Prison Terms. Houston Chronicle.

Healy, P. M., & Palepu, K. G. (2003, Spring). The Fall of Enron. Journal of Economic Perspectives, 17(2), 3-26.

Helman, C. (2010, July 9). The World's Biggest Oil Companies. Retrieved October 26, 2010, from Forbes.com: http://www.forbes.com/2010/07/09/worlds-biggest-oil-companies-business-energy-big-oil.html.

Heneman III, H. G., & Judge, T. A. (2009). Staffing Organizations (6th ed.). Boston, MA: McGraw-Hill/Irwin.

Herbert, S. (2006). Citizens, Cops and Power. Chicago, IL: Chicago University Press.

Hicks, M. J. (2007). Wal-Mart's Impact on Local Revenue and Expenditure Instruments in Ohio, 1988-2003. Atlantic Economic Journal, 35 (1), 77-91.

Innes, M., Abbot, L., Lowe, T., & Roberts, C. (2009, April). Seeing Like a Citizen: Field Experiments in 'Community Intelligence-Led Policing. Police Practice and Research, 10(2), 99-114.

Isaac, T., Zaslavsky, A. M., Cleary, P. D., & Landon, B. E. (2010). The Relationship Between Patients' Perception of Care and Measures of Hospital Quality and Safety. HSR: Health Services Research, 45 (4), 1024-1040.

Jennings, M. M. (2006). Business: Its Legal, Ethical, and Global Environment (7th ed.). Mason, OH: Thomson Higher Learning. Kartalia, J. (1999, September). Technology Safeguards for a Good Corporate Reputation. Information Executive.

Kirkwood, W. G., & Ralston, S. M. (January 1999). Inviting Meaningful Applicant Performances in Employment Interviews. The Journal of Business Communication, 36 (1), 55-76.

Lai, K., Cheng, T., & Tang, A. (2010). Green Retailing: Factors for Success. California Management Review, 52 (2), 6-31.

Lawson, L. G., Larsen, A. S., Pedersen, S. M., & Gylling, M. (2009). Perceptions of Genetically Modified Crops Among Danish Farmers. Food Economics Acta Agriculture Scandal C (6), 99-118.

Luthans, F. (2008). Organizational Behavior (11th ed.). Boston, MA: McGraw-Hill/Irwin.

Macionis, J. J. (2010). Sociology (13th ed.). Boston, MA: Prentice Hall.

Martha Stuart Living Omnimedia. (2010). Customer Service: Community Relations. Retrieved November 5, 2010, from MarthaStewart.com: http://www.marthastewart.com/community-relations.

McGuire, J. W. (1963). Business and Society. New York, NY: McGraw-Hill.

McLean, B., & Elkind, P. (2003). Smartest Guys in the Room: The Amazing Rise and Scandalous Fall of Enron. USA: Penguin Group.

Nakra, P. (2000, Summer). Corporate Reputation Management: "CRM" with a Strategic Twist? Public Relations Quarterly, 35-42.

Naughton, K., & Gimbel, B. (2004, March 15). Martha's Fall. Newsweek, p. 28.

Nelson, R. A., & Drews, J. N. (2008). Strict Product Liability and Safety: Evidence from the General Aviation Market. Economic Inquiry, 46 (3), 425-437.

Online Highways. (unk). John D. Rockefeller. Retrieved October 26, 2010, from United States History: http://www.u-s-history.com/pages/h957.html.

Papalia, D. E., Olds, S. W., & Feldman, R. D. (2009). Human Development (11th ed.). Boston, MA: McGraw-Hill.

Plambeck, E. L. (July 2007). The Growing of Wal-Mart's Supply Chain. Management Review, 11 (5), 18-25.

Rousu, M., Huffman, W. E., Shogren, J. F., & Tegene, A. (2007, July). Effects and Value of Verifiable Information in A Controversial Market: Evidence from Lab Auctions of Genetically Modified Food. Economic Inquiry, 45(3), 409-432.

Saxton, K. (1998, May/June). Understanding and Evaluating Reputation. Reputation Management.

Shannon, M. L., & Stark, C. P. (2003). The Influence of Physical Appearance on Personnel Selection. Social Behavior & Personality: An International Journal, 31(6), 613-623.

Traill, W. B., Yee, W. M., Lusk, J. L., Jaeger, S. R., House, L. O., Morrow Jr., J. L., et al. (2006). Perceptions of the Risks and Benefits of Genetically-Modified Foods and Their Influence on Willingness to Consume. Food Economics Acta Agriculture Scandal C (3), 12-19.

United States Department of Labor: Occupational Safety and Health Administration. (2010). What to do if there is a Dangerous Situation at Work. Retrieved December 9, 2010, from OSHA: http://www.osha.gov/workers.html.

United States of America V. Richard A. Causey, Jefferey K. Skilling, Kenneth L. Lay, H-25-05 (S-2) (United States District Court, Southern District of Texas, Houston Division July 7, 2004).

Walsh, D. J. (2010). Employment Law for Human Resource Practice (3rd ed.). Mason, OH: South-Western Cengage Learning.

Wilson, J. M., Tripp, D. A., & Boland, F. J. (2005, December). The Relative Contributions of Waist-to-Hip Ratio and Body Mass Index to Judgements of Attractiveness. Sexualities, Evolution & Gender, 7(3), 245-267.

* * *

PART TWO: STRATEGIC KNOWLEDGE STUDIES

2.1 GLOBAL DIMENSIONS FOR XYZ CONSTRUCTION INC.

XYZ Construction Inc. seeks to expand horizontal operations into global markets, namely into Canada, Mexico, and Asia. Management seeks information regarding potential issues or considerations relative to this initiative. Although it may seem that markets have polarized through free trade agreements, deregulation, and the high number of organizations increasing global operations, a myriad of considerations need to be considered before designing and implementing strategic plans towards this goal. This paper seeks to bring to awareness major considerations often encountered by other companies that have undertaken global expansion initiatives and to offer suggestions that may help XYZ Construction reach its goals sooner. Topics of global ethical and social issues preclude international management and cultural diversity discussions. A summary of suggestions is provided for managerial benefit and consideration.

GLOBAL ETHICAL AND SOCIAL ISSUES

Ethical and social issues from one country to another are as diverse as the customer base encountered in the homeland of XYZ Construction, including issues concerning employee treatment and wages, community support and philanthropy, governmental regulation and compliance, stakeholder prioritization and communication, as well as the economic environment and strategies. Although there exists no formalized formula for any organization to follow when crossing the global threshold, many lessons learned from mistakes and successes others have made do provide a basis for constructing useful guidelines that enable a swifter, gentler transition. Each of the issue categories mentioned above deserve further clarification and can be explored through marketing research.

Employee Treatment and Wages

Through free trade agreements and removal of other barriers, many organizations are moving at least part of their operations overseas, not so much for expansion purposes, but as cost control initiatives through reduced labor and legal compliance. Nike, for example, does not own any manufacturing facilities but takes advantage of Asian manufacturers who can produce Nike designs for a fraction of the cost of operating a plant in the United States. However, Nike has come under fire for violations of human rights by its subcontractors, including calls for boycotts against Nike products in attempt for the shoe company to take responsibility and to pressure those manufacturers into eliminating unfair work practices and to provide living wages for their workers (Carroll & Buchholtz, 2009).

Studies among union workers have also shown that although individuals join unions for personal reasons, their primary motivation for joining is to obtain fair treatment from the employer over higher wages (Pearson Learning Solutions, 2010). To help eliminate these kinds of problems for XYZ Construction during international expansion efforts, the company needs to apply these lessons to foreign workers by providing at least, if not better, living wages to workers, police actions of subcontractors toward workers, ensure basic human rights are not being violated as a result of operations, and to take responsibility when violations do occur through corrective actions.

Community Support and Philanthropy

Wal-Mart failed to integrate (expand) into Germany because the company did not understand the difference between American and German expectations for market entrants. Wal-Mart learned it must integrate into the existing culture, rather than exercise cultural ethnocentrism or californication to maintain a presence in the host environment, as it demonstrated through the acquisition of Asda in Great Britain. McDonald's diversified its menus to include regional foods in Japan and China while excluding beef from its burgers in India. Additionally, philanthropic activities do not require a company to necessarily provide financial support for a community, but gifts of knowledge, skills, or protection may suffice to gain community support. For example, outsourcing service and support functions to firms in India has helped Microsoft to concentrate on its core competencies while providing knowledge and skills to Indian workers. Wal-Mart has helped to reduce waste among manufacturers and suppliers through Green initiatives (Gielens et.al., 2008).

For XYZ Construction, providing more to the communities served than its core services may prove detrimental for successful integration to sustainability in those regions and may be accomplished through activities ranging from donated services, skill enhancement for workers (training programs), partnerships with local builders, adherence to traditional architecture, and others that enhance existing cultural norms.

Governmental Regulation and Compliance

The International Standards Organization (ISO) provides guidance and certification for construction companies desiring international presence through ISO 9000 and ISO 9001 certifications. Although not governmentally sponsored, these credentials assist construction companies with compliance among diverse techniques for quality management in the industry across international borders, currently comprising 176 of the 196 countries worldwide (International Organization for Standardization, 2011; Macionis, 2010), improving customer satisfaction and continual performance improvement. The goal here is not only "quality management" for XYZ Construction, but also reduced stresses from differences in governmental leadership (totalitarian, capitalistic, socialist), political philosophies that inhibit free trade (isolationist, protectionist, open), and employment law requirements. Careful research into each of these market areas will reduce barriers XYZ Construction may incur.

Stakeholder Prioritization and Communication

As noted in the previous section, ISO certification requires member organizations to utilize a customer-centric approach for eligibility. Recognizing owners and shareholders are not the only stakeholders in XYZ Construction will determine the success of the company internationally, as well as domestically (Pearson Learning Solutions, 2010; Cadotte, et al., 2008; Carroll & Buchholtz, 2009). Stakeholders also include employees, communities, governments, customers, and competitors alike. The trend today is for successful companies to integrate each type of stakeholder into their strategic management philosophies through triple-bottom-line accountability, rather than concentrate on financial measures alone, such as net profit or P/E ratio for sustainability (Carroll & Buchholtz, 2009). Therefore, XYZ Construction needs to prioritize stakeholder relationships that enhance these relationships, integrate these priorities into corporate strategies, and to constantly communicate these values throughout the corporate culture to ensure integration.

Economic Environment and Strategies

Drawbacks to international expansion include assuming greater risks strategically and financially, increased complexity with strategic management, and a lack of guarantees of market similarities to the home market. Advantages may outweigh these difficulties through lowered operational costs (labor, materials, etc.) that supplement domestic growth and allow XYZ Construction to become a stronger competitor in the construction market (Pearson Learning Solutions, 2010). For these possibilities to transform into realities, it is imperative management research and monitor economies entered for volatility and value. Currency exchange, inflation, and interest rates can dramatically impact strategic planning. For example, during the 1990s, Greece and Russia saw inflation exceed 2000%, while the

Chinese enjoyed higher standards of living through the spread of capitalism. The latter providing increased construction opportunities and decreased markets for the former.

International Management & Cultural Diversity

Before XYZ Construction can function internationally, management must decide upon the type of management approach that will best meet the goals of the company and those of its stakeholders concurrently (Pearson Learning Solutions, 2010). For instance, a multi-country approach requires offices and resources in each country of operations, allowing centralized control and retention of profits. However, at the other extreme, licensing or franchising XYZ Construction's name, reputation, and processes to localized contractors passes the costs of human resources, taxes, equipment, facilities, and customer acquisition to the licensee/franchisee. The latter also decreases chances of conflicts arising from cultural differences across borders (Luthans, 2008; Carroll & Buchholtz, 2009) while increasing global reputation management through branding. Prema Nakra (2000) confirmed "buyers are demanding more information about the corporation and its reputation in the market prior to making commitment to their brands or products". These can be localized faster in global markets through licensing/franchising with cultural residents than by initially attempting to build reputation as an outsider.

Cultural factors, such as religion, traditions, norms, mores, and taboos, differ immensely from one country to the next (Macionis, 2010) as demonstrated by examples provided in the previous sections. It would be improbable, if not impossible, for one company to be able to penetrate and sustain markets in every country that it seeks entry without the assistance of localized stakeholders (see the Wal-Mart discussion). In countries where the government and lifestyles of residents are based upon religious doctrines (e.g. Southeast Asia and the Middle East), it would be difficult to integrate Western building practices without amicable resistance, especially in the residential markets where the governments may tightly control innovation.

Differences in banking systems, accounting practices, technological maturity, geography, marketing techniques, and ethical philosophy also provide barriers to market success at the international level (Pearson Learning Solutions, 2010). A process that could take years to strategically implement through research and networking can be reduced to months for XYZ Construction through partnerships, outsourcing, licensing/franchising, brand building, and strategic marketing in those markets contemplated.

CONCLUSIONS

External and internal analyses are only the beginning phases for companies desiring expansion into international markets. These efforts are "limited in terms of the resources and capabilities that are available to implement [these] strategies" (Pearson Learning Solutions, 2010), none of which should be based solely upon the domestic market, but instead in conjunction with those resources and capabilities (limitations) of the markets sought. Capabilities can include conceptual barriers (religion, politics, trade embargoes, traditions, etc.) as well as physical barriers (geography, equipment, supplies, etc.), but ideally may be easily overcome by examining actions other companies have taken in the past in similar pursuits. The following guidelines summarize points discussed:

1. Provide at least, if not better, living wages to workers, police actions of subcontractors toward workers, ensure that basic human rights are not being violated as a result of operations, and to take responsibility when violations do occur through corrective actions.
2. Provide more to the communities served than core services through activities ranging from donated services, skill enhancement for workers (training programs), partnerships with local builders, adherence to traditional architecture, and others that enhance existing cultural norms.
3. Reduce stresses from differences in governmental leadership (totalitarian, capitalistic, socialist), political philosophies that inhibit free trade (isolationist, protectionist, open), and employment law requirements. Careful research into each of these market areas will reduce barriers that XYZ Construction may incur.
4. Prioritize stakeholder relationships that enhance relationships, integrate these priorities into corporate strategies, and constantly communicate these values throughout the corporate culture to ensure integration.
5. Expect greater risks strategically and financially, increased complexity with strategic management, and a lack of guarantees of market similarities to the home market as well as advantages.
6. Decide upon the type of management approach that will best meet the goals of the company and those of its stakeholders concurrently.
7. Consider licensing/franchising as a method of market entry to reduce costs of human resources, taxes, equipment, facilities, and customer acquisition toward the licensee/franchisee while also decreasing the chances of conflicts arising from cultural differences across borders and increasing global reputation management through branding.
8. Remember that cultural factors such as religion, traditions, norms, mores, and taboos differ immensely from one country to the next and that penetration and sustainment of markets in every country seeking entry may require the assistance of localized stakeholders.
9. Consider that differences in banking systems, accounting practices, technological maturity, geography, marketing techniques, and ethical philosophy also provide barriers to market success at the international level.
10. Remember that capabilities can include conceptual barriers (religion, politics, trade embargoes, traditions, etc.) as well as physical barriers (geography, equipment, supplies, etc.). ✳✳✳

2.2 BUSINESS FINANCE AND ACCOUNTING

The following twenty business and finance terms are provided for the benefit of XYZ Construction, Inc. managers in the routine operating principles of the company. Examples are provided as needed for clarification.

1. BALANCE SHEET

The Balance Sheet is one of four financial statements that reports the basic accounting equation (Assets = Liabilities + Owner's Equity) at a moment in time, usually the end of the accounting period by measuring financial position (Pearson Learning Solutions, 2010). Public corporations are required by the Securities and Exchange Commission (SEC) to make this document public as part of the reporting requirement, whereas closely held corporations usually only make the Balance Sheet known to investors, management, and owners. Assets are reported under current (held less than a year) and long-term holdings (e.g. Property, Plant, and Equipment). Accumulated depreciation, intangibles, investments, and other assets fall within this section of the document.

Long and short-term liabilities reside under the second section and include accounts payable, taxes and notes payable, wages and utilities owed, and other debts. Owner Equity then, should equal the difference between assets and liabilities, and is considered the value of the company that remains to the owners when debts are paid from the assets. Review a public corporation's Balance Sheet and notice that values for Assets total the same as Liabilities plus Equity and the groupings of items for these sections.

2. INCOME STATEMENT

The Income Statement measures operating performance by reporting revenues and expenses for the accounting period and includes net worth. This statement is one of the four required reporting financial documents by the SEC and the simplest in its format. Only the Income Statement reports revenues and expenses in this way (Pearson Learning Solutions, 2010).

3. OPERATING CASH FLOWS

A Statement of Cash Flows demonstrates how the company operates through selling goods and services to customers, how the company invests in long-term assets, and the company's need for further financing (Pearson Learning Solutions, 2010). In short, profitability is the key focus in this statement as negative entries may indicate impending bankruptcy. Financing includes stock issuance as well as money borrowed from banks. The purpose of the Statement of Cash Flows is to measure cash receipts and payments through operating activities.

4. STATEMENT OF RETAINED EARNINGS

The fourth and final financial statement, Retained Earnings, shows what the company did with its net income during the reporting period. Net income or loss carries forward from the Income Statement and it is from this entry the Board of Directors decides whether or not to pay out a dividend to stockholders (Pearson Learning Solutions, 2010). Many corporations usually have enough money to pay out these dividends as well as retain funds for reinvestment, although some retain all funds without paying dividends... sometimes a sign of financial struggle.

5. NET WORKING CAPITAL

Net Working Capital is a measure of liquidity and is represented as the difference between a firm's current assets and its current liabilities (Smart, Megginson, & Gitman, 2007) when analyzing the Statement of Cash Flows. Higher values reflect increased solvency. Reviewing a Statement of Cash Flows can show a company experienced an increase/decrease in retained earnings and investment activities. A substantial increase may be the result of going public, as demonstrated by the "Common Stock" entry on the Balance Sheet. This provides how the required reporting financial statements work together to dictate the health of the organization and meet the comparability quality for industry and other similar companies (Pearson Learning Solutions, 2010).

6. ECONOMIC VALUE ADDED

Although Economic Value Added (EVA) is generally computed annually, it may be applied to certain investments or activities to determine the difference between net operating profits after taxes (NOPAT) and the cost of funds (Smart, Megginson, & Gitman, 2007). EVA is primarily utilized in financial planning efforts and by comparing all positive EVAs. Organizations can create the highest overall EVA for stockholders. Unfortunately, there is a lapse between accrual-based accounting value and economic value, such as cost of capital and share price, that results in greater planning focus on growth rates. The concept is straightforward using the financial reports for data (Pearson Learning Solutions, 2010).

7. FIXED ASSETS TURNOVER RATIO

The Fixed Assets Turnover Ratio measures the efficiency with which an organization utilizes its fixed assets and is calculated by dividing sales by the number (in dollars) of fixed asset investment (Smart, Megginson, & Gitman, 2007). Essentially, the ratio tells how many dollars in sales are generated for every dollar of investment in fixed assets. For example, if the Income Statement shows XYZ Construction generated $825,000 in sales and held $220,000 in "All Other Assets" from the Balance Sheet, then XYZ Construction had a ratio of $825,000 / $220,000 = $3.67. So, for every $1 in assets, the company generated $3.67 in sales.

8. NET PROFIT MARGIN

Net Profit Margin is the measure of the percentage of each sales dollar remaining after deducting all costs and expenses, including interest, taxes, and preferred stock dividends and is calculated by dividing the earnings available for stockholders (Net Profit) by sales. To calculate for XYZ Corporation, divide the Net Income found on the Statement of Earnings ($45,000) by the revenues on the Income Statement ($825,000). $45,000 / $825,000 = 0.055 or 5.5% or XYZ Construction generates 5.5% net profit for each dollar in sales.

9. SALES FORECAST

The Sales Forecast is usually the first statement formed when creating pro forma, or future, financial statements (Smart, Megginson, & Gitman, 2007) and can be derived through bottom-up or top-down processing. Top-down forecasting relies more upon industry forecasts where senior managers establish company-wide objectives for sales increases, where bottom-up forecasting begins with talking to customers and establishing forecasts from sales personnel then tallying results at the senior level. While the top-down approach generally requires statistical models and analysis, many firms incorporate a combination of the two with a generated set of assumptions aggregated with customer feedback. Pro forma financial statements may look a year or more ahead and may be used by investors, but generally are tools for managers for internal planning and control purposes.

10. BREAKEVEN ANALYSIS

Breakeven analysis is a risk measurement that allows managers to establish clear goals across functional areas of a firm, such as production scheduling, market share, and variable cost control (e.g. labor). The primary goal of breakeven analysis is to avoid losses (Smart, Megginson, & Gitman, 2007) and can be defined in various ways. For example, how much labor can be expensed to a project before profits turn negative or how long must the new backhoe be commissioned before its expense no longer affects profits negatively? The general formula for breakeven analysis may be defined as dividing the fixed costs of the particular measure by the contribution margin (sales price per unit minus variable costs per unit).

As an example, let's say that a backhoe initially costs $120,000 and an additional $45 per hour to operate. How many hours must the backhoe operate before it has paid for itself if it produces $250 per hour? Fixed cost = $120,000 and variable cost is $45/hour. Sales price = $250/hour, so $120,000 / ($250/hour - $45/hour) = $120,000 / $205/hour. This gives 585.37 hours before the backhoe pays for itself through income generation and fixed costs negate and contribute to hourly profit when operating the machine at a price of $250 per hour.

11. FINANCIAL LEVERAGE

Financial leverage occurs when firms finance their operations with debt and equity and is measured using the debt-equity ratio (Pearson Learning Solutions, 2010). Leverage is the extent to which a firm relies on debt as a source of financing and can be calculated from information found in the Balance Sheet by dividing long and short-term debt by total equity. For example, the Balance Sheet indicates that XYZ

Construction had $92,000 in liabilities and $163,000 in equity. The company's leverage then is $92,000 / $163,000 = 0.56 which means that its debt is just slightly more than half of equity.

12. DOUBLE-ENTRY ACCOUNTING SYSTEM

In double-entry accounting systems, every transaction affects at least two accounts (Pearson Learning Solutions, 2010). For example, when equipment is purchased on credit, the value of the equipment asset account is increased while the accounts payable account is also increased. When a payment is made to the supplier, cash is decreased by the payment amount while the accounts payable account is also decreased by a like amount.

13. LEDGER

The Ledger is the book holding all of the financial accounts. In recent years, computerized software has replaced the traditional bound accounting books of the past to allow instantaneous and time sensitive accounting practices to occur. Accounts are arranged according to the accounting equation: Assets = Liabilities + Owner's Equity. Assets include economic resources that benefit the business in the future and consist of cash, accounts receivable, notes receivable, prepaid expenses, land, equipment, supplies, and other items of value (Pearson Learning Solutions, 2010). Liabilities include accounts payable, notes payable, and accrued liabilities. Owner's Equity records, in financial equivalents, the owner's claims to the assets of the business.

14. LIABILITIES

Liabilities are debts of the organization, or something that is owed to someone else (Pearson Learning Solutions, 2010). Asset accounts generally outnumber liability accounts for a business and record transactions involving accounts payable, notes payable, and other accrued liabilities such as taxes, interest payable, and salaries owed.

15. T ACCOUNT

The T Account, which takes the form of the capital letter T, is the most widely used form of transaction account. The title of the account is displayed at the top with debits (DR) and credits (CR) on the left and right sides of the vertical line, respectively. Debits increase an asset account while credits decrease the account. With liability and equity accounts the opposite is true (Pearson Learning Solutions, 2010). Always remember that two accounts are affected when using the double-entry accounting system.

16. BALANCE OF THE ACCOUNT

The normal balance of an account appears on the credit or debit side where an increase is recorded (Pearson Learning Solutions, 2010). For example, the debit side of an asset account or the credit side of liability and equity accounts. Because revenues increase equity, a revenue's normal balance is a credit, whereas the cash account's balance (asset) is normally a debit.

17. SARBANES-OXLEY ACT OF 2002

The Sarbanes-Oxley Act of 2002 (SOX) was passed to help restore public trust after the financial scandals of Enron, WorldCom, Tyco, and other large corporations by increasing the accuracy of information provided to board members and shareholders (Pearson Learning Solutions, 2010). This goal was achieved by overhauling incentives and the auditing process, by increasing penalties for providing false information, and by forcing companies to validate internal control processes. As a result, many companies have elected to go private, especially smaller firms who could not bear the added compliance costs of remaining public (Smart, Megginson, & Gitman, 2007)

Auditing firms now have to limit non-audit transactions and rotate audit partners every five years while companies must utilize audit committees with at least one person having a financial background. Providing false information by the CEO or CFO to shareholders can carry penalties of up to five million dollars and 20 years imprisonment, including the return of bonuses and profits for the 12 month period preceding the report. Additionally, Section 404 of SOX requires senior managers certify and validate the process through which funds are allocated and controlled along with their outcomes.

18. CASH EQUIVALENTS

While cash is a liquid asset and primary medium of exchange, Cash Equivalents include financial instruments that are easily converted to cash (Pearson Learning Solutions, 2010). Money market accounts, short-term bonds, stocks in other enterprises, in-demand equipment across the industry, inventory, and accounts receivable are forms of cash equivalents. Items that cannot be sold or liquidated quickly are not cash equivalents (e.g. long-term notes held, dated equipment by industry standards, and long-term investments). Cash, short-term investments, and current receivables (in order) are the most liquid.

19. PETTY CASH FUND

A Petty Cash Fund contains the small amount of cash and coins, or cash drawer, that an organization uses for minor purchases (say, under $50 for which a check would be cumbersome and expensive to manage) and providing change to customers. Documentation must be maintained for every purchase (transaction) that utilizes petty cash in the same way as other business income and expenses. Using petty cash slips (receipts) helps to capture these expenses so they can be used to offset income for business tax purposes. Avoiding maintenance of more cash in the drawer than is needed may deter employee theft and robbery.

20. VOUCHER

In terms of tax payments, a voucher is a form submitted with payments of tax liabilities to a governing agency, such as sales or employment taxes. The voucher accompanies payment when depositing with a bank or directly to a revenue agency.

In terms of bonds, vouchers are bonds spent only for certain purposes or goods, somewhat like gift certificates. In short, the voucher is documentation of an intent to adjust accounts in the ledger, also called a journal voucher. Vouchers are commonly used like coupons or prepaid services with customers in order to raise capital before goods or services are provided in the future.

* * *

2.3 ECONOMICS AND THE LEGAL ENVIRONMENT

XYZ Construction, Inc. owners expressed concern about the economic and legal factors that could impact the organization with particular emphasis on the essential economic and legal factors that could affect future IPO status. Macroeconomic and microeconomic factors that affect the operations of the company, legal considerations relative to equipment leases and e-contracts, and employment and labor law influences as the company grows domestically and internationally are discussed in some detail.

MACROECONOMIC FACTORS

At the macroeconomic level, especially in foreign markets, price elasticity of supplies and materials used in construction processes, including monetary exchange rates, can help XYZ Construction to forecast markets and their volatility through demand and supply responsiveness to pricing (Pearson Learning Solutions, 2010). As a general rule, as prices decrease demand increases and supply decreases, but only to the extent the market will allow before devaluing the product or service (and possibly the reputation of the company). For example, if XYZ Construction is competing with other localized builders in the residential arena, then lower package prices for new homeowners will increase demand for XYZ Construction's services and keep workers busy, but only to a point where consumers believe they are purchasing quality homes before rating the work as inferior to substitute builders. By calculating price elasticities for these homes, XYZ Construction managers can gain market share over competitors and build the brand image. Supply and demand are key elements of microeconomics. Macroeconomics involves the aggregate economy with inflation rates, GDP, and monetary exchange rates.

The other hurdle XYZ Construction must be concerned with, monetary exchange rates, can affect profitability in the home country even when being profitable in the host country (Pearson Learning Solutions, 2010). Calculating the real exchange rates of cash conversion, rather than nominal rates, is more accurate. As an example of the Canadian market of interest, it took 1.16 Canadian dollars to equal one American dollar in 2007 (Pearson Learning Solutions, 2010), or inversely, one Canadian dollar was only worth 89.6 cents in American money. So, for every $1,000 after taxed Canadian dollars of profit earned, only $896 American dollars are deposited before tax in the home accounts, significantly reducing profitability. The interaction of supply and demand affects monetary exchange rates, just as prices for products and services are, but may be monitored through an elasticity study as well.

MICROECONOMIC FACTORS

Microeconomics, or how households and firms make choices and interact with markets and how governments influence these choices (Pearson Learning Solutions, 2010), can affect how XYZ Construction performs. When interest rates increase, consumer and business spending for construction decreases, and vice versa. As incomes increase, as is happening in Asia with the industrialization boom, consumer spending for luxury goods (e.g. home add-ons and accessories like pools) increase as well. This cycle then assists the values of monetary currencies to increase in those regions. When the value of that currency falls, as has happened in the United States since the recession of late 2007, the government lowers interest rates to spark consumer spending in response for increasing the ailing currency value (Pearson Learning Solutions, 2010). In this way, XYZ Construction benefits as incomes increase and interest rates decline.

By monitoring indices, such as the Gross Domestic Product (GDP), Gross National Product (GNP), and Balance of Trade, XYZ Construction can monitor and adjust target markets for its construction business. The GDP tells how well the country is performing without international trade, the GNP adds in international performance to the GDP, and the Balance of Trade provides clues as to where incomes are coming from compared to levels of indebtedness in comparison with countries traded with.

EQUIPMENT LEASES AND E-CONTRACTS

It is important to understand that in the United States, contracts completed through electronic means (e-contracts) hold the same weight and consideration under the law as contracts endorsed through traditional ink and paper (Jennings, 2006). Although individual states vary in wording, strength, and penalty of law for these transactions, most states adopted the Universal Commercial Code (UCC) as a model structure with roots into English and Colonial common law (Pearson Learning Solutions, 2010). E-contracts traditionally found use in software licensing agreements, but evolved to Business-to-Business (B2B) and Business-to-Consumer (B2C) environments and now include nearly every form of contractual enterprise once utilized under face-to-face relationships.

To address this phenomenon, new laws were created at the federal level that reinforce acceptance of e-contractual obligation and enforcement. The Electronic Signatures in Global and National Commerce Act (E-Sign) recognizes electronic signatures "as authentic for purposes of contract formation" (Jennings, 2006, p. 298), however individual states must still decide upon validation and security rules. Additionally, the Uniform Electronic Transactions Act (UETA) and the Uniform Computer Information Transactions Act (UCITA) were created to help reduce fraud and misrepresentation in cyber transactions in support of UCC rules. To update copyright statutes, the Digital Millennium Act (DMA) amended legislation to include procedures and purpose of storing copyrighted materials such as blueprints.

Speech on the internet enjoys exactly the same protections under the First Amendment as personal, business, and political speech to include restriction by advertisers to access mailing lists of Internet Service Providers (ISP) for purposes in advertising (Cyber Promotions, Inc. v. America Online, Inc.), as so does the Securities and Exchange Commission (SEC) ruling against inflating stock prices through internet means before dumping stock.

Due process resulting from cyber transactions seems to carry the greatest burden for contractors when one of the parties exists either across state or international boundaries. To combat this dilemma, it is imperative that contracts contain a jurisdictional clause that provides right of remedy by breach of contract or other means to a specific court jurisdiction or method of confrontation, such as arbitration in lieu of trial by court (Walsh, 2010). For example, in the software license agreement for Office 2007 software between Microsoft Corporation and its licensees, the following jurisdictional clauses are included covering domestic and international licensees in legal disputes (Microsoft Corporation, 2007):

"20. APPLICABLE LAW.
a. United States. If you acquired the software in the United States, Washington state law governs the interpretation of this agreement and applies to claims for breach of it, regardless of conflict of laws principles. The laws of the state where you live govern all other claims, including claims under state consumer protection laws, unfair competition laws, and in tort.
b. Outside the United States. If you acquired the software in any other country, the laws of that country apply."

For XYZ Construction, Inc., regardless if contracts are for leased equipment used in the trade or for construction project terms, research into localized laws is imperative before any finalized documents, including e-contracts, are finalized to reduce legal problems of jurisdiction, compliance, and enforcement both domestically and internationally.

EMPLOYMENT AND LABOR LAW

Because "hourly employees belong to a union" at XYZ Construction, Inc., it is important to differentiate the scope of union membership (whether it covers only construction workers, administrative assistants, temporary workers, regular full-time workers, and so forth), the type of union representation (national, international, AFL-CIO, etc.), and the current and past relationships with this union (large numbers of complaints, harmonious, confrontational). There are many types of unions and rules across international borders that differ incessantly to how the company interacts with these unions as well as member and non-member workers (Pearson Learning Solutions, 2010).

As a private company, XYZ Construction is already familiar with labor laws in the United States due to its large labor force, such as Title VII of the Civil Rights Act as amended, the Americans with Disabilities Act (ADA), The Pregnancy Act, and the Immigration and Reform Act. However, as a public corporation individual complaints may have effects upon stock price fluctuations, even internationally, as Nike experienced when complaints soared that the company allowed contracted suppliers to run sweatshops (Bovee, Thill, & Mescon, 2007).

Working harmoniously and expeditiously with labor unions and legal attentions benefit reputation management efforts of XYZ Construction, even when foreign concerns may seem trivial or haphazard (Nakra, 2000). Although cultural and governmental laws or norms, statutes, and regulations may apply in the foreign settings, XYZ Construction, Inc., as an American company, may be held to American standards and liabilities for non-compliance in the home country for violations as is exemplified under the Foreign Corrupt Practices Act. For example, bribery may be expected in some Asian countries to expedite permits or eliminate potential fines, but the company may still find prosecution in the United States for actions in those countries (Pearson Learning Solutions, 2010).

CONCLUSIONS

Summarizing, although not all factors discussed above apply to every country in every situation, these factors do apply in most of the international regions (Canada, Mexico, and parts of Asia) that XYZ Construction has expressed consideration in its horizontal expansion efforts. The primary exclusion resides in monetary exchange rates as some Asian countries do not experience floating values because they are controlled by the banking system rather than the respective government (Pearson Learning Solutions, 2010) at the microeconomic level.

Keeping close watch on financial and cultural news items within each target market will assist decision makers within the organization with making generally accurate forecasts utilizing supply and demand price elasticity for competitiveness on price and overall brand reputation. By treating computer (electronic) formulated contracts (e-contracts) as the company would treat traditionally paper-based contracts and including jurisdictional language, XYZ Construction can avoid confusion and losses through lost time and travel expenses as well as international difference barriers.

* * *

2.4 BUSINESS LEADERSHIP AND INTEGRATION

XYZ Construction, Inc. management intends to convert the company from a closed corporation to public status in the near future. In preparation, managers sought information leading to this event in hopes of expanding the company, not only within the United States, but also globally into Canada, Mexico, and Asia, as well as horizontally into residential construction markets. Beginning with a SWOT analysis, information is baselined before moving into specific areas of concern that explores the goals and strategies for operations, specifically: marketing, employees, organizational structure, international operations, finance and accounting management, legalities, information systems, statistical controls, and leadership.

SWOT ANALYSIS

The analysis of strengths, weaknesses, opportunities, and threats that face XYZ Construction is necessary to help establish a baseline against which managers may plan, implement, and analyze business operations while investors balance these factors to evaluate investment potential (Cadotte, et. al., 2008).

Strengths

The most obvious strength for XYZ Construction is the demand for industry services, especially in Asia (Glanz & Onishi, 2011). Although the company's experience lies within the industrial arena, opportunities are present in the anticipated residential markets. By pledging Initial Public Offering (IPO) procedures, increased opportunities for capital influx exist for growth (Smart, Megginson, & Gitman,

2007). Management demonstrates capacity for intellectual leadership through careful research and analysis of potential problems prior to execution of plans including personnel, accounting, marketing, and analytical techniques.

Weaknesses

XYZ Construction management, for the time being, appears to be weak in applying statistical inference methods, but this problem may be overcome through application and experience. The company has been primarily engaged within one industry segment (industrial) within a single geographic region of the United States (northwest). As the company expands, challenges will present themselves in unfamiliar contexts, such as differing building codes and standards, regulatory complexities, and cultural diversity (Pearson Learning Solutions, 2010). By seeking out partnerships within these geographical areas, management can more quickly convert these weaknesses into strengths.

Opportunities

The positivist point-of-view stands that every action or reaction is, at a minimum, an opportunity to learn even if no tangible benefit materializes. Global expansion provides goodwill for XYZ Construction through brand enhancement (Kerin & Peterson, 2007), partnership opportunities across international boundaries, and increased profitability through reduced labor and material costs (Cadotte, et al., 2008). Industry experience across borders provides enhanced skills not available to any one geographical region, increasing innovation opportunities.

Threats

Many threats to the success of an organization are really opportunities when viewed from an innovative perspective. For instance, if sales for a particular product have declined prematurely to the expected life cycle prediction, this may inadvertently be viewed as a threat to profitability. However, turning this decline into an opportunity to enhance and roll out R&D initiatives, to expand marketing enhancements, to learn customer market expectations, and to create partnership alliances provide increased competitive advantages (Bovee, Mescon, & Thill, 2007). As an active example, XYZ Construction can convert threats of interrupted utilities in the information system into opportunities of expansion by designing improved systems or collaborating partnerships for their improvement.

Of course, political upheavals may be difficult to overcome in affected areas and strengthening of the company brand will take time to overcome, but persistence, strong leadership, skilled workers, fairness to stakeholders, and capital management will expedite the elimination of these threats (Kerin & Peterson,

2007). Cross-cultural regulations, language, property and supply values, monetary exchange rates, and similar differences may daunt management at first with global expansion initiatives, however, becoming competitive advantages once mastered.

GOALS AND STRATEGIES FOR OPERATIONS

The following sections analyze and discuss approaches to successfully implementing goals and strategies in the operations of XYZ Construction. Marketing, employees, organizational structure, international operations, finance and accounting management, legalities, information systems, statistical controls, and leadership are addressed to assist managers and stakeholders proceed with the Initial Public Offering (IPO).

MARKETING

Knowing your product or service, knowing your customers, and knowing even more your competitors is the first rule of entering new markets (Kerin & Peterson, 2007). Aside from developing a marketing plan for the overall company, XYZ Construction should develop plans for each market under consideration while completing market analyses to help better understand these markets and XYZ Construction's ability to enter them successfully. Differences in regional building codes require that crew members and project managers be familiar with local regulations and common practices to avoid costly rebuilding, as discussed later in the Compliance and Legal Considerations section.

Development and implementation of marketing plans is important for growth and expansion efforts, but not as much as correctly identifying stakeholders within each market (Cadotte, et al., 2008). Owners and shareholders expect to earn profits, employees expect fair labor practices, customers expect quality products and services at fair prices, communities expect the company to perform in a socially ethical manner, and governments demand legal compliance (Pearson Learning Solutions, 2010). Each of these stakeholders should be appropriately considered when developing marketing plans.

Geographic segmentation allows for differences in geographic markets in line with the company's strengths, weaknesses, and stakeholder expectations while providing opportunities to create alliances with competitors (Pearson Learning Solutions, 2010). This approach appears to be the best for XYZ Construction as it allows the company expansion into new markets given the constraints presented.

WORKFORCE AND OPERATIONAL MANAGEMENT

Free trade agreements and removal of other barriers enable many organizations to reduce operating costs by relocating at least part of their operations overseas through reduced labor and legal compliance overhead (Cadotte, et al., 2008). Studies among union workers have also shown the primary reason workers join unions is for personal reasons and fair treatment, not necessarily for the purposes of obtaining higher market wages (Pearson Learning Solutions, 2010).

The Compliance and Legal Considerations section below discusses why Nike improved customer and social relations by requiring subcontractors to pay living wages to workers, avoiding/ending abuses of basic human rights, and to take primary responsibility when violations do occur through termination of contracts and other corrective actions. To illustrate, The Public Broadcasting Service (PBS) aired the documentary *China Blue* as an appeal for working conditions in that country. Similar films concerning construction industry workers have been produced in cooperation with PBS and can be reviewed at the PBS website (www.pbs.org). The *China Blue* filmmakers commented:

"Workers are often required to pay for residence permits and hand over their first paychecks as a so-called deposit. They are forbidden to strike and can be fired if they get sick. Factory workers often work in hazardous conditions in environments rife with corruption, with little to no protection or recourse. Many are children under the age of 15. Workers lack unemployment compensation, health insurance and pensions. National Chinese labor laws set a minimum wage equivalent to about 31 cents an hour, but factory owners usually ignore these laws, withholding overtime and paying workers less than half of this amount" (Peled, 2005).

To help eliminate the kinds of problems created by the conditions for XYZ Construction during international expansion efforts, the company needs to apply these lessons to foreign workers:

1) providing at least (preferably better) living wages to workers,
2) policing actions of subcontractors with related workers,
3) ensuring that basic human rights are not being violated as a result of operations, and
4) taking responsibility when violations do occur through corrective and sanction actions.

ORGANIZATIONAL STRUCTURE

The primary organizational design considerations XYZ Construction Inc. will have to consider when moving from a private (closed) corporation to a public structure is loss of ownership and some decision controls (Jennings, 2006). Current ownership divides between public stockholders meaning current owners will have to relinquish some, if not most, ownership control of the company. The Board of Directors will consist of a proportionate number of outside directors for credibility (Cadotte, et al., 2008) among the public trust.

The post-SOX trend has many corporations reverting to private ownership status in order to avoid the high costs of required external auditing (Pearson Learning Solutions, 2010), with some companies reporting costs that are more than triple before the legislation (Cadotte, et al., 2008). Although moving from private to public ownership can be advantageous in terms of raising funds quickly for expansion (Cadotte, et al., 2008), careful consideration should be given to the implications of reporting requirements, outside auditing legislation, changes in control, extended costs, and personal responsibility not required of private corporations before initiating IPO procedures (Pearson Learning Solutions, 2010).

INTERNATIONAL OPERATIONS

To function successfully at the international level, XYZ Construction management has to decide upon the type of management approach that best meets the goals of the company and concurrently the goals of its stakeholders (Pearson Learning Solutions, 2010). In a multi-country approach, such as that proposed for the IPO, then offices and resources in each country of operations allow centralized control and retention of profits. However, if franchising were implemented, the XYZ Construction name, reputation, and processes would be lent to localized contractors and passing the costs of human resources, taxes, equipment, facilities, and customer acquisition to the licensee/franchisee (Pearson Learning Solutions, 2010). Franchising also decreases the chances of conflicts arising from cultural differences across borders (Luthans, 2008) while increasing global reputation management through branding.

John Macionis noted that cultural factors such as religion, traditions, norms, mores, and taboos differ immensely from one country to the next (Macionis, 2010). It is improbable that one company may be able to penetrate and sustain markets in every country that it seeks entry without the assistance of localized stakeholders (Wal-Mart failed in Germany (Gielens et.al., 2008)). In countries where the government and lifestyles of residents are based upon religious doctrines (e.g. Southeast Asia and the Middle East), it would be difficult, especially in residential markets, to integrate Western building practices without amicable resistance where the governments may tightly control innovation (Pearson Learning Solutions, 2010).

Barriers to market success at the international level may also be differentiated in banking systems, accounting practices, technological maturity, geography, marketing techniques, and ethical philosophy (Pearson Learning Solutions, 2010). Processes can be reduced to months for XYZ Construction through partnerships, outsourcing, licensing/franchising, brand building, and strategic marketing in those markets contemplated that would normally take years to strategically implement through research and networking alone (Pearson Learning Solutions, 2010).

FINANCIAL AND ACCOUNTING MANAGEMENT

Initiating an IPO for XYZ Construction creates financial and accounting considerations not previously required for the company under the Sarbanes-Oxley Act (SOX) and reporting requirements levied by the Securities and Exchange Commission (SEC) (Pearson Learning Solutions, 2010). Foreign operations may also mandate reporting requirements within those markets beyond those of the home country, differing in format as well as input (Smart, Megginson, & Gitman, 2007); for example, GAAP in the United States versus IFRS in Canada, Hong Kong, Taiwan, and Japan.

The Sarbanes-Oxley Act particularly mandates that the CEO, CFO, and other key executives be held personally accountable for violating fiduciary responsibilities to shareholders through penalties of lengthy prison terms (Moran, 2008), repayment of bonuses and incentives (Pearson Learning Solutions, 2010), and equity-based compensation. Restrictions are also placed upon auditing requirements in that auditor relationships are narrowed in length and scope through periodic rotation, restricted additional company assignments, and board membership (Stice & Stice, 2006).

Many managers and businesses increasingly take interest in triple-bottom-line accounting that not only reports financial measures, but also environmental and social reporting through the implementation of a balanced scorecard (Pearson Learning Solutions, 2010). The Canadian Imperial Bank of Commerce (CIBC) published that this system attempts to balance financial and non-financial measures, including objectives set by the organization "for society, clients, employees, community, environment, suppliers, and corporate governance". Establishing which measures affect XYZ Construction and its stakeholders is a continual process involving careful managerial and market analyses (Bovee, Mescon, & Thill, 2007).

COMPLIANCE AND LEGAL CONSIDERATIONS

Aside from the economic compliance and legal considerations discussing financial and accounting management in the preceding section, XYZ Construction, especially as a potential global organization dealing in the construction markets, must consider legalities within each territory the company operates (including local differences within the U.S.) (Moran, 2008). Issues regarding human resources/labor (recruitment, hiring, and retention), building codes, and contractual compliance (tort, service, and product) carry significant influence upon the success of the company.

At the labor level, laws concerning employer/employee relationships constantly change, such as the controversial law that currently limits collective bargaining privileges for unionized government workers in Wisconsin (Newman, 2011). Although an act or omission may be encouraged or allowed in one region, it may be illegal in another with declining benefit to the company through damaged reputation and lost productivity. For example, Nike does not physically produce any of its own products, outsourcing all manufacturing processes to foreign labor markets. When it was discovered that some of these contractors were violating human rights of their workers (practices legal in the host countries) through actions that would otherwise be against the law in the United States, activist groups quickly utilized media outlets to inform the American public and call for boycotts on Nike products (Bovee, Mescon, & Thill, 2007). The result was Nike began inspecting contractor facilities to rectify these problems and terminated contracts with those companies who did not comply. Currently within the U.S., federal legislation, such as the Americans with Disabilities Act (ADA) and the National Labor Relations Act (NLRA), and more stringent state and local level statutes prohibit many of the abuses against employees now common in other countries.

At the industry level, global building codes can vary. Many attribute the low death toll in Japan after the reported 8.9 earthquake and following tsunami in 2011 to the country's reputation for having the strictest building codes in the world (Glanz & Onishi, 2011). Regardless of the specific location, XYZ Construction would benefit from utilizing localized team members for each area served to ensure experienced compliance with regional building codes to reduce warranty and initial construction costs, liability issues, and to increase demand compliance.

Contract law also varies by location served. In the U.S., a defendant is innocent until proven guilty by means of failing to eliminate doubt, whereas in England and many Asian countries, guilt is assumed unless proven innocent by a preponderance of the evidence (Carroll & Buchholtz, 2009). For this very reason, many companies accused of wrongdoing will make a first effort to avoid prosecution through denial and other proactive defensive techniques (lying, reverse blame, avoidance, etc.) although in the United States, taking responsibility is admired and often rewarded at the consumer market and government levels, such as when Johnson and Johnson initiated tamper-resistant packaging for Tylenol (Carroll & Buchholtz, 2009).

INFORMATION MANAGEMENT AND TECHNOLOGY

The use of information systems (IS) requires planning, implementation, and evaluation and control. These systems include the hardware, software, and telecommunications networks that link people in collecting, creating, and distributing useful data for the purposes of meeting organizational goals (Pearson Learning Solutions, 2010). Transforming the raw data into ultimate wisdom through the usage of this information across the organization leads to success for the system implemented. A proper system minimizes conflicts and maximizes interoperability among employees, managers, customers, and other stakeholders by adding value through increased productivity and profitability (Pearson Learning Solutions, 2010). Total costs of ownership (TCO) may be reduced through outsourcing non-critical systems that do not exercise strategic competitiveness or provide economic as well as architectural, operational, and compliance values for the organization (Pearson Learning Solutions, 2010).

Consideration by XYZ Construction management into developing components of the information system that provide competitive advantage in-house, extending the duration of any advantage since pre-packaged components are also available to competitors (eliminating the advantage) may assist the company in gaining market share.

Concerns over infrastructural integrity draw questions to economically depressed locations where interruptions in power grids, political upheaval, water quality, and employee safety may inhibit XYZ Construction's efforts at growth and profitability. The implementation of well-managed databases and internet presence may help to eliminate some of these distractions of business for security, maintainability, and transaction speed (Pearson Learning Solutions, 2010).

INTERNAL CONTROL AND EVALUATION

Internally, XYZ Construction is limited only by the imagination (and math skills) of its managers. For example, descriptive statistics may be utilized to benefit the organization in terms of (but by no means limited to) determining warranty periods of construction projects or utilization for comparative marketing (Pearson Learning Solutions, 2010). Safety standards of materials and qualities of workmanship are often measured and determinations made using statistical analyses of variance and hypothesis testing. Care must be taken in that the sample size utilized in the calculations is large enough to establish a reasonable baseline representing the entire line or service, and that enough time has passed representative of warranty period claims for validity and reliability (Cadotte, et al., 2008).

Customer satisfaction and market evaluation measures resemble these techniques except that managers need to be careful when working with nominal or ordinal scales, especially when comparing across markets. Direct comparisons may prove meaningless for inferential analyses, especially across product lines, when calculated using misaligned sample data (Pearson Learning Solutions, 2010).

LEADERSHIP

The second element of leadership is "leadership is goal directed and plays an active role in groups and organizations" (Pearson Learning Solutions, 2010, p. 1352). This definition infers that organizational leaders, foregoing their respective leadership style, must be goal oriented; a common characteristic of organizational effectiveness (Cadotte, et al., 2008). In other words, XYZ Construction management sets organizational goals through marketing plans, vision and mission statements, project deadlines, and so forth and the real leaders provide direction among subordinates and partners to meeting or exceeding those expectations.

The first and third elements of leadership dictate that respectively, leadership is a group phenomenon and leadership presence assumes that some form of a leadership hierarchy exists, whether it exists as a formal structure or is implied by action (Pearson Learning Solutions, 2010). XYZ Construction crews operate within the team format indicating a lack of hierarchy, although studies indicate that successful self-managed teams, with a definable group leader, tend to operate more efficiently and productively than teams with a more restrictive leadership structure (Cadotte, et al., 2008). Successful leaders of self-managed teams often follow an authoritative leadership style, applying democratic principles the bulk of the time, yet asserting influence and power during periods of team conflict (Macionis, 2010). In the managerial ranks, some form of hierarchy is essential to balance power and corruption (Pearson Learning Solutions, 2010), but leaders who work with a team orientation tend to reach organizational goals more frequently than those organizations who abide strictly to rank-and-file orientations (Cadotte, et al., 2008).

CONCLUSIONS

For XYZ Construction, Inc. management to follow-through with intentions of converting the company from a closed corporation to public status in the near future, managers need to prepare by seeking information that leads to this event as well as expansion within the United States and globally into Canada, Mexico, and Asia. Consideration into horizontal residential construction markets is of equal importance. Beginning with a SWOT analysis, information gathering and processing must be baselined before moving into specific areas of concern that explores the goals and strategies for operations, specifically: marketing, employees, organizational structure, international operations, finance and accounting management, legalities, information systems, statistical controls, and leadership.

* * *

PART TWO REFERENCES

Bovee, C. L., Thill, J. B., & Mescon, M. H. (2007). Excellence in Business (3rd ed.). Upper Saddle River, NJ: Pearson Prentice Hall.

Cadotte, E. R., Bruce, H. J., Gardial, S. F., Garval, D., Gilbert, K. C., Jacobs, J. D., et al. (2008). The Management of Strategy in the Marketplace. Knoxville, TN: Innovative Learning Solutions.

Carroll, A. B., & Buchholtz, A. K. (2009). Business & Society: Ethics and Stakeholder Management (7th ed.). Mason, OH: South-Western Cengage Learning.

Cyber Promotions, Inc. v. America Online, Inc., 948 F. Supp. 436.

Gielens, K., Van De Gucht, L. M., Steenkamp, J.-B. E., & Dekimpe, M. G. (2008). Dancing with a Giant: The Effect of Wal-Mart's Entry into the United Kingdom on the Performance of European Retailers. Journal of Marketing Research, XLV, 519-534.

Glanz, J., & Onishi, N. (2011, March 12). Japan's Strict Building Codes Saved Lives. Retrieved March 19, 2011, from The New York Times: http://www.nytimes.com/2011/03/12/world/asia/12codes.html?_r=1&pagewanted=all.

International Organization for Standardization. (2010). ISO 9000 - Quality Management. Retrieved January 21, 2011, from ISO: http://www.iso.org/iso/iso_catalogue/management_and_leadership_standards/quality_management.htm.

Jennings, M. M. (2006). Business: Its Legal, Ethical, and Global Environment (7th ed.). Mason, OH: Thomson Higher Learning.

Kerin, R. A., & Peterson, R. A. (2007). Strategic Marketing Problems: Cases and Comments (11th ed.). Upper Saddle River, NJ: Pearson Education, Inc.

Lai, K., Cheng, T., & Tang, A. (2010). Green Retailing: FACTORS FOR SUCCESS. California Management Review, 52 (2), 6-31.

Luthans, F. (2008). Organizational Behavior (11th ed.). Boston, MA: McGraw-Hill/Irwin.

Macionis, J. J. (2010). Sociology (13th ed.). Boston, MA: Prentice Hall.

Microsoft Corporation. (2007). Microsoft Software License Terms Office 2007. Redmond, Washington.

Moran, J. J. (2008). Employment Law: New Challenges in the Business Environment (4th ed.). Upper Saddle River, NJ: Pearson/Prentice Hall.

Nakra, P. (2000, Summer). Corporate Reputation Management: "CRM" with a Strategic Twist? Public Relations Quarterly, 35-42.

Newman, A. (2011, March 19). Outrage as Judge Blocks Wisconsin Union Law. (G. Benoit, Ed.) Retrieved March 19, 2011, from The New American Magazine: http://www.thenewamerican.com/index.php/usnews/politics/6758-outrage-as-judge-blocks-wisconsin-union-law.

Pearson Learning Solutions. (2010). SKS7000 – Executive Concepts in Business Strategy. Boston, MA: Pearson Learning Solutions.

Peled, M. X., Chen, S. (Producers), & Peled, M. X. (Director). (2005). China blue [Motion Picture].

Smart, S. B., Megginson, W. L., & Gitman, L. J. (2007). Corporate Finance (2nd ed.). Mason, OH: Thomson South-Western.

Stice, E. K., & Stice, J. D. (2006). Financial Accounting: Reporting and Analysis (7th ed.). Mason, OH: Thomson Higher Education.

Walsh, D. J. (2010). Employment Law for Human Resource Practice (3rd ed.). Mason, OH: South-Western Cengage Learning.

* * *

PART THREE:
LEGAL ISSUES IN HUMAN RESOURCES MANAGEMENT

3.1 ANTIDISCRIMINATION LAW

This paper examines changes, some significant, that have occurred in federal antidiscrimination legislation since 1990. Other than the Pregnancy Discrimination Act of 1991, no new major legislation has been enacted. However, existing laws receive daily scrutiny and re-definition within the court system. These changes affect American workers as a culture alongside the organizations that employ them. Exploration begins with jurisdictional clarification into shared liability for organizations (and individuals), moves into clarification of disability questions for employers, notices a trend in sexual harassment cases, and then provides a twist encountered through age discrimination for federal workers.

SHARED LIABILITIES

In 1994, courts ruled that employers were still bound to legislative jurisdiction under Title VII of the Civil Rights Act and the ADA even though they may not otherwise qualify under minimum employee requirements... if that employer jointly serves in a subcontractor's hiring/firing decision of an employee and that subcontractor does qualify (Joseph D. Jendusa v. Cancer Treatment Centers of America, Inc. and Midwestern Regional Medical Center, Inc. and Richard Stephenson, 1994). In other words, if business partnerships collaborate with employee decisions, they also share liability and responsibility for those employees under legislative enactments.

This ruling carries a plethora of anti-discriminatory implications that force changes from contemporary business mindsets toward worker-friendly environments. Contracting individuals and organizations no longer can demand that certain protected classes of people who are qualified to perform particular services through a contracted agency be restricted from working on projects without a bona fide exemption. For example, if an individual hires a roofing company to replace the shingles on their home, but informs the contracting supervisor "not to bring any Asians on my property while doing this job", then that individual becomes jointly liable under Title VII for racial discrimination if that roofer complies by denying workers of Asian descent employment on that roofing job. Similar situations apply to disabled workers, traditionally gendered occupations, and any class of workers protected by federal legislation.

The Jendusa ruling, one can argue, also helps with the elimination of glass ceiling effects by reducing biased outside influences upon personnel decisions. Using the previous roofing example, businesses may complain about profit losses incurred from lost sales, however, more Asians enjoy advancement opportunities through experience attainment while the roofing customer realizes conformity (tolerance) resulting from need (roof) and compliance (liability threat).

EMPLOYER RESPONSIBILITIES WITH NEW DISABILITIES

Business textbooks frequently discuss issues concerning the employment of new employees (Jennings, 2006; Moran, 2008) but sparingly tackle problems concerning existing workers who become disabled while employed within an organization. Qualifications for liability differ under ADA for employers within each category as ruled in Wayne A. Meyer v. Southern Eagle Sales and Service, Inc. When hiring new individuals with disabilities, employers find restrictions with accommodation, job modifications, and possible realignment of positions. This case further defined interpretation of the Americans with Disabilities Act toward protection of employers when current workers incur disability as detailed within the legislation.

The ruling declared that employers are not required, in some circumstances, to adjust the organizational or job structures to accommodate the new disability if those changes will not reasonably allow the worker to perform those duties at the same levels previously executed. In Meyer's case, he was a salesperson in a position that required extended periods of walking and standing until his disability precluded these capabilities. The court decision favored the employer in that it could not provide an accommodation that would allow Meyer to perform those essential job duties and was not "required to relieve [Meyer] of any essential functions of the job, modify the actual duties, or reassign existing employees or hire new employees to perform those duties".

The message to workers signifies that light duty then is a voluntary accommodation, intended as temporary assistance, on behalf of the employer in hopes the employee will soon return to previous job outcomes. The employer is under no obligation under the ADA to permanently alter job duties, reassign the worker, or to move other employees if those outcomes cannot be achieved. For instance, if a welder goes blind, then that welder is not protected under anti-discrimination legislation from termination because that welder can no longer perform his/her duties with any kind of reasonable accommodation. The Meyer's ruling failed to provide increased opportunities for disabled persons under the ADA, but it does protect the existing workforce from unscrupulous workers that prey upon disability claims for reduced workloads.

SEXUAL HARASSMENT

Sexual harassment cases plagued the courts throughout the 1990s and early 2000s (Jennings, 2006). One such case in which the Equal Employment Opportunity Commission (EEOC) involved itself concerned a two-edged blade of training males and females together in one-on-one situations. Fearing complaints of sexual harassment from trainees, Swift Transportation attempted to avoid conflict by requiring males reside only with males and females only with females while on over-the-road excursions. This reasoning backfired on Swift when students felt the policy was maliciously biased towards gender as a few cited that most experienced driver-trainers were men, providing a disadvantage to the women seeking the same level of training. Although Swift entered a consent decree and voluntarily lifted the segregation policy, the court refused to penalize the transportation company claiming the EEOC failed to prove malicious intent underlying the original decision (EEOC v. Swift Transportation Co., Inc., 1999).

This case reinforced the need of each party in an anti-discrimination suit to prove their respective parts for effective claims while demonstrating the courts understand the complexity of the issues for organizations. Likewise, eliminating damned-if-you-do scenarios proves difficult; however, the courts are recognizing these attempts at compliance with ADA initiatives and subsequently decreasing the fluency of punitive measures in these cases.

AGE DISCRIMINATION

Review of age discrimination cases since 1990 reveals that many resulted from acts of retaliation from former employers after the ex-employee filed a complaint. The 2008 case of Myrna Gomez-Perez versus Postmaster General, as eventually heard by the Supreme Court, concluded that although the Age Discrimination in Employment Act (ADEA) only described the private sector in terms of retaliation, federal employers share equal inclusion of liability. Gomez-Perez asserted that her previous employer reduced her work hours and made false reports after she complained of age discrimination. Lower courts granted judgment to the Postal Service citing lack of verbiage concerning retaliation. The Supreme Court disagreed in that Title IX of the Education Amendments of 1972 did provide further protection for federal employees.

This case was a turning point for employees of federal agencies seeking equal protections as private sector workers; now everyone (over age 40, of course) could complain of age discrimination without fear of retaliation efforts from employers. As a secondary message to employers, the ruling also reinforced the notion that although one legislative enactment may lack discussion of a particular point, other subsequent works apply when either an absence occurs, or the older legislation contradicts newer applications.

CONCLUSIONS

Anti-discrimination laws enforced by the EEOC (Equal Employment Opportunity Commission, 2012) primarily cover topics exploring age, compensation, disability, genetics, race, religion, pregnancy, and sex. The commission recommended literally thousands of cases for legal action since 1990 with little decline in the number of annual complaints. The majority of cases handled by the EEOC incur outside settlements, precluding trend documentation as well as public and academic awareness (Moran, 2008).

Each new case situation provides opportunity for refinement of legislative intents and interpretations, sometimes with cultural impact, but always affecting organizational structures to some degree. Culturally, American workers feel relief that outsiders endure a share of the liability when work status decisions are influenced, whereas additional assurance arises from knowledge that if an older law excludes them, then other legislative actions may provide needed coverage. Refinement occasionally assists organizations at the other end of the continuum as well: those companies making conscious efforts towards compliance find relief when situational contradictions back them into corners.

Globally, these changes arguably hinder competitive advantage for American organizations when similar worker rights laws do not exist abroad, but compliance strengthens political and brand awareness in core operations (Jennings, 2006). Conversely, further advantages arise the minute foreign organizations attempt domestication when originating from countries lacking rights considerations.

* * *

3.2 ADA AS EMPLOYMENT LAW

This paper examines the historical development of the Americans with Disabilities Act of 1990 (ADA) and how it has undergone revision and refinement since. This examination includes amendment during 2008 as well as subsequent legislation altering the ADA indirectly. Specifically, attention focuses upon the drivers forcing changes and the impacts incurred because of judicial interpretations and applications. As such, landmark court cases are reviewed within their affects upon organizations, employees, and society as a whole in relation to these rulings and perceptions.

ADA DEVELOPMENT

The Americans with Disabilities Act of 1990 originated as an addendum to the Civil Right Act of 1964 in response to the need for provisions in coverage of disabled persons in the workplace. Employment discrimination for the disabled lacked attention within the civil rights legislation and excluded a large proportion of the workforce. The intercessory Rehabilitation Act of 1973 enacted protections for federal workers, this time failing the larger private sector. The year following (1991) the creation of the ADA, amending of the Civil Rights Act forced changes in sections 101, 102, and 509 of the ADA "to provide for the recovery of compensatory and punitive damages in cases of intentional violations of Title VII, the ADA, and section 501 of the Rehabilitation Act of 1973" (Equal Opportunity Employment Commission, 2012).

By 2008, legal challenges to the ADA lead to the congressional passing of the Americans with Disabilities Act Amendments Act of 2008 (ADAAA). These amendments considered landmark cases like Toyota v. Williams and Sutton v. United Airlines (Equal Opportunity Employment Commission, 2008) to narrow the scope of protections and definitions intended by Congress. The intent of these changes served primarily with assisting courts in the interpretations of vague language constructs for proper applications. The last formal transformation of the ADA occurred in 2009 with the adoption of the Lilly Ledbetter Fair Pay Act of 2009 (LLFPA). The LLFPA clarified periods in which victims of discrimination may challenge and recover for discriminatory compensation decisions or other discriminatory practices affecting compensation. The sections that follow concentrate upon the major court cases leading to adoption of the ADAAA and subsequent narrowing of ADA applications within the court systems.

NEW V. PRE-EXISTING DISABILITY

As discussed in a previous writing, modern textbooks often ignore problems employers face when current employees incur disabilities during their tenure at the organization. Courts distinguished qualifications for liability under the ADA for employers discerning differences with potential and hired employees (Wayne A. Meyer v. Southern Eagle Sales and Service, Inc., 1999). Judicial seats remarked that in some instances, employers are not required to adjust organizational or job structures to accommodate new disabilities, if those changes will not reasonably allow the worker to perform those duties at the same levels previously executed. Meyer's was a salesperson requiring extended periods of walking and standing until his disability disallowed these personal capabilities. The decision favored his previous employer asserting that it could not provide an accommodation that would allow Meyer to perform those essential job duties and the employer was not "required to relieve [Meyer] of any essential functions of the job, modify the actual duties, or reassign existing employees or hire new employees to perform those duties".

Light duty, therefore, is a voluntary accommodation intended as temporary support on behalf of the employer in anticipation the employee will quickly return to previous job outcomes. Altering job duties and work reassignments serve without obligation or permanence under the ADA for employers if those expected employee outcomes cannot enjoy achievement.

PROSTHETICS AND DISABILITY

Simply obtaining and utilizing a prosthetic device does not prove disability under ADA definitions, especially if that device appears to remove that person's inability to perform major life activities, such as working (Sutton v. United Airlines, Inc., 1999). Eyeglasses, dentures, hearing aids, and other devices that restore sight, eating ability, hearing, and respective activities to an individual's life statutorily eliminate any disability status incurred or claimed before utilization and restoration. Disabilities incur two elements: 1) a physical or mental impairment; and 2) a substantially limited life activity common to most people. The Sutton v. United Airlines case conveyed to definition that when a prosthetic device eliminates the second element, the disability fades with it under ADA reasoning. For example, if a worker wears eyeglasses that corrects their vision, then that employee no longer has a claim to visual impairment.

The ruling also acknowledged a statutory loophole designed to reduce stereotyping of workers based upon appearance of perceived disabilities. Even if an employee lacks a definitional physical or mental impairment, if that employer acts in discriminatory ways believing a person is disabled, then that worker may utilize that employer's belief in the claim as if the impairment really existed. Additionally, the court recognized the right of employers to service minimal physical and mental requirements remarking that persons who fall below the thresholds do not meet any disability; their ability to work is not hampered, just the opportunity to hold that particular job.

REASONABLE ACCOMMODATION

Nearly every case brought to the courts involving discrimination under the ADA involves the topic of accommodation in some form or other (the next subsection involves life activities and accommodations). Here the topic delves into how accommodation can collide with traditions and abuse by employees. In PGA Tour, Inc. v. Martin, the golf organization generally expected qualified participants to walk the course as they played, ignoring possibilities that players may have ADA-protected inabilities to walk great distances or to stand for long periods. When Martin requested a golf cart to travel the course, PGA Tour denied his request, essentially in the name of tradition. Eventually, the Supreme Court ruled in Martin's favor citing the organization should reasonably have allowed Martin to ride the course since the cart provided no unfair advantages over other players.

On the flip side, and contradictory to the outcomes previously discussed concerning new disabilities (New v. Pre-Existing Disability), an employee attempted to use reduced and exempted workloads in lieu of job qualifications (Toyota v. Williams, 2002). Williams was diagnosed with a disability that precluded her from performing her full job duties, refused corrective treatments (Leeds & Richards, 2008): albeit she accepted therapies – but she still refused available corrective procedures and demanded selective work duties to accommodate her decisions, not her inabilities. Realizing that Williams was abusing Toyota's accommodation attempts to alter her job duties permanently, the Supreme Court applied its 1999 ruling that accommodation is temporary on behalf of the employer and exempted Williams from auxiliary ADA protection.

These landmark cases further defined the Americans with Disabilities Act and its application of accommodations. Employees could no longer abuse protections to alter their job duties while employers were forced to set aside tradition for inclusion of qualified membership. These attitudes reflect how the ADA works in the combined interests of organizations and their members alike.

LIFE ACTIVITIES V. ABILITY

Although Toyota v. Williams aided with further definition of reasonable accommodation, the case more importantly provided clarification for the differences between Activities of Daily Living (ADL)

(Phillips, et al., 2011) and one's ability through qualification to perform their job duties. These were the changes implemented within the ADAAA. Under ADAAA redefinitions, a person fails to prove a disability using ADLs if those inabilities do not affect qualifications for the particular job or, conversely, if the losses of physical and mental bona fide work qualifications missed the mark to inhibit ADLs common among most persons. The ruling completed the question lower courts disagreed upon, whether ADLs and job qualifications existed as mutually exclusive, or mutually inclusive, and just what constituted an ADL.

Acceptance of the medical classification for ADLs removed doubt from interpretations while restricting the scope of inclusive ailments. For example, short-term conditions, such as curable diseases (e.g. alcoholism) and sprained ankles cannot be justifiable claims whereas a department store manager terminated for contracting the AIDS virus may prove disparate treatment (Bragdon v. Abbott, 1998). Whether disparate treatment or disparate impact, Toyota v. Williams also reiterated the need for courts to apply appropriate reasoning when deciding similar cases under ADA litigation, else improper outcomes result.

HEALTH

Questions often arise whether a proposed work qualification offends the ADA if that qualification prevents injury or illness to workers. Most often, the answer rebounds in the negative, however inquisitions occasionally repose if an employer has the right to deny workers if those persons willingly assume risks that endanger themselves (Chevron v. Echazabal, 2002), and to what extent. The Supreme Court ruled in favor of employers demarking not only the right, but also the responsibility of organizations to protect their members, quoting "[organizations are] to assure so far as possible every working man and woman in the Nation safe and healthful working conditions". For Echazabal, this meant that Chevron's right (responsibility) to deny employment that would further cause him bodily harm superseded Echazabal's right to decide if he was willing to assume the risk.

Social views contend that organizations should celebrate disability through acceptance and accommodation while medical opinions spot disabilities as offensive traits necessary of elimination (Muller, 2011). Whereas it seems that the ADA takes side with social perspectives at first glance, closer examination reveals a trend by the courts to incorporate medical reasoning into their decision-making processes. Not only does the Chevron case exemplify this congruence of ideas, the ruling supports the rationale underlying the ADA that health weighs more heavily than free will when personal rights are at stake.

CONCLUSIONS

In relationship to its parent, the ADA is young within the legislative and judicial arenas, barely two decades old. In spite of this newness, the ADA has undergone revision and constant redefinition in terms of its purposes and protective assurances. Points to what constitutes a claimable disability, when that disability is applicable to the workplace, what should or should not be done by employers and organizational members, and exactly how long the perceived disability matters have each found treatment since inception.

Traditions undergo forced change in long-standing organizations while persons attempting to abuse the protections afforded find deserved recompense. The same reconciliations apply when prioritizing personal rights to free will and the rights of organizations to protect themselves and their members: social perspectives and medical opinions have come together to balance incongruity. It will be of interest to see how future technologies and ideas affect application of principles interpreting ADA developments.

* * *

3.3 ERISA AND THE STATES

This paper examines the primary components of the Employee Retirement and Income Security Act of 1974 (ERISA), namely pension plans and healthcare. Largely unchanged since its inception, differences with enforcement, control, and judicial interpretation sever the Act into distinct arenas. While the pension component enjoys the same activity and ownership as most other Congressional legislations, the healthcare section appears to endure the greatest amount of subsidiary adaptation, reformative adjustment, and scrutiny since the Civil Rights Act of 1964. Exploration begins with analysis of the healthcare component, moves toward a discussion of pension plans under ERISA, and then examines the battle between proponents. Review of three benchmark court cases precedes final summative commentary.

HEALTH DEVELOPMENTS POST-ERISA

Michael S. Gordon, an initial drafter of ERISA, commented on the question of why Congress intentionally failed to cover employee healthcare plans outside of welfare benefits within the regulatory instrument. "Unlike pension plans there was no crisis in health plans in 1974... there was no evidence of overwhelming red tape blocking participants or their beneficiaries from obtaining needed medical treatment or any other health benefit" (Borzi, 2008, p. 661). Essentially, Congress did not foresee the myriad of HMOs, exuberant inflation of medical costs, and active demands for employer healthcare reform coming within the following decade that left ERISA outdated almost immediately.

The Consolidated Omnibus Budget Reconciliation Act of 1985 (COBRA) addressed the issue of vanished coverage when employees lost their jobs. Additionally, estranged family members of former workers could also elect to continue healthcare policies for a limited time at their expense. The unfortunate truth-of-consequence for those eligible under COBRA lies in practicality of affordability. Low-income participants without substantial savings cannot afford the modern costs of premiums, plus the allotted administrative fees permitted, making COBRA worthless to the majority of unemployed and unskilled workers.

The next eleven years witnessed enactment of the Health Insurance Portability and Accountability Act (HIPAA). This legislation modified ERISA by creating rights of portability to covered workers and restricting usage of preexisting condition exclusions or limitations within group markets by their insurers. HIPPA modernized discrimination definitions to include coverage, enrollment, and premiums related to health status, age, and gender. The Emergency Economic Stabilization Act of 2008 (EESA) expanded mental health coverage and provided inclusion for women who had undergone mastectomies. Under heated and continued opposition by the states, The Patient Protection and Affordable Care Act (ACA or commonly known as "Obama Care") also required all persons, employed or not, to obtain medical insurance by 2014 or face annual fines payable (if required to file returns under Internal Revenue Service guidelines) through taxation measures. ACA may eventually further affect ERISA in as far as employer-provided health plans after the Act fully enacts the remainder of its components by 2016.

CHANGES IN PENSION PLANS

ERISA was originally designed to protect pension plans, primarily the welfare benefits portions (Moran, 2008). As Gordon pointed out, when ERISA was enacted in 1974, the drafters could not foretell dramatic life expectancy increases and the effects caused by the baby boomer generation on pension funding. Combined with global recession, significant reductions in 401(k) balances, and uncertainties with reform of healthcare many workers find they need to work longer than traditional retirement ages. A surge in phased retirement programs emerged in response drawing attention by the Internal Revenue Service (IRS).

In 2004, the IRS proposed regulations aligned with ERISA geared toward phased retirement programs maintaining that plans must be aligned with a company's benefits program in such a way that retirement benefits were not negatively affected and employees were not penalized for working part-time (Noble & Harper, 2010). Specifically, workers could retire at age 59 ½ if they reduced workloads by at least 20%. Retirees could not elect lump-sum distributions, accepted reduced periodic benefit amounts (not to exceed total benefit amounts), and were required to continue contributions to the plan with any earned income from part-time work. In comparison to Social Security's graduated retirement age, phased retirement meant employees could begin retirement as much as 15.5 years sooner. At the employer level, skilled workers were retained longer but compliance required additional monitoring efforts.

The Pension Protection Act of 2006 (PPA) legislated the IRS regulations with provisions against discrimination by employers. In most cases, the PPA recognized age 62 for early retirement, but honors 59 ½ under defined contribution plans (e.g. 401(k) plans). Noble and Harper commented on the realization of the impact the aging workforce has upon retirement programs and the apparent need for more collaborative efforts to address underfunding problems of pension plans in the United States. From here one may safely assume that state and federal disagreements follow expectation.

STATES V. FEDERAL CONTROLS

The leading proponent to healthcare reform, including the ACA and ERISA, tends to be the states (Leonard, 2011). One reason is that ACA mandates the states to utilize their administrative capacities for implementation of various programs. The aforementioned regulation requiring all individuals to obtain healthcare insurance by 2014 drew the most attention, citing encroachment upon state's rights. As a result, 40 states either outright refused to adopt and enforce specific components of the Act or they attempted to pass "amendments and resolutions purporting to nullify the federal laws".

The subordinate issue concerning allocation of power between the central government and the sovereign states serves the unexpected effect of deliberation before the voters and the American public. Agreeing with Leonard, Jacobson (2008) cited the trend of the Supreme Court to side with the states since 1980 in cases of power delegation, but in this particular matter refused judiciary intervention, receding behind the Commerce Clause of the Constitution. This exemption allows the Supreme Court to bow out of judicial decisions when it feels the matter is social policy, effectively forcing Congress to address any deficiencies found in markets or legislations. At least on the healthcare side of ERISA, very little, if any intervention by the courts may overshadow the power debates. However, with pension plans the courts regularly entertain settlement under ERISA's primary objective.

JUDICIAL DEVELOPMENTS WITH ERISA

Failure of many pension plans for American workers led to bankruptcy for many companies (Moran, 2008). To alleviate underfunding and termination of pension plans, ERISA incorporated fiduciary responsibility for plan administrators, termination insurance requirements, and minimum funding requirements while the pension plan is active. In no case, even before vesting, may a plan pay out less in total benefits than the employee is entitled. Xerox's retirement fund sought to reduce payouts drastically for retirees (to overcome future underfunding problems?) by as much as 90% (Miller v. Xerox Corp. Retirement Income Guarantee Plan, 2006). The fund attempted to deduct, erroneously, values of previously discontinued profit sharing plan distributions from accrued pension amounts. The court ratified ERISA with the conclusion that accrued pension benefits cannot be devalued.

Fiduciary duties of the plan administrator require that person to act in the best interests of the investor, not the company. Similar to the breach of duty exercised by the Xerox fund administrator, the fiduciary of Varity Corporation misled plan investors into transferring out of the program using false information (Varity Corp. v. Howe, 1996). Since the employer fraudulently coerced succession, the courts ruled that beneficiaries could be reinstated. Similarly, printed language that attempts to exclude certain classes of workers from benefits also violates ERISA, including severance packages (Anstett v. Eagle-Picher, 2000).

CONCLUSIONS

Although the Department of Labor (DOL) is responsible for ERISA enforcement, seldom does it involve itself with health matters, sticking to pension alignment and leaving healthcare to the states. Very little has changed since the creation of the Act in favor of the DOL's preference, but continual reform and debate encircle health matters. The latest Congressional changes delivered such intense debate that some states threatened union recession and the Supreme Court invoked its right to exclude itself from the controversy. In essence, the majority of states claimed infringement of their rights to sovereignty and countered with refusals to enforce the new initiatives and providing non-enforcement statutes for their residents.

On the other side of ERISA, the courts continually intervene with pension plan enforcement. Attempts by unscrupulous companies to forego paying accrued benefits and scheming to discriminate against classes of workers find higher costs with penalties than if compliance had occurred in the first place. The next few years will be interesting for human resource personnel as the divisions in ERISA components continue to diversify.

* * *

3.4 FMLA AND THE COURTS

This paper examines the historical purpose and development of the Family and Medical Leave Act of 1993 (FMLA). Several court cases helped to define usage for employers while enhancing assigned responsibilities shifted to workers. No longer did organizations endure all the burden of compliance now that employees were tasked with steps to follow. Analysis begins with a brief review of the Act's development and review of benchmark cases affecting human resource personnel. Guidelines assisting each participant category offer information leading to maximal compliance for organizations and opportunity for employees to ensure optimal conformance on their parts.

FMLA BACKGROUND

The traditional androcentric perspective within the workplace essentially dictated that workers were expected to have outside others care for family members while they remained dedicated to the employer's needs. Beginning in 1978 with passage of the Pregnancy Discrimination Act (amended in 1991), employers realized that women were increasingly entering the workforce and destined to overcome their minority status with more than 60% of American women working today (Macionis, 2010). Couple with this transition the increased expectancy of men to equally engage with household and childrearing duties (Papalia, Olds, & Feldman, 2009) and single-father households (opposed to traditional single-mother households), an equilibrium erupted the androcentric mindset of the labor force.

States had already begun passing legislation geared toward striking a balance between family needs of employees and operational concerns among employers, however many deficits remained unresolved that demanded federal intervention. The Family and Medical Leave Act of 1993 (originally titled "1991" but vetoed twice by President George H.W. Bush until passed by President Bill Clinton in 1993) required employers with at least 50 workers (less restrictive than other Acts) to provide at least 12 weeks of unpaid leave for bona fide and verifiable medical reasons to qualified employees and certain family members. For example, fathers could take leave when their children were born or both parents when a doctor certified the necessity of their presence during the convalescence. Employers benefited in the Act required advanced notice when possible, vacation and sick day usage served as inclusive perquisites to the 12-

week period, and the leave counted within any twelve-month period without resetting every calendar year. The latter prevented abuse by employees attempting to take a continuous six-month absence overlapping calendar years.

Considering the levity granted, employers and workers alike often attempt coercion of the legislative parameters in circumvention of cultural and societal changes through discrimination or other organizational expectancies. The next section reviews court cases that recognized these problems and further framed FMLA.

LEGAL DEVELOPMENTS

In line with the recognition that cultural expectancies demand a decline with androcentric perspectives discussed earlier, Joseph Scamihorn requested a leave of absence after his sister was murdered (Scamihorn v. General Truck Drivers, 2002). Scamihorn's father fell into clinical depression, forcing Joseph to temporarily leave work in psychological support of his father. When Scamihorn returned to work, his employer (Albertson's) notified him that he had lost all seniority status and was treated as a new employee. The Circuit Court emphasized, on Scamihorn's behalf, that psychological care of his father constituted coverage under FMLA and employees using the benefit must return to their former positions (or equivalent) without interruption in seniority status up to the time leave was taken.

Recognizing the employer was attempting to circumvent FMLA provisions by eliminating affected job positions, the Southern District Court of New York ruled in favor of workers foregoing retaliation by their employers (Brenlla v. Lasorsa Buick, 2002). Although not generally considered for disparate impact under terms of other discrimination statutes, the disparate treatment of the case conveyed for the further definition of disability under the Americans with Disabilities Act protects workers who become unable to work temporarily.

In a landmark case, the District Courts ruled that misinformation concerning FMLA benefits by employers and failure to communicate these rights in general persuades rulings in favor of employees (Butler v. Illinois Bell Telephone Company, 2006). As Illinois Bell Telephone Company discovered, if the employer makes the worker believe coverage extends beyond that entitlement period, then that employer is bound to that misinformation if it would adversely affect employment status. Relatively, silence on behalf of the organization, according to the Court, also constitutes lying.

GUIDELINES FOR WORKERS

Employees retain responsibilities of compliance with FMLA as well as their employers. Failure to comply may prove detrimental to their cases should judicial intervention occur. Five guidelines workers should understand for maximizing their benefits under FMLA include:

1) seeking information from employers;
2) communicating intentions in a timely manner;
3) providing required certification documentation;
4) understanding which family members they may take leave for; and
5) realize that FMLA uses up sick days and accrued vacation time first.

As previously demonstrated, employers are required to furnish timely and accurate information to workers in need of FMLA coverage. Reciprocity of this consideration entails that workers should provide their employers with the same respect under the Act's provisions. Requests for entitlement information and providing the necessary documentation ensure communication occurs. FMLA covers parents, spouses, children, stepchildren, and adopted children only, so if an uncle becomes ill, then coverage does not apply. This restriction prevents abuse of the entitlements by workers for just anyone. Most importantly, employees need to realize and justify the costs involved. Sick time and vacation days are used first and count toward the 12-week benefit period. Additionally, costs for medical insurance during the leave of absence become the responsibility of the worker taking off while no income from the employer accumulates.

GUIDELINES FOR EMPLOYERS

Employers find the burden of compliance with FMLA provisions can, at times, envision complexity (Moran, 2008) with application in spite of the appearance of simple terminology. Resource personnel require experience to supplement training among the myriad of possible situations organizations encounter with employees attempting leaves from work. Aside from knowing and communicating the guidelines afforded workers, employers further compliance by following these guidelines:

1) Realize that some employees will attempt to abuse medical leave to avoid work so keep accurate records;
2) Refrain from discouraging workers from utilizing their benefits proved by the Act;
3) Avoid questions concerning plans to change family size;
4) Make the workplace safe for pregnant workers rather than create isolation policies; and

5) Ensure that reassignments of personnel maintain at least equal pay, seniority, and other benefits of the previous position.

Accurate record keeping always trumps opinion and memory from a legal compliance perspective. If two recollections of events find conflict, then the testimony closest to the written record enjoys more believability and credibility than the other does. Discouraging workers from pursuing rightful benefits or protections brings perceptions of deception on behalf of the employer or coercion to avoid compliance in the employee's best interests. Inquiry into plans for parenthood may not only violate FMLA, but also the Pregnancy Discrimination Act of 1991.

Being safe is top priority of many legislative initiatives, such as the Occupational Safety and Health Standards Act. Talking safety is not enough, so providing workspaces that exceed the speech demonstrates conscious efforts at compliance without creating opportunity for isolative discrimination practices.

Lastly, organizations avoid complications if they fill positions held by persons on FMLA leave and have to reassign those persons upon return. This practice is allowable only if the employee loses no benefits, pay, or seniority previously enjoyed when reassigned. However, the worker accrues none of these status benefits (Moran, 2008) during the duration of their absence.

CONCLUSIONS

Occasionally, complying with federal laws is a slippery slope and the Family Medical Leave Act of 1993 leaves no exception. The greatest confusion arises from understanding the scope and diffusion of responsibilities for workers and employers alike with organizations tasked with ensuring that employees know their roles. Although ambiguity appears to offer opportunity for workers to abuse the system and employers to attempt plausible deniability, built-in checks ensure the FMLA's role as an extension to previous legislation for coverage. Following prescribed guidelines for compliance assists organizations with maximal compliance initiatives and workers with opportunity for informed decisions as well as assurance to receive entitlements.

* * *

3.5 WORKPLACE DISCRIMINATION

This paper examines the historical purpose and development of the Family and Medical Leave Act of 1993 (FMLA). Several court cases helped to define usage for employers while enhancing assigned responsibilities shifted to workers. No longer did organizations endure all the burden of compliance now that employees were tasked with steps to follow. Analysis begins with a brief review of the Act's development and review of benchmark cases affecting human resource personnel. Guidelines assisting each participant category offer information leading to maximal compliance for organizations and opportunity for employees to ensure optimal conformance on their parts.

RELIGION

The Civil Rights Act of 1964 (as amended) provided protection for workers from discrimination in the workplace because of personal religious beliefs, either beliefs of the workers or beliefs forced upon them by employers. The only exception provided through the First and Fourteenth Amendments of the Constitution relay to religious organizations and their abilities to hire persons of the same faith for promotion of the organizational goals (Moran, 2008). This includes clergy, but not janitorial, administrative, or other positions a person may otherwise be qualified to perform. The following four policies demonstrate practices disallowed for government and private employers and the detrimental effects that could befall managers resulting from violations.

Hiring or Termination of Workers

With the wars in Afghanistan and Iraq, anti-Muslim sentiments plague the American public with misinformation. As global history depicts, practicing Islam does not make a person any more likely to perform terrorist acts than a person engaged in the Christian or Jewish faiths (e.g. The Spanish Inquisition, stories from the Old Testament Bible, The English Crusades, The Salem Witch Trials, and so forth). In compliance with the Civil Rights Act, the policy in this organization forbids failing to hire (or terminating) Muslim persons who may be otherwise qualified because of their religious affiliation.

Predating legislative enactments, the tenancy of religious freedom was upheld by the Supreme Court (Torcaso v. Watkins, 1961) when the State of Maryland was forbidden to ask religious affiliation as a requirement for employment. In addition, creating or failing to protect these workers from hostile environments within the workplace constitutes violations of equal importance in legal terms of disparate treatment and retaliation.

Accommodating Religious Beliefs

Employers are legislatively required to accommodate religious beliefs that do not cause undue hardship for the organization, compromise the rights of others, or require more than minimal costs to implement. Within these limits, the policy for this organization is reasonable consideration of written requests on a case-by-case basis. The majority of requests stem from observations of religious holidays or the placement of religious relics in their workspace (Moran, 2008). Examples of undue hardship for the organization include allowing retail workers time off during the busy Christmas holiday sales season not afforded to their peers, and the dissemination of religious paraphernalia by workers to the organization's customers.

The Equal Employment Opportunity Commission recommended (U.S. Equal Employment Opportunity Commission, 2008) employers deal with scheduling conflicts, allow shift swapping between employees and flexible scheduling, or laterally transfer workers when possible to alleviate problems. In all cases, communication between the employee and employer must first exist before actions are taken.

Religious Harassment

Religious harassment rears in two guises; the first when employees impose their religious beliefs upon coworkers or customers, and the other when a non-religion based organization imposes religious doctrine or practices upon its employees. Practices can include dress codes, displays of religious bling (Daniels v. City of Arlington, Texas, 2001), the passing of religious literature, and of course, speech. Although the First Amendment to the Constitution provides free speech, the intention behind this law envisioned deliberation between individual citizens and the government, not "say anything you want – when you want – to whomever you want" within the private sector (Walsh, 2010).

The organizational policy telling discriminatory religious jokes, passing or posting religious literature to other employees or customers, providing religion-based reasons for supervisory actions/inactions, and proselytizing in the workplace as strictly prohibited helps to ensure compliance with Civil Rights legislation. Failure to comply may result in hostile workplace claims, lost customers and revenues, or other discriminatory outcomes.

Religion, the Workplace, and Socialization

Many sociologists argue the workplace is a social institution which builds societies and provides an atmosphere for fictive kinship as well as economic stability (Macionis, 2010). Legal perspectives disagree, however, and view organizations solely as economic entities (Moran, 2008). This treatment from the legal system allows people to associate only with persons of similar faith if they choose, and on their own time, but protects workers from unfair behaviors at work caused by differences in religious beliefs. Because of this legal perspective, the organizational policy that employment decisions concerning homosexuality (male or female) or other personal preferences initiated outside the workplace cannot derive from religious tenants stands firm. Contrastingly, prohibitions of behaviors by workers that negatively affect the organization, including sexual affinity, are allowed for reasons not legally protected, especially sexual harassment of coworkers and customers by same sex persons.

COMPENSATION

The Fair Labor and Standards Act was amended by the Equal Pay Act of 1963 (EPA) to regulate child labor, minimum wage, and overtime pay. Many states have tightened these standards, e.g. minimum wage requirements. In alignment with the Civil Rights Act, the EPA prohibited differing wages for men and women performing the same job as well as prohibiting age discrimination. Additionally, persons working overseas for an American company became entitled to pay differentials that equated their wages to a domestic position, if higher. The topics of glass effects, physical sex (not gender – a social construction) pay disparity, age discrimination, and reverse discrimination follow.

Glass Effects

While glass ceiling effects generally refer to minorities and women (not a minority in the work world today) who find they are restricted from higher-level positions for discriminatory reasons, glass escalator effects provide the opposite effects. Generally, the latter include males working in traditional female jobs who tend to excel more rapidly than their feminine coworkers. Although no laws currently exist covering glass effects (Milkovich & Newman, 2008), Congress acknowledged these problems by forming the Glass Ceiling Commission (GCC) through a 1991 amendment to the Civil Rights Act. The group looks at advancement preparedness, opportunities available, and promotional policies of organizations (Moran, 2008) indicating that future amendments will cover these shortcomings in discriminatory workplace practices.

In anticipation to fairness, the organizational policy requiring a standards-based promotional system to include knowledge, skills, abilities, and experience rather than referential promotions insures that minorities and women enjoy the same promotional opportunities. GCC studies indicate women average two reporting levels below the CEO while African-Americans generally experience four levels in managerial positions within elitist organizations.

Pay Disparities (Sex)

The Equal Pay Act of 1963 attempted to close the gap between wage differences of males and females performing the same job. The advent of job descriptions initially served as a two-edged concept in that employers argued that although males and females held the same job title, slight changes in the wording of descriptions constituted reasoning for pay differences (Milkovich & Newman, 2008). In response, the EEOC and the courts developed the policy of "substantial differences", meaning that skills required, physical and mental effort exerted, responsibility as accountability, and environmental working conditions were considered and weighed when determining if similar jobs were eligible for different pay rates (Perales v. American Retirement Corp., 2005).

To avoid ambiguity in definition and appearances of sexual discrimination, the policy of many organizations is that unless jobs are substantially different in terms of skills required, physical and mental effort exerted, responsibility, and environmental working conditions then each employee in that position will hold the same job title and approximate pay level, regardless of their sex. Failure to properly classify and pay employees can result in cases of sexual discrimination and remuneration.

Age Discrimination

Economic recessions occasionally require organizations downsize their workforces to equilibrate cash flow demands. The Age Discrimination in Employment Act of 1967 (ADEA) amended the Civil Rights Act and the Equal Pay Act by protecting workers over the age of 40 from replacement by younger employees receiving lower salaries. Using other termination reasons for discharging older employees during downsizing serves as no defense unless the cutbacks occur across the board and affects employees of all ages within the organization (McKennon v. Nashville Banner Publishing Co., 1995; Carlton v. Mystic Transportation, 2000). Additionally, refilling downsized positions with younger employees, even if the replacement is over age 40 (O'Connor v. Consolidated Coin Caterers, 1996), also may constitute age discrimination.

It is the policy within certain organizations that if downsizing operations occur among personnel, these cutbacks will occur across the board, regardless of age or tenure, and that rehire priority will first be granted to those discharged employees from those positions. This policy removes any chances of age discrimination disputes while maintaining repertoire in personnel relations and ensuring experienced personnel pools.

Reverse Discrimination

More a phenomenon than a legal concept (Milkovich & Newman, 2008), reverse discrimination often results in consequence to attempts to relieve liabilities for direct discrimination. In other words, majority workers find themselves excluded from employment, promotional, and other work-related opportunities when an organization takes actions for minorities and women without applying those actions across the workforce. Current legislation disallows quota programs for reasons of disparate treatment and impact that often result without hiring or promoting the best qualified person for the job, essentially denying equal protection of the law (University of California Regents v. Bakke, 1977).

An organizational policy recommended stands that no quotas or policies shall apply to any singular category of workers, including race, pay, sex, and any other protected class of workers. Violations can inadvertently cause unintended discrimination toward other categories of workers, defeating the original intended purpose. This policy also applies when resolving pay differential discrepancies that may arise in that all categories of workers should be considered.

APPEARANCE

The District of Columbia and San Francisco as local jurisdictions and the State of Michigan, exclusively, handle physical appearance within anti-discrimination laws, including grooming, weight, attractiveness, and other personal characteristics. Physical appearance is not a protected class under federal legislation, however, many "protected class - plus" (Walsh, 2010, p. 199) instances fall within the scope of discrimination with a basis stemming from physical body characteristics. Usually the Americans with Disabilities Act (ADA) receives the most attention when dealing with these issues.

Weight

Until 2011 (EEOC v. Resources for Human Development, Inc., 2011), the EEOC and the courts only considered severe obesity, meaning a person is more than twice the expected body weight of the average person of their height (and at least 100 pounds), as a qualifying disability under the Americans with Disabilities Act. The catch was that such persons had the burden of proof in showing the underlying cause of their obesity was medically induced and not preventable as a matter of lifestyle or lack of willpower (Walsh, 2010). Now the burden of proof is no longer necessary nor required (U.S. Equal Employment Opportunity Commission, 2012) as existence of the condition itself serves as the qualifying factor for worker rights protection under the ADA. For other body weight classes, including persons considered underweight, sex-plus cases have prevailed in the courts.

As a matter of policy within this organization, body weight (overweight or underweight), will not be a deciding factor for any job related criterion unless the condition obviously places the worker or other persons at risk for physical injury within the scope of their duties. Additionally, the condition must impair that individual's ability to physically perform those duties at expected and common performance levels. Failure to demonstrate qualifications within these criteria may result in discrimination claims and high settlement costs.

Grooming and Attractiveness

Grooming standards imposed upon employees generally lack protection if those requirements are generally accepted by the public, such as hair length differences among males and females, and those standards do not impose upon other protected rights of those workers. Asking women to wear sexually explicit clothing in office settings and forcing African-Americans to accept only stockroom positions has failed sexual and racial discrimination defenses (Cutler, 2004) as grooming standards expected by customers and necessary for business purposes.

Grooming policies within this organization shall not impose upon protected characteristics of workers and will be weighted in accordance with socially acceptable standards of the community served. Each policy should carefully consider trending within the changing norms imposed by society (Macionis, 2010). Violations may incur severe legal penalties and reparations in accordance with the law.

Sex Stereotyping

Sex stereotyping, or forced gender roles, by employers is not acceptable and leads to disparate treatment for males and females alike. Transsexuals cannot be forced into gender roles generally accepted as appropriate for their sex (Smith v. City of Salem, Ohio, 2004). Under the Americans with Disabilities Act, gender identity disorder is a protected mental disease precluded from discrimination. For example, if a male firefighter chooses to wear dresses to work, then as long as the dresses are allowed for females, then the employer must allow the behavior. This exception stems from the Women's Liberation Movement when females began wearing slacks, rather than full-length dresses, in retaliation to sex stereotyping during the early twentieth century.

The policy of organizations, therefore, is to take possible sex stereotyping into consideration when developing any dress codes or other grooming policies for workers. In severe cases that interfere with coworker perceptions, issues concerning business purpose and necessity, work and production quality, and other pertinent issues will be considered before actions are taken. Failure to comply with this policy may result in sexual or disability discrimination suits against the organization.

Other Personal Characteristics

Aside the obvious outward characteristics attributed to workers, employers often assess mental capabilities, historical backgrounds, behavioral traits, familial obligations, and a myriad of others. Although most have no direct attribution or coverage under personnel legislation, many have proved discriminatory in terms of disparate impact treatments. For example, sexual discrimination can be proven if the majority of single-mothers in an organization are passed over for promotion in proportion to other classes of workers. Therefore, the prominent policy of organizations is all evaluative procedures concerning employees endure comparative analyses to ensure minimal disparate impact opportunities.

ILLINOIS WORKPLACE PRACTICE

This paper examines the Fair Labor and Standards Act (FLSA) and the Equal Pay Act (EPA), their limitations for protections against discrimination and economic equalities, and examination of how states attempted remediation by expanding the federal mandates to suit their individual needs. Illinois, in particular, ratified the FLSA and EPA when the state legislature enacted its own versions (IFLSA and IEPA, respectively). Over time, the state realized other shortcomings and created the One Day Rest in Seven Act (IODRSA), the Wage Payment and Collection Act (IWPCA), and the Prevailing Wage Act (IPWA) as compensatory measures on behalf of workers (Note: the preceding "I" is added to acronyms to distinguish state legislation from their federal counterparts).

Prior to the Civil Rights Movement, states began enacting antidiscrimination laws as early as 1945 (Delton, 2007), with 28 states showing initiative by the time the Civil Rights Act was enacted in 1964. However, many states remained powerless with enforcement efforts until the federal government joined the movement. The three decades that followed experienced an explosion of human rights laws, including fairness of wages and other work-related principles. Although the states varied within the scope and enactment of these problems, these modifications rooted in the federal foothold of enforcement initiatives via the Department of Labor (DOL).

No federal guidelines exist, other than establishment of a variable federal minimum wage, as to how wages should be calculated for particular occupations. Usually, organizations influence wage markets as a reflection of their organizational values (Phillips, 2011). For example, a university desiring to hire only top-notch instructors may offer pay packages exceeding industry norms whereas a community college may strive for instructors who will work for minimal pay and benefits. This social trend at the organizational level stirred debates between minimum pay standards at non-farm labor rates, the minimum wages dictated by the FLSA, and the more common living wage argument. Table 1 demonstrates the hourly rate prescribed by each standard.

Table 1
Hourly Wage Comparison

Non-Farm Production Wage	FLSA Minimum Wage	Living Wage
$19.04/hour	$7.75/hour	$12.13/hour

Note: Adapted from "A Living Wage for Research Subjects" by T.B. Phillips, 2011, Journal of Law, Medicine, and Ethics, p. 243.

Obviously, the non-farm production wage induces economic influences upon small businesses, runaway inflation for staple commodities, and wage discrepancies between skilled and unskilled labor trades. The minimum wage established by the FLSA finds dependency upon the particular group (some exclusion applies) and fails to consider cost-of-living differences by geographic location. Employers of unskilled labor forces generally subscribe to this standard to keep labor costs minimal and profit margins wider. The living wage model raises labor costs by at least 36% in an attempt to alleviate persons enduring extreme poverty, with more than 140 cities conforming (Phillips, 2011), however, reluctance endures on larger scales. Many industrial and service organizations prefer to meet FLSA and living wage half way at about $10 per hour, e.g. Walmart and Fram Filtration.

The Illinois FLSA

The Illinois Fair Labor Standards Act extended its federal parent by defining inclusion to organizations having four or more employees. An additional test for exemption status required these employees earn at least $455 per week or $23,600 per year. In essence, part-time executives earning less than this threshold became hourly employees entitled to overtime compensation "at one and a half times the proportional rate of their weekly salary" (Jackson Lewis, LLP, 2004, para. 3) during weeks they worked more than 40 hours. Minimum wage was set at $8.25 per hour, excluding exempt, commissioned, and tipped employees, with students and persons under age 18 set at $7.75 per hour. All of these minimums exceeded the federal guidelines but provided additional burdens upon employers. Comp time, where workers trade paid days off for working overtime, was abolished, yes abolished, for state employees as a legal business practice statewide.

The Illinois One Day Rest in Seven Act

The IODRSA established two simple rules concerning break periods for workers not covered under the FLSA. The first declared a 20 minute break be provided for every 7 ½-hour work period no more than five hours into the shift. For businesses that operate around the clock, employers could not schedule anyone to work more than six days in any seven-day period, unless that employee volunteered. Any other break periods offered by the organization were considered as good faith benefits.

The Illinois Wage Payment and Collection Act

The old adage, "you break it – you bought it" does not apply to Illinois workers under the IWPCA. No longer could retailers deduct register shortages or costs of goods damaged from employees' paychecks, unless the worker agreed to the deduction. Additionally, the agreement required written authorization at the time the paycheck was cut, so blanket authorizations were outlawed. Other common practices banned by the IWPCA included holding final paychecks for any reason, to include awaiting return of organizational equipment and uniforms. All final checks for terminated employees required payment by the next scheduled payday to prevent payroll audit and fines by the Illinois Department of Labor.

In the case of equipment not returned, the Department advises organizations to sue the former employee in claims court, or to take civil action when the employer can prove damages were intentional; otherwise, these losses are exempt under the amnesty provisions betrothed to workers by the IWPCA.

Only four possible situations exist (Illinois Department of Labor, 2012) for payroll deductions:

1) when required by law (such as taxes);
2) to the benefit of the employee (such as health insurance premiums, union dues etc.);
3) a valid wage assignment or wage deduction order is in effect; and
4) made with the express written consent of the employee, given freely at the time the deduction is made.

The Illinois Prevailing Wage Act of 2011

On a county-by-county basis, the IPWA ensures that residents (at least 90%) obtain employment on state-funded projects. The wage paid must align with the prevailing rates, regardless if the employee is a laborer or maintenance worker, paid to similar workers within the public sector. Private subcontractors also endure liability for compliance with definition to include smaller public government sectors (e.g. cities and counties) and public schools. This law forced many public organizations to review and adjust wages for all employees to match those of private organizations and served in prelude to Illinois becoming a right-to-work state in 2013. The provision required organizations within the state to hire resident applicants in priority to non-residents with at least 90% of the total workforce maintaining residency.

CONCLUSIONS

States often enact different approaches when adjusting federal legislation toward perspectives relevant to their regional workforces, e.g. minimum wage standards. Large cities incur niching of specialty jobs within particular neighborhoods, and in turn, employers occasionally seek out these workers (Ellis, Wright, & Parks, 2007). Unfortunately, it is difficult to prove racial or other discriminatory intentions in these situations in the name of labor relations. Although discrimination does not exist within the workplace at the levels it did when the Civil Right Act was passed, hundreds of complaints are still filed each year with governing and enforcement agencies showing organizations have yet a long way to develop. In response, the states have refined federal standards within their own jurisdictions and attempted to tackle other shortcomings within the laws.

As far as wages, federal law "fails to resolve the question of what is fair pay or impose a general requirement employees be paid fairly" (Walsh, 2010, p. 367). One could argue on behalf of gender inequality or disability, but still no resolution exists as to how much any particular job is worth. Illinois began to act with its Prevailing Wage Act, limiting the scope of reach to its internal public workforce. Perhaps the hesitance stems from declining to manipulate wage markets or from a broader fear of enticing socialist politics. Regardless of social or economic reasoning, acknowledgement of the problem has formally begun to enter the political arena. It will be interesting to see if other states adopt policies enacted within Illinois and to what degree these changes affect federal legislation. For human resource personnel, the multitude of state-level (and sometimes local) differences within employment laws can complicate national operations, requiring constant attention.

* * *

3.6 FUTURE VISION

This paper examines possible future trends among antidiscrimination issues at the local and global levels. Attention is given to age discrimination, gender and sex discrimination, racial discrimination, affirmative action, and equal pay discrimination. Although many developments evolve characteristic to real versus model idealizations, others predictably emanate from psychological and social principles. Understanding these changes within the workplace assist managers and human resource personnel with adaptation and expectations promulgated from legislative bodies at all levels surrounding the organization.

AGE DISCRIMINATION

Age discrimination may reasonably increase in frequency as the proportion of older workers continues to overcome those under the age of 40 in the United States. Currently, the Civil Rights Act of 1964 protects these workers from disparate impact (as a group) and disparate treatment at the individual level by banning practices of replacing older employees with younger and cheaper help, by reducing positions held only by older persons, and by preventing their exclusion from hiring and promotions. The Employee Retirement Income Security Act (ERISA) expanded the Civil Rights Act provisions with protections in the handling of pensions and other retirement benefits enjoyed by older workforces.

Aging populations can be found throughout the world as global phenomena. As a result, many countries have enacted anti-discrimination laws within the last couple of decades covering older workers, including the United Kingdom, Sweden, and Norway. Similar to the United States, the UK recognizes direct (treatment) and indirect (impact) disparities within legislation (Forunes & Mykleton, 2010). During 2010, approximately 40% of European workers qualified for coverage under variances of legal remedies for age discrimination.

GENDER DISCRIMINATION

In the United States, "gender discrimination" more accurately defines as "sex discrimination". While the term sex refers to the biological distinctions between males and females, gender encompasses the psychosocial aspects of what it means to function in male and female roles (Papalia, Olds, & Feldman, 2009). No federal law protects workers from gender discrimination whereas many, including the Civil Rights Act, the Fair Labor Standards Act, and the Americans with Disabilities Act include definitions based upon the biological characteristics of workers, all incorrectly utilizing the terms "gender" and "sex" interchangeably.

Over the last fifty years society witnessed sex reassignment surgical procedures (male to female (MTF) and female to male (FTM)), the "coming out" and growth of the gay community, transsexual lifestyles (not necessarily gay – they may just dress that way), and the reversal of traditional gender roles (Macionis, 2010) within the family unit. The latter holding that more women are entering traditionally male occupations while more men are accepting greater household responsibilities traditionally reserved for females (cooking, house cleaning, childcare, etc.). In any of these cases, gender (from the psychosocial perspective) outgrew legislative protection except under civil liberty violations categorized beneath hate crimes. For example, "gay bashing" equates to battery, and public transsexualism may be labeled as a mental disorder protected under the ADA. Actually, until 1981, homosexuality was medicalized as a mental disorder (Coon & Mitterer, 2010), when the lifestyle choice lost ADA coverage.

In the workplace, transgender persons are those "whose gender identity expression does not align with traditional gender norms" (Dispenza et.al., 2012, p. 65). These persons experience sex discrimination in the form of hostile environments within the workplace and high rates of unemployment (refusal to hire), demotions, and terminations. Unfortunately for them, these cases prove difficult within the courts, if at all (Walsh, 2010), in terms of discrimination, but occasionally find remedy at the state and local levels. For example, Washington, D.C. protects physical appearances while San Francisco prohibits discrimination against sexuality preferences. Many states have recognized gay marriage as of this writing, including Illinois and Michigan, however, the Supreme Court declined New York's resolution allowing unmarried domestic (especially same-sex) partners to share employment benefits.

RACIAL DISCRIMINATION

Since the 1920s, France had been known as a country honoring racial tolerance for African descendants and still religiously, in the 21st century, among Muslims. Surrounding European countries, including those in the United Kingdom, retained discriminative attitudes through racial biases that remain thriving in the workplace. For example, after World War II the UK formed the National Health Service, which recruited foreign nurses. Darker skinned nurses received lower pay, fewer advancement opportunities, and restricted training programs than their Anglo coworkers received; practices that remained active through 2011 (Batnitzky & McDowell, 2011).

Fortunately, in the United States, social and congressional changes beginning in the 1950s began processes that changed socialization within the workplace. Racial prejudices may never completely disappear, but aggressive enforcement against previous practices lessened opportunities for the resurgence of oppressive behaviors – a common tenant of operant conditioning. Although racial discrimination cases continue to surface within the judicial system, with even more settled outside the courts, the number of cases pursued today is far less than in previous decades.

AFFIRMATIVE ACTION

Affirmative action programs originally brought misconceptions of needs for quota systems to the workplace. Employers believed that to avoid legal prosecutions in the name of disparate impact, they could in-state minimum numbers of workers from each racial category. The courts disagreed, implying that quota systems discriminated against all races by denying fair opportunities to the most qualified individuals and degraded the workforce by employing persons because of skin color rather than abilities.

Today, employers should seek proportional numbers of employees from each racial category represented in the local population. However, they should avoid reserving positions to specific categories (Walsh, 2010). In other words, strive to attain a balance as close as possible by proportion, but fill positions by qualifications regardless of racial background. Beginning with the Reagan administration, government branches pursued the attitude that discrimination would not be tolerated, "but affirmative action is not all that important or critical" (Marlow & Rowland, 1989, p. 549).

Economic fluctuations, especially at the global level, affect market forces and how employers recruit, hire, train, and promote minorities and women (Marlow & Rowland, 1989). During upswings, the demand for workers increases while the availability pool for qualified applicants declines, causing disparities in affirmative action pursuits. This phenomenon predicts that during the global recession of the early 21st century that as demands for employees faded, the available pool of qualified workers elevates and further balances racial proportioning within the workplace.

EQUAL PAY DISCRIMINATION

Until recently, primary concern had been given to the discrepancy in pay rates between men and women performing the same job. Females received as little as 60% of the pay and benefits provided to males (Macionis, 2010), especially in managerial positions. Great strides occurred, primarily in southern states such as Georgia, until the inverse was true with women earning an average of 131% of their male counterparts in Atlanta by 2008. Obviously, more work needs to be done before equilibration is achieved.

Focus of attention turned from sex differences in pay discrimination to occupational fairness. Illinois enacted its Prevailing Wage Act in 2011 requiring state contractors to pay all persons within a particular occupation the same wage, and by 2013 to ensure all employers, public and private, comprise at least 90% of their workforce from state residents. This Right-to-Work initiative correlates to Marlow and Rowland's 1989 observation that economic conditions correlate to affirmative action results. As a global comparison, the concept discussed earlier where the UK was studying pay discrepancies among nurses within its National Health Service (as well as race and national origin) indicates the occupational shift from sex-based discrimination.

CONCLUSIONS

The United States was among the first countries to recognize, predict, and act upon possible age discrimination post-WWII when it enacted the Civil Rights Act of 1964. Other western cultures, including the United Kingdom, are just realizing the impact of the greying workforce in combination with global economic recession. Gender and sex discrimination follow suit as the U.S. gravitates beyond male and female differences and moves into the psychological meaning of gender roles. No longer do Americans argue in terms of what biology provided them so much as what they choose to be (or not to be) over choices of lifestyle.

Although racial discrimination exists, the number of civil suits declined... a model for European nations to follow when importing labor. The days of affirmative action programs may be limited in the United States over the next few decades. Social demands appear to be shifting from the specific to the general in terms of organizational equality, at least at the state level when dealing with pay disparities and employment rights. The next decade may witness equilibration issues moving towards all workers as a unit rather than specific groups within the United States, while other nations attempt to catch up.

* * *

3.7 INTERNATIONAL HUMAN RESOURCE POLICY

This paper examines issues relevant for organizations contemplating multinational expansion of operations, especially within China, from the perspective of employee treatment. Administrators and human resource personnel may find surprise with the realization that foreign employees are protected by American legislation, such as the Americans with Disabilities Act, The Civil Rights Act, and most others. Exploration turns toward review of Chinese legal and political perspectives and compares these with American Congressional and Presidential views on these issues. Recommendations originating from these arguments are provided to guide organizational human resource personnel tasked with multinational preparation.

CHINESE POLITICAL PERSPECTIVES

The traditionalist perspective of the Chinese people and government dictates high resistance to change and outside influence. Likely acceptance of contradictory practices proves slow within the social mindset of the society, however, occurring dramatically once initiated. These concepts historically demonstrate themselves repeatedly within regional partitions of the United States, such as with issues of slavery, racial and gender discrimination, and medicalization of psychological habits (drugs, alcoholism, etc.). Although tensions grew over decades of deliberation that sometimes lead to bloodshed, actual application of acceptances resulted from sudden top-down initialization processes, usually at the government level. For instance, over a century had passed since the abolishment of slavery, but oppressive attitudes saw no drastic changes until after enactment of the Civil Rights Act of 1964. The following 30 years witnessed more change than the previous 300 years combined for the oppressed categories of people.

China, currently criticized for its human rights treatment of workers and citizens, serves as no exception to the pressures of top-down influences. The difference lies in the thick-walled barriers imposed by its communist and communal leadership characteristics compared to the critical democratic societies demanding reform in exchange for global economic participation. Capitalism encroached upon the median living standards of the Chinese people converting the economy from farm-based agrarians to bustling condominium dwellers almost overnight (Macionis, 2010). Social-conflict theorists point out that as economies improve, moves toward equalities arise from within a capitalist society while structural-functionalists argue socialist societies endure external pressures derived from competitive socialization.

Until recently, trade negotiations between the European Union (EU) and China remained strictly economic and commercial, but since 1998, the EU has sought to broaden the relationship with political and legal implications by imposing a human rights clause. Although facially signed, the Chinese government failed to ratify the clause fearing legal ramifications at the global level (Hua, 2008). Additional arguments included refusing EU partner interference like the "brutal methods of the Americans" through sanctions, embargoes, and military interventions for noncompliance at interpretive levels. By this reasoning China does not refute discriminative human rights practices within its society, however, as structural-functionalists predicted, the government proclaims the "whatever happens in Vegas" attitude via an attempt at soft power coercion from the EU through "interference in China's internal affairs".

Likewise, the growing market economy within China bilaterally grows pressures from its citizens for human rights reform, especially among workers. It is not uncommon for factory employees to work 24 hours or more at a time or for employers to utilize child labor in unsafe conditions with overall employment similar to slavery (Bovee, Thill, & Mescon, 2007). Chinese proponents argue that China should concede to a few demands of the human rights clause, but utilize bargaining tactics to obtain other beneficial concessions from EU partners in exchange (Hua, 2008). For example, to avoid American-style punishments, recommendations trend toward Article 96 of the Cotonou Agreement providing for lengthy bilateral consultations (arbitration) if either party should fail to meet its obligations, and setting out the principle that sanctions should be proportionate to the infraction concerned while changes in labor practices occur slowly and gradually.

UNDERSTANDING CHINESE REFORM

Ultimately the question of which judicial jurisdiction an organization falls, host or domestic, when cases concerning human rights arise. In most cases, the host country retains jurisdiction, but on occasion global courts intercede. Such was the case when the Inner London Education Authority was challenged by Ahmad concerning whether modern interpretations should prevail over original intent when the law was created (Ahmad v. Inner London Education Authority, 1978). In a decision for the plaintiff, Lord Justice Scarman wrote in his brief the importance of developing the law as society changes "not against a background of the law and society of 1944 but in a multiracial society which has accepted international obligations and enacted statutes designed to eliminate discrimination on grounds of race, religion, [color] or sex." The American Congress applied the same reasoning when it amended the Civil Rights Act in 1991 through accounting for the evolution of social and moral concepts, including the demands and expectations of modernized societies.

Legal applications and interpretations change with time and China appears no differently. As the country moved from imperial dictatorship towards communism, so too has it further grasped capitalism (albeit under communist leadership) and integrated free markets within its economies. Combined with traditionalism and hence resistance for change within its base culture, China must eventually accept transformations within its government, legal and financial systems, and of course the way it does business on the global scale. Although change occurred over centuries or decades in the past, China experienced the fast-paced rigor of capitalism and demands of inequality created by the new system (e.g. wealthy versus extreme poverty) as explained through social conflict theory. Altering the infrastructure of the economic and cognitive views of the society dictates that reforms in organizational practices should follow as they did in the United States and England.

The chaos created within the single largest populated country understandably brings with it the realities of difficulties undertaken by organizations desiring operations within China. Rights expected and protected by people and their organizations originating from democratic nations often fail fruition in collectivist cultures that denounce the individuality enjoyed as a social norm (Macionis, 2010) by those who welcome economic disparity. Outside pressures from foreign organizations, either refusing to do business in China or boycotting Chinese products due to poor human rights practices (Carroll & Buchholtz, 2009) appears to speed the attention and gravity of these issues by Chinese leadership as well as global partners.

REPERCUSSIONS FOR AMERICAN ORGANIZATIONS

American companies operating within China have been targets of accusations characterized by low pay (for the region), unsafe working conditions, utilization of child labor, and other exploitations of workers. Social Accountability International (SAI), a global standards organization, created SA2000 as an addendum to the International Standards Organization (ISO) initiatives disallowing certified members to employ persons under age 15, to utilize prison labor, to promote safe working conditions, to avoid discrimination (race, caste, origin, religion, disability, gender, sexual orientation, union or political affiliation, and age), to limit working hours, and to pay supportive wages. Violations are reported globally with subsequent offenders disbarred from doing business with other member organizations.

The Alien Tort Claims Act (ATCA) of 1789 allows foreign nationals to sue American-based multinational companies within American courts for that organization's actions performed abroad, including violations of international laws and treaties. Current cases generally involve companies performing business in countries with oppressive governments (Carroll & Buchholtz, 2009) and hosting human rights abuses. This legislation overrules cultural relativism by holding American companies legally liable for actions/inactions exercised overseas, especially when these laws fair more restrictive than those of the host nation, such as China. Regardless of China's human resource legislation, this equates to American companies treating Chinese employees as if they were also Americans subject to federal benefits (unless strictly prohibited by Chinese law?).

PRESIDENTIAL EXECUTIVE POSITION

Unlike the previous Bush administration, President Obama explicitly mostly agreed with the Chinese position concerning the human rights intervention initiatives previously discussed. In summary, the Chinese made three demands:

1) Non-brutal sanctions for non-compliance ("play nice");
2) Arbitration proceedings before retaliation ("talk to us first"); and
3) Separation of governmental influences with internal affairs ("we won't tell you how to tend your house if you don't mess with ours").

The first two issues received response during Obama's acceptance speech when he accepted the Nobel Peace Prize in 2009.

"The promotion of human rights cannot be about exhortation alone. At times, it must be coupled with painstaking diplomacy. I know that engagement with repressive regimes lacks the satisfying purity of indignation. But I also know that sanctions without outreach—condemnation without discussion—can carry forward only a crippling status quo... First, in dealing with those nations that break rules and laws, I believe that we must develop alternatives to violence that are tough enough to actually change behavior" (Obama, 2009).

The final demand met reserved compliance:

"Those regimes that break the rules must be held accountable. Sanctions must exact a real price. Intransigence must be met with increased pressure - and such pressure exists only when the world stands together as one... The same principle applies to those who violate international laws by brutalizing their own people" (Obama, 2009).

In this case, Obama limited collective action on life-threatening situations, making clear the types of rights violations that merit action: genocide, brutalization, and violent repression (Etzioni, 2011) while implying that lesser offenses commonly acclaimed by activists will endure no cause for direct interference, but may still undergo diplomatic interventions. For the most part President Obama (and apparently the Nobel Prize Committee) supports the Chinese position concerning interference, but concedes that China still needs to act on changes in its human rights policies before obtaining universal acceptance within the free market system. Unfortunately, as of this writing, a possible administration change is possible within weeks, possibly allowing a turnaround in Presidential policy.

CONGRESSIONAL LEGISLATIVE POSITIONS

During the 1990s, China was the target of 32% of all speeches concerning human rights violations in the House of Representatives and the Senate combined (Cutrone & Fordham, 2010). Of those 898 arguments, 88% held negative connotations while 47% recommended imposed sanctions until compliance. The actual position of the legislator making complaint relied upon whether that person merely endorsed the agendas of their constituents or the pursuance of humanitarian initiatives.

Results showed that members from import-sensitive districts were more likely to speak out about human rights violations whereas members from export-oriented districts were less likely to do so. In the case of China, evidence revealed members targeted human rights violators with whom their constituents competed. Floor remarks demonstrated support for limited sanctions only in order to avoid actions that were more serious - trending in favor of President Obama and China's positions concerning aggressive oppression. The implications of humanitarian concerns for the activity of individual members are not as strong as associations of economic interests because international human rights conditions do not vary across members of Congress as their constituents' interests do.

In terms of American political interests, human rights violations are downplayed when they are committed by friendly or strategically important nations, but become politically important when countries have hostile political relations with the United States commit them. For example, Soviet restrictions upon Jewish immigration received little attention concerning trade in comparison to embargoes imposed upon Iran with open media threats to "annihilate Israel". Regardless of differences based on ideology, Cutrone and Fordham's research showed international political conditions exerted (Ahmad v. Inner London Education Authority, 1978) the same influence on each member of Congress.

RECOMMENDATIONS

Organizations preparing to go multinational are faced with laws and regulations geared toward solutions needed by their respective human resource departments. Differences in generational issues, discrimination, labor laws, immigration, and so forth should be addressed as far in advance for preparation as possible. The following recommendations serve as a guide when addressing these issues and originate from the issues discussed previously.

1. Treat all foreign employees as well as domestic workers under the guidance of current legislation imposed within the United States, even if not required by the host country. Failure to do so could result in litigation within the American court system under the Alien Tort Claims Act while, drawing international attention to the organization.

2. If possible, seek certification under SA2000 to show the global community the organization chooses to be socially responsible toward human rights in terms of discriminatory practices. Avoid discrimination in the host country for race, caste, national origin, religion, disability, gender (sex), sexual orientation, union or political affiliation, and age. Certification delves beyond these common types by including issues of child labor, prisoner exploitation, and safe working conditions normally covered by the Fair Labor Standards Act and the Occupational Safety and Health Act.

3. Seek to understand the Presidential position concerning worker rights at home and abroad. During presidential terms where the administration chooses to endorse and enforce stances toward international relationships, organizations may find increased difficulties with building and growing their business internationally, especially if those positions differ significantly from those of the host country.

4. Realize organizations which import products from or rely upon operations within countries known to violate human rights standards fair far worse under American legislation than exporters. Countries deemed as hostile in terms of human rights likely may endure global sanctions under congressional actions affecting the organization. For organizations operating in those regions, human rights violations may be attributed and scrutinized to the organizations themselves.

5. Understand the cultural and historical influences affecting outcomes of human rights legislation of the host country in relation to domestic expectations. Traditionalist cultures tend to increase resistance for change more than democratic societies do, whereas cultures experimenting with capitalism are more likely to embrace theories and practices of individualized equality once the economic system is in place.

CONCLUSIONS

It is extremely difficult to apply American legislation, such as the Americans with Disabilities Act or the Civil Rights Act, to organizations desiring multinational growth, especially when a host country may not support the concepts enacted by the foreign legislation. China represents a rare example of a large global presence that desires to at least work with occupying nations, even if relations appear somewhat limited. Within a century, China moved from an imperial dictatorship, to a communist regime, to a country trading collective ideals for individual wealth; a transition many western societies never imagined possible. It is no wonder that confusion and reservation prevails in root of societal resistance among the leadership.

Operating within China turns into an experience of ethical issues more than one of legal obligations. For American practitioners, issues that many domestic workers take for granted may find themselves as null points from the Chinese perspective, yet those problems become legislative obligations regardless of geographic location when challenged in the American court system.

Cultural relativism, in terms of legalities, flows both ways or communication fails. When one nation demands dominance in the global marketplace, negotiations break down leaving intended changes for the benefit of workers uncompleted. Employees may lose or experience delayed protections from discrimination, safety, and fairness in compensation. Just as the United States expects freedoms for workers under the myriad of legislative enactments, so too do lawmakers extend the intensions of these rights to the employees of multinational organizations working abroad. Multinationals represent their home country with the expectation that through modeling of these concepts, foreign governments recognize and adopt the ideals through their own lawmaking processes (Cutrone & Fordham, 2010).

Although macro-perspective in nature, the recommendations provided assist human resource personnel (and their administrators) with understanding and application of concepts provided by law to foreign operations. Some reciprocity exists when collaborating with foreign governments and cultures for maximum effectiveness (e.g. understand the history and culture of the foreign country as well as domestic implications). Essentially all American legislative Acts apply when employing foreign nationals, even China. Employers should check with their respective state laws for extended applications similar to the Alien Tort Claims Act.

* * *

PART THREE REFERENCES

Ahmad v. Inner London Education Authority, 1 QB 36 (Queen's Bench (England) 1978).

Anstett v. Eagle-Picher, 203 F.3d 501 (7th Circuit 2000).

Batnitzky, A., & McDowell, L. (2011, March). Migration, Nursing, Institutional Discrimination and Emotional/Affective Labour: Ethnicity and Labour Stratification in the UK National Health Service. Social & Cultural Geography, 12(2), 181-201. doi:10.1080/14649365.2011.545142.

Borzi, P. C. (2008). There's "Private" and Then There's "Private": ERISA, Its Impact, and Options for Reform. Journal of Law, Medicine & Ethics, 660-669.

Bovee, C. L., Thill, J. B., & Mescon, M. H. (2007). Excellence in Business (3rd ed.). Upper Saddle River, NJ: Pearson Prentice Hall.

Bragdon v. Abbott, 524 U.S. 624 (Supreme Court of the United States 1998).

Brenlla v. Lasorsa Buick, LEXIS 9358 (S.D. New York 2002).

Butler v. Illinois Bell Telephone Company, LEXIS 76123 (N.D. Ill Eastern Div. 2006).

Carlton v. Mystic Transportation, 202 F.3d 129 (2nd Circuit 2000).

Carroll, A. B., & Buchholtz, A. K. (2009). Business & Society: Ethics and Stakeholder Management (7th ed.). Mason, OH: South-Western Cengage Learning.

Chevron v. Echazabal, 536 U.S. 73 (Supreme Court of the United States 2002).

Coon, D., & Mitterer, J. O. (2010). Introduction to psychology (12th ed.). Belmont, CA: Wadsworth.

Cutler, J. E. (2004, November 12). Abercrombie & Fitch Settles Race, Sex Discrimination Lawsuits for $50 Million. Daily Labor Report (218), pp. A-2.

Cutrone, E. A., & Fordham, B. O. (2010). Commerce and Imagination: The Sources of Concern About International Human Rights in the US Congress. International Studies Quarterly (54), 633-655. doi:10.1111/j.1468-2478.2010.00603.x.

Daniels v. City of Arlington, Texas, 246 F.3d 500 (5th Circuit 2001).

Delton, J. (2007). Before the EEOC: How Management Integrated the Workplace. Business History Review (81), 267-295.

Dispenza, F., Watson, L. B., Chung, Y. B., & Brack, G. (2012, March). Experience of career-related discrimination for female-to-male transgender persons: A qualitative study. The Career Development Quarterly, 81, 65-81.

EEOC v. Resources for Human Development, Inc., F. Supp. 2d WL 609560 (Eastern District of Louisiana 2011).

EEOC v. Swift Transportation Co., Inc., 45 F. Supp. 2d 1036 (Oregon 1999).

Ellis, M., Wright, R., & Parks, V. (2007). Geography and the Immigrant Division of Labor. Economic Geography, 83(3), 255-281.

Equal Opportunity Employment Commission. (2008, September 25). ADA Amendments Act of 2008. Retrieved from Equal Employment Opportunity Commission: http://www.eeoc.gov/laws/statutes/adaaa.cfm.

Equal Opportunity Employment Commission. (2012). Titles I and V of the Americans with Disabilities Act of 1990 (ADA). Retrieved from Equal Opportunity Employment Commission: http://www.eeoc.gov/laws/statutes/ada.cfm.

Equal Employment Opportunity Commission. (2012, August 2). Discrimination by type. Retrieved from U.S. Equal Employment Opportunity Commission: http://www.eeoc.gov/laws/types/index.cfm.

Etzioni, A. (2011). Obama's Implicit Human Rights Doctrine. Human Rights, 12, 93-107. doi:10.1007/s12142-010-0164-9.

Forunes, T., & Mykleton, R. J. (2010). Age discrimination in the workplace: Validation of the Nordic Age Discrimination Scale (NADS). Scandinavian Journal of Psychology (51), 23-30. doi:10.1111/j.1467-9450.2009.00738.x.

Hua, Z. (2008). The problem of the clause on human rights and the Sino-European agreement on cooperation. (8), 40-47. (M. Duchâtel, Trans.).

Illinois Department of Labor. (2012). FAQ: Wage Payment and Collection Act. Retrieved from Department of Labor: State of Illinois: http://www.state.il.us/agency/idol/faq/qawage.htm.

Jackson Lewis, LLP. (2004, April 8). Illinois Rejects Changes to Proposed Overtime Regulations. Retrieved from Jackson Lewis: http://www.jacksonlewis.com/legalupdates/article.cfm?aid=566.

Jacobson, P. D. (2009). The Role of ERISA Preemption in Health Reform: Opportunities and Limits. Journal of Law, Medicine & Ethics, 88-100.

Jennings, M. M. (2006). Business: Its legal, Ethical, and Global Environment (7th ed.). Mason, OH: Thomson Higher Learning.

Joseph D. Jendusa v. Cancer Treatment Centers of America, Inc. and Midwestern Regional Medical Center, Inc. and Richard Stephenson, 868 F. Supp. 1006 (E.D. Ill. 1994).

Leeds, H. S., & Richards, E. P. (2008). Legal Issues in Accommodating the Americans with Disabilities Act to the Diabetic Worker. The Journal of Legal Medicine, 29, 271-283. doi:10.1080/01947640802297546.

Leonard, E. W. (2011). Rhetorical Federalism: The Role of State Resistance in Health Care Decision-Making. Journal of Law, Medicine & Ethics, 73-76.

Macionis, J. J. (2010). Sociology (13th ed.). Boston, MA: Prentice Hall.

Marlow, E. K., & Rowland, K. M. (1989). Affirmative action: Federal support, Supreme Court decisions, and human resource management. Human Resource Management, 28(4), 541-556.

McKennon v. Nashville Banner Publishing Co., 513 U.S. 352 (Supreme Court of the United States 1995).

Milkovich, G. T., & Newman, J. M. (2008). Compensation (9th ed.). New York, NY: McGraw-Hill/Irwin.

Miller v. Xerox Corp. Retirement Income Guarantee Plan, 464 F.3d 871 (9th Circuit 2006).

Moran, J. J. (2008). Employment Law: New Challenges in the Business Environment (4th ed.). Upper Saddle River, NJ: Pearson Prentice Hall.

Muller, J. F. (2011). Disability, Ambivalence, and the Law. American Journal of Law & Medicine, 37(4), 469-521.

Myrna Gomez-Perez v. Postmaster General, 553 U.S. 474 (Supreme Court of the United States 2008).

Noble, F. P., & Harper, E. (2010). Strategy and Policy for Phased Retirement. Benefits Quarterly, 11-14.

Obama, B. (2009). Remarks by the President at the Acceptance of the Nobel Peace Prize. Retrieved from The White House: http://www.whitehouse.gov/the-press-office/remarks-president-acceptance-nobel-peace-prize/.

O'Connor v. Consolidated Coin Caterers, 517 U.S. 308 (Supreme Court of the United States 1996).

Papalia, D. E., Olds, S. W., & Feldman, R. D. (2009). Human development (11th ed.). Boston, MA: McGraw-Hill.

Perales v. American Retirement Corp., Lexis 22630 (Western District of Texas 2005).

PGA Tour, Inc. v. Martin, 532 U.S. 661 (Supreme Court of the United States 2001).

Phillips, C. D., Patnaik, A., Dyer, J. A., Naiser, E., Hawes, C., Fournier, C. J., & Elliott, T. R. (2011). Reliability and the Measurement of Activity Limitations (Adls) for Children with Special Health Care Needs (CSHCN) Living in the Community. Disability & Rehabilitation, 33(21), 2013-2022. doi:10.3109/09638288.2011.555596.

Phillips, T. B. (2011, Summer). A Living Wage for Research Subjects. Journal of Law, Medicine, and Ethics, 243-253.

Scamihorn v. General Truck Drivers, 282 F.3d 1078 (9th Circuit 2002).

Smith v. City of Salem, Ohio, 378 F.3d 566 (6th Circuit 2004).

Sutton v. United Airlines, Inc., 527 U.S. 471 (Supreme Court of the United States 1999).

Torcaso v. Watkins, 367 U.S. 488 (Supreme Court of the United States 1961).

Toyota v. Williams, 534 U.S. 184 (Supreme Court of the United States 2002).

University of California Regents v. Bakke, 438 U.S. 265 (Supreme Court of the United States 1977).

Varity Corp. v. Howe, 516 U.S. 489 (Supreme Court of the United States 1996).

Walsh, D. J. (2010). Employment law for human resource practice (3rd ed.). Mason, OH: South-Western Cengage Learning.

Wayne A. Meyer v. Southern Eagle Sales and Service, Inc., Lexis 365 (E.D. Lou. 1999).

* * *

PART FOUR: INDUSTRIAL – ORGANIZATIONAL PSYCHOLOGY

4.1 THE GENESIS AND IMPORTANCE OF INDUSTRIAL – ORGANIZATIONAL PSYCHOLOGY

Understanding the origins and research methods commonly employed among industrial and organizational psychology researchers is fundamental to expanding the knowledge of the field of Industrial/Organizational (I/O), application of new research activities, and professional growth of the researcher. Discussion of these origins is highlighted with the introduction of new terminology before explaining the scientific approach as utilized by I/O psychologists. Contrast of the most common research designs, through elaboration of the advantages and disadvantages of each type, emphasizes further understanding of the field of I/O psychology.

ORIGINS

Much debate exists as to the exact origin and originator of I/O psychology as changes in academic perspectives continue to seek recognition. Landy (1997) failed to recognize pioneering women in his vast array of historical writings where Koppes (1997) provided elaborate resumes of eccentric (albeit impressive) model women psychologists that inspired her own career. This familiar argument mirrors the Gilligan/Kohlberg controversy of male bias in research (Papalia, Olds, & Feldman, 2009) and the rejection by many psychologists of the generalizability of Freudian research since his primary subjects of study included only a limited number of affluent women; not men, children, or persons residing in the lower socioeconomic statuses (Coon & Mitterer, 2010).

This equalization of recognition transition (ERT) exists in no unique practice for industrial/organizational psychology, or for any other discipline, but instead as a global social trend. The definition of ERT is presented here as the social (transitive) tendency for cultures, organizations, out-groups, and individuals to seek personified recognition of their perspectives as inclusive to social perspectives of established historical phenomena, requiring adaptation or change to the original perspective of that historical phenomena.

For example, Native-Americans and African-Americans continue to postulate for rewritten secondary school history books to include their historical perspectives of American history (opposed to primarily Anglo-American) just as biological sciences moved away from creationist idealism (religion-based) over the last few decades while debated in the controversial blurred-line separations of church-and-state political issues.

As noted with Landy and Koppes, Landy recognized Germany's Wundt and America's James as cofounders of I/O psychology as a sub-discipline (Landy, 1997) and Koppes looked up to Gilbreth as the "mother of industrial psychology" (Koppes, 1997). Unfortunately for both of them, Muchinsky noted that W. L. Bryan first formally published in 1897 concerning the discipline and addressed the American Psychological Association (APA) long before the others completed implementations of their respective programs of study (Muchinsky, 2006).

The truth of the matter into who is the actual "father" or "mother" of I/O psychology lies only in the context of the question. In the spirit of ERT, those persons seeking acclaimed recognition as either the founder, or follower of the true founder (e.g. neo-Piagetian), the answer helps to boost egocentric personalities in cognitive social circles. However, to the introductory student of psychology, the reality inquisition of "Who cares?" infers just as well to the seasoned industrial and organizational psychologist who concerns himself/herself with the reliability, validity, and utility of contributions over argument of who was first.

Building upon this position, the rest of this paper focuses on the different types of research designs I/O psychologists rely upon with minimal regard for the cognitive perspectives of their origins.

IMPORTANCE OF RESEARCH

Research by industrial and organizational psychologists carries three primary purposes, description, prediction, and explanation (Muchinsky, 2006). The added fourth dimension of control (Coon & Mitterer, 2010) finds attention depending upon the context of the research purpose. Whichever dimensions the researcher includes, understanding the hypothesis under consideration stands as the goal.

Description

The first step to solving any problem incurs upon recognizing a problem actually exists, then stating in definable terms, the nature of the problem. Analyses into the literature allows the researcher to ascertain whether the problem was previously solved, whether someone studied similar phenomenon needing further examination, or whether the topic remains unexplored. The literature review then dictates if deductive (data available) or inductive (new data needed) methods necessitate the research design. Discussion of design systems follows later.

Once data analysis and review of the findings occur, the researcher attempts to make sense of these findings through application of the hypotheses; however, the "why" lingers undiscovered at this point (Coon & Mitterer, 2010).

Prediction

Like description, prediction enjoys application in the setup and analysis phases of the research. During hypothesis building, the researcher attempts to build hypotheses that predict outcomes for the question at hand. Conversely, after research completion and analyses conduction, the adjusted hypotheses attempt to predict future behaviors or outcomes given a certain set of circumstances (Field, 2009). For the I/O psychologist, prediction mandates utility of research outcomes.

For example, how well does the personality test predict aggressiveness in applicants, if hired, and is that a desired trait for the position tested for? When designing the test, the I/O psychologist may hypothesize whether answers to particular questions accurately predicts the aggressive trait in test-takers.

Explanation

The explanatory dimension attempts to explain the "why" behind a behavior or probable solution. Expanding upon the aggressiveness behavior trait, the researcher develops a theory (correct or not) that helps to explain how the test predicts future aggressiveness in applicants. This phase is the most difficult part of the research process (Muchinsky, 2006) as exceptions occur, biases mislead analyses (Papalia, Olds, & Feldman, 2009), and knowledge of the subject may be limited in scope.

Imagine trying to explain why positive responses to the statement, "I was abused as a child", positively correlate to authoritarian leadership styles and dictatorship tendencies (Macionis, 2010). In the end, sharing this information with peers, colleagues, and the scientific community through publication assists other researchers.

Control

"[C]ontrol simply refers to altering conditions that affect behavior... If you suggest changes in a classroom that help students learn better, you have exerted control." (Coon & Mitterer, 2010). Control as a dimension of research provides valid goals for conducting the study in the first place. If the goal of the industrial and organizational psychologist developing a test that eliminates aggressive personalities from the hiring pool motivates research into test development, then control is exerted when a valid and reliable test finds utility for that purpose. As a fourth dimension of research, control exhorts its invaluable context.

TYPES AND DESIGNS OF RESEARCH

The design of a research problem is merely the plan for conducting the study (Muchinsky, 2006) and many techniques are available to researchers for execution, mostly depending upon cost and availability of resources (Heneman III & Judge, 2009). Laboratories coincide with controlled studies, natural settings (workplaces, communities,) entertain naturalistic studies, and libraries or private settings provide relaxation for meta-analyses.

While the first two settings are common for primary research, the latter combines previous research (data and/or results) to yield secondary research activities and encumbers the lowest cost, but also provides the least amount of variable control. Laboratories, unless funded through a generous benefactor, endure the highest costs but provide the highest degree of control. For these reasons, most industrial and organizational psychologists undertake naturalistic settings due to lowered costs and the ability to observe subjects in natural work settings. In fact, consultants enjoy compensation for conducting research studies for private employers.

Laboratory Experiments

In laboratory experiments, researchers design the study to control for certain variables that may not be possible to control in a natural setting. For example, the Hawthorne Studies, although a natural setting, attempted to utilize the factory as a laboratory setting by varying the lighting levels of the factory (control variable) to test for changing levels in worker production (dependent variable). Unfortunately, the intended measures failed, but the researchers realized that when workers know they are under study, the workers will perform at levels contrary to reality, but in accordance with levels they would be expected under ideal conditions (Muchinsky, 2006; Heneman III & Judge, 2009). This drawback of laboratory studies is known as the Hawthorne effect. The "why" this effect occurs is debatable but fear from employer scrutiny commonly finds citation.

A primary advantage of laboratory experimentation includes random assignment of subjects into control and study groups. This practice helps to eliminate bias and type errors associated with participants (Field, 2009) in that participants do not know (and sometimes neither do researchers in double-blind studies) to which group they are assigned to. The controlled environment of the laboratory enables researchers to better find causal links between study variables. For an I/O psychologist, laboratories are common for paper-based research (personnel testing) and curriculum development (training research) activities.

Quasi Experiments

Quasi experiments combine the laboratory with the field or naturalistic environment to make participants feel as if they are not in a laboratory. The controversial Biosphere 2 experiment required persons to reside inside a man-made environment within the Arizona desert over a two year period to test whether humans could sustainably survive and maintain a restricted biosphere in space. The timespan allotted conceivably helped the participants to overcome the laboratory feel of the environment and to consider the biosphere as their home.

Unexpectedly, the participants divided into disputing factions and began consuming emergency supplies, explained as an effect of isolation (Poynter, 2006). Quasi experiments sometimes reveal unintended information that benefits researchers, just as in the Hawthorne Studies, but the Hawthorne case was not a quasi-experiment because in that study, manipulation of the natural environment occurred rather than the laboratory.

Questionnaires and Surveys

Questionnaires and surveys, with careful use of the internet or small organizations, can provide inexpensive means of obtaining anonymous data. Use of mailed forms incurs higher costs and reduced participation. Although respondents are more likely to reply to personal questions, they believe cannot identify them than in interviews or tracked data forms, several drawbacks can skew data results (Muchinsky, 2006). Respondents tend to answer questions in a way they feel the researcher desires (Field, 2009), many purposely enter bogus responses to retaliate against the line of questioning (an anti-spam technique), and less than 50% return rate is expected... 31% if mailed (Muchinsky, 2006).

Questionnaires and surveys find popularity among I/O psychologists, but Muchinsky warns that wording of these instruments should match the reading level of the participant sample, that researchers carefully plan for generalizability if needed, and that cross-cultural needs be identified and accommodated.

Observation

Landy and Koppes reported that the earliest industrial and organizational psychologists utilized observation (naturalistic setting) as a primary research technique (Landy, 1997; Koppes, 1997). Gilbreth exhorted observation in the workplace as valuable when conducting simulation studies and testing of applicants while James believed that observation was fundamental to understanding behavior. A primary benefit of observation flows from the concept that it further generates ideas for testing with other research methods. Aside from the aforementioned disadvantages involving workplace observation, the method continues today as a successful research method (Muchinsky, 2006).

SUMMARY OF RESEARCH DESIGNS

No single method of research design finds universal acceptance and it is up to the researcher to choose the method, or combination of methods, that best fits the hypothesis under test. Of the methods described, laboratory experiments allow the highest level of control but endure the lowest level of realism. Quasi experiments tolerate moderate control and high levels of realism due to their structure; however, questionnaires and observation perceive the lowest controllability. Between the latter two, observation of course provides the highest realism while participants report that questionnaires provide moderate realism, even without interaction (Muchinsky, 2006).

CONCLUSIONS

While many researchers concern themselves with the vanity of who was responsible for creating the sub-discipline of industrial and organizational psychology over 100 years ago, we cannot overlook the important fact that everyone who works takes part in its continued development; I/O psychologists, cross-discipline researchers, employers, and most importantly, the workers alike. ERT helps to explain why so many people attempt to rewrite history from a multi-faceted perspective rather than following the traditional golden rule of social influence, "He/she who has the gold makes the rules".

Through the dimensions of description, prediction, explanation, and control, researchers in the field of industrial and organizational psychology utilize the scientific method to further advance the sub-discipline as a viable and valuable tool that governments and private industry alike can better understand workers and their respective organizational cultures. Without this process, research attempts fail in validity, reliability, and more importantly, utility.

Laboratory experiments are best suited for situations where variable control is necessary, but at the expense of realism. The quasi experiment attempts to bring some of this realism into the laboratory and can yield unintended discoveries, sometimes at the expense of the initial research project. The growing popularity of questionnaires and surveys, especially with the low cost of internet delivery, demonstrates flaws in reliability, but still lags behind the use of naturalistic observation as the dominant form of research design. Observation appears in the earliest literature and has matured through seemingly countless trial-and-error documentations and provides the basis for many future research queries.

* * *

4.2 DISCUSSION OF PERFORMANCE APPRAISAL

Over the last three decades of my working life, only my current employer performed any kind of formalized evaluation of my work performance. In fact, the one evaluation completed last year served no compensatory purpose although ratings exceeded average worker scores. The evaluation is state mandated bi-yearly for all adjunct instructors for the purpose of eliminating poor performers.

Promotions depend upon application and hiring into advanced positions, but new hires receive the same base rate of pay (hourly or salary) as tenured seniority. An administrative assistant just graduating from a school program starts at the same wage as an administrative assistant with 20 years of experience. Because my employer is a community college, the thought pattern purports that persons in lower positions take advantage of free tuition (for employees) to move into higher positions.

Many of my previous employers either drew concern in cases of possible screw-ups, but all based wage increases upon annual cost-of-living-adjustments (COLA) and time-in-service (TIS). For example, a 3.2% COLA raise for all employees and/or a $1 raise in base pay after the probationary period totaled raises. The same truth for my current employer continues except TIS substitution with advanced education level payments of $1,000 is specified for every 12 semester hours completed beyond the Master's degree.

CONCLUSIONS

Unfortunately, no real-world experience application exists within my work-life that matches any of the performance evaluation concepts described by Muchinsky (Muchinsky, 2006), Heneman, or Judge (Heneman III & Judge, 2009). However, I believe that merit raises or bonus offerings by the college based upon the mandated performance evaluation may assist in declination of turnover and improve teaching performance of adjunct instructors. Smith (2011) determined three inter-related constructs in a recent study supporting this determination:

1. Intrinsic factors primarily motivate instructors.
2. Motivation increases through extrinsic factors (such as bonuses or merit raises), although instructors found motivation through intrinsic factors (love of job).
3. Instructors did not feel that policies and procedures [alone] effectively motivated them.

* * *

4.3 ASSOCIATE SELECTION

The practice and research surrounding the selection of associates in the workplace brings as much diversification to the field of industrial and organizational psychology as there are employers. In fact, no two employers use exactly the same culmination of processes and methods for personnel selection (Heneman III & Judge, 2009). These differences lay in the choice of methods preferred and modification within specific utilities. For example, intelligence test form variations and in the training of interpreters for these tools (Muchinsky, 2006).

Other dissimilarities in personnel selection result from the position level sought by the applicant (engineer v. general laborer). We would not ethically endure a general laborer the embarrassment of sitting through an engineering exam for which they likely would not maintain knowledge or experience nor would we require a structural engineer to partake in a chemistry understanding evaluation to test job knowledge in building bridges.

The requirements of validity and reliability of chosen selection methods holds utmost importance (Muchinsky, 2006). Selection methods should measure the intended attribute of the applicant that matches the job analysis and do so consistently across the applicant pool.

Sometimes the best selection method fails the requirement of feasibility in application, especially for smaller organizations. Costs outside the budget, lacks in trained human resource and/or administrative personnel available, and fears of legal or governmental intervention often provide explanation for lacks in adoption of better known (higher validity) methods.

The purpose of the sections following is to compare and contrast various research designs associated with determining the validity and utility of personnel techniques. Although primarily written from an American cultural perspective, exploration into some cross-cultural concerns in applicability of techniques novel attention.

SOCIAL CONTEXT

I/O psychologists typically find reputation for development of assessments, conducting validation research, and consequential explanation of instrument usage (Muchinsky, 2006). These professionals rarely undertake implementation of personnel selection programs individually and require the cooperation of key organizational personnel, such as managers and supervisors of prospective applicants, human resource personnel, and other employees. Even though associate selection arguably begins with a careful job analysis (Heneman III & Judge, 2009), employees and supervisors experienced with the position need to provide critical task information before the analysis comes to fruition.

Human resource personnel bring detrimental guidelines incumbent to the success of the organization to the analysis while providing historical feedback that enables I/O psychologists to view larger perspectives of the organizational culture.

Selection criteria not only identify person/job matches, but also person/organization matches to ensure organizational fit of the applicant within the personnel culture. This aspect of personnel selection depends more upon rater intuition without validation or quantification since these selection factors derive from empirical experiences between the rater and applicant (Muchinsky, 2006). Alternatively stated, "gut feelings" lack validation due to inability by researchers to quantify measurement and therefore do not generalize across applicants or organizations.

The story of Stanley offering explanation for completing a task differently than the traditional method used within the organization (Ritti & Levy, 2007), "Well at Company X we did it this way" meeting immediate resistance through, "You are not at Company X anymore, so do it our way" demonstrates variability within organizational cultures even within the same industry.

I/O researchers draw limitations within their work socially by the communities and other stakeholders they serve. Common or acceptable associate selection practices in the United States conversely receive criticism and rejection in other countries due to religious influences (e.g. Muslim controlled countries honor Sharia law over capitalistic ideals), nepotism (India and other caste system countries), and resistance to change traditions (China). Jennings (2006) sourced the latter as a component cause within the U.S. of the glass ceiling effect where women endure denial with advancement into managerial positions. This cross-cultural rejection leads to narrowed implementations of sound research.

Socially enacted laws, such as the Americans with Disabilities Act (ADA) and Title VII of the Civil Rights Act, formulate rules into not only how research by I/O psychologists may be conducted on living persons, but also limit implementation of outcomes through legislation to prevent adverse impact (4/5 Rule) and other forms of discrimination. These laws do not exist merely for providing a scope of limitation, but to uniformly deliver frameworks for the advancement of the field.

AGREEABLENESS IN VALIDITY

One practical dilemma that researchers face is in the determination of cutoff (criterion) scores for assessments deemed valid against the related predictor. Since reliability is necessary for validity, questionable validity occurs when selection measures incur questionable reliability (Heneman III & Judge,

2009). To further complicate interpretations of validity, some I/O psychologists cannot agree upon standardized levels of acceptance in the magnitude of validity coefficients.

Heneman and Judge, for example, stand firmly that validities above 0.15 dictate moderate usefulness while those over 0.30 maintain high measures of usefulness. However, Muchinsky adds that most of the higher validity scores average between 0.30 and 0.40, with coefficients above 0.50 rarely observed in the field of I/O psychology.

Face validity, in contrast, does not include mathematical schemas but instead draws upon empirical constructs that define usefulness of a measure (Heneman III & Judge, 2009). Because a study indicates high validity for a specific assessment does not point to that assessment as useful or acceptable under face validity. Social construction deems the assessment invalid due to inappropriateness.

For example, the practice of I/O psychology observes an increased likelihood that individuals bring legal challenges against companies they feel utilize unfair or irrelevant materials and content (and win), regardless of assessment content validity (Muchinsky, 2006). When face validity prevails over content validity then utility of the assessment diminishes.

Given these circumstances, the challenges and complexity of determining cutoff scores increase with the development of each new assessment tool. To reduce the probability of situations occurring that involve adverse impact, the procedure of banding, or placing cutoff criterion into ranges of predictive scores, dominates the field as an acceptable reduction method for challenges.

APPLICATION VERSUS HIRING

Predictors for assessments enjoy more usefulness when selection ratios decrease (Heneman III & Judge, 2009) due in part to costs involved with the selection process, in part to the sheer number of applicants within the hiring pool, and in part to the job in question (Muchinsky, 2006). Obviously, when elaborate or expensive assessment centers dominate the hiring process of associates, high numbers of applicants exponentially increase the costs of selection.

Testing 1,000 applicants means 10 times the cost of testing 100 applicants. The expenditure can reveal dramatically expensive overhead, especially when only a few positions need filled. Smaller organizations simply cannot endure the expenditure and forfeit the benefits associated with the higher priced assessments through selection of lower cost alternatives.

Preferred employers obtain more accepted job offers while jobs that entail fewer demands require less selectivity, time, and cost to fill. Economics, locally or globally, helps determine if a company pursues applicants or if applicants flock to the company seeking employment. Whatever the case, or combination of factors surrounding the organizational situation, the higher the position needing occupied or the more qualifications required filling a position, the longer the time essential to adequately screen applicants.

Muchinsky (2006) noted that potential employers and applicants maintain mutual stakeholder relationships throughout the recruitment process because both assess one another to determine the degree of fit with each other. For example, an incumbent may turn down a job offer in retort to face validity or utility of components within the assessment process, for empirical data experienced during the process, or simply for dissatisfaction in the offer itself (Jennings, 2006).

Although selection ratios find manipulation by a number of factors, industrial and organizational psychologists continue to research the best combinations of methods needed for assessment centers in various scenarios. Difficulty arises when matching costs, time, and utility of preferred measures against validity, reliability, and empirical data to employer/applicant necessities. Cross-discipline research by I/O psychologists aids in discovering solutions that apply concrete issues to real-world settings (Seijts & Latham, 2003).

RESEARCH DESIGNS

The relationship between how well people perform on tests and on the job reflects the validity of the selection tool. In 1998, the most valid predictor in this relationship of job performance stood out as general mental ability (g) with a correlation coefficient of r =0.51 (Schmidt & Hunter, 1998). This particular meta-analysis sparked re-examination of previous research within job performance criterion (such as work samples) and arrived at drastically different conclusions in some cases (Roth, Bobko, & McFarland, 2005). Validity for work samples declined by half, from the previously reported (Asher & Sciarrino, 1974) 0.54 to 0.26, once error corrections in the original statistical analysis began. Further analysis by Roth, Bobko, and McFarland revealed that when combined with general mental ability, predictable validity of work samples for job performance increased significantly to 0.32.

The lesson to understand here lies in the complexity of the research design rather than on the individual components. When combined, the sum of the parts of the selection criteria enhances the outcome in greater proportion than the distinct components alone. Muchinsky summarized this phenomenon best; "Personnel selection is predicated upon a complex mix of technical and social factors embedded in a legal framework" (Muchinsky, 2006, p. 173).

Since most research in I/O psychology entertains the workplace, difficulties in validation through sampling plague research designs due to small sample sizes, especially in proprietary organizations that limit research information. Issues involving sharing of data and results may lead to inconclusive or incomplete scientific investigation within certain industries and occupations.

Toyota, for example, receives fame for integration of Kaizen principals into the manufacturing environment and development of the Just-In-Time (JIT) supply chain management method of assembly line manufacturing. This technique required extensive study of personnel capabilities, attributes, and motivation followed by alignment of these results to arrive at a workable solution. Although widely studied on a global scale, public knowledge of JIT forced the automaker giant to clamp down on information security. Today, all applicants sign non-disclosure statements that include information regarding employee relations and practices as a condition of employment. Hence even though the employee sample numbers in the tens of thousands, access to human resource information remains confidential within the company and out of reach among other I/O psychologists.

Research designs cover other assessment types: polygraphs (limited usage), drug testing, letters of recommendation, biographical information, situational exercises, interviews, and job-specific skills tests, to name a few. Of these, letters of recommendation maintain the lowest validity, although widely used. Interviews remain favorites among employers (and some social researchers) as having the most utility with their empirical feedback capability. Regardless of the combination of assessment types considered, the I/O researcher culminates responsibility in determining the research design that provides the most value containing validity and utility (Muchinsky, 2006).

CONCLUSIONS

The practice and research of I/O psychology persists as diversified today as the sub-discipline did at its inception. Differences in people and the cultures they share through places of employment provide difficulty in generalizing attributes across industries, let alone organizations within a single industry. Finding the right mix of measurable attributes within an applicant that proves predictability in successfully becoming a productive and reliable associate daunts the foundations of the field.

Social constraints in law and tradition predicate the evolution of I/O psychology. The United States has endured reforms not only in employment law, but also in the ethical and practical applications of research. Other regions of the globe disagree amongst themselves sometimes incorporating prejudicial or even superstitious reasoning into employment practices. From this it becomes clearer as to why face validity sometimes prevails over content validity as the source of judicial interpretation.

Other times cost and lacks in availability of resources force the best selection research to take back seat to the most economical means. The more qualifications demanded of associates, the higher the costs in obtaining the best qualified applicants to fill those positions. The smaller the company and the tighter the security around employee information, the more difficulty I/O psychologists stake in obtaining valid and reliable data to complete research yielding the highest possible utility.

Regardless, industrial and organizational psychologists must continue to observe, to record, to analyze, and to share research for enhanced understanding of the mutual employee/employer relationships within the limits imposed by societies and the organizations who serve them.

* * *

4.4 DISCUSSION OF MOTIVATION

Muchinsky (2006) described seven theories of motivation concerning employees and work. He summarized each by detailing how they compare towards one another, how they enable the field of industrial/organizational psychology, and how they stand the scrutiny of utility for business practitioners. One of these theories, composed of a combination of theories, grasps attention for dominance: Self-Regulation Theory.

The primary concept behind Self-Regulation Theory lays the understanding that generalization of motivational concepts (overall) among job classes, as well as between individuals across jobs, carries discrepancies. Not every person feels motivated by the same constructs leading to performance increases (Milkovich & Newman, 2008). Most employees temporarily respond effectively from monetary incentives; however, applying Maslow's Hierarchy of Needs Theory demonstrates that over time, money alone fails sustainability in meeting higher needs (Muchinsky, 2006).

Adaptability provides strength in support of Self-Regulation Theory. As new motivational theories conceptualize, complexity of the system grows in response through inclusion of these ideas or replacement over weaker concepts. For example, Muchinsky noted that Goal-setting Theory exists as a component although it "is among the most valid and practiced... in organizational psychology". This perception within Self-Regulation Theory enables research findings with higher validity and generalizability than individual components studied in standalone applications.

CONCLUSIONS

Many states banned smoking in various settings (public places, businesses,.) during the first decade of the 21st century. The challenge for employers relies upon legal compliance in conjunction with combinations of employee "needs" to smoke, cessation training, and changes in hiring practices. Moon and Jang-Han (2011) employed Self-Regulation Theory using Personality-Trait Theory, Reinforcement Theory, and Emotional Theory (not Emotional Intelligence) to determine that emotional states in the presence of certain personality traits predict whether positive or negative reinforcement influences individuals to smoke. Any of the component theories could not draw similar conclusions when studied alone.

This information, for I/O psychologists, helps to indirectly narrow legal compliance and personal gaps among employees and demonstrates the dominant preference for Self-Regulation Theory.

* * *

4.5 THE NOVELTY OF TEAMS

Predictions abound by industrial and organizational psychologists that usage of teams within public, government, and private industry cannot escape avoidance as norms in society. Emergence of studies within social psychology, sociology, and I/O psychology break down the studies of teams to understand the mindset behind successful and failed team projects as well as the mechanical workings that provide benefits over traditional manager/subordinate individual models.

The following sections overview the research behind selection, performance appraisal, decision making, and interpersonal processes at the team level in contrast to work performed by individuals.

SELECTION

Similar to I/O psychologists who rarely undertake implementation of personnel selection themselves (Heneman III & Judge, 2009); self-managed teams require the cooperation of key personnel when hiring new members. Unlike traditional selection methods encompassing individuals however, the team as a whole assumes responsibility for choosing new team associates rather than involving outside placement through say, a human resources department (Russell & Jacobs, 2008). Of course, this statement is not entirely correct as HR typically prescreens or verifies applicants to meet organizational standards before referral and hiring of applicants at the organizational level (e.g. drug screen, background check, etc.).

Russell and Jacobs noted 16 activities that self-managed teams might perform where individuals or semiautonomous teams (work groups) traditionally lose empowerment to managers:

1. Set their own work schedules and plan their own work.
2. Allocate task responsibilities among team members.
3. Coordinate work among team members.
4. Determine training needs; acquire needed training.
5. Coordinate work with other teams or departments.
6. Engage in multi-skilling and job rotation.
7. Set production quotas or performance targets.

8. Deal directly with external customers.
9. Conduct performance appraisals of team members and provide feedback to each other.
10. Directly deal with their vendors or suppliers.
11. Purchase equipment or services directly.
12. Do own budgeting.
13. Recruit, select, and hire own team members.
14. Discipline and fire team members as the need arises.
15. Inspect own work.
16. Change the nature of their work to improve quality.

Points numbered 13 and 14 summarize the empowerments given to self-managed teams when dealing with employment issues. In contrast, semiautonomous teams or groups generally encounter restrictions with hiring and firing individuals at the organizational level. Other characteristics demonstrate the need for balanced KSAOs within the team for success. To achieve the proper mix, the team considers acculturation characteristics (teamwork skills) of the prospective applicant as well as ability to do the job (taskwork skills) (Muchinsky, 2006).

Research in the area of personnel selection for teams embraces personality traits, productivity, operating costs, job satisfaction, motivation, compensation, and interoperability (Muchinsky, 2006; Russell & Jacobs, 2008). For example, researchers discovered that conscientiousness, emotional stability, and extraversion predict an individual's willingness to back up team mates and 38% of companies that utilized teams reported improved work quality.

PERFORMANCE APPRAISAL

Performance appraisal at the team level takes account of additional factors not found at the individual level (Muchinsky, 2006). Perceived control over one's ability and actions determine acceptance levels of the individual within the team. Less control spawns more sympathy and assistance from team members while increased control lessens team sympathies, sometimes to the point of alienation or exclusion. Albeit this phenomenon occurs at the individual level among coworkers, but teams generally operate as a personnel unit that depends upon member contributions for success. In this respect teams have more at stake when a member falters and find strength in the weakest link (Jackson & LePine, 2003).

Social loafing often receives causal attribution through lacks of incentives (Muchinsky, 2006). Milkovich and Newman (2008) boasted that incentive plans boost productivity with exceptions to tasks involved, organizational commitment to the team, and the work environment. All agreed that free-riding plagues groups, especially when incentives relate to compensation. Research indicated that good performance measurement techniques lessened free-rider problems because social loafing detection increased.

When teams reorganize, shift individual responsibilities, or set new priorities, Russell and Jacobs (2008) suggested that teams clarify member roles and responsibilities through task analyses, SWOT analyses of the team's work, create plans for cross-training, and provide periodic feedback and review of member contributions to the team effort. Difficulty arises for semiautonomous teams where individual members perform multiple jobs, rather additional jobs outside the team but within the organization. In these cases, staffing occurs to recruit and select applicants for both job-specific KSAOs (competencies). Measurement objectives in applicant flexibility, adaptability, and speed for learning new skills paramount the selection process with supplementary difficulty (Heneman III & Judge, 2009). Essentially, singular applicant hiring for two separate jobs occurs simultaneously: one for the organization and the second as a member of a team.

DECISION MAKING

Decision making probably stands out as the most studied concept for teams among industrial and organizational psychologists. Implications of team decisions range from the military where every employee enjoys membership in at least one team, to the government (Iraq War weapons of mass destruction claim), to technology development, and to productivity levels within the manufacturing sector. For various reasons, most researchers agree that team membership of five to eleven persons (in an odd-numbered configuration) provides the greatest effectiveness, depending on the team's purpose (Russell & Jacobs, 2008).

Four basic types of decision-making undergo scrutiny: autocratic, democratic, consensus, and unanimous. Russell and Jacobs concluded with recommendation that teams primarily utilize consensus for most decisions, but understood that other types occasionally bring necessity. This style allows for majority agreeableness while leaving room for disagreement and further scrutiny; effectively providing voice for every member.

Autocratic type decisions lag for specific situations requiring immediate decisions or those outside the scope of the team's ability. Implication here suggests that traditional managerial intervention, like that employed at the individual level, back up team decision making processes when teams cannot reach consensus or when situations disallow team involvement.

Groupthink and other conformity issues abound the literature in relation to decision making outcomes. Only one conclusion seems to come to fruition in avoidance of groupthink; (1) do not select 'yes men' (persons who consistently succumb to group or leadership pressures even when they have contradictory information to provide) as team members where input is vital, and (2) as a team member, speak up (Luthans, 2008).

The classical Milgram studies into group conformity by individuals initially showed how groupthink affected many persons to conform to even grotesque group pressures and recent history revealed similar real-world situations (Space Shuttle Challenger). Luthans claimed that current research into conformity lacks maturity, resulting in preemptive conclusions.

Leadership studies relatively fit into lessons of decision making and influences from conformity. The style of leadership, the division of power within leadership, and the attributes of followers comprise and influence decisions teams form depending upon the purpose and composition of the particular team (Muchinsky, 2006). Some members may dominate while others fear rejection by the group (Russell & Jacobs, 2008). The same conclusions occur with individuals in non-group employment statuses although teams can predictably measure success or failure of the group by leadership styles employed (Luthans, 2008).

INTERPERSONAL PROCESSES

Overall performance of teams relates to influences by interpersonal processes in communication, conflict, and cohesion (Muchinsky, 2006). Virtual teams depend upon communication technologies for planning and member cooperation, especially in a global perspective. At the micro level, in-group communication between team members provides essential information that allows coordination and completion of task objectives. Communication therefore sees limitations stemming from leadership styles and dysfunctional influences.

Different types of conflict within teams can provide benefit, competition, or problems. Conflict in itself does not translate into negativity. Beneficial conflict interprets to conflict expected for growth and advanced understanding where competitive conflict occurs between members in judgment of who is better or who is correct. When directed toward out-groups, the latter benefits the team through senses of accomplishment and cohesion whereas within the team feelings of discord and contention likely result (Luthans, 2008).

Cohesion among team members manifests in task performance as related to the accepted interdependence among members (Muchinsky, 2006). Cohesive teams view decisional dissent among members as non-threatening, however, less cohesive teams suffer subjectivity to groupthink or rejection of further pertinent information. Macionis (2010) suggested that bonding at the fictive-kin level describes this relationship among team members within military and self-managed groups. Trust in other teammates, the belief that members behave in beneficial ways toward other members when the situation lacks control by those other members, integrates as a support mechanism for cohesion. Of the interpersonal processes studied by I/O psychologists, trust excels as the least understood.

Building on interpersonal processes, research into socialization and team building techniques arise in need of incorporating new members into existing teams as well as enhancing their longevity (Luthans, 2008). Some applicants display unwillingness or apprehension about joining teams making the recruitment process more difficult. Once acculturated however, team hires tend to perform at higher levels than they initially did, just as individuals do.

CONCLUSIONS

Team studies involve the same concerns that individuals face with additional considerations. Member composition includes individuals so the trick is to meet the needs of each member while encouraging the team to work, think, and feel as a single unit. Improved models evolve to meet this need that help I/O psychologists and employers to enhance and improve these relationships while providing more efficient output processes.

In essence, selectivity, performance appraisal, decision making, and interpersonal processes draw upon one another through inter-related concepts making defined conclusions immature. Perhaps over time, as Luthans noted, correlational studies may refine the usage of teams to de facto standards, becoming the norm rather than the exception.

* * *

4.6 DISCUSSION OF LABOR RELATIONS

Mediation, fact-finding, and arbitration dominate as solutions when unions and management reach an impasse during labor disputes in the United States. An impasse correlates in terms of a standoff where none of the proponents concede and each believes their particular position prevails as the most correct. Although union strength is diminishing in political terms (Grier, 2011) and membership (Muchinsky, 2006), employers still see these forces and deal with them regularly.

Unlike trends with standard service contracts that increasingly include clauses requiring arbitration, especially in cases involving interstate or international disputes (Walsh, 2010) unions prefer mediation. Mediators reduce formality and provide further options for either party than arbitrational decisions, which are absolute and binding.

Fact-finding appears more of a tactical decision since the mediator publishes findings/decisions. The belief is that an impasse sways by public opinion toward either party from pressures to accept dominant opinions. Historically, fact-finding techniques generally fail this intended purpose and dramatic measures, such as strikes, tend to follow (Muchinsky, 2006).

In arbitration, the neutral third-party presides as an unofficial judge, but with the same binding authority. Arbitration may follow with legal due process if either party meets the burden of proving an unfair advantage in the process. For example, the union solely chooses the arbitrator (Walsh, 2010). Interest arbitration increasingly finds inclusion within public union contracts, but no difference within private union contracts takes notice (Muchinsky, 2006).

CONCLUSIONS

Admittedly, this author takes an anti-union stance from an ethical point-of-view. The belief is that if an employer is so unjust that employees need to hire (pay dues) a team of lawyers (union representatives) to make sure that employer treats them fairly, then they should not want to work there anyway. I once worked for an open shop company where employees fared better than union employees did after the vote-in. The unionized employees then worked twice as hard for the same pay as they were pre-union, where those of us who refused to join enjoyed the same work level as before. For example, before the union these workers averaged 27 hour workweeks at 40 hour pay; afterwards it was 40:40 for them.

* * *

4.7 STRESS MANAGEMENT WITHIN THE WORKPLACE

In attempt to address the causes of workplace stressors at the organizational level, rather than simply clean up the aftermath through individual counseling and other treatments, preventive measures deserve discussion. Topics including drug and alcohol testing, flexible working schedules, adequacy in sleep schedules, worker economic concerns, role and family conflict management, and models of mental health follow for assisting managers in reaching plausible solutions. Caution prevails in that no specific solution generalizes to every situation encountered by the organization. However, combinations show lowered costs at the bottom line (Pearson Learning Solutions, 2010).

DRUG AND ALCOHOL TESTING

Detected illegal drug use in the workplace decreased steadily since 1988 from 13.6% nationally over a 20 year period to a stabilized 3.8% of those workers tested (Korkki, 2008). This trend reportedly saw equivalent reductions in economic costs of healthcare, lost earnings, and indirect expenses between 1998 and 2006 within the state of Oregon. Over the eight year period, losses estimated at $185 billion statewide from alcohol abuse and $180 billion from drug abuse significantly reduced to $3.24 billion and $2.69 billion, respectively (Whelan, Josephson, & Holcombe, 2008). Unfortunately, even these losses overshadowed Oregon's forestry, agriculture, fishing, and hunting industries combined income of $3.77 billion for 2006.

Drug and alcohol testing do not provide valid predictors for job performance, good or poor, but they do predict other behaviors such as absenteeism, accidents, and counterproductive activities (Heneman III & Judge, 2009). Therefore, postemployment losses decrease resulting from successful pre-employment testing programs for illicit drugs and alcohol use/abuse. Ensuring against adverse impact, age discrimination (Muchinsky, 2006), and other Title VII concerns, Heneman III and Judge provide six recommendations for organizations:

1. Emphasize drug testing in safety-sensitive jobs and those where the link between substance abuse and negative outcomes supplies documentation.
2. Use only reputable laboratories for testing; not in-house testing personnel.
3. Obtain consent before testing, inform test results, and provide an appeal procedure.
4. Retest positive samples.
5. Maintain the individual's right to privacy throughout the testing procedures and results.
6. Conduct program reviews against relevant criteria (accidents, absenteeism, turnover, and job performance) to prove utility of the program if challenged.

Elimination of potential employment candidates who abuse illicit drugs and/or alcohol relieves stresses by workers for fears of potential accidents, workplace violence, personal production losses, and absenteeism that may affect their own safety or performance. Testing existing employees maintains social controls that such behaviors remain intolerable during employment with the organization although legal mandates for some positions exists (truck drivers and federal employees).

Additionally, organizations that provide effective substance abuse rehabilitation programs enjoy reduced costs of turnover within the organization, but then discover further restrictions under the Americans with Disabilities Act (ADA) if future termination deems warranted (Walsh, 2010).

FLEXIBLE WORKING SCHEDULES

Flexible working schedules, by definition (Muchinsky, 2006), exclude compressed workweeks, split-shift schedules, voluntary working hours (volunteer overtime), and similar employee scheduling under direct control of the employer. Conversely then, flextime includes arrangements between employers and employees to complete core work activities during alternative times. Muchinsky reported flextime scheduling alleviates many problems with family commitments, recreation, second jobs, commuting, and stress. Tardiness obviously becomes a nullable factor if the shift begins with arrival of the worker.

Many researchers agree that flextime benefits hourly employees more than persons holding professional positions as the latter group may enjoy this scheduling informally as exempt members of the organization. Workers provided flexible hours by their employers tend to work more intensely than counterparts maintaining rigid office hours (Kelliher & Anderson, 2010). The equity theory of motivation explains this quality/production increase by demonstrating that employees assert an obligation toward the employer in exchange for the added benefit. Reserve soldiers (active two weeks per year) outscoring Regular-duty soldiers during training exercises is not uncommon. Essentially, reduced stressors through forced scheduling (monotony) translate to increased motivation and production quality and lowered costs for the organization.

ADEQUACY IN SLEEP SCHEDULES

Just as summer vacations in grade school originated from the need of traditional farm families (as the dominant occupation of the time) to remove children from school to work family farms, the more common shift schedule of 7 AM to 3 PM rooted to accommodate parents with childcare preparations around school hours. Other variations accommodate traffic congestion and added social problems stemming from these roots. Complexities between schedules, extended scheduling, and long commutes related to work mandate shortened periods of sleep for many workers. Eleven aversive characteristics ranging from physical disorders, to mental disorders, to poor work quality identify effects of sleep deprivation within research literature (Muchinsky, 2006).

Evolutionary theory dictates that humans endure biological programming in terms of circadian rhythms to remain awake during daylight hours and then sleep at night. The theory fails to explain why some people prefer the inverse and thrive just as well (Coon & Mitterer, 2010). When neuroscience discoveries about the hormone melatonin combine with outcomes surrounding production-level studies (e.g. Hawthorne Studies), we now know that increased levels of lighting intensify melatonin production and causes wakefulness. Hence, with brighter light follows night adaptation. For example, most traffic collisions involving sleepy drivers occur in poorly lit areas near or outside of cities.

Increased energy costs recently caused many facilities to remove lighting from areas not in regular use by employees, such as hallways and corridors at the Toyota production plant located south of Princeton, Indiana (personal observation, July 2011). In such cases, recommendation goes to re-illuminating these areas if employee usage increases or production/quality levels of employees within adjoining areas decrease.

WORKER ECONOMIC CONCERNS

Cuba Gooding, Jr. summed up the primary motivation for most anyone seeking or continuing a job with "Show me the money!" (Crowe, 1996). "I need food; I need shelter; I need clothing. I need money to provide these things and therefore I need a job". Maslow's Hierarchy of Needs demonstrates at the most fundamental level why workers seek employment with explanation into the types of work sought, expounded by the expectation of personal gratification. We constantly hear workers state if they won a lottery their first task would be to quit their job; not because they wanted to open a position for someone else that may need employment, but due to no longer needing employment himself or herself.

Research reveals that properties of situations can reduce negative effects of stress (Muchinsky, 2006). Obtaining employment reduces stress for unemployed persons while gaining adequate pay (promotions and raises), needed benefits (health insurance), and reduced environmental stressors (harassment, disparate treatment, etc.) significantly reduce personal stress (Heneman III & Judge, 2009).

Other stress management initiatives aimed at reducing or eliminating organizational stress include on-site physical fitness facilities, meditation, biofeedback, yoga, counseling, social support programs, and employee assistance. For example, an Illinois employer recently prevented a key employee's home from entering foreclosure by providing a means to make reduced mortgage payments, thus retaining the worker.

ROLE AND FAMILY CONFLICT MANAGEMENT

When a motivated drive (ambition) stumbles from blockage before reaching a desired goal, frustration occurs. Frustration exhibits as overt (visible) and covert (mental-sociopsychological) spilling over into the workplace as violence, aggression, withdrawal, moonlighting, absenteeism, or turnover (Luthans, 2008). Sources comprise encounters inside and outside the realm of work such as dead-end jobs, high degrees of job specialization, supervisory conflict, family conflict, and role conflict outside the workplace.

Roles of women changed dramatically over the last century from supporting working husbands while maintaining households and rearing children to joining the workforce without leaving previous roles behind. Today, 60% of married women and 85% of adult women hold jobs in the United States; 72% of these work full time (Macionis, 2010). College enrollment by sex reversed since 1960. In fact, 92% of my students average out as females in social science courses unrelated to pink-collar occupations (jobs traditionally held by women). Not only did women increase role sets of mother, wife, house cleaner, cook, and so forth to include employment role sets (colleague, worker, professional, income earner, etc.), but males were forced to change theirs in response as well. Papalia, Olds, and Feldman (2009) reported that men increasingly share in household and parental duties while their partners work.

Role conflicts, relative to traditional expectations, continue to increase as gender roles move toward equilibration. Modern concerns illuminate in popular media and films like Tootsie (Pollack, 1982) and Daddy Daycare (Carr, 2003). The first movie depicts a man secretly assuming female roles in order to maintain relationships with his estranged children while maintaining his normal roles in the workplace, sometimes with great difficulty. A decade later in the second movie, two men assume traditional women's roles with children while their wives hold jobs normally worked by men.

As roles converse, stressors not encountered within previous generations increase until workers learn to adapt. Courts increasingly award child custody to parents with resources and abilities to best care for the children (Walsh, 2010) unlike previous generations where judges awarded children primarily to women, sometimes forcing the family into poverty. The shift shows up in workplaces with nearly as many single fathers as single mothers. My previous workplace consisted of four such fathers and one single mother. Hopefully, the steady decline in divorce rates since 1980 (Macionis, 2010) will be attributed in future studies to the sharing of family and work responsibilities.

Employers that recognize these societal changes and respond accordingly to reduce stressors enjoy employees who tend to show up for work, stay with the organization, maintain productivity, and display lower levels of aggressive or reclusive behaviors (Luthans, 2008). Counseling, childcare assistance, flextime scheduling, and other social support programs benefit employees and employers as previously discussed in the Worker Economic Concerns section above.

MODELS OF MENTAL HEALTH

An accepted model of stress for mental health categorizes stress using seven inter-linked groups (Kahn & Byosiere, 2006). Complex associations among antecedents, individual responses, and consequences of stress dictate how organizations choose to understand and respond to situations involving employees. Organizational causes of stress, such as downsizing and cutbacks, serve as antecedents the organization controls when reducing stress among affected employees. Understanding how workers respond to the antecedents provides opportunities for developing methods or programs to eliminate unnecessary stress as well as unwanted consequences (violence, theft, etc.).

CONCLUSIONS

Many benefits exist for organizations that understand stress affecting workers and take action to reduce or eliminate it. Reduced absenteeism, reduced turnover, reduced probability of workplace violence, and increased happiness among employees allows the company more productivity and profitability. Although no one solution generalizes to every situation, combinations as needed prove invaluable.

* * *

4.8 RETENTION OF QUALITY ADJUNCT FACULTY

Bad instructors do not exist if those teachers enjoy the sustenance of willing mentors, supportive administration, and forum for development. With transition from tenured professors to as much as 65% (up from 40% a decade ago (Maynard & Joseph, 2008)) of courses now taught using adjunct instructors, colleges and universities struggle to hire and retain quality educators. Cost-savings through lower per course wages and denial of non-reimbursable benefits (medical insurance, vacation pay, etc.) enable increased profits while maintaining tuition and fee charges to students. This paper analyzes historical differences and current trends to offer suggestions to Illinois Eastern Community Colleges (IECC) administration for improvement with adjunct initiatives.

JOB SATISFACTION

IECC employs two basic types of adjunct instructors: those who work part-time as a preference (voluntary), and those who teach less than full-time desiring tenured-track employment (involuntary). This distinction dispels the myth that adjuncts, in general, dislike their jobs since research indicates that voluntary part-time teachers report equal satisfaction levels that full-timers demonstrate (Maynard & Joseph, 2008). Essentially, part-time faculty members do not comprise a homogeneous group with a shared set of desired working conditions and uniform job attitudes.

Employees of IECC reported that 19% of survey takers did not feel empowered to complete their jobs successfully; 30% felt undercompensated for the work they performed; 28% failed to find opportunities for advancement or promotion; and 19% concluded the employee evaluation process lacked constructivism without encouragement to enhance job performance (Illinois Eastern Community Colleges, 2010). Given the research findings of Maynard and Joseph, safe assumption prevails that among instructors, the majority of displeased persons likely reside within the involuntary adjunct category. However, distinction needs verification.

JOB PERFORMANCE

Landrum's (2009) study comparing job performance between full-time and part-time instructors tested differences in student evaluations among trainers and leniency of grading between the groups. Results indicated that no significant correlation existed for employment status and student ratings. Correlation between status and grade distributions also revealed no significant difference. However, allocation of resource availability and actual outcomes showed that adjunct instructors achieved this equilibrium utilizing fewer resources. For example, many part-timers did not facilitate offices, school sponsored email addresses, equipment availability, and on-campus classroom space normally allocated to their full-time counterparts. Landrum cautioned interpretation of findings not to mean that adjuncts do more with less, but do the same work with fewer resources as tenured counterparts in terms of student evaluation and grade distribution outcomes.

INTRINSIC AND EXTRINSIC MOTIVATION

Collegiate instructors find drive to persevere primarily through intrinsic rewards (Smith, 2011). These internally motivate the teacher to develop, refine, and continue working significantly more than extrinsic factors alone. As colleges continue to evolve and demand continual professional improvement, outside benefits increasingly enhance intrinsic factors and motivate instructors. A simple example using Maslow's Hierarchy of Needs validates the need for extrinsic motivators: merely loving one's work fails to pay the bills and purchase groceries.

The old adage, "Scratch my back and I'll scratch yours", roots in equity theory in how hard a person is willing to work results from comparisons of that workload to the efforts of others, in this case the employer. Essentially, the more adjunct instructors put into their work (education, experience, skill, and effort) the more they expect in return in the forms of pay, benefits, working conditions, seniority, and so on (Muchinsky, 2006). The tradeoff of extrinsic rewards theoretically increases intrinsic value that translates back to high performance outcomes on behalf of the students and college.

During the early and mid-twentieth centuries, workers expected job security as an intrinsic psychological reward for a lifetime of service to the organization (Luthans, 2008). Economic transition and global competition extending into the twenty-first century dismayed employees with downsizing, facility and process relocation, administrative hierarchy flattening, and benefit reductions. Explosive growth rates of information systems forced college libraries and classroom technologies to adapt or die, virtually eliminating job security from instructors who failed to keep up. Faced with this dilemma, many colleges have responded by revoking tenure of professors and adapting seniority systems through at-will employment scenarios such as that utilized by the University of Southern Illinois at Edwardsville. The upside reigns benefit for adjunct instructors by including them in seniority systems after a set number (36 at USI-E) of semester hours taught.

Unfortunately, IECC recently provided 4% pay increases for all employees, but boasted $700,000 savings in wages (Illinois Eastern Community Colleges, 2011) by cutting many courses taught by adjuncts. This event contrasts equitable reasoning... "Here's a raise, but we're cutting your hours to pay for it".

DISCONNECTEDNESS

Meixner, Kruck, and Madden (2010) surveyed adjunct instructors to better understand the qualitative experiences of part-time faculty. Nearly half of the respondents claimed no invitational opportunity to attend an orientation session while another quarter reported no rescheduling opportunity due to conflicts. When asked if mentoring would prove beneficial, 43% affirmed with open-ended explanations like "Knowing at least one [full-time faculty] member could help part-timers feel less isolated" and "How is a new person, at any level, going to know what their expectations are without mentoring?"

The authors concluded with four recommendations that mentors can provide to adjuncts for development and transition into the professional/organizational culture:

1. General and specific technology assistance (e.g., Blackboard, distance learning, presentation techniques)
2. Peer review and sharing of teaching strategies with other part-time faculty (e.g., informal get-togethers, peer review of papers, ability to conduct research with others)
3. Course planning strategies (e.g., how to plan, implement, and evaluate a course in its entirety)
4. Motivating students (e.g., understanding students' developmental skill sets, keeping students on task)

Adjunct instructors with IECC also commonly complain about the isolation felt from disconnectedness with lack of mentoring, overwhelming expectations of course development without formal training, lacks in professional development opportunities, nonexistence of formalized peer review and collaboration, and understanding student motivation initiatives.

INITIATIVE PROPOSAL

The Illinois Equitable Pay Act of 2003 further defined the federal legislation (Equitable Pay Act) previously enacted for the benefit of equitable pay between genders. The Illinois law extended fair pay beyond gender barriers to include any employee (of employers with four or more workers) within the state holding the same position. As a result, monetary pay (salaries, etc.) of adjunct instructors working for IECC leveled with adjuncts teaching at comparative schools within Illinois. Therefore, pay levels cannot reasonably contribute further to this discussion.

The question at hand, "How can IECC recruit and retain quality adjunct instructors without significant costs?" requires asking current part-timers what it takes to achieve that goal. The pre-implementation answer involves directives involving improvements that enhance intrinsic motivation, lessen effects of isolation, and prevents costly extrinsic factor expenses without encroaching upon earned tenured benefits.

The first step requires development of an open-ended questionnaire that allows adjunct instructors to freely voice their concerns. Closed-ended surveys whisper attitudes within respondents toward limited potential outcomes in favor of administration, restrictive choices of solutions by means of either/or alternatives, and misleading interpretations of intent through context (Heneman III & Judge, 2009). Tabulation allows quantification for prioritizing respondent replies in order to narrow bridging adjunct concerns with viable outcomes.

Utilizing acknowledged factors, research into accessible beneficial alternatives IECC can offer need identification. For example, if respondents desire inclusion into college-sponsored activities (say, Student Appreciation Day) then email adjuncts invitations with details that include ways to participate on behalf of the college as a faculty sponsor, rather than merely posting notices on bulletin boards that equate part-time instructor participation with that of a student. This phenomena psychologists term equal status contact and it stems from equity theory (Coon & Mitterer, 2010). Off-campus instructors generally suffer additional social isolation by never seeing bulletin board notices or communicating regularly with on-campus personnel.

Interaction between researcher and administrative personnel is critical at this stage for development of a second survey compositing organizational offerings without postulating unintentional outcomes among respondents (does not infer unfeasible solutions in the minds of survey-takers). Feedback then allows for matching acceptable offerings with desired outcomes to produce a listing of recommended alternatives. Coordination and implementation of approved programs follow feedback.

Of course, the primary objectives cannot declaratively end here. Periodic monitoring through feedback surveys to determine changes in levels of motivation, individual program acceptance and utilization, levels of feelings of disconnectedness, and organizational impact must follow up.

CONCLUSIONS

Utilization of adjunct faculty through inclusive initiatives provides approach-approach conflict avoidance. Adjuncts win in terms of reduced feelings of isolation, increased opportunities for acceptance by joining organizational activities, and camaraderie among peers. IECC draws upon existing resources to reduce turnover, to retain quality instructors, and to strengthen the existing organizational culture. Administration must consider impacts upon the existing full-time employee consortium so that perceived encroachments remain minimalized. Low/no cost alternative benefit programs enhance IECC culture, student outcomes, and strategic goals while utilizing existing resources and personnel.

* * *

PART FOUR REFERENCES

Asher, J. J., & Sciarrino, J. A. (1974). Realistic Work Sample Tests: A Review. Personnel Psychology, 27, 519-533.

Carr, S. (Director). (2003). Daddy Daycare [Motion Picture].

Coon, D., & Mitterer, J. O. (2010). Introduction to Psychology (12th ed.). Belmont, CA: Wadsworth.

Crowe, C. (Director). (1996). Jerry McGuire [Motion Picture].

Field, A. (2009). Discovering Statistics Using SPSS (3rd ed.). Thousand Oaks, CA: Sage Publishing, Inc.

Grier, P. (2011, March 2). Wisconsin union fight: Which Side Does US Public Support? Retrieved from The Christian Science Monitor: http://www.csmonitor.com/USA/Politics/The-Vote/2011/0302/Wisconsin-union-fight-Which-side-does-US-public-support.

Heneman III, H. G., & Judge, T. A. (2009). Staffing Organizations (6th ed.). Boston, MA: McGraw-Hill/Irwin.

Illinois Eastern Community Colleges. (2010, November 16). Board News: 11-16-10 (Press Release). Olney, IL: Illinois Eastern Community Colleges.

Illinois Eastern Community Colleges. (2011, September 22). Board News: 09-22-11 (Press Release). Olney, IL.

Jackson, C. L., & LePine, J. A. (2003). Peer Responses to a Team's Weakest Link: A Test and Extension of Lepine And Van Dyn's Model. Journal of Applied Psychology (88), pp. 459-475.

Jennings, M. M. (2006). Business: Its Legal, Ethical, and Global Environment (7th ed.). Mason, OH: Thomson Higher Learning.

Kahn, R. L., & Byosiere, P. B. (2006). Stress in Organizations. In P. M. Muchinsky, Psychology Applied to Work (8th ed., p. 352). Belmont, CA: Thomson Wadsworth.

Kelliher, C., & Anderson, D. (2010, January). Doing More with Less? Flexible Working Practices and the Intensification of Work. Human Relations, 63(1), 83-106.

Koppes, L. L. (1997). American Female Pioneers of Industrial and Organizational Psychology During the Early Years. Journal of Applied Psychology, 82(4), 500-515.

Korkki, P. (2008, March 16). Drug Tests as a Window on Workers. New York Times, pp. BU-2.

Landrum, R. E. (2009). Are There Instructional Differences Between Full-Time and Part-Time Faculty? College Teaching, 57(1), 23-26.

Landy, F. J. (1997). Early Influences on the Early Development of Industrial and Organizational Psychology. Journal of Applied Psychology, 82(4), 467-477.

Luthans, F. (2008). Organizational Behavior (11th ed.). Boston, MA: McGraw-Hill/Irwin.

Macionis, J. J. (2010). Sociology (13th ed.). Boston, MA: Prentice Hall.

Maynard, D. C., & Joseph, T. A. (2008). Are All Part-Time Faculty Underemployed? The Influence of Faculty Status Preference on Satisfaction and Commitment. Higher Education (55), 139-154.

Meixner, C., Kruck, S. E., & Madden, L. T. (2010). Inclusion of Part-Time Faculty for the Benefit of Faculty and Students. College Teaching (58), 141-147.

Milkovich, G. T., & Newman, J. M. (2008). Compensation (9th ed.). New York, NY: McGraw-Hill/Irwin.

Moon, J., & Lee, J.-H. (2011). Predicting Cigarette-Seeking Behavior: How Reward Sensitivity and Positive Emotions Influence Nicotine Cravings. Social Behavior & Personality: An International Journal, 39(6), 737-746.

Muchinsky, P. M. (2006). Psychology Applied to Work (8th ed.). Belmont, CA: Thomson Wadsworth.

Papalia, D. E., Olds, S. W., & Feldman, R. D. (2009). Human Development (11th ed.). Boston, MA: McGraw-Hill.

Pearson Learning Solutions. (2010). SKS7000 - Executive Concepts in Business Strategy. Boston, MA: Pearson Learning Solutions.

Pollack, S. (Director). (1982). Tootsie [Motion Picture].

Poynter, J. (2006). The Human Experiment: Two Years and Twenty Minutes Inside Biosphere 2. New York, NY: Thunder's Mouth Press.

Ritti, R. R., & Levy, S. (2007). The Ropes to Skip and the Ropes to Know: Studies in Organizational Behavior (7th ed.). Hoboken, NJ: John Wiley and Sons.

Roth, P. L., Bobko, P., & McFarland, L. A. (2005, Winter). A Meta-Analysis of Work Sample Test Validity: Updating and Integrating Some Classic Literature. Personnel Psychology, 58(4), 1009-1037.

Russell, J. E., & Jacobs, J. D. (2008). Group Dynamics, Processes, and Teamwork. In E. R. Cadotte, H. J. Bruce, S. F. Gardial, D. Garval, K. C. Gilbert, J. D. Jacobs, et al., The Management of Strategy in the Marketplace (Pp. 49-75). Knoxville, TN: Innovative Learning Solutions.

Schmidt, F. L., & Hunter, J. E. (1998). The Validity and Utility of Selection Methods in Personnel Psychology: Practical and Theoretical Implications of 85 Years of Research Findings. Psychological Bulletin, 124, 437-454.

Seijts, G. H., & Latham, B. W. (2003). Creativity Through Applying Ideas from Fields Other Than One's Own: Transferring Knowledge from Social Psychology to Industrial/Organizational Psychology. Canadian Psychology/ Psychologie Canadienne, 44(3), 232-239.

Smith, M. (2011). Examining Factors That Influence Employee Motivation in a South West Virginia University. (Unpublished doctoral dissertation). Prescott Valley, AZ: Northcentral University.

Walsh, D. J. (2010). Employment Law for Human Resource Practice (3rd ed.). Mason, OH: South-Western Cengage Learning.

Whelan, R., Josephson, A., & Holcombe, J. (2008). The Economic Costs of Alcohol and Drug Abuse in Oregon in 2006. Portland: ECONorthwest.

* * *

PART FIVE:
ADVANCED TOPICS IN
ORGANIZATIONAL
BEHAVIOR

5.1 APPRAISE ORGANIZATIONAL BEHAVIOR

Fred Luthans (2008) modernized the general definition of organizational behavior as "the understanding, prediction, and management of human behavior in organizations". Borrowing from theoretical perspectives in other disciplines, such as sociology, allows researchers in the field to understand and predict many behaviors. However, the management of behavior in the organizational setting makes the study unique from other disciplines. Effective management then requires an understanding of the changing characteristics of organizations. King, Felin, and Whetten identified at least 27 of these criteria (King, Felin, & Whetten, 2010).

Common topics found within the literature over the last five years show researchers find interest in the areas of organizational commitment, organizational justice, socialization, prosocial and antisocial organizational behaviors, kaizen, expectancy, adaptability, trust, teamwork, and leadership.

CHARACTERISTICS OF ORGANIZATIONS

Organizations exist as unique entities enduring a birth and an unlimited lifespan with eventual mortality. In varying ways, organizations serve as social actors who influence social and physical environments by shaping communities and the individuals comprising them. As such, organizations are legally recognized by governments and, likewise, held accountable for their choices. Their persistence stems from maintaining goals or purposes related to associated markets providing distinctive identities among competitors and other social actors. The focuses on roles (market leader, employer, activist) provide inheritance of inferred status or referent power to either use or confer authority (King, Felin, & Whetten, 2010).

Organizations can positively (through lobbying) or negatively (e.g. Enron and others) shape regulation that causes change within it. Accordingly, conflicts occur which the organization must deal with that can either enhance solidarity or cause losses in sovereignty. The internal culture influences its members, and at times, those members change the culture, such as when a retail store enters a new market region or undergoes management takeover. The organization imprints identities upon members (e.g. the "former CEO of" or the "janitor at").

ORIGINS OF ORGANIZATIONAL BEHAVIOR

Review of historical background into the development of organizational behavior studies is appropriate for understanding how the discipline advanced to where it is today. Early pioneers tended to ignore the human aspect of behavior in management and emphasized the roles of hierarchal structure, specialization, planning, and controlling – essentially treating organizations as machines (Luthans, 2008). The first documented experiment exploring organizational behavior in a social context was the 1924 Hawthorne Studies, where effects on people encouraging production levels revealed that not only does lighting levels matter, but also the fact when workers know they are under study, results become skewed.

It was not until World War I respectability came to the field when military organizations commissioned the development of measures that selected and assigned recruits based upon morale, motivation, psychological problems, and discipline (Muchinsky, 2006). Dozens of companies followed suit. During World War II, situational stress tests were developed applying behavioral concepts to work with the development of the flight simulator. Subspecialties sprang up post-war providing credence to behavioral study as a scientific discipline. The last fifty years witnessed government application to organizations in response to the Civil Rights Movement. With the advent of the Information Age, specialization went a step further to witness global economic influences and the need to seek solutions to organizational change through behavioral understanding, predictability, and manageability.

COMMITMENT

It was common after World War II that after a worker hired into a new organization that person remained committed to their job and organization for many years, possibly even their entire working life. The mindset, under expectancy theory, evolved into the notion employment would be available... graduate high school, get a job with a reputable company, and remain until retirement (Muchinsky, 2006). Global economic changes awakened the realization, however, that organizations were volatile in their existence and job security was relative to the organizational environment. As a result, commitment began to wane and the average number of jobs held by a worker during their lifetime increased significantly. Today, turnover, quality, and production issues provide primary concerns in many industries with blame pointed at the lack of commitment by employees.

Recent studies have shown leaders who allow subordinates to share in supportive decision-making activities enjoy higher rates of commitment (Cerit, 2010). Correlational results indicated high significance ($p < .01$) rates ranging between .623 and .932 between the variables of valuing people, staff development, community involvement, authenticity, leadership, and of course, commitment.

ORGANIZATIONAL JUSTICE

Organizational justice traditionally resided on issues of employment status and benefits with the advent of labor unions. Today, with legislation covering equality and fairness with employment in the aftermath of the Civil Rights Act in the United States, the country has witnessed the decline in membership threefold, down to about 12.4% (Macionis, 2010). Similar issues remain with American employers taking residence on foreign soil in terms of sweatshops, economic equivalence in pay levels, and physical abuse of workers. The domestic focus has swayed instead toward gender equality, e.g., elimination of the glass ceiling effect and age discrimination with the graying of the average population.

Recent research showed managers tended to view organizational justice behaviors within the group more positively than other members (Titrek, 2009). Younger persons also perceived less justice than older workers, due mainly to experience levels. Feedback and cooperation of managers with subordinates reduced ill perceptions in all categories towards leadership behaviors.

PROSOCIAL AND ANTISOCIAL BEHAVIOR

Recent decades witnessed mass violence episodes, such as the Columbine High School Shooting and the origin of the term "going postal" in response to several postal workers shooting their fellow constituents. Nearly every case involved one or more disgruntled organizational members who were alienated to the point of social retaliation. Many secondary schools have increased security measures, not to detect symptoms of organizational violence, but to reduce chance occurrences. Questions for researchers arose in how to detect, predict, and intervene with antisocial behaviors before escalation to violence, especially on mass scales.

Supporting the assumption that breakdowns in perceived rewards by organizational members leads to escalated antisocial behaviors, Hornung (2010) calculated that alienation is negatively correlated with a perceived absence of justice in both organizational rewards and procedures. Also, he noted procedural justice appeared to enhance morale while participative decision-making was more preventive against alienation than material rewards for compliance.

KAIZEN / GOING GREEN

Toyota first introduced the concept of kaizen, or waste elimination, from manufacturing processes, resulting in the Just-In-Time (JIT) business model (Krajewski, Ritzman, & Malhotra, 2007). Modifications and enhancements to the concept, in conjunction with global warming theory, led organizations to adopt behaviors that reduce wastes, increase recycling initiatives, and seek alternative means for efficiency that did not increase negative environmental impacts. For instance, thinner trash bags for use in landfills, biofuels as renewable resources, and hybrid vehicles evolved in response to the Green Movement.

Environmental uncertainty refers to the frequent and unpredictable changes in customer preferences, technological development, and competitive behavior perceived by managers (Lin & Ho, 2010). A study by Lin and Ho revealed a moderate -0.135 (t = -2.487, p < 0.05), significant and negative influence on the green practice adoption by organizations and perceived environmental uncertainty.

EXPECTANCY

Expectancy theory states as we accumulate more, we expect more. Application of this concept holds true with wages and benefits, workloads, and qualifications for tasks (Heneman III & Judge, 2009). For example, many Americans expect higher than minimum wages and vacation pay although neither of these benefits find mandate by law, yet remain accepted through cultural tradition. It is not uncommon for workers to complain if productivity quotas increase or for businesses to raise minimal hiring qualifications for positions requiring updated skills.

Educational laws now require public schools to integrate those children who test as learning disabled into regular classrooms at least half the school day. Teacher's complain that classes slow with progress in order to accommodate these children. However, McMullen, Shippen, and Dangel argued that expectancy violations from teachers and students create the actual conflict. Teachers, in turn, need training programs that ease integration, and the students need a clear, explicit, and measurable framework of organizational expectancies for exhibition of the desired organizational behaviors.

TRUST

Relative to teamwork, organizational culture, turnover, and other aspects can infer negative connotations for an organization while issues of trust complement these areas of concern as a factor of consideration. Lacks of trust from organizations for its members leads to enhanced security measures, increased employment screening tactics, and lockouts during union strikes. At the other extreme, employees may even go so far as to record telephone conversations (e.g., Lewinsky V. Clinton). Most organizations, however, reside in the middle on these issues. Trust is considered a reliable and valid factor in establishing processes to predict organizational commitment, job satisfaction, performance, and intentions to leave the organization (Altunas & Baykal, 2009). The findings by Altunas and Baykal indicated the organizational trust members had in their institutions, managers, and coworkers influenced the organizational citizenship behaviors of conscientiousness, civic virtue, altruism, and courtesy, whereas it had no effect on sportsmanship behavior.

CONCLUSIONS

Organizational behavior relies upon other disciplines to accomplish its primary strength of application. These tasks entail realization of the multitude of characteristics that describe the components involved with the existence and functionality of organizations. As market changes, legislation, and globalization affect their existence, the scope of research adapts in search of solutions for improvements. Just as no single theory of behavior explains how or why elicited actions/reactions occur and default to other theories for assistance, organizational research findings carry over in context to other situations. The Green Movement resulted from the recognition behaviors needed to change, but in turn, served as solutions for ailing organizations that desperately needed alternative efficiency angles. Recent research for education, health, manufacturing, and benefit industries demonstrate the diversity covered by organizational behavior studies.

* * *

5.2 APPLYING ORGANIZATIONAL THEORY

Applying a single organizational theory when attempting consultation with an organization proves difficult, and sometimes, unjustified. The sciences of organizational theory and its spawn, organizational behavior, are relatively new to academic acceptance, yet they yield profound results for organizations when applied through consultation guidelines. Before examining applications for each, understanding definitional differences calls to order.

ORGANIZATIONAL BEHAVIOR VERSUS ORGANIZATIONAL THEORY

Organizational Behavior (OB) often finds definition as the understanding, prediction, and management of human behavior within organizations (Luthans, 2008). Like other recognized disciplines, understanding and prediction stem from usage of accepted scientific methodology. The key difference between OB, human resource management (HRM), organizational development (OD), and organizational theory (OT) lies in OB's application focus through management practices and processes.

Similar to organizational theory, OB remains reliant upon a theoretical base, however, mostly at the micro level of analysis. In conjunction with cross-discipline origins, a few pioneering researchers believe the field has stagnated from innovation and originality (Oswick, Fleming, & Hanlon, 2011). Other prominent leaders argue understanding and explaining individual and group behaviors depends upon recognition of other behavioral science frameworks (Luthans, 2008).

Organizational Theory resides at the macro end of the analytical spectrum with emphasis toward organizational structure and design. It attempts to explain the "why" of acts, events, structures, and thoughts occurring with emphasis on the nature of causal relationships by looking closely at underlying processes (Sutton & Straw, 1995). Of course, drawbacks to theory development and testing include their simplification of reality and exclusion of factors potentially affecting points under consideration during the earliest stages (Hambrick, 2005) and misapplication of borrowed concepts (Oswick, Fleming, & Hanlon, 2011).

Due to the opposite scopes of organizational theory and organizational behavior as defined here, applying analyses of a single theoretical approach in a consultation scenario without inclusion of both perspectives results in decreased validity for the application. Therefore, discussion of OT and OB perspectives is necessary for fuller understanding of the scenario that follows.

SCENARIO

Mr. Johnny Dee of ABC Oil Services contacted Dr. Nichols concerning high rates of absenteeism, poor performance, and suspected illicit drug use among field workers. Dr. Nichols met with Mr. Dee at the primary job site to explore organizational needs and to gather observational information firsthand. In consideration of the primary data intake, Dr. Nichols assessed he could assist ABC Oil Services with overcoming potential root problems. Following contract negotiations, Dr. Nichols arranged with Johnny Dee for details upon how he would enter the organization and interact with current employees. They agreed Dr. Nichols would pose as a temporary part-time employee so he could gain reliable positional/psychological feedback and understand the various positional responsibilities within the client system. However, Dr. Nichols stipulated he would not identify employees who admitted to, or were suspected of, engaging in illicit drug activities, except dealing during working hours.

Over the next 30 days, Dr. Nichols worked with the field workers carefully noting patterns of suspected drug activity, reasons for absenteeism, motivational concerns, work ethics, and general aptitude. Meeting with Mr. Dee to analyze the data, they discovered the problem as multifaceted and requiring adaptations across the organization. Over the next week, they established basic goals related to overcoming these issues and generated preliminary intervention strategies to complete the diagnosis stage of consultation (Dougherty, 2009). Dr. Nichols prepared a formal analysis to present to ABC Oil Services' Board of Directors outlining the identified problems, goals, and organizational commitment requirements. The presentation also demonstrated the phases of implementation in addition to the expectancy roles of organizational members for successful consultation.

Results of Analysis

Dr. Nichols and Mr. Dee, during the diagnosis stage of the consultation, realized the problems facing ABC Oil Services with absenteeism, performance, and suspected illicit drug usage were valid and interrelated. The time Dr. Nichols spent working alongside the field workers revealed sources affecting these behaviors rooted in organizational perspectives of Theory X dominance, contrasted with expectancy theory among employees. Of course, not all drug usage could be accounted for beyond personal considerations of some employees, but acceptance (tolerance) by nonusers relied upon other explanations. Initiatives then, necessitated changing mindsets of non-drug users as well as regular users.

Motivation proved low among field crews with evidence of decreased work ethics among new hires the longer their employment duration had elapsed, further contributing to reduced performance levels. Crewmembers complained wages remained substandard within the industry, work hours seemed unpredictable and weather dependent, they used outdated equipment with poor maintenance records, and continued employment was contingent upon the mood of the site supervisor.

Viewing the organizational problems from opposing perspectives (Theory X and Expectancy Theory) allows for assessment of the organization through OT and OB, respectively, at the macro and micro levels.

Theory X

Theory X purports employees generally exhibit behaviors of irresponsibility, they lack ambition, they hate to work, and as a result, managers must use coercion (Bovee, Thill, & Mescon, 2007). In 1923, when Frederick Taylor proposed his scientific management perspectives, the United States was still in its industrial phase and workers were considered as cogs in the manufacturing process. Managers undertook a task rather than holding a person orientation and assumed workers needed goading to maintain productivity (Coon & Mitterer, 2010). Psychological efficiency (good morale, labor relations, employee satisfaction, etc.) took no less to precedence over work efficiency (maximum output at lowest cost).

Mr. Dee reported ABC Oil Services began in 1939 during an extremely competitive oil boom and survived through "maintaining the business model and consistent business practices". Reviewing crewmember complaints revealed ABC Oil Services fits the Theory X business model. Costs incurred via repairs to outdated equipment, productivity losses from absenteeism, continually restocking an unskilled labor pool, and especially, supervisory complaints indicated these bills pass in the form of lower wages to employees. In contrast, research consistently shows employers who take an employee-centered approach tend to have the happiest and most productive workers (Wright & Cropanzano, 2000).

Overcoming Theory X

Frederick Taylor also proposed Theory Y. This theory propagated opposing assumptions; namely, people are industrious, creative, rewarded by challenging work, enjoy autonomy, and appear willing to accept responsibility (Coon & Mitterer, 2010). These employers posture that workers add value to the organization through senses of freedom and responsibility with career mindsets. Crew members who feel they can voice issues of quality control and safety tend to demonstrate responsibility for their work. When employees take ownership of established goals, productivity and quality increase. Where Theory X emphasizes authority, Theory Y promotes growth, commitment, and self-direction (Bovee, Thill, & Mescon, 2007).

Through goal setting, Mr. Dee and Dr. Nichols established primary objectives that transition ABC Oil Services at the macro level into an employee-centered organization:

1) adopt a pre- and post-hire drug screening program;
2) increase wages to at least competitive rates for the region;
3) create an attendance bonus program tied to achievable performance initiatives;
4) establish supervisor performance and training guidelines with administrative and/or subordinate peer review; and
5) query employees for other areas of concern through periodic anonymous surveys.

Expectancy Theory

Expectancy Theory links employee motivation to outcomes in proportion to their inputs. This widely accepted explanation is an expansion of equity theory in that it links efforts to performance and rewards to individual goals (Bovee, Thill, & Mescon, 2007). Three primary factors influence the amount and quality of effort that crewmembers put forth:

1) their expectations in their own abilities;
2) responsive rewards from the organization for their efforts; and
3) the value of those rewards as perceived by the worker.

In simplest terms, if an employer wants to motivate employees, it needs to provide achievable incentives workers value as worthwhile.

Data analysis by Dr. Nichols and Mr. Dee uncovered issues negatively affecting crewmember motivation. Aside from, but related to, key points understood through Theories X and Y, workers admittedly exalted discontentment with ABC Oil Services as an employer. They expressed concerns they were unvalued and unappreciated as individuals that actively contributed to the successes of the organization... "Not even so much as a thanks or job well done. All you ever get is an [buttocks] chewing if something isn't perfect!"

Goal setting includes micro level initiatives coinciding and supporting the transition of ABC Oil Services into an employee-centered organization. Mostly behavioral, each goal provides the cause and effect, action and reaction, incentive and reward required by expectancy theory:

1) treat each employee with respect;
2) establish and arrange mental/drug/family counseling service availability for employees and their families;
3) hold supervisors accountable for their relations with employees;
4) establish an open door policy between supervisors and employees; and
5) establish an employee recognition system for reaching performance goals, including attendance.

CONCLUSIONS

For ABC Oil Services to continue as a viable and profitable enterprise, it must embrace and adjust to the environmental changes surrounding it. Just as processes within methodologies, technologies, and markets force adaptations to the business model, so too do employee relationships. Threats of unionization have decreased in the United States by more than two-thirds since the Depression Era (Pearson Learning Solutions, 2010) with new membership attributed to white-collar professions. Many scholars believe implementation of advanced labor laws over the last few decades decreased the need for representation for workers, in addition to globalization and losses within manufacturing and mining industries. Without recognition and application of organizational and behavioral theory, ABC Oil Services' applicant pool will likely dry up, forcing alternatives for its customers to meet their own demands.

* * *

5.3 WORKER PRODUCTIVITY AND JOB SATISFACTION

Worker productivity and job satisfaction are relational terms and sometimes ambiguous until defined for the particular application. For instance, productivity may often find utilization as an antonym for "not just sitting around", or finitely receive measurement as a ratio of output (pieces per time, inputs vs. outputs, etc.). Similarly, job satisfaction viewed in Maslow's hierarchal terms of employment meeting basic needs of the worker (money to purchase food, pay rent, etc.) does not offer the psychological implications inferred through stress, burnout, or organizational culture expectations. Research has suggested satisfied, or happy, workers deliver higher rates of productivity to the organization (Wright & Cropanzano, 2000; Tarris & Schreurs, 2009), although definitions of the components and measures vary. The discussion that follows explores the context of these facets, differing values and morals of workers, cognitive dissonance, and other factors relating to the connections between productivity and job satisfaction.

DEFINITIONS OF HAPPINESS AND PRODUCTIVITY

For purposes here, worker happiness and worker satisfaction interchangeably refer to the same concepts. Although information gathering typically originates at the subjective level through surveys, questionnaires, and interviews of individual workers, the summative applications find objective residence at the collective level within the organization. For example, if 95 of 100 people reported they were "extremely satisfied" with a pay increase, managers may ambiguously report, "nearly all employees are happy as a result of the recent pay raise". Unfortunately, this statement implies universal satisfaction toward the organization when taken out of context by ignoring the five percent not fully satisfied with the pay increase and other factors (work environment, leadership styles, fringe benefits, etc.) influencing total acceptance. To these ends, researchers find themselves probing for significant variables to explain the total concept of satisfaction and the implications these factors contribute to organizational value.

Productivity, as restated from above, includes quantitative and qualitative characteristics, that when combined, form the measure of performance (Tarris & Schreurs, 2009). Objective, or quantitative, measures analyze the difference between the goal to be reached and the efforts toward reaching the goal in terms of numerically observable criteria. Qualitative productivity types conversely concentrate upon process-oriented measures, like satisfaction, and other cognitive (covert) criteria.

Therefore, worker happiness measures fall within the realm of qualitative study, but cannot find full utility without observing the quantitative relationships that provide context within performance. For the statement "happy workers are productive workers", other factors define "happy" and "productive" require consideration for the particular contextual situation. If workers receive a pay raise, do they necessarily become more productive? For how long does the increase last and how much more productive are they? Does providing pay increases work for all professions? How much of a wage increase is required to detect noticeable change in productivity levels? What is the optimal pay increase in relation to overall performance? Answers to these questions demonstrate the complexities involved for researchers when studying the interconnectedness and variability of the importance of the facets of job satisfaction.

Pay Increases

As stated previously, pay increases positively affect performance through qualitative analysis of performance measures, namely job satisfaction. However, a perfect correlation does not exist (Yang et.al., 2008) for pay increases and happiness alone, implying that other factors need inclusive consideration. Under the definition of job satisfaction that it widely refers "to the extent of which people like or dislike their job", Yang, Miao, Sun, Liu, and Wu queried Chinese soldiers before and after a salary increase and found overall job satisfaction for the soldiers rose by only 11.3% while satisfaction with the raise increased threefold by 31.1%. The latter number remained lower than expected considering wages doubled. Given the economic changes within China over the last few decades, rises in costs-of-living may explain the discrepancy.

Besides satisfaction with the pay increase, Yang, Miao, Sun, Liu, and Wu also recorded enhanced satisfaction in relations with supervisors (6.7%), colleagues (5.4%), subordinates (4.8%), and self-perspectives within themselves (15.8%). Valuable correlational information was missing from the study to determine levels of relatedness, if any, of these satisfaction factors to one another. The study also begs the question if the perceived changes, especially social relations with subordinates who did not receive raises, resulted from relaxed personal (financial) stressors that changed intrapersonal behaviors or from temporary biopsychoscocial influences of the significant pay raise.

Firm Size, Gender, Unionization, Performance Pay, and Other Relationships

Artz (2008) asked if since performance pay (bonuses or piece rates) increased performance, whether job satisfaction jointly increases or decreases from the added labor involved. He also wondered if males and females shared equal feelings and if the size of the organization or unionization mattered. Concurrent studies by Green and Heywood (2008) showed performance pay negatively correlated, albeit slightly and insignificantly, to job satisfaction (-0.03), but concluded intrinsic motivations remain for workers when presented with opportunities for financial gain. Artz agreed with Green and Heywood that overall, performance pay appeared as an insignificant influence upon motivation, but disagreed with them citing males and unionized persons show moderate correlations (0.35, 0.30, $p < .05$) when examined individually.

Six significant factors among all workers, according to Artz' study, demonstrate relationships with job satisfaction. In order of importance to workers, these include work itself (0.51, $p < .01$), work variety (0.51, $p < .01$), promotion prospects (0.38, $p < .01$), supervisor relations (0.26, $p < .05$), employer-provided training (0.17, $p < .05$), and fringe benefits (0.14, $p < .05$). Union workers shared satisfaction in the same factors, except fringe benefits, however, demonstrated more emphasis. Additionally, unionized persons stressed pay (0.35, $p < .05$), amount of work (0.63, $p < .01$), and their commute (0.37, $p < .01$) with dissatisfaction in opportunities to use their abilities (0.64, $p < .01$) and the amount of work (0.63, $p < .01$) in relation to job satisfaction. Surprisingly, nearly perfect correlations existed for employer-provided training and variety of work.

In contrast, non-unionized workers placed emphasis upon supervisor relations (0.60, $p < .01$) and the efficiency of management (0.41, $p < .01$). They also considered hours worked (0.33, $p < .05$) and a bit of the friendliness of coworkers (0.05, $p < .05$) as satisfying factors.

Many organizations find difficulties with staffing professions (nursing, construction, etc.) that historically served primarily single-gendered roles. As trends and interests of males and females change, so must organizations desiring to maintain qualified staffing levels (Heneman III & Judge, 2009). It may seem egocentric to say males place high emphasis on being able to use initiative (0.87, $p < .01$), while females do not express significance with this factor upon their job satisfaction, but that is exactly what Artz found. The differences cannot be explained through personality traits as no significant dissimilarities in the Big Five exist in terms of job satisfaction (Foulkrod, Field, & Brown, 2010). Females tend to place three times the concern with variety in their work (0.89, $p < .01$) as males, and unlike their counterparts, stress efficiency in management (0.40, $p < .01$) and the amount of work (0.89, $p < .01$) when considering their job satisfaction (Artz, 2008).

Job Stress and Burnout

One might expect teachers who work with special education children may experience higher levels of job-related stress and potential burnout, given the extreme differences in mental and physical characteristics of their clientele, and the specialized curriculum needed for accommodating educational objectives. Fortunately, research reveals contrary to that assumption, special education teachers do not experience high levels of stress, and perceived emotional exhaustion generally runs low (Platsidou & Agaliotis, 2008). Now the question evolves to "why not?" when obviously some do burnout.

Inquisition into this parallax revealed intrinsic rewards among the teachers ranked highest in burnout prevention. Feelings of accomplishment (-0.45, $p < .01$) superseded low pay and promotional prospects among special education teachers in leading to burnout. In terms of job satisfaction, however, the job itself drew an equally high negative correlation (-0.45, $p < .01$). Collaborations with other teachers and administrators reduced job stress significantly with a moderate negative relationship (-0.23, $p < .01$). Therefore, as intrinsic rewards and help from others increased, burnout potential decreased leading to higher potential for overall job satisfaction.

Studies from healthcare fields showed similar findings (Hamidi & Eivazi, 2010). Among these workers, however, the only significant stressor appeared to be concerns with pay, although the professional culture rates moderate stress in comparison to other common private-industry fields.

Acculturation and Values

Acculturation exists in two primary forms, accommodation and assimilation (Macionis, 2010). The first occurs when a person adapts their current culture, values, and beliefs to fit those of a foreign influence. This happens when an invading force occupies a new territory and the original inhabitants adopt some of the invader's characteristics, or when a person starts a new job and must adjust to fit in with the new organizational climate. Assimilation involves trading one cultural perspective for another, such as when immigrants immerse themselves in the new culture. Over time, accommodation transforms into assimilation at the organizational level with bureaucratic tendencies, argots, and traditions. Think of the process of a new soldier recruit who assimilates military life, then accommodates learned characteristics of that culture with civilian life after leaving service (neatness, manners, haircuts, and so forth).

Organizations often try to minimalize these transitions by seeking job candidates requiring little adjustment through performing person-organization and job-person fit analyses. The person-organization fit correlates with job satisfaction (0.46, $p < .01$) and without turnover intentions (-0.33, $p < .01$) when controlled for other factors like age, gender, position level, and education (Liu, Liu, & Hu, 2010). It is important to note as persons age, their values change in response to psychosocial development (Papalia, Olds, & Feldman, 2009) and the longer they remain with an organization. Likewise, turnover intentions diminish with age (-0.50, $p < .05$).

Cognitive and Emotional Dissonance

The previous discussion about acculturation and changing one's values leads to questions concerning cognitive and emotional dissonance, or the conflicts created when one thought or emotion conflicts with that of another, namely the organization. Emergency workers, soldiers, police officers, and other professions deal with these issues regularly as part of their jobs. Physicians must honor religious beliefs of their patients even when they conflict with their own and soldiers are trained to kill other people, often in conflict with religious and civilian practices. The requirement to hide their true emotions, or emotional faking, can lead to job dissatisfaction (-0.28, $p < .01$) and higher levels of emotional exhaustion (0.39, $p < .01$) (Pugh, Groth, & Hennig-Thurau, 2011). Recommendations for relieving cognitive and emotional dissonance include changing job structures that minimize contact with stressor agents, training workers in building confidence skills and emotional management techniques, and prescreening job candidates for adaptability.

CONCLUSIONS

Achievement of an organizational culture free from job dissatisfaction is extremely complex and improbable given the myriad of influential factors and types of specializations available. Everyone is bound to be unhappy with their jobs at some point in time, whether it is from problems at work, or extrinsic factors affecting their quality of production. Through research, employers are learning how to identify and manage work stressors, good candidates, and how to adapt to environmental changes affecting success. Assumptions made based upon ethnocentric views sometimes prove false and require adaptations to allow for growth.

* * *

5.4 FACTORS OF MOTIVATION

Searching through the literature reveals a wealth of information on the topic of work motivation. Debates ensue (some for decades) over the validity and utility of theories, while still none stands out as dominant over the others or all encompassing. Herzberg wrote about his Two-Factor Theory of Motivation in 1966 (Gardner, 1977), proclaiming academics should approach motivational questions from two parts: those variables that increase satisfaction, and those that decrease dissatisfaction. This paper looks at Herzberg's reasoning, controversies surrounding it, and offers another avenue for understanding and application in combination with works written more recently.

HERZBERG'S TWO-FACTOR THEORY

Herzberg's Two-Factor Theory, or Motivational-Hygiene (M-H) Theory, states motivation is measured in two parts: through motivators and hygienes. Motivators are those factors (six identified by Herzberg) that increase a person's level of job satisfaction, whereas hygienes (10 found by Herzberg) reduce that same person's levels of job dissatisfaction. He was clear factors relate as they apply to the employee, not to the employer or process, and satisfaction and dissatisfaction do not exist as polar opposites. For example, just because a salary increase (hygiene) may reduce dissatisfaction in a particular job for a person, does not mean that person's satisfaction levels increased proportionately (Luthans, 2008; Gardner, 1977). What it does mean is the worker does not necessarily like their job more, but they apparently dislike it a little bit less. As discussed in the next section, this rationale confuses many researchers, such as Bockman (1971), who attempt validation into M-H Theory, with occasional precarious results (Gardner, 1977).

Herzberg asked two primary questions of workers:

1) "What makes you feel good about your job?" and
2) "What makes you feel bad about your job?".

He noted replies seemed consistent with good descriptions geared toward job content while bad terms related to job context, or situations. Herzberg labeled content descriptors as *motivators* and the others as *hygienes*. Since hygienes relate to environmental factors, they correlate to Maslow's Needs Hierarchy at the lowest level (Luthans, 2008) by bringing motivation to the zero level to prevent dissatisfaction. Hygienes do not improve motivation directly, as motivators do. According to Luthans, challenging content (hint: content = motivators) motivates a person in their work while improving work conditions (the context) merely reduces dissatisfaction.

Overall, M-H Theory provides insight into the reasoning when employers enhance jobs through extrinsic factors alone, such as high wages or other hygiene factors, motivation fails to increase when measured in productivity levels – intrinsic motivating factors are still needed.

CONTROVERSIES AND DEVELOPMENT

Controversy surrounds M-H Theory's simplistic model in treating motivation with only two divisions when regression analyses tell researchers they still do not know enough when imperfect correlations exist (Luthans, 2008). However, the structure of this theoretical model explains this concept by noting plurality of factors within each division. Bockman (1971) demonstrated other researchers complain that *when they deviate* from the model, more than two divisions, specifically motivators and hygienes, exist (another implied validator for Herzberg – not following his directions and arriving at differing conclusions).

Misunderstanding seems to appear as an underlying theme among many opponents of M-H Theory. As noted previously, Bockman attempted to redefine (incorrectly) the relationship between satisfaction and dissatisfaction, saying these terms implied exact opposites. Personal experience has witnessed this style of confusion among psychology students with the terms *habituation* and *dishabituation*; again, not opposites, but procedural complements (Papalia, Olds, & Feldman, 2009). The following section attempts to further simplify confusion with classifying factors as motivators or hygienes by building a procedural model that follows Herzberg's original definitions.

CATEGORIZATION MODEL FOR DUAL-FACTOR ANALYSIS

King attempted to develop a model for understanding Herzberg's Two-Factor Theory from a mathematical premise in which he showed five possible interpretations (Gardner, 1977). Unfortunately, this work exposed relationships between motivators and hygienes without showing how to determine exactly how one knows if a factor categorizes as content or context. For example, was Herzberg correct in saying salary was not an intrinsic motivator that increases job satisfaction? Maslow probably would have agreed salary meets a base requirement of need when pursuing employment, the foundational premise of M-H Theory (Luthans, 2008), but that prospect does not explain volunteer workers who receive no wages.

Following King's mathematical model concept, review of the definitions provided by M-H Theory, 13 representations for motivators and hygienes can be extrapolated. Four always proved true for motivators and one for hygienes, although four additional hygiene descriptors relate in a mutually exclusive manner. Two other descriptors, when related to either factor, negate classification for either factor category. The last descriptor applies to negating hygienes since their definition requires that hygienes "decrease job dissatisfaction" (Luthans, 2008).

Although Table 5.4.1 may be helpful for identification at the property level, understanding the flow process can still prove difficult when discerning correct classifications. For this purpose, Figure 5.4.1 provides a flow chart which transforms the descriptions into a logical order of assessment, allowing for quick categorization of factors as either motivator, hygiene, or needing further analysis. Using the known salary hygiene as an example, a walkthrough demonstrates the simplicity for application of factors into M-H Theory categorization.

First, we assume analyses for the salary variable were previously completed and correlations established for significance, controlling for influencing factors such as age, gender, and so forth. Our purpose here is to establish if the viable factor of *salary* is a motivator, hygiene, or neither. Using the flow chart, Step 1 first allows for elimination of obvious disqualifiers (the first two in Table 5.4.1). We determine from the previous research salary increases or decreases do not lead to decreases in job satisfaction and dissatisfaction simultaneously, nor does removing one's salary cause both job satisfaction and dissatisfaction at the same time.

Step 2 tests the common situational (context) aspect for classifying factors. Knowing some people work without pay in volunteer positions, the affirmative guides progression to Step 3 where we can affirm an increase in salary eases dissatisfaction, again depending upon the situation (a dollar per hour has a greater affect than a penny per hour). A negative reply here additionally confirms the last disqualifier from Table 5.4.1. The final inquisition confirms converting a volunteer employee to a salaried asset also decreases dissatisfaction. In summary, salary meets the qualifications of a hygiene factor.

If Step 2 had failed, we would have skipped to the Step 4 tests in search of motivator status. Negative replies to any Step 3 or Step 4 question disqualify that step and call for further research, after which the process begins again.

RELATING JOB ENRICHMENT TO MOTIVATION-HYGIENE THEORY

M-H Theory does not directly attempt to explain the relatedness of performance and job satisfaction (Luthans, 2008) in the process of proposing workers have the basic need of avoiding unpleasantness while filling their need for growth (Martin, 2009). Other theories build upon Herzberg's work, sometimes indirectly, such as Vroom's Expectancy Theory, Skinner's Operant Conditioning (particularly scheduling), Adams' Equity Theory, and Kelley's popular Attribution Theory (Smerek & Peterson, 2007). Although M-H Theory preceded most of these works, it operates best as a check-and-balance system against those mechanisms when testing variability against satisfaction and dissatisfaction.

To test this framework, the job enrichment question arose whether inclusion of adjunct instructors within administrative planning concepts reduced job dissatisfaction levels and motivated these instructors within their jobs (Martin, 2009). Studies showed a negative correlation existed (-0.45, p < .05) between when teachers were included in planning activities, and the declination of disengagement (withdrawal from the job). These results implied an indication of relatedness to motivation and dissatisfaction; however, which one remained unclear.

Using Expectancy Theory, interpretation of the correlation calls that the teachers were motivated toward engagement because of the desire for inclusion in the planning process – the filled expectation yielded a motivating outcome (Luthans, 2008). Scrutiny begs the question "Was the inclusion a motivator that increased job satisfaction, or a hygiene that reduced dissatisfaction?" Employing the flowchart located in Figure 5.4.1, the assumption follows the teachers were surveyed and results indicated dissatisfaction decreased only when the planning content directly related to that teacher's courses (a reasonable assumption for our purposes here). The answer to Step 1 sounds in the negative, arriving at Step 2, where the situational nature found dictates progression to Step 3. Here the result shows the original research provided positive replies to both parts, and surprisingly, inclusion in planning is not a motivator for these instructors, only a hygiene factor.

To answer the original research question then using Motivational-Hygiene Theory as a check, inclusion of the teachers can reduce job dissatisfaction although it cannot enjoy consideration as a motivator. Of course, these findings may not generalize across the field, but the polled employer better understands its workforce, a contribution to human resource management.

CONCLUSIONS

Herzberg's M-H Theory, when understood, works well in retrospect after analyzing motivation variables utilizing theories suited for the particular research question. Conclusions previously classified as motivators realistically exist in the realm of improving the context of the job rather than the content motivation truly hinges upon. When uncertain, the included flow chart assists managers and researchers with knowing when further questions need asking, and with categorization of specialized factors.

* * *

5.5 MATRIX OF ORGANIZATIONAL INSTRUMENTS

Many authors argue corporate culture deserves attention as the most important source for sustained competitive advantage (Sackman, 2007) since it is unique to the organization and difficult to replicate. Research into corporate culture attempts to link performance, employee satisfaction, product quality, and other corporate characteristics. These multi-directional objectives derive measurement instruments with varied scopes, purposes, benefits, and applications making direct comparisons difficult.

The focus of this paper hinges upon developing a matrix for discussion of five instruments that pervade marketing initiatives among consultation firms utilizing corporate culture in their analytical models. Table 5.5.1 (Appendix) summarizes the purposes, benefits, costs, and verifiable case studies associated with the chosen devices found in the following sections. The final section concludes by reiterating the diversity of corporate culture studies and the relativity of differences to practical applications.

CORPORATE CULTURE QUESTIONNAIRE

The Corporate Culture Questionnaire (CCQ) marketed by DMA Synergetics Management Consultancy as an instrument that looked at the culture of an organization by reviewing how dominant practices and beliefs matched managerial objectives (DMA Synergetics Management Consultancy, 2012). For undisclosed reasons, the original developer, SHL Limited of Surrey, England, changed business models after a merger with PreVisor in 2011 and no longer offers the CCQ product (SHL Limited, 2012). Benefits of the instrument included insuring administrators understand consistency of values across organizational departments while improving communication and morale to enable guidance of change within corporate strategy (DMA Synergetics Management Consultancy, 2012). All information concerning the CCQ, including case studies, is no longer available for review or comment by SHL Limited.

DENISON ORGANIZATIONAL CULTURE SURVEY

Denison and Neale developed the Denison Organizational Culture Survey (DOCS) at the heart of the Denison Model as a means for linking organizational culture and bottom-line results (AvoLead LLC, 2012) by providing a measure of an organization's progress toward achieving a high-performance culture with optimum outcomes. DOCS measures the specific aspects of an organization's culture based on four cultural traits and twelve management practices of the Denison Model and then links these traits to bottom-line performance measures, such as profitability, quality, innovation, and market share. Organizations benefit from associated reports written in the language of business, making the analyses powerful user-friendly tools. Unfortunately, DOCS fails maximum effectiveness as an analytical tool without subsidy from the Denison Leadership Development Survey (DLDS) to link bottom-line measures of Return of Investment (ROI), Return on Assets (ROA), sales growth, quality, and employee satisfaction (Denison Consulting, 2012a). Costs to implement DOCS begin at $1,500 for up to 50 surveys, increasing by $15 for each additional survey, plus $200 per hour for consultation and miscellaneous fees (Discovery Learning, 2012). Case studies may be reviewed on the Denison Consulting website (Denison Consulting, 2012b).

ORGANIZATIONAL CULTURE INVENTORY

Human Synergistics International and its global subsidiaries tout the simply titled Organizational Culture Inventory (OCI) as the leading and most researched instrument for measuring organizational culture (Human Synergistics International, 2012a). Beyond measuring operating culture, the current form purposes assessments of key outcomes: individual member satisfaction, intention to stay, role clarity and role conflict, and perceptions of the organization's service quality. At a starting cost of $2,251 plus $24 for each analyzed survey, Human Synergistics trains an organizational member to administer and analyze the OCI, and then to apply concepts for organizational change throughout the organizational culture (Human Synersitics International, 2012c). Other benefits of the OCI include (Denison Consulting, 2012a):

1) signaling and/or validation in the need for cultural transformation;
2) it allows planning and monitoring of organizational development programs;

3) supports programs designed to enhance strategy implementation, employee engagement, organizational learning, quality and reliability, and/or customer service;
4) it facilitates mergers, acquisitions, and strategic alliances;
5) it enhances managers' understanding of culture and sustainability;
6) it provides management of diversity and corporate responsibility; and
7) the OCI measures culture for teaching and research purposes.

Case studies and other research documents are publicly available (Human Synergistics International, 2012b).

ORGANIZATION ASSESSMENT SURVEY

The Organization Assessment Survey (OAS) examines the internal structure of the organization and assesses how employees are working together to meet organizational goals. Additionally, the instrument allows understanding the current climate, environment, and individuality of the organization. To these ends, the OAS core concepts remain intact while specifics are tailored to individual organizations (United States Office of Personnel Management, 2012). For example, the U.S. Office of Personnel Management works with other governmental agencies and Authenticity, Inc. prefers non-profit organizations for clientele (Authenticity Consulting, LLC, 2012) that benefit from coverage of 26 assessment topics and free online access to the instrument. National Business Research Institute, Inc. charges nominal fees to for-profit companies and allows review of case studies (National Business Research Institute, Inc., 2012).

KENEXA CULTURAL INSIGHT

Kenexa purchased rights to the former Organizational & Team Cultural Indicator in 2008 and aptly changed the instrument's name to Kenexa Cultural Insight (KCI) (Kenexa, 2012a). Kenexa contends the KCI purposes as a cultural assessment that defines an organization's strengths, weaknesses, and subconscious elements to improve employee retention. With this singular goal, benefits include clarity of strategy, alignment and engagement of organizational internal communications plans, and creation of authentic recruitment advertising. Contradicting the instrument's purpose, the company claims the KCI provides administrators insight into cultural matches or mismatches before completing a merger or acquisition. Inquisition to Kenexa's sales department into pricing of the KCI receives further marketing efforts for purchase of consultation services without direct price quoting. However, case studies may be reviewed on the company's website (Kenexa, 2012b).

ALTERNATIVE INSTRUMENTS

Meta-analysis of the literature by Jung and colleagues revealed more than 70 qualitative and quantitative instruments available for organizational culture assessment (Jung, et al., 2009). Of these, only 48 survived scrutiny of psychometric assessment and the majority of those were in early stages of development. The researchers concluded although no singular assessment seemed ideal, users should choose, if needed, an instrument serving purposes closer to the organization's needs, paying close attention to the context of application.

To demonstrate, both the Kenexa Cultural Insight and the Organizational Culture Inventory instruments boast the benefit of facilitating mergers and acquisitions. The first tool serves the basic purpose of reducing turnover, whereas the latter also provides the intentions of measuring service quality. If a client needs to measure service quality as a component of organizational culture in face of a merger or acquisition, then the OCI is the better option, according to Jung and associates. Additional requirements by the client may realistically find better service through rejection of both options and obtaining another, or combining instruments to achieve desired outcomes.

CONCLUSIONS

The study of organizational/corporate culture is relatively young, gaining recognition for viability mostly after the 1980s (Sackman, 2007). Internally, organizational culture studies look to increase profitability while externally views transition across national borders within industries (Sanders & Cooke, 2005). This differentiation lead to myriads of instruments with purposes as varied as the organizations served. Some managers want to measure and control employees through cultural stabilization, while others look to the internal culture as a means to understand rates of turnover or employee satisfaction factors. Whatever the case, no one solution exists for every situation and managers should review or develop an instrument suited to the needs and goals of the organization.

* * *

5.6 ORGANIZATIONAL STRUCTURES

In order to change the culture of an organization, researchers must first find ways to identify and define the matrix of elements that comprise the "way of life" before searching among possibilities for solutions. This paper attempts to demonstrate this concept using a case scenario centered upon a community college district, the complexities involved in evaluation, and the scope of perceptions required. Attainment begins with discussion of elements found in a strong organizational culture and continues with concerns about changing those norms in beneficial ways.

ELEMENTS OF A STRONG ORGANIZATIONAL CULTURE

King, Felin, and Whetten (2010) argued organizations, and their relative cultural components, exist dynamically and depend upon markets served for growth and continuity as each organization survives with the individuality known representative of those persons and groups that comprise them. These researchers identified at least 27 characteristics common to organizations, spanning macro descriptions to micro-analytic behavioral processes. For example, while retail companies "sell stuff", salespersons who do the selling may require training – a micro process - in common psychological principles (e.g. foot-in-the-door technique) to reach organizational goals. Conversely, many retailers may abhor a specific technique or require indirect methods toward reaching similar goals; again, an organizational culture characteristic.

Globalization and increased competition forced organizations to question if, and to what extent, corporate culture and economic success of a business were related. As demonstrated by the Carl Bertelsmann Prize, the answer endured increasing importance and remained in the interests of corporate leaders (Sackman, 2007). Successful companies within their respective industries across the globe "leave no doubt that they consider their specific culture as it is lived in, and supported by, the company relevant for their success", (p. 9).

Defining the elements of strong organizational culture for any successful organization requires the entity explore instruments that:

1) capture strengths as well as weaknesses (Sackman, 2007);
2) reflect as much of the total culture as possible (Jung, et al., 2009);
3) demonstrate relativity (validity) to the organization's industry (Sackman, 2007); and
4) provide application toward organizational goals (Sackman, 2007; Jung, et al., 2009).

Just as each organization differs from all others, selection, interpretation, and intervention of solutions demand equal consideration in context of the applicable situation. No one instrument (to date) enjoys globalized standardization across industries, organizational types, or even team situations (King, Felin, & Whetten, 2010).

Referring to the point of strengths and weaknesses, organizations that understand their stronger qualities capitalize through competitive advantage, while those that recognize their weaknesses and work to convert these failings into assets demonstrate growth (Krajewski, Ritzman, & Malhotra, 2007). However, those organizations which realize the potential opportunities of working both spectrums grow faster than those organizations who dwell on one approach or the other. The second requirement for choosing an instrument, reflect as much of the culture as possible, enables successful constituents to recognize and approach their strengths and weaknesses appropriately. Of course, a cultural assessment designed for use among a chain of retail stores could not accurately reflect the organizational culture with a fleet of over-the-road truck drivers, so some validity within the industry calls for relevance. Likewise, if the assessment fails to contribute toward organizational goals, then resources (time, money, etc.) turn into waste. The following section discusses changing the organizational culture (implementation) once the assessment develops.

CHANGING ORGANIZATIONAL CULTURE

Designing organizations enables better understanding of organizations, and how to improve those organizations (Dunbar & Starbuck, 2006). Organizations flourished over the last two centuries raising questions on their effects within societies (e.g. governments and economics) and the extrudable benefits (jobs and community support) available from their existence. Improved efficiency, increased productivity, equity of financial rewards, and means to reduce social stratification emerged under Marxist theoretical bases that still persist at one extreme (Macionis, 2010) and recent changes in corporate bureaucracy processes under the law at the other (Title VII of the Civil Rights Act, Sarbanes-Oxley Act, etc.). Today, the focus of organizational study has shifted toward intra-organizational perspectives in the hopes of changing structures from within rather than the forced compliance (Dunbar & Starbuck, 2006) instantiated through legal reform, social demand, and market shifts.

Studies conducted by Russo and Harrison (2005) acknowledged this transition when they showed environmental performance improved in U.S. electronics facilities when it was linked to plant manager's pay, but not for lower-level managers who felt the situation was beyond their control. From an organizational culture perspective, efficiency improved when elements of initiatives related directly to appropriate individuals, but not when applied to members of the organization as a whole.

Strategically, mission statements describe the core activities of the organization (Fugazzotto, 2009), however vague and generalized many seem. Traditionalists often argued organizations intent on making money had one mission "to make money for the shareholders or owners", even non-profits (Friedman, 1970). Modern thinking transformed to recognize communities, employees, and customers as stakeholders without the interests of whom, the organization likely failed to exist (Bovee, Thill, & Mescon, 2007). Retrospectively to the controversial matters surrounding Enron and similar companies in the early 2000s, organizations were forced to re-evaluate their purposes and methods of operations leading to revisions in their missions to include these other stakeholders.

For instance, Walmart Stores, Inc. revised its statement that begins, "Saving people money to help them live better" (Wal-Mart Stores, Inc., 2012) to reflect commitment to customers as a primary mission. Continuing, the company recognizes the result of this purpose with an economic impact clause following: "Walmart's overall impact on the retail industry and beyond has changed the way business is conducted globally, and increased consumer benefits — regardless of where they shop."

One of the largest industries undergoing transition, when reviewing the literature, is education - where studies in team implementations attempt exploration into organizational culture changes relating to shifts in purpose (mission) as well. For example, James and Connolly (2009) developed a model that linked organizational culture of the staff (as a group) in 12 British schools to performance as measured by pupil attainment. They realized understanding organizational culture is difficult and complex and that culture of itself did not determine performance.

Similarly, Merton et.al., (2009) examined how organizational culture influenced curricular change processes at a midwestern engineering and science college. They found that how well change strategies aligned with the organizational culture of the institution directly influenced success or failure of the effort (measured by perpetuation of the program).

Following this theme, the remainder of this paper focuses on the higher education industry by building a case study surrounding a community college district in southeastern Illinois. Examining the description of the organizational culture precedes analyses of the elements needed for cultural strength and the steps necessary for change within organization.

CASE STUDY FOR A COMMUNITY COLLEGE

Illinois Eastern Community Colleges (IECC) is a state-sanctioned community college district covering eight counties in southeastern Illinois. Four campuses exist, each with its own administration (President, Dean of Instruction, etc.), full-time faculty, and staff. Daily functions, such as recruitment and retention of students, project planning, and community service outreach programs serve under the responsibility of each campus in their respective geographic service areas.

The Board of Trustees, which includes the District CEO, resides in a centralized location separate from any one campus. The Board decides all final hiring and termination decisions for full-time employees since everyone within the college district is considered as an IECC worker with assignment to a specific campus. Campus Deans hire adjunct faculty as the singular exception to needed Board approval and only adjunct faculty travel between campuses for teaching assignments.

Campus Presidents attend monthly Board meetings where issues concerning District matters commence, however Presidents must defend reasoning for program creations and adjustments, budget changes, facility usage, interagency collaborations, and other matters concerning their specific campuses before any actions may find authorization. In other words, Presidents have no authority in matters that could differentiate their respective campus from the others without permission from the Board.

Despite controls initiated by the Board, internal methods of operations function quite differently. For instance, an adjunct professor working at two campuses can expect to utilize two different textbooks for the same course, to expect different equipment (projectors, etc.) at each location, and to endure opposing social atmospheres although no more than 40 miles separates most campuses.

Aside from an all-inclusive college catalogue published by the Board of Trustees concerning student expectations, a Procedural Manual guides each campus into the expectations and communications with the Board. Employee handbooks exist by employee classification: tenure-track instructors, adjunct instructors, staff, and administration. Unfortunately, these handbooks fail in terms of brevity with no mention of campus culture since preparation resides with the Board.

Case Analysis

Macneil, Prater, and Busch (2009) conducted a study where they explored the question if organizational culture made a difference between "Acceptable" and "Exemplary" schools in terms of student achievement. These researchers found Exemplary schools outperformed the Acceptable schools anywhere from 20% to 50% in nine of ten dimensions: Goal Focus, Communication, Power Equalization, Resource Utilization, Cohesiveness, Morale, Innovativeness, Adaptation, and Problem Solving. The tenth dimension, Autonomy, appeared more prominent at the lower-end schools. This can be expected in education settings with lower student-teacher ratios, such as community colleges in comparison to universities. Although these findings apply to students, the bottom-line demonstrates how culture influences organization-wide trickle down to other stakeholders, namely students as customers.

Tenure-track faculty demonstrates no differences over adjuncts when significantly evaluating school climates (Roby, 2010), however, each share in concerns with leadership, isolation, trust, and support. At IECC, isolation of adjuncts is obvious with lack of invitation to participate in campus/district activities (graduation, recruitment, planning, etc.). Many adjuncts cannot identify tenured instructors in their own departments after years of service. Just as acknowledged in the Roby study, many IECC adjuncts distrust some administrative personnel, seeking support from other sources. Rumors and discussions about struggling campuses plague the cultures at stronger facilities.

In attempt to control administrative uniformity across the Districts colleges, the Board failed to integrate organizational culture, providing an acceptable level of consistency with employees. To remedy this problem, the District should collaborate with the four campuses and evaluate the organizational culture. As mentioned beforehand, the process endures a multilevel complexity of design, implementation, and analysis before interventions may effectively prevail. Recommendation goes to applying the military Warning Order concept (reverse planning from result to preparation) by identification of organizational culture elements affecting students in their best interests (Does IECC want to be exemplary or acceptable?). Next, selection and evaluation of cultural elements relevant to employee groups that facilitate the student culture require analysis.

Based upon findings using these specialized instruments (by internal design or outsourced), an ideal organizational culture emerges where collaborators design interventions that integrate desired changes across the organization. Concerning the initial problem with employee handbooks, each campus could write their own set that engrosses the unique aspects of that particular campus in conjunction with common district cultural expectation components. Then if an instructor changes campuses, reduced efforts at adaptation may occur. Other aspects (isolation, trust, etc.) should also find approaches to resolution as well.

CONCLUSIONS

Perceptions of the organizational culture at IECC differ significantly between employee groups at all levels. Just as the maintenance staff may visualize their parts in the group culture from the bottom upward in comparison to administrators, adjunct faculty see themselves looking inward in relation to tenured instructors. Changing these perceptions involves removing those cultural elements identified as barriers, and enhancing others realized that improve the organization in directions needed to obtain sustainable goals (e.g. exemplary status).

* * *

5.7 STRUCTURAL ANALYSIS

This paper reviews current literature in search of current research affecting organizational design and structure. Application of these findings to a real-world organization frames the mindset of organizational change over the last few decades.

ORGANIZATIONAL DESIGN AND STRUCTURE

Traditional bureaucratic organizations contained a hierarchal structure designed to facilitate and control flows and processes of information, products, and people. By the 1980s, these hierarchies began to flatten, reducing the steps and costs involved in maintaining the structures. Today, flexibility in networks of information and people forces organizations to recognize patterns of interactions and coordination that links technology, tasks, and human components in order to accomplish its purposes (Luthans, 2008). Rather than departments or teams that focus upon, and remain within, specialized areas of the organizations with managers serving as links, these sections interact in ways that speed coordination and innovation without the barriers inflicted through bureaucratic processes. Many organizations no longer represent their structures with triangular flow charts; realizing atomic models better demonstrate the interactions and flexibility encountered within their operational structures.

One such organization undergoing this transformation process is Frontier Community College (FCC). In 1995, the school utilized a hierarchal structure consisting of a Chancellor, a President, a Dean, several departmental directors, and layers of seniority-based employees. Currently, the design eliminates the Chancellor and all but two directive positions, leaving a few associate deans, and discontinuation of seniority statuses (tenure is undergoing phase-out by state legislation). Day-to-day operations require interactions across departments with leadership serving in referee positions. For example, instructors work with library staff directly to plan relative material acquisitions without approval or reporting to department heads or administration.

Group and interpersonal/intrapersonal processes, communication, political behavior, power structures, decision-making processes, and stress issues likewise evolved rapidly within organizations affecting the general cultures. Discussion continues for each area with reflection upon Frontier Community College.

GROUP AND INTERPERSONAL PROCESSES

Ife (1995) listed five issues that encourage participation in group affairs:

1) People will participate if they feel the issue or activity is important.
2) People must feel that their action will make a difference.
3) Different forms of participation must be acknowledged and valued.
4) People must be enabled to participate, and supported in their participation.
5) Structures and processes must not be alienating.

The first two principles relate intra-personally to the organizational member by instilling purpose and goals, respectively, whereas the last three provide interpersonal strengths of membership, empowerment, and cohesiveness. The entrenchment of intrapersonal and interpersonal issues within an organization reflects in the view that understanding context is necessary to scrutinize the processes connecting individuals with their environment (Radermacher et.al., 2010). Although Ife's principles primarily relate to individualized perspectives, intrapersonal processes translate to the skills and competence needed by the individual to perform effectively within the organization. Interpersonal processes similarly enable team dynamics and the individual's ability to function with other organizational members. For instance, when conflict and tension among workers relating to mixed agendas arise, individual needs supersede those of the organization. Therefore, in this case, actions by leaders and other members that align with the last three principles identified by Ife can alleviate goal conflicts.

At FCC, retention of quality adjunct faculty heightened concerns for administration with the firing of all except six full-time faculty members in 2011. After completing real-time work-sample evaluations using new state guidelines, many adjuncts also lost their jobs. Remaining instructors were surveyed in line with current research results in order to understand the scope of the problem and to assert obtainable goals. Two implications revealed adjuncts desired more inclusion into college-sponsored activities and improved orientations that enhanced the autonomy required by the organizational structure, supporting Ife's principles. Some progress had been made by inviting adjuncts to participate in graduation ceremonies, revamping the orientation process, and inclusive participation with college-wide surveys affecting organizational culture.

COMMUNICATION

No doubts in argument persist that organizations changed with the incorporation of internet-enabled technologies. Practices of international travel for purposes of face-to-face meetings now entail turning on a conference screen at each end for live communications. Email and cellular telephones allow members of the organization to send messages and contracts in minutes rather than days or weeks, and to telecommute from nearly anywhere. In fact, by 2005, 50 million employees worked outside formal and traditional organizational settings (Schaeffer, 2010). Most secondary schools in the United States today integrate computer skills into their curriculums while collegiate institutions offer entire degree programs online.

Peacock (2008) showed how studying the evolutionary aspects in technological changes of organizational websites reveals artifacts of organizational change processes where organizational and technological factors combine dynamically and symbiotically. The implication here posits that organizations with little technological change also demonstrate comparative changes within their cultures. This research begs the question of transparency and community: Do organizational websites offering little information and interactivity for stakeholders share the same traits within their cultural identities?

Despite noticeable advantages in communication technologies, concerns emerged from interaction theorists about workplaces centering as sources for friendships and extending work availability around the clock; however, mothers and fathers returning to the homes, the increases in worker autonomy, and increases in job satisfaction rates tend to offset the negatives (Hirsch & DeSourcey, 2006).

When first introduced, online course development at FCC was reserved to full-time instructors by invitation of administration after polling students college-wide for feasibility and profitability. Recently with staffing changes, the program opened to any adjunct or full-time instructor. The process entailed the instructor first developing the course and then submitting their finished product for approval by a review committee. Upon approval, the course was scheduled and enrollment determined feasibility, regardless if other instructors already provided the offering. Additionally, the Dean of Instruction mailed personal letters to all instructors requesting that traditional courses add online components (gradebooks, student chats, etc.). Communication processes moved from traditional channels to mostly online with coursework, human resources, and other daily operations.

POLITICAL BEHAVIOR, POWER, AND DECISION-MAKING

"Organizational politics is implicated in all levels of organizational functioning... from power structures and informal interactions to individual identity" (Davey, 2008, p. 650). Women's studies centralized upon organizational politics showed that political activity links to the performance, achievement, and maintenance of power of individuals within the organization, especially for career-minded minority members. The covert (hidden) socio-cognitive processes involved with organizational politics assist in the maintenance of identities by excluding cultural misfits who attempt to undermine existing power structures. Although an inverse relationship exists between power and politics, the two concepts intertwine in a close affiliation (Luthans, 2008). For example, those who lack power utilize increasingly more political strategies as means in competing for limited resources, whereas those with power need fewer political maneuvers.

Power and politics at the organizational level see constant scrutiny in terms of behaviors affecting compensation, promotional opportunities, and leadership when contrasting gender stratifications. Glass ceiling and glass elevator effects, respectively, describe barriers to cross-gendered positions and gender-related accelerations among career choices (Schaeffer, 2010)... males entering female-dominated fields are more likely to enter administrative roles. Since Gilligan expanded Kohlberg's work showing males utilize justice as a driver with administrative decision-making and females lead with a care aspect (Papalia, Olds, & Feldman, 2009), other research (Davey, 2008) indicated that women represent politics within the organization "as irrational, aggressive, competitive and instrumental, leading to individual, not organizational, success" (p 650); thus, enhancing the glass ceiling effect in organizations led by males.

Generally, the effectiveness of leaders is defined by their abilities to make sound and beneficial decisions on behalf of the organization. Newer thinking claims that high-performing leadership involves influencing individuals (organizational members) to transfer their short-term self-interests into a contribution to long-term performance of the group, essentially leaders build a team and guide it to outperform competition (Kaiser & Overfield, 2010). This alternate perspective arose after Kaiser and Overfield studied individual leaders over successful companies. Noticing that CEOs accounted for 14% of the variability in firm financial performance, they queried an explanation for the link between individual leaders and organizational performance using value chain logic – the *how* these leaders achieved effectiveness rather than personal characteristics.

The President of Frontier Community College has a reputation for disliking confrontation and promoting females who support his ideologies. Over the last three years, males with offices or classrooms in the administrative building found themselves terminated, relocated to another building, and passed over for promotional opportunities when the positions required personal interaction and the employee previously interjected in discussions. Research noted above indicates the President understands the gender differences and utilizes political behaviors to maintain his power and control over decision-making.

STRESS

Shared stressor refers to workplace stressors affecting moderation of relationships at the group level and the direct outcomes the strain poses for individuals directly (Griffin, 2010). For instance, although an organization undergoing downsizing targets specific classes or geographic workers (e.g. sports program at a high school), other workers may feel threatened by increased workloads or further anticipatory reductions (Luthans, 2008). This trickle-down effect, initiated by the antecedent stressor, evolves into a shared condition within the organization although individual members may or may not receive direct implication. Other common shared stressors, by this definition, include impending union strikes, primary product discontinuations, hierarchal realignments, natural disasters, technological lags (or competitive advancements), impending industry legislations, and mergers or acquisitions. In laymen's terms using contagion theory, although a specific event or situation provides no direct implication upon most members of a group or organization, those persons attempt to prevent the stressor from spilling over into their own lives by moderating the relationship the stressor may have on them personally; thus, a shared stressor.

With the hierarchal, communication, and general organizational structure changes encountered by remaining FCC employees, shared stressors increased worrisome behaviors dramatically over short periods. Cutbacks, firings, procedural changes, course content requirement enhancements, and similar actions kept employees concerned that spillover may force unwanted change in their personal lives.

CONCLUSIONS

Organizational structures transformed exponentially over the last couple of decades, leaving few, if any, untouched. Collegiate institutions felt the full force of the "adapt or die" mentality alongside the businesses, industries, and communities they served. Since organizations cannot exist without the people that socially construct them (Schaeffer, 2010), trickle down effects changed the personal lives of their members as well. Technology developments and extreme global competition generally receive the bulk of the driving blame in academic literature for these phenomena; however, one cannot discount the personal needs of organizational members as motivation that drives organizational survival. It will be interesting to see if the rates of change continue or level out in establishment of a new base organizational definition.

* * *

5.8 ORGANIZATIONAL BEHAVIOR: CULTURAL IMPACT

Mergers of American organizations in Eastern Europe and Asia rarely enter the American news media. In South Korea, for example, under the US-South Korean Free Trade Agreement signed in 2011, American firms cannot merge or hire South Korean lawyers until 2017 (Law Business Research Ltd, 2012), severely impacting mergers and acquisitions in that country. Uncertainty of economic and market trends in Europe forced declines in the rates of mergers and acquisitions across most industries since peaking in 2007. Spin-off creations and demergers increased in attempts to streamline organizations where Cargill, Marathon Oil, Kraft Foods, and ConocoPhillips reduced their asset bases in order to raise capital, to reduce debt, and to refocus on their core services.

United Parcel Service (UPS) found a way to expand within Asian markets without direct merger or acquisition attempts within those markets by merging with a Northern European competitor that already held a significant market share (Robinson, 2012). Unification with TNT Express increases UPS from 10% to 16% of the Asian markets, in comparison with FedEx's 21% and DHL's 36% market shares in Asia.

The focus of this paper is the examination of issues facing UPS concerning organizational behavior impacts resulting from the merger with TNT Express in view of the Asian and Northern European cultural impacts. Exploration into foundational theory, context of modern organizations, individual processes, interpersonal processes, and organizational processes serve for comparison of issues of organizational design, change, and international issues affecting this merger. Suggested methods of adoption and procedural implementation follow each sectional topic.

PROSOCIAL AND ANTISOCIAL IMPLICATIONS

UPS hopes not only to gain market shares under control of TNT Express, but also to maintain and grow them in conjunction with current strengths through merging the companies. In essence, UPS must appropriately deal with conflicts that enhance solidarity within the new organization or face loss of market shares. The combined internal culture influences its members who in turn reform the culture, and then imprints those identities upon the organizational members. Global economic changes imprint the realization of the volatility of the organization requiring higher quality of products and services combined with supportive leadership (Muchinsky, 2006). Although managers tend to visualize organizational justice more positively than other members (Titrek, 2009), feedback and cooperation of managers and subordinates in terms of leadership behaviors tend to reduce poor perceptions. Hornung (2010) remarked that participative decision-making helped to prevent feelings of alienation more than material rewards for compliance while procedural justice procedures served to enhance morale.

Rather than providing immediate restructuring of pay scales and other material incentives, research therefore suggests UPS negotiate with employees of TNT Express while integrating the companies. Remaining fair and consistent in employee relations provides the best results in gaining leadership support. This multifaceted approach decreases biased assumptions extending from differences in perceptions relating to organizational commitment.

EXPECTANCY AND TRUST

Expectancy theory claims people want more as they accumulate more, especially in terms of benefits and reduced workloads (Heneman III & Judge, 2009). When a benefit, such as regular wage increases, decrease in volume or frequency and work quotas increase, people complain more. Issues of declined trust ensue between organizational leaders and subordinates. Higher turnover rates, poorer quality of goods and services production, lower job satisfaction, and other factors affecting organizational commitment predictively deteriorate the core of the organizational culture. Trust reliably validates established processes when predicting organizational commitment, job satisfaction, performance, and intentions to leave the organization (Altunas & Baykal, 2009). Sportsmanship behavior, as predicated by traditional thinking in work ethic and participation efforts, shows no effect on trust by organizational members, including managers. More specifically, the behaviors of conscientiousness, civic virtue, altruism, and courtesy, however, demonstrate impact of trust on members in their institutions, managers, and coworkers.

During the TNT Express merger, UPS should expect issues of distrust in the new management hierarchy from acquired employees and managers. Changes in operational procedures may negatively affect acculturation mandates if those changes create drastic fluctuations in workloads or expected benefits previously enjoyed under TNT Express management. Careful examination of critical aspects should entail preclusion of any actions that contradict expectancies in order to reduce issues concerning declining trust.

WORKER PRODUCTIVITY AND JOB SATISFACTION

Worker productivity and *job satisfaction* serve as relational terms needing definition for the particular application. Differences for these measures rely upon the particular organization, even within the same industry. Where one manufacturing company may measure productivity as pieces per time, another manufacturer may quantify productivity as a ratio of asset turnover (Krajewski, Ritzman, & Malhotra, 2007). Likewise, job satisfaction from an employee perspective may indicate the overall ability of outputs received from the job to satisfy the needs of the worker when the employer looks for reduced turnover and intentions to remain with the organization. Taken together, these factors suggest satisfied workers deliver higher rates of productivity to the organization (Wright & Cropanzano, 2000). Either way, *productive* and *satisfied* demand evaluation of the context used and consideration of qualitative and quantitative characteristics, to provide consistent meaning.

Although performance pay only provides a slight negative correlation (-0.03) to performance, job satisfaction endures with increased intrinsic motivations, such as opportunities for future financial gain (Artz, 2008). This research also indicated workers placed importance upon (in descending order) the work itself, work variety, promotion prospects, supervisor relations, employer-provided training, and then fringe benefits. Similar studies (Platsidou & Agaliotis, 2008) demonstrated how intrinsic rewards reduce and prevent burnout, especially when workers feel a sense of accomplishment (-.045, $p < .01$). These findings also help to explain the relationship expectancy and trust play in the roles between managers and their subordinates, as discussed in the previous section.

When merging with TNT Express, UPS should consistently evaluate the qualitative and quantitative factors that define worker satisfaction and productivity in terms of the acquired workforce, in contrast with the existing organization, striking a balance between the two. Emphasis upon intrinsic values align with the company's objectives of efficiency and dependability, in particular, those that provide training not only for current TNT Express employees into the UPS culture, but also for current UPS employees in understanding differences in regional operations. TNT Express workers should feel they have equal opportunities for advancement and promotion within the new organizational hierarchy without fear of feelings of succession behind UPS dominance.

ACCULTURATION, ASSIMILATION, AND DISSONANCE

When forcing a person to adapt their current culture, values, and beliefs to fit those of a foreign influence, acculturation (or "californication" in the western United States) is said to occur (Macionis, 2010). Acculturation frequently disrupts the operations, missions, and routines, respectively, in organizations merged or acquired by outside influences. From a voluntary perspective, assimilation occurs when those characteristics integrate by choice. Assimilation, therefore, can effectively exist as a tool with fewer repercussions when the desire to implement change in organizational culture deems necessary (e.g. make it *their* idea).

Dissonance, the conflicts created when thoughts or emotions struggle with one another, transpires normally in many professions, but more so during transitional periods of acculturation. When people are forced to hide their true beliefs or feelings (emotional faking), job satisfaction decreases (-0.28, p < .01) alongside higher rates of emotional exhaustion (0.39, p < .01) (Pugh, Groth, & Hennig-Thurau, 2011). Minimizing contact with job stressors and implementing confidence training help to alleviate these problems.

No doubts exist employees of TNT Express will experience feelings of cognitive and emotional dissonance (and to some degree, employees of UPS) relating to the takeover, especially with UPS as the dominant organization. Asian employees may struggle more than European counterparts due to the extent of imposed acculturation, but these effects can be minimalized. Training programs focused to redirect the acculturation process into assimilation aspects reduce transition stressors and time while increasing employee confidence toward UPS. In other words, design the programs to show how UPS operations, mission, and routines comparatively outweigh existing methods and the TNT employees will more likely adapt more easily, embracing the changes on their own.

MOTIVATION

Recent literature abounds with research on motivation, however, to date no singular theory can explain all of its aspects. As mentioned in the previous section concerning acculturation, assimilation, and dissonance, job satisfaction decreases under stress. Additional consideration goes to the counterpart, job dissatisfaction, which is not a polar opposite. Herzberg originally distinguished the two concepts by noting that although a salary increase may lower dissatisfaction through hygiene factors, the overall level of job satisfaction may remain unchanged (Luthans, 2008). Technically this means the person may not like their job (work process) more, but may dislike it (possession or position) less. To use simpler terms, what the two-factor theory contributes is provision of a means to the notion that removing bad things from a job is as important as adding good things.

As explained using expectancy theory, job satisfaction, and the often-ignored job dissatisfaction, contribute to performance. Workers expect the work they trade for salary and benefits will contribute to their basic needs in supporting themselves. These concepts tie further to Herzberg's work when the realization materializes that workers avoid unpleasantness while filling their needs for growth (Martin, 2009).

When evaluating the TNT Express workforce, UPS should appraise components of current packages to determine which factors contribute to the context of the job (reduce dissatisfaction), and which factors enable motivation by increasing job satisfaction. Application of this method to current UPS employee positions may also serve to improve retention rates by plummeting turnover and refining the general culture of the merged organization. Correct identification of satisfiers (motivators) and non-satisfiers (hygiene) serves as the key to success.

INSTRUMENTS FOR CULTURAL DEVELOPMENT

The corporate culture is unique to the organization and difficult to replicate by competitors, giving rise that corporate culture deserves attention as the most important source of sustained competitive advantage (Sackman, 2007). Research attempts to link performance, satisfaction, quality, and other organizational characteristics to organizational culture using instruments specific to the application holding varied scopes, purposes, and benefits. This diversity requires reiteration into the relativity of practical applications and therefore cannot remain unnoticed in importance.

The Denison Organizational Culture Survey (DOCS) provides a means for linking bottom-line results and organizational culture by providing a measure of the organization's progress toward achieving optimum outcomes (AvoLead LLC, 2012). Specifically, twelve management practices and four cultural traits link to measures of profitability, quality, innovation, and market share. Other subsidy analytic tools enhance understanding and intervention for measures of return of investment (ROI), return on assets (ROA), sales growth, quality, and employee satisfaction. Unfortunately, costs for large organizations to implement DOCS and its subsidiary tools can reach high proportions unless used to maximum benefit.

The Organizational Culture Inventory (OCI) adds to DOCS by assessing individual member satisfaction, intentions to stay, role clarity and conflict, and perceptions of the organization's service quality into the base assessment. Overall costs run comparable to DOCS with its optional components, however, a local member of the organization can be trained to evaluate and interpret results (Human Synersitics International, 2012). Additional benefits of the OCI include signaling the need for organizational change, planning and development of development programs, and facilitation of mergers and strategic alliances.

For an instrument tailored more specifically to the organization, the Organizational Assessment Survey (OAS) examines the internal structure of the organization and assesses how employees work together toward organizational goals. Other factors include understanding the current climate, environment, and individuality of the organization, totaling 26 assessment topics (United States Office of Personnel Management, 2012). Costs vary for individualized treatment, although, free implementations exist for non-profit organizations.

More than 70 instruments available for organizational culture assessment reside in the research literature, with 48 surviving scrutiny of psychometric assessment (Jung, et al., 2009). Conclusively, no singular instrument seems ideal for determining overall organizational culture and attention to the context of the application is needed. Realistically, combinations of instruments or home-development may serve the desired outcomes.

Justification for analysis of the organizational culture at UPS and TNT Express clearly stands out from previous discussions. Of the commercially available products described here, the Organizational

Culture Inventory promises the closest match to the UPS business model and objective for merging TNT Express. Most importantly, opting to train managers in concepts of application, training, and organizational development revealed by the instrument provides additional competitive advantage for the organization. Although the OCI likely will not comprehensively cover all aspects of the organizational culture in terms of all desired outcomes, the experience gained enables in-house refinement and development of an instrument compatible to the needs of UPS.

CHANGING ORGANIZATIONAL CULTURE

Researchers identified 27 common characteristics of organizations (King, Felin, & Whetten, 2010) that span micro-analytic and macro-analytic behavioral processes. These traits dynamically exist and depend upon the specific markets served for growth and continuity. Corporate leaders understand the increasing importance of how corporate culture and economic success relate with increasing global competition (Sackman, 2007). Definition of a strong organizational culture requires exploration into instruments that capture strengths and weaknesses of the culture, reflect as much of the culture as possible (see the *Instruments for Cultural Development* section), demonstrate validity to the particular industry, and provide application toward organizational goals.

Organizations that recognize their weaknesses and work to convert them into assets show growth, just as understanding stronger qualities allows capitalization through competitive advantage (Krajewski, Ritzman, & Malhotra, 2007). Actually, those organizations that realize potential opportunities of developing strengths and weaknesses grow faster than those organizations that concentrate on one or the other.

The focus of organizational study shifted toward intra-organizational perspectives for purposes of changing organizational structures from within rather than relying on forced compliance measures (Dunbar & Starbuck, 2006) demanded by legal reform, social developments, and shifts in markets. Efficiency improves when elements of initiatives directly related to appropriate individuals within the organization, rather than the members of the organization as a unit (Russo & Harrison, 2005). For example, improved mileage and vehicle efficiency occurs when the responsibility is placed upon the drivers in a fleet, rather than the individuals who load the trucks.

Today, mission statements are strategic tools for describing the core activities of the organization (Fugazzotto, 2009) rather than reaffirming pre-traditional ideals like, "to maximize profits for shareholders and owners" (Friedman, 1970). In contrast, these devices now include employees and communities as stakeholders in recognition the organization would fail to exist without their presence (Bovee, Thill, & Mescon, 2007). In response, organizations across all industries are revamping their mission statements to coincide with stakeholders and impacts, such as retail (Wal-Mart Stores, Inc., 2012) and education (James & Connolly, 2009; Merton et.al., 2009).

UPS can expect acquired personnel from TNT Express to share in some level of distrust in UPS administrators during the transitional period (Roby, 2010). Perceptional change involves removing those elements of the organizational culture identified as barriers (hygiene) and then enhancing elements known to improve (motivators) the organization in directions determined to reach sustainable goals. Evaluation of the UPS mission statement may reveal a need to revamp for inclusion of stakeholders at the macro-analytic level and then to provide training at the micro-analytic level to reinforce these ideals. By self-initiating changes when needed, UPS reduces risks of forced compliance from legal and social demands and excels competitively within its industry.

ORGANIZATIONAL STRUCTURE

As traditional hierarchal organizational models (pyramids) flatten (Luthans, 2008), many administrators realize their organizations act more like atomic models or spherical webs. This design perspective better demonstrates how interactions and flexibility operate as networks within operational structures rather than a chain-of-command format with defined (and limited) lines of communication. The following sections discuss this transition in terms of group and interpersonal processes, communication, politics, power, and decision-making.

Group and Interpersonal Processes

Five principles encourage participation in group affairs (Ife, 1995):

1) people participate if they feel the issue or activity is important;
2) people must feel their action will make a difference;
3) different forms of participation must be acknowledged and valued;
4) people must be enabled to participate with support in their participation; and
5) structures and processes must not be alienating.

The first principle instills purpose and the second reinforces goals as interpersonal relations to the organizational member. The latter three principles address interpersonal strengths of membership, empowerment, and cohesiveness. Scrutiny of the processes connecting individuals with their environments is reflected in the depth of interpersonal and intrapersonal issues within an organization (Radermacher et.al., 2010). These intrapersonal processes equate to the skills and competence required by individuals needed to perform effectively within the organizational culture, while interpersonal processes enable team dynamics and the ability of individuals to work with others.

As UPS integrates TNT Express personnel, careful consideration should be applied with interpersonal and intrapersonal processes by including those employees in the transformation process. Acknowledgement of ideas and concerns they may have, individually and as a group, through timely action and response build confidence in membership and cohesiveness. TNT Express employees will need to feel empowered (e.g. open-door policy) to effect the changes surrounding them or alienation and withdrawal may occur. The more problems involved during the transitional period, the more reflectivity of image placed upon UPS within the new markets. TNT Express employees also reside in the market communities acquired and their relationship with UPS transfers into the mindsets of those communities as stakeholders affecting levels of market volatility.

Communication

Networks allow formal messages to flow in controlled (upward, downward, and horizontal) and uncontrolled (inside/outside to/from unplanned points) directions. The external components link the organization to its environment, such as word-of-mouth advertising or rumors of community reputation, and find exponential supplementation through mediated communication (e.g. Facebook) (Ruben & Stewart, 2006). The result of this communication is the creation of the organizational climate.

Organizational websites display the evolution of technological change processes where organizational and technological factors combine dynamically and symbiotically (Peacock, 2008). The position is that changes within the organizational culture, and its current state, reflect in the website, be it internet or intranet for customers or employees. Colleges and universities show this process with the advent and implementation of online degree programs and intranet access for faculty to maintain course records.

With the integration of TNT Express employees and takeover of its served Northern European and Asian markets, UPS will have to integrate this diversity into its communication networks. Differences in languages and preferred communication techniques add to the challenges of assimilation (Ruben & Stewart, 2006). The UPS website will require modification to incorporate the languages in daily operational procedures, including online training program initiatives, for maximum efficiency and minimal confusion. Although UPS currently serves the broadness of these regions, it is probable that many languages in subcultural areas lack incorporation into the company systems. Failing to serve these diversifications adequately can lead to losses in those market shares.

Politics, Power, and Decision-Making

Gender studies demonstrate political activity links the performance, achievement, and maintenance of power of individuals within the organization from perspectives of women and minorities (Davey, 2008). Socio-cognitive processes covertly involved with organizational politics contribute to the maintenance of identities by eliminating persons who undermine existing power structures. Those persons who lack power tend to use more political strategies when competing for limited resources in contrast to those persons in power (Luthans, 2008).

Effective leaders are generally defined by their abilities to make sound decisions that benefit the organization. High-performing leaders influence organizational members to performance levels that contribute to the long-term performance of the group, rather than short-term self-interests (company survival versus bigger bonus). When combined with a global presence, historical passages teach that influences from governmental and traditional norms add difficulty to maintaining and stabilizing a dynamic power base, hence confounding decision-making processes.

As UPS expands its markets with the TNT Express merger, the organization can expect additional political influences to affect administrative decision-making processes. Disputes of gender employment constructs and other social issues derived from localized thinking diversify the difficulties expected. Inclusion of these groups and individuals within the UPS power structure strengthens leadership through political balances and overall sustainability of UPS in those markets. Within the organizational structure, inclusion at the administrative levels reduces chances of external political maneuvering that hinders organizational goals.

CONCLUSIONS

United Parcel Service already holds a greater market share of the Asian market within its industry. However, a merger with the Northern European TNT Express provides complex issues on a global scale concerning organizational behavior. From integrating employees in all markets influenced by the acquired company, to satisfying customers within those markets, to handling political influences and their differing perspectives, UPS needs to understand how these behavioral stimuli function so that it may achieve its goals of sustainable growth into the future. Taking a leadership stance into the how these aspects work provides insights into how they can work together to form a stronger organizational culture.

An organization is only as strong as the individual stakeholders that comprise its existence. By careful identification of the macro and micro-analytic factors surrounding UPS, the company can ease the transition of people, values, and resources involved and reach goals through flexible and dynamic interventions that provide assimilation rather than acculturation and rebellion.

* * *

PART FIVE APPENDIX

Table 5.5.1

Matrix of Five Common Organizational Culture Instruments	
Instrument	**Description**
Corporate Culture Questionnaire (CCQ)	
Company Contact:	DMA Synergetics Management Consultancy
Primary Source:	http://www.dmasynergetics.com/hrm/assessment/motivation/index.htm
Purpose:	Gives an in-depth look at the culture of an organization, looking at its dominant practices and beliefs and how closely these match the objectives of the company. CCQ identifies any areas in an organization that do not line up with the organization's desired culture and helps to implement the required change.
Benefits:	1) Ensure that understanding of the company's values is consistent across departments and locations
	2) Improve communication across the organization
	3) Improve the morale of staff
	4) Guide any changes in corporate strategy.
Case Studies:	http://www.shl.com/OurClients/CaseStudies/Pages/TheAmbulanceServiceofNewSouthWales.aspx
Costs:	No Longer Available (Author changed research focus)
Denison Organizational Culture Survey (DOCS)	
Company Contact:	Denison Consulting
Primary Source:	http://www.avolead.com/assessment-tools/denison-culture-survey
Purpose:	Links organizational culture to bottom-line results. DOCS provides a measure of an organization's progress toward achieving a high-performance culture and optimum results. It measures the specific aspects of an organization's culture based on four cultural traits and twelve management practices of the Denison Model then links these traits to bottom-line performance measures such as profitability, quality, innovation, and market share.
Benefits:	The DOCS and related reports are written in the language of business, making them powerful and user-friendly tools.
Case Studies:	http://www.denisonconsulting.com/resources/CaseStudies.aspx
Costs:	$1,500 up to 50, +$15 ea + $200/hr + fees
Organizational Culture Inventory (OCI)	
Company Contact:	Human Synergistics International
Primary Source:	http://www.humansyn.com/Solutions/TransformingOrganizations/OrganizationalCultureInventory.aspx
Purpose:	Beyond measuring operating culture, the current form assesses key outcomes: individual member satisfaction, intention to stay, role clarity and role conflict, and perceptions of the organization's service quality.
Benefits:	1) Signals and/or validates the need for cultural transformation.
	2) Plans and monitors organizational development programs.
	3) Supports programs designed to enhance strategy implementation, employee engagement, organizational learning, quality and reliability, and/or customer service.
	4) Facilitates mergers, acquisitions, and strategic alliances.
	5) Enhances managers' understanding of culture and sustainability.
	6) Manages diversity and corporate responsibility.
	7) Measures culture for teaching and research purposes.
Case Studies:	http://www.humansyn.com/ResearchandPublications/Publications.aspx
Costs:	$2,251 + $24/Survey (includes training)

Continued next page...

Organizational Assessment Survey (OAS)	
Company Contact:	National Business Research
Primary Source:	http://www.nbrii.com/products/employee-surveys/organizational-assessment-surveys/ http://cts.opm.gov/pdf/OAS%20Description.pdf
Purpose:	Examines the internal organizational structure; assesses how employees are working together to meet organizational goals; allows understanding the current climate, environment, and individuality of the organization.
Benefits:	Covers 26 topics and may be customized to meet an organization's specific needs.
Case Studies:	http://www.nbrii.com/products/employee-surveys/organizational-assessment-surveys/
Costs:	Free for non-profits. Others vary by client base.
Kenexa Cultural Insight (formerly Organizational & Team Cultural Indicator)	
Company Contact:	Kenexa
Primary Source:	http://www.kenexa.com/employment-branding/cultural-insight-survey
Purpose:	A cultural assessment that defines an organization's strengths, weaknesses, and subconscious elements to improve employee retention.
Benefits:	1) Clarity of strategy for management around an organization's strengths, weaknesses and subconscious cultural elements
	2) Alignment and engagement of organizational internal communications plans
	3) Creation of authentic recruitment advertising
	4) Realization of necessary cultural fit components for personal assessment tools
	5) Understanding of appropriate alignment of the organizational culture
	6) Insight into cultural matches or mismatches before completing a merger or acquisition
Case Studies:	http://www.kenexa.com/survey/proven-results
Costs:	Varies with marketed consultation packages.

Note: All data was supplied through marketing resources and may include biased product descriptions specifically designed for these purposes, especially Benefits as these characteristics appear subjective.

Table 5.4.1

Motivator and Hygiene Classification Descriptors

Property (Annotation)	Description
Motivators	
$\uparrow F \rightarrow \uparrow JS$	Increasing the factor leads to increasing job satisfaction.
$\downarrow F \rightarrow \downarrow JS$	Decreasing the factor leads to decreasing job satisfaction
$+ F_e \rightarrow \uparrow JS$	Addition or existence of the factor leads to increased job satisfaction.
$-F_e \rightarrow \downarrow JS$	Removal or non-existence of the factor leads to decreased job satisfaction.
$-S$	The factor is not situational (context) dependent.
Hygienes	
$\uparrow F \rightarrow \downarrow JD$	Increasing the factor leads to decreasing job dissatisfaction.
OR	OR
$\downarrow F \rightarrow \downarrow JD$	Decreasing the factor leads to decreased job dissatisfaction.
AND	AND
$+ F_e \rightarrow \downarrow JD$	Addition or existence of the factor leads to decreased job dissatisfaction.
OR	OR
$-F_e \rightarrow \downarrow JD$	Removal or non-existence of the factor leads to decreased job dissatisfaction.
$+S$	The factor is situational (context) dependent.
Disqualifiers	
$\Delta F \rightarrow \downarrow JS$ AND $\downarrow JD$	Changes in the factor lead to decreased job satisfaction and job dissatisfaction simultaneously.
OR	OR
$\Delta F \rightarrow \uparrow JS$ AND $\uparrow JD$	Changes in the factor lead to increased job satisfaction and job dissatisfaction simultaneously.
$\uparrow JD \neq H$	Any factor that increases job dissatisfaction is not a hygiene.

Figure 1. Herzberg's Two-Factor Theory: Model for Categorization

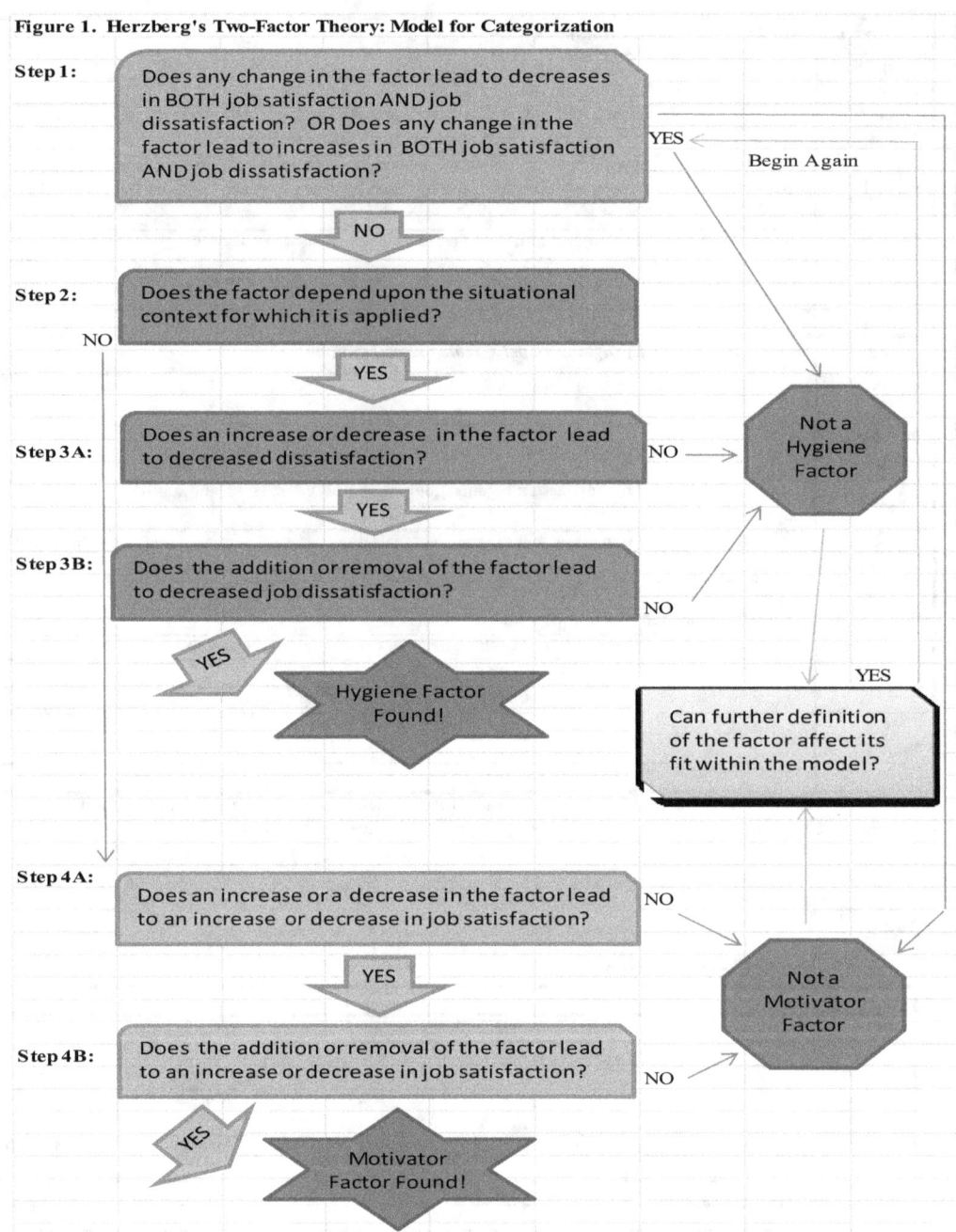

Figure 5.4.1. The model for classifying factors into Herzberg's Two-Factor Theory provides a tool to ease confusion and misclassification of Motivators, Hygienes, or determining if a factor needs further clarification for fit. Step 1 eliminates obvious paradoxes of satisfaction and dissatisfaction. Step two leads into the primary difference between motivators and hygiene factors; the situational or contextual aspect of the factor. Step 3 analyzes for qualification of hygiene factors while Step 4 identifies motivators. In accordance with the theoretical process, failures return to redefinition and application of the model.

PART FIVE REFERENCES

Altunas, S., & Baykal, U. (2009). Relationship Between Nurses' Organizational Trust Levels and Their Organizational Citizenship Behaviors. Journal of Nursing Scholarship, 42(2), 186-194. doi:10.1111/j.1547-5069.2010.01347.x.

Artz, B. (2008). The Role of Firm Size and Performance Pay in Determining Employee Job Satisfaction Brief: Firm Size, Performance Pay, and Job Satisfaction. Labour, 22(2), 315-343.

Authenticity Consulting, LLC. (2012). Nonprofit Organizational Assessment. Retrieved from Survey Monkey: http://www.surveymonkey.com/s.asp?u=3754722401.

AvoLead LLC. (2012). The Denison Organizational Culture Survey® Assessment Consultants. Retrieved from AvoLead Abundance Evolution Leadership: http://www.avolead.com/assessment-tools/denison-culture-survey.

Bockman, V. M. (1971). The Herzberg Controversy. Personnel Psychology, 24, 155-189.

Bovee, C. L., Thill, J. B., & Mescon, M. H. (2007). Excellence in Business (3rd ed.). Upper Saddle River, NJ: Pearson Prentice Hall.

Cerit, Y. (2010). The Effects of Servant Leadership on Teachers' Organizational Commitment in Primary Schools in Turkey. International Journal of Leadership in Education, 13(3), 301-317. doi:10.1080/13603124.2010.496933.

Coon, D., & Mitterer, J. O. (2010). Introduction to Psychology (12th ed.). Belmont, CA: Wadsworth.

Davey, K. M. (2008). Women's Account of Organizational Politics as a Gendering Process. Gender, Work and Organization, 15(6), 650-671. doi:10.1111/j.1468-0432.2008.00420.x.

Denison Consulting. (2012a). Denison Advantage Overview. Retrieved from Denison: http://www.denisonconsulting.com/home.aspx.

Denison Consulting. (2012b). Denison case studies. Retrieved from Denison: http://www.denisonconsulting.com/resources/CaseStudies.aspx.

Discovery Learning. (2012). Denison Organizational Culture Survey Project Management. Retrieved from DocStoc Documents & Resources for Small Businesses and Professionals: http://www.docstoc.com/docs/42793735/Denison-Organizational-Culture-Survey%C2%AE-Project-Management.

DMA Synergetics Management Consultancy. (2012). Culture & Motivation. Retrieved from DMA Synergetics Management: http://www.dmasynergetics.com/hrm/assessment/motivation/index.htm.

Dougherty, A. M. (2009). Psychological Consultation and Collaboration in School and Community Settings (5th ed.). Belmont, CA: Brooks/Cole.

Dunbar, R. L., & Starbuck, W. H. (2006). Learning to Design Organizations and Learning from Designing Them. Organization Science, 17(2), 171-178. doi:10.1287/orsc.1060.0181.

Foulkrod, K. H., Field, C., & Brown, C. V. (2010). Trauma Surgeon Personality and Job Satisfaction: Results from a National Survey. The American Surgeon, 4, 422-427.

Friedman, M. (1970, September 13). The Social Responsibility of Business is to Increase its Profits. New York Times Magazine, pp. 32-33, 122-124, 126. Retrieved October 1, 2010, from University of Colorado at Boulder: http://www.colorado.edu/studentgroups/libertarians/issues/friedman-soc-resp-business.html.

Fugazzotto, S. J. (2009). Mission Statements, Physical Space, and Strategy in Higher Education. Innovations in Higher Education, 34, 285-298. doi:10.1007/s10755-009-9118-z.

Gardner, G. (1977). Is There a Valid Test of Herzberg's Two-Factor Theory? Journal of Occupational Psychology, 50, 197-204.

Green, C., & Haywood, J. S. (2008). Does performance pay increase job satisfaction? Economica, 75, 710-728. doi:10.1111/j.1468-0335.2007.00649.x.

Griffin, B. (2010). Multilevel Relationships Between Organization-Level Incivility, Justice and Intent to Stay. Work and Stress, 24(4), 309-323. doi:10.1080/02678373.2010.531186.

Hambrick, D. C. (2005). Just How Bad Are Our Theories? A Response to Goshal. Academy of Management Learning and Education, 4(1), 105.

Hamidi, Y., & Eivazi, Z. (2010). The Relationships Among Employees' Job Stress, Job Satisfaction, and the Organizational Performance of Hamadan Urban Health Centers. Social Behavior and Personality, 38(7), 963-968. doi:10.2224/sbp.2010.38.7.963.

Heneman III, H. G., & Judge, T. A. (2009). Staffing Organizations (6th ed.). Boston, MA: McGraw-Hill/Irwin.

Hirsch, P. M., & DeSourcey, M. (2006). Organizational Restructuring and Its Consequences: Rhetorical and Structural. Annual Review of Sociology, 171-189.

Hornung, S. (2010). Alienation matters: Validity and Utility of Etzioni's Theory of Commitment in Explaining Prosocial Organizational Behavior. Social Behavior and Personality, 38(8), 1081-1096. doi:10.2224/sbp.2010.38.8.1081.

Human Synergistics International. (2012a). Organizational Culture Inventory. Retrieved from human synergistics international: http://www.humansyn.com/Solutions/TransformingOrganizations/OrganizationalCultureInventory.aspx.

Human Synergistics International. (2012b). Research and Publications. Retrieved from human synergistics international: http://www.humansyn.com/ResearchandPublications/Publications.aspx.

Human Synersitics International. (2012c). Organizational Culture Inventory Report. Retrieved from Human Synergistics International: http://www.hscanada.com/Organizational%20culture%20assessments.pdf.

Ife, J. (1995). Community Development: Creating Community Alternatives - Vision, Analysis and Practice. Melbourne: Longman.

James, C., & Connolly, M. (2009). An Analysis of the Relationship Between the Organizational Culture and the Performance of Staff Work Groups in Schools and the Development of an Explanatory Model. International Journal of Leadership Education, 12(4), 389-407. doi:10.1080/13603120902980804.

Jung, T., Scott, T., Davies, H. T., Bower, P., Whalley, D., McNally, R., & Mannion, R. (2009). Instruments for the Exploration of Organizational Culture: A Review of the Literature. Public Administration Review, 69(6), 1087-1096. doi:10.1111/j.1540-6210.2009.02066.x.

Kaiser, R. B., & Overfield, D. V. (2010). The Leadership Value Chain. The Psychologist-Manager Journal, 13, 164-183. doi:10.1080/10887156.2010.500261.

Kenexa. (2012a). Employment Branding: Cultural Insight Survey. Retrieved from Kenexa: http://www.kenexa.com/employment-branding/cultural-insight-survey.

Kenexa. (2012b). Surveys: Global 100 Banking and Financial Services Company Employee Survey Case Study. Retrieved from Kenexa: http://www.kenexa.com/survey/proven-results.

King, B. G., Felin, T., & Whetten, D. A. (2010). Finding the Organization in Organizational Theory: A Meta-Theory of the Organization as a Social Actor. Organization Science, 21(1), 290-305. doi:10.1287/orsc.1090.0443.

Krajewski, L., Ritzman, L., & Malhotra, M. (2007). Operations Management: Processes and Value Chains (8th ed.). Upper Saddle River, NJ: Pearson Education, Inc.

Law Business Research Ltd. (2012, March). Research Trends and Conclusions: Mergers & Acquisitions 2012. Retrieved from Who's Who Legal: http://www.whoswholegal.com/news/analysis/article/29549/research-trends-conclusions-mergers-38-acquisitions-2012/.

Lin, C.-Y., & Ho, Y.-H. (2010). The Influences of Environmental Uncertainty on Corporate Green Behavior: An Empirical Study with Small and Medium-Size Enterprises. Social Behavior and Personality, 38(5), 691-696. doi:10.2224/sbp.2010.38.5.691.

Liu, B., Liu, J., & Hu, J. (2010). Person-Organization Fit, Job Satisfaction, and Turnover Intention: An Empirical Study in the Chinese Public Sector. Social Behavior and Personality, 38(5), 615-626. doi:10.2224/sbp.2010.38.5.615.

Luthans, F. (2008). Organizational Behavior (11th ed.). Boston, MA: McGraw-Hill/Irwin.

Macionis, J. J. (2010). Sociology (13th ed.). Boston, MA: Prentice Hall.

Macneil, A. J., Prater, D. L., & Busch, S. (2009). The Effects of School Culture and Climate on Student Achievement. International Journal of Leadership in Education, 12(1), 73-84. doi:10.1080/13603120701576241.

Martin, A. (2009). Motivation and Engagement in the Workplace: Examining a Multidimensional Framework and Instrument from a Measurement and Evaluation Perspective. Measurement and Evaluation in Counseling and Development, 41, 223-243.

McMullen, R. C., Shippen, M. E., & Dangel, H. L. (unk). Middle School Teachers' Expectations of Organizational Behaviors of Students with Learning Disabilities. Journal of Instructional Psychology, 34(2), 75-80.

Merton, P., Froyd, J. E., Clark, M. C., & Richardson, J. (2009). A Case Study of Relationships Between Organizational Culture and Curricular Change in Engineering Education. Innovations in Higher Education, 34, 219-233. doi:10.1007/s10755-009-9114-3.

Muchinsky, P. M. (2006). Psychology Applied to Work (8th ed.). Belmont, CA: Thomson Wadsworth.

National Business Research Institute, Inc. (2012). Organizational Assessment Surveys: Employee Survey White Papers. Retrieved from NBRI: http://www.nbrii.com/products/employee-surveys/organizational-assessment-surveys/.

Oswick, C., Fleming, P., & Hanlon, G. (2011). From Borrowing to Blending: Rethinking the Processes of Organizational Theory Building. Academy of Management Review, 36(2), 318-337.

Papalia, D. E., Olds, S. W., & Feldman, R. D. (2009). Human Development (11th ed.). Boston, MA: McGraw-Hill.

Peacock, D. (2008). Weaving the Web into Organizational Life: Organizational Change and the World Wide Web in Cultural Heritage Organizations. The Journal of Arts Management, Law, and Society, 38(1), 89-95.

Pearson Learning Solutions. (2010). SKS7000 - Executive Concepts in Business Strategy. Boston, MA: Pearson Learning Solutions.

Platsidou, M., & Agaliotis, I. (2008). Burnout, Job Satisfaction, and Instructional Assignment-Related Sources of Stress in Greek Special Education Teachers. International Journal of Disability, Development and Education, 55(1), 61-76. doi:10.1080/10349120701654613.

Pugh, S. D., Groth, M., & Hennig-Thurau, T. (2011). Willing and Able to Fake Emotions: A Closer Examination of the Link Between Emotional Dissonance and Employee Well-Being. Journal of Applied Psychology, 96(2), 377-390. doi:10.1037/a0021395.

Radermacher, H., Sonn, C., Keys, C., & Duckett, P. (2010). Disability and Participation: It's About Us but Still Without Us! Journal of Community and Applied Social Psychology, 20, 333-346. doi:10.1002/casp.1039.

Robinson, A. (2012, March 19). UPS – TNT Express Merger – Real Gains for UPS Come in Asia. Retrieved from Courier Express and Postal Observer: Industry News and Commentary: http://cepobserver.com/2012/03/ups-tnt-express-merger-real-gains-for-ups-come-in-asia/.

Roby, D. E. (2010). Teacher Leaders Impacting School Culture. Education, 131(4), 782-790.

Ruben, B. D., & Stewart, L. P. (2006). Communication and Human Behavior (5th ed.). Boston, MA: Pearson Education.

Russo, M. V., & Harrison, N. S. (2005). Organizational Design and Environmental Performance: Clues from the Electronics Industry. Academy of Management Journal, 48(4), 582-593.

Sackman, S. A. (2007). Assessment, Evaluation, Improvement: Success Through Corporate Culture (2nd ed.). (B. Stiftung, Ed.) Gütersloh, Germany: Verlag Bertelsmann Stiftung.

Sanders, E. J., & Cooke, R. A. (2005, June 6). Financial Returns from Organizational Culture Improvement: Translating Soft Changes into Hard Dollars. Retrieved from Human Synergistics Belgium: http://www.humsyn.be/Financial%20Returns%20from%20Culture.pdf.

Schaeffer, R. T. (2010). Sociology (12th ed.). New York, NY: McGraw-Hill.

SHL Limited. (2012). Who We Are. Retrieved from shl: http://www.shl.com/uk/company/who-we-are/.

Smerek, R. E., & Peterson, M. (2007). Examining Herzberg's Theory: Improving Job Satisfaction Among Non-Academic Employees at a University. Research in Higher Education, 48(2), 229-250. doi:10.1007/s11162-006-9042-3.

Sutton, R. I., & Straw, B. M. (1995). What Theory Is Not. Administrative Science Quarterly, 40, 378.

Tarris, T. W., & Schreurs, P. J. (2009). Well-Being and Organizational Performance: An Organizational-Level Test of the Happy-Productive Worker Hypothesis. Work & Stress, 23(2), 120-136. doi:10.1080/02678370903072555.

Titrek, O. (2009). Employees' Organizational Justice Perceptions in Turkish Schools. Social Behavior and Personality, 37(5), 605-620. doi:10.2224/sbp.2009.37.5.605.

United States Office of Personnel Management. (2012). Information About OPM'S Organizational Assessment Survey. Retrieved from The Center for Talent Services: http://cts.opm.gov/pdf/OAS%20Description.pdf.

Wal-Mart Stores, Inc. (2012). Our Purpose. Retrieved from Walmart Corporate: http://walmartstores.com/AboutUs/9538.aspx.

Wright, T. A., & Cropanzano, R. (2000). Psychological Well-Being and Job Satisfaction as Predictors of Job Performance. Journal of Occupational Health Psychology, 5(1), 84-94.

Yang, H., Miao, D., Sun, Y., Liu, X., & Wu, S. (2008). The Influence of a Pay Increase on Job Satisfaction: A Study with the Chinese Army. Social Behavior and Personality, 36(10), 1333-1340.

* * *

PART SIX:
ADVANCED TOPICS IN ORGANIZATIONAL DEVELOPMENT

6.1 CULTURAL AND GLOBAL INFLUENCE

McDonald's Corporation (McDonald's) survives as the oldest and largest fast food restaurant chain in the world. Understanding the organization's structure enables further inquiry into the cultural impacts imposed on a global scale using diverse regional manifestations. Although very few studies exist in the literature concerning the massive enterprise, an understanding of its organizational structure enables clarification of longevity, breadth, and impact upon its environment.

ORGANIZATIONAL DESIGN AND STRUCTURE

The way employees and managers make decisions, communicate, and accomplish tasks is predisposed by the organizational structure. The framework influences achievement of organizational goals by distributing responsibilities and accountability to reduce waste, confusion, and frustration for stakeholders. Maintenance of company-wide authority at the top levels enables the organization to control and systematize marketing and focus upon immediate goals. The decentralized nature of McDonald's flattened hierarchal leadership structure (Brewer, 2008) allows the organization to move decision-making authority down to lower organizational echelons. Increased controls at the store level helps to account for global growth, giving McDonald's presence in 119 countries (McDonald's Corporation (a), 2012) across 33,000 restaurants with 80% of the spread through franchise opportunities.

The diversified global presence creates problems with marketing McDonald's limited product offerings. Departmentalizing the corporate structure geographically recognizes cultural differences in the customer base, ultimately promoting brand recognition through tailored menus, advertising expectations, and exploration of localized customs. For instance, McDonald's signature Big Mac sandwich in India contains no beef, using a vegetable-based product instead that is spiced heavily to localized tastes; whereas in Japan, chicken-based products dominate the menu. Hong Kong stores sport 24-hour delivery service in accordance with customary practices of the region.

Larco (2009) documented how organizations desiring to succeed in foreign countries must compromise with the dominant host culture, expecting forms of accommodation from it rather than complete assimilation of the foreign concepts. Wal-Mart experienced first-hand failure in Germany by refusing to adapt organizational practices (Gielens, et. al, 2008).

Functionally, McDonald's touts its organizational structure as a team-focused operation, although its "crews" do not meet any definitional organization of a recognized team format. Perhaps functionally cross-training individuals to perform most jobs needed in the restaurant may intend motivational perspectives in meeting organizational goals of standardization, speed, quality, and conformity, as well as enable promotion-from-within.

Just as in most corporate structures, the top management echelon of McDonald's divides into functional departments, e.g. Legal and Supply Chain. The difference succumbs to further departmentalization with store assignment under continental geographic managers (Asia, Europe, Australia, etc.) before sectioning by country of presence. The United States region divides into Central Division, East Division, and West Division before aligning strategically into smaller regions. This system enhances the benefits of decentralization discussed earlier.

McDonald's lacks many of the expected structural components generally accepted today as requisite for survival. None of the organizational websites (e.g., U.S., Japan, India, Hong Kong, and Australia) provides access or information for current employees as stakeholders. Virtualization gears toward customers and investor information (U.S. only) with similar social network branding on Facebook, Twitter, YouTube, and Flickr. Organizational Systems Theory explains this procrastination of changes within one or more parts of a complex system implies changes for the others (McCann, 2004). Fluctuations with employment laws provide added difficulties, especially at regional levels, in development and maintenance of personalized information on a large scale. When cultural and traditional factors reason in, the complexities endure exponentiation. The question of effectiveness arises against adaptation since the organizational parts of the system reside in a constant state of change.

MARKET INFLUENCES

Organizations, including McDonald's, suffer susceptibility to market and social influences in a causal relationship (King et. al., 2010). The restaurant giant was forced (just in the United States alone) to change product packaging in response to the green movement, to change product labeling in response to legal threats ("Contents Are HOT"), and to alter product composition and offerings over dietary concerns within the last couple of decades. Reviewing product photographs and nutritional reports on the Hong Kong, Japanese, Indian, and Australian corporate websites reveals spillover of these concepts into the foreign markets with low-fat, high-nutrition foods, especially those marketed to children. These lessons reinforced the principle that globalized organizations need to focus upon intermediate outcomes and target superior financial performance only as a long-term measure of success (Hult et. al., 2007). In this context, organizational structure mediates the relationship between strategy and performance.

SOCIAL INFLUENCES AS AN ACTOR

One of the characteristics of an organization is the ability to endure beyond the lifespan of its owners (shareholders). So far, McDonald's has surpassed its founders, the McDonald brothers, and subsequent purchaser Ray Kroc, who died in 1984. Ray Kroc finds credit as the developer of standardized business processes across multiple business locations (Macionis, 2010). The bureaucratic formula found adoption within other industries (e.g. Ford and Wal-Mart), eventually leeching into governmental and other societal processes, giving rise to the McDonaldization of Society.

As previously mentioned, McDonald's changed not only the way it packages its products, but also the requirements throughout the industry due to legal ramifications (Jennings, 2006). Changes initiated by McDonald's as a social actor on its legal, industrial, and societal environments exemplifies globally in the way the world conducts business through standardized practices and hence its own organizational structure.

DIVERSITY WITHIN THE ORGANIZATIONAL STRUCTURE

When discussing McDonald's as a global figure, consideration in matters of diversity draws attention. McDonald's self-reports that 70% of American employees reside in feminine and minority statuses (exact composition not reported). In contrast, only 25% (globally) hold managerial positions, but 45% of franchise ownership belongs to women and minorities (McDonald's Corporation (b), 2012). In the U.S., these numbers could potentially indicate instances of disparate discrimination in violation of the 80% rule (Heneman III & Judge, 2009) in relation to employees and managerial position holdings, but the units of measurement differ in scale (U.S. versus global) and accurate inference cannot be assumed.

In 2009, McDonald's initiated an organization-wide program to relieve issues of disparate impact that "supports the recruitment, development, and advancement of women at all levels of the company while creating [an organizational] culture where women have the opportunity to succeed and grow" (McDonald's Corporation (c), 2012). In 2011, the program earned McDonald's the Catalyst Award in recognition as an innovative and systemic means through which women can thrive. By facilitating organizational structure changes through diversity initiatives, McDonald's continues to exert social change as an organizational actor.

CONCLUSIONS

Organizations manage rapid change through agility and disruptive change by means of resiliency (McCann, 2004). McDonald's demonstrated it can handle both situations through the structure of its organization and continues this focus through self-initiative and global expansion efforts. The four dimensions of resiliency identified by McCann help to explain how McDonald's persists as a global leader, not only within the fast food industry, but also as a model organization for other organizational structures. These dimensions summarize the topics mentioned in this paper and include:

1) Absorbing shocks and surprises;
2) Creatively exploring alternatives;
3) Broadly assessing resources; and
4) Executing transformational change.

The organizational structure of McDonalds, through mutual inclusion, enabled reciprocal development and persistence of the organization's goals and existence.

* * *

6.2 ORGANIZATIONAL DEVELOPMENT THEORIES

This paper sets out for understanding of how to motivate students to pursue common goals of mastering course materials for application in their lives and careers. Achievement theory attempts explanation through identification of learning goals that inspire critical thinking, collaboration, and communication extending beyond the classroom by encouraging mastery as an organizational norm at all levels of the curricular spectrum. Discussion begins with identification of base theoretical concepts involved with motivation, performance and mastery goal relationships, and an applicable demonstration. Enhancement through affiliation with studies of closure, internal and external motivation, and political motivation further encompass the relationship of achievement theory beyond academic realms into other organizational applications.

ACHIEVEMENT THEORY

Achievement theory seeks to understand and explain motivation of students in educational settings. Originally, researchers sought to determine the better conditions between mastery and performance goals in terms of student motivation, however evolution of perspectives led focus upon approach and avoidance goals as well as plausible combinations for effectiveness (Senko et. al., 2011). Focusing upon the original theoretical basis, Table 6.2.1, *Motivation and Goals in Achievement Theory*, summarizes current findings between motivation and goal setting using performance and mastery goals when set by students, instructors, and both working together.

While achievement goals may find generalized definition as the purposes individuals describe for task engagement, the differing impacts of the person's pursuit of achievement varies the structure and processing of the relevant information (Harlow et.al., 2011). Mastery goals indicate an individual's view toward developing new skills, retention of an understanding of their work, improving levels of personal competence, or finalizing their sense of mastery based upon self-imposed standards. With performance goals, those individuals try to obtain favorable judgments (within themselves or from others) or to avoid negative judgments of their competence.

Students who pursued mastery goals when beginning courses demonstrated increases in motivation throughout courses, whereas students endeavoring toward performance goals had tendencies with spurious motivation, ignoring task focus, problems with collaborative learning, and higher incidences of cheating. Rather than ask questions or practice in the direction of mastering concepts, these students would "do what it takes" to get through the task or take avoidance steps from probability of failure (Senko et.al., 2011).

In contrast, when instructors set either performance or mastery goals in the classroom for their students, mixed results predominated. Performance-oriented goals demonstrated increased motivation levels when set by the instructor rather than the students, although lower academic performers demonstrated higher failure rates. For mastery goals, success of student attainment depended upon the instructor's ability to compensate for differing abilities of the students. Those learners with whom the instructor could adapt their teaching style showed higher levels of motivation toward mastering necessary skills, otherwise motivation levels decreased among struggling students.

Groups of instructors and students who collaborated performance goals displayed higher levels of motivation throughout the courses than either group (students/instructors) leading goal obtainment individually. Unfortunately, unlike combinations that sought mastery goals, motivation among performance goal students did not exceed beyond the classroom. The indication here is when students and instructors work together at mastery goal attainment, motivation endures beyond the coursework and spills over into the student's lives – an indication of true learning (learning equals a change in behavior) (Papalia, Olds, & Feldman, 2009).

RELATIONSHIP TO ORGANIZATIONS

In 2009, Macneil, Prater, and Busch reported their study exploring the question if organizational culture made a difference between "Acceptable" and "Exemplary" rated schools by means of student achievement. These researchers concluded that *Exemplary* schools outperformed *Acceptable* schools in nine of ten dimensions (Goal Focus, Communication, Power Equalization, Resource Utilization, Cohesiveness, Morale, Innovativeness, Adaptation, and Problem Solving) by 20% to 50%. As expected in smaller classrooms at community colleges, the dimension of *Autonomy* dominated at the smaller education institutions. Note the initial nine dimensions share as qualities found in students commonly expected to utilize critical thinking behaviors in their academic work as well as meeting characteristics known for skill mastery (depending upon the required skill, of course).

Typically, academic institutions known for mastery of academics (Harvard University, Stanford University, Massachusetts Institute of Technology (MIT), etc.) enjoy reputations as exemplary schools with private fortune and government organizations actively seeking their graduates. Motivation, combined with goal-achievement strategy skillsets, demonstrates how these personal assets translate to cultural influences, and in turn, rely upon the organizational structure at micro and macro levels.

TESTING ACADEMIC THEORY – AN APPLICATION

During the spring 2012 academic semester at a community college, an instructor (yours truly) designed courses to test the applications of performance and mastery goal settings in relation to motivation and subsequent enrollment in advanced courses. Psychology 101 students were not encouraged by the instructor to employ mastery of the concepts, but left to decide performance or mastery goal approaches on their own. Common replies to instructor inquisitions consisted of "I don't know" answers and failure to engage in meaningful dialog, even with cueing. Midterm and final examinations for the course consisted of filling in copies of worksheets of which the instructor provided answer keys to each student immediately after initial due dates. The majority of students, 56%, failed the exams with scores ranging between 22% and 64%. Only the two "A" students in the course subsequently enrolled for Psychology 109 with that instructor the next semester.

The second course, Psychology 109, consisted of the instructor engaging students one-on-one with dialogic and comprehensive discussions of the course material, incorporation of a variety of media that demonstrated material application to the real world, and a partnership atmosphere between the students and instructor toward mastery goals. Examinations and homework consisted of essay-type questions graded using a "critical thinking" rubric. All except two students achieved an "A" for the course with 75% subsequently enrolling in a Microbiology course the following semester facilitated by that same instructor.

This simplified experiment demonstrated the concepts tabulated in Table 6.2.1 by showing partnered goal setting between instructors and students increased learning motivation within the students and spilling over into other academic disciplines. Meanwhile, performance goals established by students alone lacked the same degree of motivation and failed to carryover past the course, except by the higher achievers.

For other organizations, these results essentially translate to active engagement across levels of the structural hierarchy (with mastery goal orientations) may result in higher levels of motivation and achievement, affecting the overall organizational culture.

EXTENDING ACADEMIC THEORY

Closure includes the desire for a firm answer to a question, the removal of ambiguity, and the extent to which people desire knowledge about the world in which they live in; in terms that are clear and unlikely to change (Harlow, DeBacker, & Crowson, 2011). The need for closure may cause persons to accept the first plausible response (immediacy) or to freeze upon or safeguard past knowledge. Since closure positively correlates with shallow processing, students not engaged with mastery goal formations report difficulty in coursework required for foundational expertise in their programs of study. In fact, these students generate fewer hypotheses or perspectives when asked to solve practical problems.

Internal motivation relates to an interior value of that individual to work, of itself, whereas external motivation represents an outward value based upon personal values and expectations not related to the work (Liu & Fang, 2010). The willingness to share information correlates to a person's practice of sharing that information, but only slightly (exact statistics unavailable). Seniority and position within the organizational hierarchy exhibit no direct influence upon sharing behaviors, but do associate with levels of communication and mutual interaction. These behaviors help to explain the differences between motivation levels in relation to goal-processing type.

Studies into power and political relationships generally reside within sociological studies, however, these studies contribute to academic theory, especially when sharing knowledge or training other professionals. When members of individual professions feel they need to protect their sense of identity, they may endure interference with their abilities to learn in a collaborative manner (Baker et.al., 2011). In turn, the organization suffers and divisions remain intact concerning power structures. For example, if a physician feels that he/she is a leader and therapists may only serve subordinately, then that physician may withhold interactive teaching experiences with therapists, thus retaining their leadership status. Conversely, the same therapists who share information with nurses may describe a collaborative team orientation for that relationship. Instructors who maintain the former philosophy may be more likely to refrain from mastery goal relationships with their students, preferring instead that students assume full responsibility for their learning.

CONCLUSIONS

Regardless of the goal approach utilized, instructors and professionals who share information with colleagues engage in application of academic theory. Although not comprehensive due to its infancy, academic theory helps with explanation of motivational understanding in relation to goal setting initiatives, as well as providing guidance for application. Theoretical extensions enable development into the realm of organizational culture and structural integrity by addressing when a perspective may or may not work and alternative approaches.

Even when differing studies emerge, leaders find empowerment for refinement of current paradigms for relieving barriers to achievement in potential exploration of solutions concerning motivation. Centralized organizations can use academic theory as a tool toward decentering managerial hierarchies and empowering subordinates to fill expectancy gaps. With trends in globalization, collaborative relationships may find strength when cultural barriers preclude information sharing and teamwork requirements.

* * *

6.3 GLOBALIZATION AND ORGANIZATIONAL STRUCTURE

This paper engages educational market opportunities within a global perspective. Community colleges within the United States traditionally offered vocational training matching community demands and cost-effective pre-baccalaureate programs aimed to boost students in reaching higher educational aspirations. However, globalization influences arising in the 21st century changed how communities and the businesses that support these neighborhoods function operationally and competitively in hopes of sustainment, let alone growth. Reason stands that community colleges cannot remain immune to globalization, either through academics geared toward filling positions within transformed international producers, or competitively as actors within the education industry.

Analysis into reasoning of globalization-focused change via risk assessment precedes recommendation to move the Illinois Eastern Community Colleges (IECC) district forward in the current global competitive environment.

ORGANISATION FOR ECONOMIC CO-OPERATION AND DEVELOPMENT (OECD)

OECD promotes policies intended to improve the economic and social well-being of people around the world as its primary mission (Organisation for Economic Co-operation and Development (OECD), 2012). The organization measures productivity and global flows of trade and investment, analyzes and compares data to predict future trends, and sets international standards. Additionally, OECD looks at issues directly affecting the lives of ordinary people, such as comparing how different countries' school systems are readying their young people for modern life.

The half-century old global organization takes initiative in the latter by comprising annual statistical data allowing direct comparisons of global educational investments in relation to studied countries throughout the world, and publishes these findings in an annual report, *Education at a Glance [year]: OECD Indicators*. As of this writing, the 2011 report was available for citation and reveals the following judgments:

1. Just over 40% of Americans finish some level of college education – ranking number 16 per capita internationally. Korea (unified), Canada, Japan, and Russia, respectively, lead the world in educational completion rates among 25-64 year old's.
2. At the current rates, France, Japan, Ireland, and Korea are expected to grow in proportion to per capita educational attainments at the college level, while Austria, Brazil, and Germany are anticipated to fall further behind in the rankings. The United States can expect little to no growth if the current trend continues.
3. By the end of 2009, the United States held the highest market share of international students attending its colleges and universities (26%), slipping drastically to an 18.3% global market share two years later.
4. More females (25% more) graduated college than males in Iceland, Poland, and the Slovak Republic. Germany, Mexico, and Switzerland experienced no gender gap during 2011, while Japan and Turkey graduated mostly males. The United States primarily demonstrated gender proportions similar to Poland.
5. The United States ranked second world-wide for the number of Associate degrees awarded (34%) in comparison to types of degrees offered, behind Turkey. In all, Associate degrees comprised 7% of all diplomas awarded from only 10 countries (Turkey, United States, Korea, Ireland, Denmark, Norway, Iceland, Sweden, France, and the United Kingdom).

The OECD findings clearly demonstrated market share availability for American community colleges on a global scale. Over one-third of Associate degrees awarded originate in the United States, capturing more than one in twenty of all academic degrees granted in the world. In combination with IECC's endeavor to elevate academic standards, the opportunity to grasp the gaps created by the downslide in global academic market shares among American schools increases IECC's probability of sustainable growth.

ORGANIZATIONAL RESTRUCTURING

Currently, only one of IECC's four campuses provides incentives for international student enrollment, namely Wabash Valley College (WVC). Although Olney Central College (OCC) also provides student housing, only WVC offers dedicated ESL facilities for students who do not speak English fluently. Both campuses offer athletic programs, however, community involvement and support are minimal at best. Unfortunately, the other two campuses, Frontier Community College (FCC) and Lincoln Trail College (LTC), lack resources needed to accommodate foreign students seeking two-year programs. It appears obvious then that some organizational restructuring precludes attempts by IECC to capture available global market shares in the academic industry.

"Redesigning an organization to take advantage of today's sources of wealth creation isn't easy, but there can be no better use of [an administrator's] time" (Bryan & Joyce, 2007, para. 1). Gaining competitive advantage through strategic (long-term) planning by incorporating organizational design into the central strategy most often goes overlooked by organizational leaders. Bryan and Joyce's analogy summarizes the holistic perspective necessary for globalized modernization and capitalization returns; "Executives may not be able to control the weather {market outcomes}, but they can design a ship {organization} and equip it … [to] navigate the ocean {industry} under all-weather {market} conditions". By expanding and nurturing the ability to host international students throughout its multi-campus structure, IECC can competitively gain globalized market share as a competitive advantage. IECC international student costs of attendance (books, tuition, medical insurance, housing, etc.) already compare with Canada's lowest priced universities accommodating foreign students, the number two academic leader of the world.

VOCATIONAL VERSUS ACADEMIC FOCUS

As previously noted in the 2011 OECD report, Austria and Germany are expected to fall further behind in the global academic ratings. Trampusch (2010) discovered that when vocational programs in these countries were politically tied to the size of influential organizations, the types of transformative change affecting the collegiate institution varied in scope. For example, the interests of large firms became more important to academic outcomes at German universities as these firms collaborated program redesigns of the skill system (vocational programs), in alignment with personalized corporate needs. In response, German legislation altered two-year vocational training programs at all German universities to meet minimal standards that fail to end in vocational certifications for graduates; requiring instead that alumni complete apprenticeships beyond academic basics asserted (as is common within the particular industry).

The lesson for IECC administrators applies two-fold. First, when designing vocational or academic programs, tailoring these products to specific corporate influences can prove detrimental to the overall academic system, unless those influences generalize to the particular industry as a whole. Secondly, accepting excessive corporate influence upon design of vocational or academic programs may cannibalize attempts by IECC to expand globalization efforts of the college district. Economies need a continuous increase of skills and knowledge base in order to integrate into the global production process (Vos, 2010). Preparing workers for future job markets involves strengthening skill development and active labor market policies, beginning with the training institution.

COMPETITIVE MOVEMENT

Administrators of one private university elected to pursue globalization by increasing reputation through the hiring of prestigious professors and changing course program offerings in response to student market inquisitions abroad (Stromquist, 2007). The twist was local expectations and those of the poorest regions of the world were ignored. In other words, the university chose wealthier foreign markets in a globalized perspective over localized traditions. As a result, the institution endured high rates of turnover, unpredictable curriculum offerings, and unstable sources of investor income.

The case study reaffirms that stakeholders should be included as integral parts of the organizational culture to avoid unforeseen negative impacts when pursuing strategic goals. In the end, bringing together organizational design and development requires advocating a culturally sensitive approach to organizational structuring (Bate, Khan, & Pye, 2000), whether the intent remains localized, or pursues globalized expansion.

CONCLUSIONS

Recommendation goes to the development of IECC's International Student Program with emphasis on:

1) enhancing international recruiting efforts;
2) facility development across all district campuses; and
3) curricular refinement that allows globalized application of academic and vocational offerings from perspectives of
   a) domestic students working international positions,
   b) foreign students returning abroad, and
   c) foreign and domestic students collaborating internationally.

Declines in American market shares within the globalized community, in conjunction with an overall acceleration of foreign universities as academic leaders, provides rare opportunity for IECC to turn the negative trends into competitive advantages. By transforming IECC's organizational design through globalized development, the college district can emerge as a world leader within its established primary academic markets.

* * *

6.4 TEAMING AND BUSINESS SITUATIONS

This paper sets out to develop an organizational team model purposed to assist localized and multinational organizations in the formation and implementation of effective teams. Discussion begins with differentiation of teams from workgroups and leads into analysis of four basic team types. Advantages and disadvantages for adoptive consideration of team implementations preclude inherent issues with characteristic member affiliation to help round the organizational influences comprising the developed model.

TEAMING PURPOSE VERSUS TYPE

Throughout the process of narrowing down the type of team model desired, managers must assess:

1) the purpose and goals of the team's existence;
2) the autonomous scope of the team's decisions and actions (reliance upon management);
3) communication and other resources allocated to the team;
4) the advantages/disadvantages of using teams within the organization; and
5) compositional characteristics of individual team members for optimum success (Russell & Jacobs, 2008).

The following subsections analyze each of these criteria for advice, production, project, and action teams. However, first noting the managerial influences distinguishing workgroups from self-managed and virtual teams provides understanding the second criterion, regardless of the team type.

By definition, unless the group of individuals (as a unit) meets the following benchmarks, that group is merely a workgroup and not a team (Katzenbach & Smith, 1993):

1) Shared leadership roles – any hierarchal structure of authority, such as having a clearly focused leader, indicates a managerially controlled workgroup.

2) Individual and mutual accountability – a lack of accountability as a group indicates nonexistence of cohesiveness of membership or shared responsibility.

3) Collective work products – reliance on the sum of each individual's work rather than a joint effort indicates the presence of traditional work flows.

4) Performance measured by assessing collective work – when performance is measured by influence of outside influences, such as organizational financial ratios, the indication is that team performance is not assessed.

5) Discusses, decides, and performs work together – workgroups may discuss tasks and make decisions (same as managerial meeting task), but they delegate work to others rather than perform in a collective manner toward task goals.

In the manager-led workgroup, administrators control the group's activities, responsibilities, structure, staffing, and task procedures. Semi-autonomous workgroups are sometimes granted control of some of these aspects, but not all. Conversely, self-managed teams may control their own work schedules, allocation of responsibilities among team members, determine and implement their own training needs, do their own budgeting, and inspect their own work, among others (unlimited). Self-managed teams find empowerment through increased ownership of their processes, from planning and coordinating the job to self-governance and hiring of members (Russell & Jacobs, 2008). In essence, these teams are authoritative divisions of the organization.

Advice Teams

Advice teams, commonly referred to as quality circles, committees, advisory councils, and employee involvement groups, exist temporarily for the purposes of enhancing managerial decisions through information. Generally, members need only low levels of technical specialization and, therefore, collaboration entails equalized coordination efforts. Rarely are advice teams empowered as self-managed due to their scope of purpose and longevity. Most often team members are appointed in interest of and by the creating organization with semi-autonomous controls. For example, government agencies often create committees and advisory councils temporarily to address a particular set of questions and private companies utilize quality circles to quickly generate new ideas (Bovee, Thill, & Mescon, 2007) aimed at innovation.

Production Teams

Production teams serve purposes in assembly systems, manufacturing, mining, and aircraft crews and find responsibility for completing day-to-day operations. In simpler applications, production teams often do not require extensive technical skills for specialization, but they do depend upon communication and collaboration between themselves and other work units in repeated continuity (Russell & Jacobs, 2008). Aircraft crews collaborate continuously on successful flights with ground crews as well as between themselves, although stewards and baggage handlers require little specialization to accomplish their tasks in relation to pilots or air traffic controllers.

Project Teams

When highly specialized skillsets and coordination efforts find need through problem solving and specialized expertise, project teams temporarily form to create solutions. Project engineers, task forces, and research groups demonstrate the concept of project teams, especially in cross-functional roles (Russell & Jacobs, 2008) that differ for each new project. Planning and building a span bridge across a wide body of water requires architects and engineers with specific skills to collaborate extensively using work cycles, unlike those utilized with previous projects. Project teams are most often entrusted with self-management through accountability for their actions/inactions.

Action Teams

Action teams provide similarity to project and production teams with the exceptions that work cycles tend to be brief, repeatable, and require extensive training (Russell & Jacobs, 2008). Most action teams necessitate highly technical specialization and collaboration like that found within surgical teams, military squads, and sports teams. These teams operate in a semi-autonomous manner. For example, although a military squad may retain decisiveness for the completion of its mission, commanders retain control for planning and other operational parameters aimed at the context of the mission.

Virtual Teams

Virtual team composition ranges from members across floors of an office building who collaborate via email, telephone, and whiteboard applications to international teams whose members network through technological means. For effectiveness, virtual teams need to preplan collaborations with little or no informal interaction (Russell & Jacobs, 2008) in contrast to regular face-to-face communication offered by conventional teams. Virtual collaboration often dictates that teams endure less time, more pressures, and tighter work schedules. Although these teams can be implemented as advice, production, or action teams, most often project teams fair better virtually due to their flexibility and ease for changing structurally in response to customer demands.

ADVANTAGES AND DISADVANTAGES OF USING TEAMS

Work teams enable organizations to better meet competitive goals than individual workers do. Members tend to display flexibility, self-discipline, and a wider array of skills in exchange for senses of empowerment, commitment, and increased job satisfaction (Sheng, Tian, & Chen, 2010). Other advantages include increased productivity and work quality; greater focus on task problems; reduced costs, turnover, and absenteeism; improved creativity and innovation; and fewer incidences of conflict.

Of course, these benefits only surface when the team concept is implemented properly. The size of the team depends upon the goals or tasks under consideration by the organization. Groups that become too large find themselves susceptible to poor communication, social loafing, indecisiveness, hierarchies, and groupthink (Russell & Jacobs, 2008). Although no specific formula exists to determine team size, research showed membership between five and eleven persons, with an odd-numbered enrollment, usually provided the greatest effectiveness.

MEMBER CHARACTERISTICS

Creating effective teams obviously indicates staffing these groups with people who possess qualities in the proportions expected within their membership role. Persons living in western societies typically demonstrate individualistic orientations, whereas eastern cultures traditionally enjoy collectivist personalities. The indication here suggests that collectivist-oriented persons adjust to team concepts easier than westernized individuals do (Gauthier, Pettifor, & Ferrero, 2010).

Weighting needed characteristics to the work role assists with placement of potential team members. For instance, ideally a person's ability to learn determines value to the team if that person is suitable for multiskilling and job rotation, while high attention to detail demonstrates potential to contribute a focus on continuous improvement (Wellins, Byham, & Wilson, 1991). Additional personal characteristics to weight include a candidate's abilities to analyze information, to communicate orally, to influence others, to solve problems, to tolerate stress, to organize work tasks, to demonstrate initiative, to operationalize work standards and proficiency, and overall compatibility for working with others.

TEAMING MODEL

Figure 6.1 (Appendix) depicts the overall model useful for firstly, determining the need to utilize team concepts; secondly, building an appropriate team formation, and then following through implementation. Team creation when/where workgroups should be utilized can doom the effectiveness of the implementation, so the first step proposes the initial test of need. Once the decision enters appropriateness, Step 2 begins the process of determining which type of team should be utilized. Comparing factors into purpose, duration, skill requirements, empowerment levels, and membership control assists leaders with decisions concerning advice, production, project, or action team creation that meets organizational goals. Virtual teams are purposely excluded from this model, as these groups are merely extensions of the other team types with dependency upon available resources and communication alternatives.

Step 3 involves determining the characteristics of individual members within the selected team. Exact descriptions for each member of every type of team lies outside the scope of this discussion and requires careful planning and research upon the parts of those persons responsible for team assembly. Likewise, the last step entails designing measurable outcomes for obtaining feedback to administrators and team members concerning effective operations. As previously stated, these measures need to provide meaningful information directly related to team processes rather than overall organizational performance.

CONCLUSIONS

The developed organizational team model summarizes the processes managers need to create and implement team structures within their organizations. Regardless if the teams remain localized or cross international borders, this basic tool serves as a practical guide in reaching organizational goals beyond those attainable via workgroups. Organizations that span global existence benefit from team orientations, when implemented properly, usually in a virtual extension of transformed advice in the form of production, project, or action teams.

Improbability reigns in the development of a team model oriented toward activating prepackaged team schemas (one size fits all), since not only are organizations unique, but also are the goals and implementations driving demand for efficiency. The overall advantages of successful team formation orientations far outweigh the disadvantages, especially in light of ongoing research initiatives helping organizations to transform their negatives into positive assets.

* * *

6.5 JOB DESIGN

This paper discusses job design in relationship to competencies and the knowledge, skills, abilities, and other factors requisite of employees when designing an effective job design process. Demonstration of key principles through the analysis of an existing program at a community college district provides basis for evaluation of this relationship in a real-world scenario. The importance of collaboration in the design process distinctly shows the levels of effective outcomes toward organizational goals.

KSAOS

Workforce quality, or human capital, is defined as the knowledge, skills, abilities, and other characteristics (KSAOs) of people and their motivation to use them successfully on the job (Heneman III & Judge, 2009) in pursuit of organizational goals (Bryan & Joyce, 2007). KSAOs entail the job requirements, or basic qualifications, needed by personnel to perform the job effectively and span the recruiting, deployment, and retention phases of the employment cycle. The relationship between these qualifications and organizational goals serve foundationally with issues concerning recruitment, evaluation, and retention of employees at the staffing level, and qualitatively at the organizational level among other stakeholders (e.g. customers). For example, if customers view the employee's work performance abilities within a negative perspective of expectations, this quality (pun intended) eventually carries over into the customer's perception of the overall organization.

Knowledge includes the conceptual, factual, and procedural information that apply directly to performance tasks and tends to focus toward the job, occupation within the career field, and the organization. *Skills* relate to measurable competence in performance of particular tasks, relying upon experience, as observed by others. *Abilities* change less over time and prove useful in transfer to other tasks as fundamental traits of the person. Factors important to the success of the organization that fail to fit the other three categories lump into *Other Characteristics*. Respective KSAOs for a college instructor may include a degree in the subjects taught, use of technological equipment related to the coursework, keeping course syllabi updated, and having values consistent with the academic culture. Each component relates to the employee's ability to effectively perform the job and concurrently fulfill the goals of the organization.

MEASURABLE CHARACTERISTICS

Within the job design process, measurable characteristics influence successful implementation and management of program cohesiveness. This paper focuses only upon collegiate instructors as a general category of jobs within the organization owing to differences of specialties, however, core competencies shared between instructor specialties deserves attention. With this distinction made, development of KSAOs is refined when employing measurement techniques deriving from core competencies of all instructors as well as specialty considerations (Patterson, Ferguson, & Thomas, 2008).

During pre-employment initiatives, knowledge is generally measured when the applicant accomplishes minimum verifiable factors; such as holding a master's or doctorate degree (for the organizational level) within their field of expertise (for the job specialty level) and obtainment of pre-determined scores on knowledge assessments. These assessments may be written or orally administered during a structured interview process (Kirkwood & Ralston, 1999) and add value for selecting individuals who meet person-job and person-organization fit (Heneman III & Judge, 2009). After employment, completion of additional training measures the individual's knowledge and potential for retention initiatives.

Skill measurement entails evaluation of experience and implies depth of application of knowledge. How long a person worked in a particular field, how often they repeated a task, and the spectrum of work experiences during an employee's career assess characteristics that set apart persons with equivalent knowledge qualifications. For instance, a new graduate from a master's program probably would not understand problem possibilities, argots (language of the field), diversity in solution approaches, and human communication skills that a person with equivalent education would have after working for five years (Ritti & Levy, 2007).

Cognitive, psychomotor, physical, and sensory abilities most commonly find room for measurement in organizations to meet qualifications of fitness of the person to the job and institution. Measurements in quantitative, speed, endurance, and speech clarity abilities respectively carry varying weights (Heneman III & Judge, 2009), among dozens of others, for each job classified. As previously defined, these factors typically remain constant for an individual; however, they can incline/decline with training and time. This relationship implies abilities are positively correlated with knowledge and experience and therefore indicative of value to the organization. Pencil and paper, computerized, and observational tests measure applicable abilities prior to employment and periodically post hoc (e.g. annual military MOS testing). One ability qualification within American universities is verbal proficiency in the English language. An instructor who cannot communicate effectively with the predominant student body detracts value from organizational goals and customer expectations (Jennings, 2006).

The final category may include legal, availability, and character requirements. These factors do not question whether the person physically can or cannot perform the job duties directly, but indirectly serve as minimums to protect organizational and stakeholder interests. For example, an instructor without transportation likely may prove undependable. As such, many of these factors measure in a have/have not qualification status with little grey area for negotiation.

KSAO INTEGRATION WITH COMPETENCIES

Competencies contribute to job performance and organizational success as contributing characteristics of the individual (Heneman III & Judge, 2009). As with any KSAO requirement, competencies are specific to a particular job, but usually generalize to multiple jobs (e.g. technical expertise or adaptability). The primary benefit of using competencies over KSAOs is flexibility across job categories, a characteristic needed for successful team implementations where members perform multiple roles. For the organization, adopting competency-based requirements allows alignment of all jobs with the mission and goals (e.g. customer focus). However, measurement of competencies can prove difficult (Patterson, Ferguson, & Thomas, 2008; Daniels & de Jonge, 2010).

Dorenbosch, van Engan, and Verhagen (2005) demonstrated that employees who undertook a multifunctional perspective (.221, P < .01) were significantly more likely to take ownership in their organizational operations (.417, p < .01) than employees who worked in redundant occupations (.050, p < .05). This research helps to explain why competencies, which allow an organization-wide (multifunctional) integration of workers, provides greater flexibility and success for organizations that do not rely upon KSAOs alone in job designs. Therefore, the position organizations should integrate KSAOs and competencies into their job designs, rather than just one model or the other, seems appropriate if those organizations desire greater success levels with members who take ownership in their jobs. When the organizational mission integrates into the job design, jobs take focus toward common goals.

APPLICATION OF JOB DESIGN PRINCIPLES

Figure 6.3 (Appendix) depicts the current job description for a full-time instructor at Illinois Eastern Community Colleges (IECC). It is important to note that adjunct faculty teaches approximately 80% of courses and no job description exists for this position at IECC. Additionally, no similarity exists for any two job descriptions organization-wide. For these reasons, emphasis in this examination relies upon analysis of the full-time instructor position.

The short mission statement of IECC states, "The mission of Illinois Eastern Community Colleges District 529 is to provide excellence in teaching, learning, public service, and economic development." (Illinois Eastern Community Colleges, 2012). Under the *Job Duties* heading of the job description in Figure 6.3, the phrase, "Design and effectively use learning systems" indicates the competency derived from the mission statement. All instructors, regardless of field, should have this shared competency in meeting the institutional goals of "providing excellence in teaching, learning..." Subtopics (a through i) proceed with providing measurable KSAOs deemed necessary for an instructor to possess in order to fulfill this competency. For example, subtopic b ("Knowledge essential to the subject being taught") is a knowledge factor measured by documentation (transcripts) on file for the instructor. Likewise, subtopic f meets the definition of a skill, subtopic d is an ability, and subtopic a does not neatly fit into one of the other three categories. From this point on within the job description, job duties seemingly intermix competencies and KSAOs with the intentions of using full-time instructors as cross-functional employees in administrative and clerical roles.

Aside from needing revision of the *Job Duties* for full-time instructors, the job description completely ignores minimum qualifications required of all instructors. This section remains blank but easily may endure compilation from the listed job duties. Although it is unclear who prepared the job analysis, the Director of Human Resources and the district CEO signed the document. Did these persons perform the job analysis or did they collaborate with instructors and supervisors (appropriate Deans)? The entire process requires careful organization and coordination with the people involved (Heneman III & Judge, 2009). Overall, job design at IECC appears drastically incomplete and in need of further development.

CONCLUSIONS

Job design within an organization is a complex process involving the goals of the institution, the people within it, and measurable outcomes. Whether jobs are individually focused or team-focused, the organization benefits most when jobs are designed collaboratively toward a unified end result. Although research has shown competency-based models outperform those models restricting themselves to KSAOs, competency models still require the KSAOs as "how-to" instructions for effective implementations of goal achievement. The analysis of IECC's job design outcomes demonstrates the importance of collaboration, integration, and application of competency/KSAO fundamentals when designing jobs. With considerably more work, IECC could reasonably develop an integrated approach toward meeting organizational goals through its job design process.

* * *

6.6 ETZIONI AND ORGANIZATIONAL DESIGN

This paper evaluates Etzioni's three approaches to power and the influences these have upon the organization's development. Using an organizational chart from a community college district, an attempt to validate the chart as an organizational design and development tool through Etzioni's approaches seeks merit. Discussion begins through dialogue of his approaches, continues with application of these principles to the organizational chart, and then proceeds with discussion of Etzioni's underlying inferences affecting the application results. Before concluding, related issues of power and commitment through compliance aid in the understanding of how developments, since Etzioni conducted his studies, affect the overall supposition.

ETZIONI'S APPROACHES TO POWER AND COMPLIANCE

In 1964, Etzioni published *Modern Organizations*, a book in which he concluded organizational leadership existed in three types, namely normative, coercive, and remunerative (utilitarian) (Etzioni, 1964). Application of each of these power types, respectively, depended upon the nature of the organizational membership class whether moral, alienated, or calculative. "Moral membership" essentially means members view the overall organization positively, whereas at the other extreme, 'alienated membership' dictates group members not only hold negative perceptions of the organization, but also may take hostile actions (e.g. employee theft, sabotage, work slowdowns, etc.). Somewhere in the middle, persons associated with 'calculative membership" tend to weigh benefits against limitations and strike a balance.

Based upon membership classification, Etzioni argued that application of the appropriate power level by leadership leads to congruent uses of power within the organization. Coercive power uses force to intimidate members into doing something, such as when dictators like Suddam Hussein, ordered the deaths of residents who opposed his regime, or when police officers make arrests for law violations.

Utilitarian power, such as seen within traditional organizations in association with employees or marketing to customers, provides incentives in hopes organizational members comply with the power initiative. Modern infomercials apply this tactic with offers in terms of "Buy our product and we will send you not one, but two at the same low price... and as an additional bonus you get these other trinkets, too." The power in this case relates to manipulation of customer purchase decisions as well as market shares for their products.

Normative power receives the most research attention as it can have not only positive effects, but also detrimental negative consequences because normative power uses peer pressure to influence members. In other words, normative power exploits member mindsets through expectations to act according to the overall wishes of the group. Although individuals remain free to make their own decisions, in team situations groupthink and social loafing may occur (Russell & Jacobs, 2008).

Obviously, no single organization totally relies upon any particular power structure for every organizational problem, or even routine operational activities. In fact, although one form may dominate in leadership terms, all three draw dependency from the situation at hand and the desired outcomes. In the previous infomercial example, utilitarian structures deal with customer mindsets while employees endure coercive techniques to remain employed ("Show up and do your work our way or lose your job."). Concurrently, these same employees may partake in brainstorming sessions where they develop new marketing ideas.

Review of the organizational chart provided in Figure 6.2 (Appendix) reveals how a flattened organization encompasses each of Etzioni's power structures. Note that although four campuses exist in District 529, only Frontier Community College is provided for redundancy elimination. At the top of each portion, the CEO leads the flattened structure with dozens of deans, directors, and other key personnel reporting directly to him, implying normative structures exist where each director is expected to perform a particular organizational process (finance, campus operation, etc.). Each subordinate then supervises one or more employees empowered in support of that role. The largest group of employees, the faculty, facilitates no subordinates and reports directly to the Dean of Instruction, an implication of power equality with other department (process) heads. Unfortunately, the organizational chart fails to demonstrate coercive political implications throughout the administrative chain and remunerative tactics employed in aid of compliance with utilitarian power. At the faculty level, matters of seniority and skill level also fail to materialize within the organizational chart. Essentially, organizational charts depict levels of authority, not power (Kocev, 2002).

POWER AND COMMITMENT

Etzioni defined his power structures as a synthesis of systems that organizations adopt to secure member compliance. The focal interest sought by Etzioni was the manner in which people within organizations conform to organizational requirements and follow the standards of behavior expected. Today's goal-oriented, performance directed organizations require the compliance of members in reaching those goals, however, the problem occurs when deviance from these standards results from weaknesses in member commitment.

Commitment studies reveal a multifactorial nature. Studies have shown conclusively closure (Baker et.al., 2011), deviance from tradition, alienation, lack of knowledge (competency), lack of advancement opportunities (goal stagnation), and many other intrinsic factors affect organizational member commitment. It makes sense then, under Etzioni's correlation, that when these factors falter commitment, declines and power structures meet difficulties.

STRATEGIES WITHIN ORGANIZATIONAL DESIGN

Bryan and Joyce (2007) wrote that "meaningful change [to organizational design] usually involves difficult personality issues and corporate politics" (para. 2). Again, resistance to change alters commitment, which limits power of leadership. Learned during the Vietnam War, the military now trains soldiers in the psychological phenomena that humans typically follow the path of least resistance, so when in a foreign combat zone, they should avoid this temptation by treading only where the local people move about ("When in Rome..."). The Viet Kong were aware of this aspect of human nature and placed land mines where enemy soldiers might take a shortcut. Likewise, CEOs within organizations generally choose easy structural modifications over longer-termed options (Bryan & Joyce, 2007). This way resistance, corporate politics, and effort required remain minimal rather than necessarily better for the strategic goals of the organization.

The organizational chart for District 529 (Figure 6.2, Appendix) depicts an additional benefit – an observer can view the distribution of major core competencies throughout the organization needed to accomplish intermediate processes. For example, most high-level positions require an administrative assistant (secretary) to liaison the administrator's duties within the organizational structure. The position of the assistant implies proficiency level. Financial administrators perform different functions than recruiting, but require core competencies in finance, reporting, and interpersonal skills. Although specific competencies reside outside the scope of the organizational chart, the major distribution becomes evident. This can be especially important for similar organizations seeking changes to their organizational structure.

CONCLUSIONS

Recommendation for using the organizational chart as an indicator of power structures lies largely unwarranted. At best, the chart provides a glimpse into the vastness of power struggles within the organizational structure and the diversity of core competencies needed to understand organizational processes. After writing his book, Etzioni changed career focus without emphasis on power structures, relying more on issues of morality and human rights. Although his conclusions serve as a basis for studies into power, the topic leads to leadership developments deemed at resolving efficiency issues. Organizational charts therefore, indicate chains of authority with the political emphasis and should not endure reliance as an organizational design tool. Instead, these charts work best as maps for authoritative flows within the organization.

* * *

6.7 VALUE OF INNOVATION

This paper looks at innovation and the effects it has on organizations at the micro and macro levels. Specifically, 3M and Apple, Inc. are examined using both approaches to innovation with respect to how the organizations developed. Additionally, factors affecting innovation approaches, including centralization of power, resource availability, social networking, and culture are examined in accordance with their influences on innovation. Finally, distinctions and implications between micro-innovation and macro-innovation are applied to the Apple methodologies of organizational development.

3M AND INNOVATION

3M operates internationally within 65 countries as a multi-billion dollar organization supporting 84,000 employees (3M, 2012). The company targets six specialty areas, including healthcare, graphics, communications, security, transportation, and business products with stress upon shared technologies that increase speed and efficiency. The primary organizational development system adopted by 3M revolves around these flexibilities, concentrating on innovation as a core value. Marketing efforts attempt reflection through correlation of "Innovation" with the organizational name (e.g., "3M Innovation" or "3M, now that's Innovation").

Consumer and industrial products endure constant change through composition as well as usage. Leadership recognizes this transformative focus while describing the organization:

"3M is a global innovation company that never stops inventing. Over the years, our innovations have improved daily life for hundreds of millions of people all over the world. We have made driving at night easier, made buildings safer, and made consumer electronics lighter, less energy-intensive and less harmful to the environment. We even helped put a man on the moon. Every day at 3M, one idea always leads to the next, igniting momentum to make progress possible around the world." (3M, 2012).

Codotte (2008) taught in his management courses at the University of Tennessee that continual innovation "will be necessary to keep the product in the forefront of the end-user's mind" (p 121). He was referring to the product life cycle and how products that stagnate tend to be replaced by cheaper knock-offs as they begin to become similar to these other brands. By maintaining a zone of indifference through continual innovation, products and services can maintain exceptional performance and indefinite lifespans. This concept, of course, must be ingrained into the organizational system for maximum effectiveness, as exemplified by 3M.

INNOVATING APPLE

In the early years of Apple, Inc., the world knows the organization's focus was architectural competition against IBM's personal computer (PC) in hopes of capturing dominant market share as a computing standard. Although not completely unsuccessful, the company eventually lost dominance to the rival standard due to incompatibility and ease-of-use issues, especially among operating systems, software, pricing, and extensibility categories within consumer markets. In essence, Apple's products just did not play well with others and incurred higher costs.

Apple administrators realized *sustainability* was an acute term and the organization needed ways to create demands for its products using innovative techniques that incorporated existing standards. Computing architectures were adapted to utilize operating systems and software compatible with competing markets, such as Microsoft's Windows operating system in place of the proprietary OSX. The result was really not innovative, but it did provide sustainment long enough to develop new product lines that proved successful. Between 2003 and 2007, Apple introduced the iPod, the tablet PC, and the iTunes music service, catapulting revenues from one billion to over 150 billion dollars annually (Chen & Chen, 2009) during the four-year span. These products introduced the world to realities of science fiction (tablet PC), assisted the ailing music industry with methods of increasing revenues through royalties and sales (iTunes), and provided consumers with a way to increase accessibility to their musical products (iPod).

Apple learned the only way for a company to gain and maintain competitive advantage is to upgrade facilities and activities constantly in the name of innovation (Drew, 1997). Like 3M, this meant adapting these ideas for incorporation by more than one market, namely industry, as well as consumer markets. This phenomenon can find explanation in the principle that customer-oriented companies can use innovation to design more customer value, but they cannot easily create competitive technical products (Chen & Chen, 2009) without the assistance of complement organizations.

FACTORS AFFECTING INNOVATION

Academics generally agree that centralized organizations actually impede innovation, while decentralized and informal organizations encourage flexibility and creation of new ideas. Subordinates that work in participatory environments demonstrate higher levels of motivation and involvement with decision-making, awareness, and commitment (Khan & Manopichetwattana, 1989). Companies often realize increased innovativeness when the hierarchal structures flatten to enable information transfer within the company and thus a freer exchange of ideas (Chen & Chen, 2009) occurs with the decreased internal resistance.

Resource availability and allocation enhance innovation and commercial successes, especially at globalized echelons. Social networking technologies not only permitted faster exchanges of ideas, but also collaborative and cooperative coordination of activities within the organization. Although smaller organizations endure prohibitions with lacks in resources, the prominence of these technologies allow increased opportunities for growth and quality enhancement with equal footings to responses for changing organizational demands. In effect, social networking provided organizations of all sizes to better interact inter-organizationally and externally with immediate customer demands. Both 3M and Apple utilize social networking technologies within their organizational processes.

Studies into cultural influences support the notion that social networking, even non-electronic, enhances the organization's ability to capitalize and succeed (Ibata-Arens, 2008). The region of Kyoto, Japan is infamous for successful start-ups in proportion to the socioeconomic status of its residents. Ibata-Arens found that bonds created through personal relationships allowed organizations to flourish with mere pocket money in lieu of the westernized tradition of seeking outside capital.

MICRO AND MACRO INNOVATION

Macro-inventions serve as radical new ideas (van der Veen, 2010) while micro-inventions enhance existing products or services. In either case, these inventions (or more appropriately, steps of innovation) affect not only the product or service intended, but also the management practices of the acquiring organization. In a similar sense, *micro-innovation* encompasses only a particular segment of an organization, such as a product line or internal process, whereas *macro-innovation* embodies the affects and development systems of the whole organization. This distinction implies micro-innovations can occur sporadically and without intentions while macro-innovation cannot occur without direct effort of the organizational members in a planned fashion. For example, as noted earlier Apple changed its computer architecture to handle competitor software in response to customer demands; a micro-innovation due to unintended causes and lack of company-wide change. However, when Apple changed its organizational practices to accommodate new market approaches, macro-innovation occurred as a result of deliberate and planned organization-wide execution. Merely changing the product lines would not have been innovative, just adaptive.

CONCLUSIONS

Studies consistently demonstrate organizations which do not employ innovation at the organizational level self-destruct with an expiration date. Similarly, organizations that stagnate their products or services meet a similar demise in those business areas. Only by incorporating innovation as a core fundamental of organizational practices do indefinite life terms come to fruition. Innovate organizations tend to enjoy open communications with members who feel empowered by management and then deliver increased productivity through ideas in response.

Apple refused to abandon its computer market and chose to adapt it to competitor's standards. However, by refocusing the company to assist other industries, innovative ideas transformed Apple into a multi-billion dollar company almost overnight. On the other hand, 3M chose to embrace innovation at all levels of the organization and managed to create a synonymous relationship between its name and the concept. Akin to the lesson Apple learned, 3M realized early about the necessity of targeting outside industries for growth.

By understanding the factors that drive innovation, organizations can develop models that effectively produce growth and remove the stigma (threat) of sustainability. Macro-innovation, therefore, is a best practice for organizations desiring development systems that produce maximum effective goal attainment while exceeding competitive pressures.

* * *

6.8 ORGANIZATIONAL DEVELOPMENT CONCEPTS AND THEORIES

This paper embarks the task of examining the Illinois Eastern Community Colleges (IECC) district in terms of its organizational structure to determine best practices for developing the structure to meet the needs of its stakeholders by extending and compiling previous discussions. Students, faculty, and administrators of the district reside primarily within four campuses: Wabash Valley College (WVC), Frontier Community College (FCC), Olney Central College (OCC), and Lincoln Trail College (LTC). Although each campus maintains its own organizational structure from the President's position on down, each President reports directly to the district (IECC) Chief Executive Officer (CEO), who further oversees the district office. The CEO then reports to (and serves as the chair of) the Board of Trustees.

Analysis begins with description of the organizational structure with emphasis upon market, global, and outside influences that shape the current organization. Achievement theory analytics describe internal components of the stakeholders leading to discussion of issues with teaming and job design, before summing with implementation recommendations for IECC.

ORGANIZATIONAL DESIGN AND STRUCTURE

The structure of an organization influences ways employees and managers conclude decisions, communicate internally and externally, and accomplish tasks. Reducing waste, confusion, and frustration for stakeholders through distribution of responsibilities and accountability as organizational goals influences achievement throughout the framework. The organization controls and systematizes marketing through control and focus by top-level managers and maintenance of organization-wide authority structures.

Decentralized management structures, with their flattened hierarchies, most often succeed over traditional pyramidal arrangements due to the flexibility of moving decision-making authority down to lower echelons (Brewer, 2008). Campuses of IECC can attribute the operational diversity of their organizational structures and unique cultural experiences among faculty and students alike to the decentralized control given them by district management. No two campuses operate identically nor do they enjoy the same level of organizational success as measured by Full Time Equivalents (FTE), the customer base, and program (product) availability options. Examination of the organizational flow charts for the district office, versus that of the FCC campus (Figure 6.2; Appendix), reveals a 5:3 ratio in hierarchy levels. Where, at the campus level, three hierarchy levels exist. The district hierarchy is comprised of five levels in the structural system, indicating far fewer bureaucratic measures to task accomplishment at the campus. The only shared position between campuses and the district is the CEO, signifying that district departmentalization supersedes no direct authoritative control over individual campus operations. This further allows campuses to diversify from one another on similar issues, with CEO approval, of course.

With these points in mind, Organizational Theory miscarries explanation into how changes within one campus fails to imply changes for the other three, although the system appears complex (McCann, 2004). The WVC and OCC campuses continue to thrive while FCC and LTC face further cutbacks in operational spending. Despite efforts at facility improvements and radio and print advertising, FCC is facing a 22% reduction in student enrollment over the previous year for the 2012-2013 academic season (Boyles, 2012). Campus administrators calculate reasoning to economic downturns within the local economies in spite of constant hiring campaigns and growth reporting from the largest community employers: Fram Filtration, Airtex Corporation, and Elastec Marine.

MARKET INFLUENCES

Market and social influences create susceptibility for organizations as direct causal relationships (King, Felin, & Whetten, 2010). Where Organizational Theory fails these findings, when applied to campuses singularly, it explains the differential outcomes. Boyles, the Dean at FCC, noted that as the economy falters and businesses weaken, former workers return to school in hopes of upgrading or learning new skills to prepare themselves for other (and perhaps better) employment opportunities. The inverse observation predicts that when the economy suffers, enrollment strengthens, but should decline as community economic situations improve. Further research into this phenomenon require further study for confirmation as to whether community-based finances affect the academic industry as a whole and which factors involved could lessen the impact.

Because of the drastic enrollment decline previously mentioned, a few instructors at FCC have personally taken initiatives to develop marketing campaigns targeting their specific courses. If successful, these strategies not only assist with turnover prevention among those instructors, but also increase enrollment for the campus. The flattened organizational structure provides teachers with incentive and authority to undertake self-preservation initiatives that benefit the district and campus. Similar to global establishments, the principle that organizations should focus upon intermediate outcomes, while leaving financial performance a strategic measure of success (Hult et.al., 2007), delineates the relationship between strategy and performance as mediated by the organizational structure. As noted by McCann (2004), organizations manage rapid change through agility, and disruptive change by their resiliency, as demonstrated via district consolidation and personal advertising, respectively.

GLOBALIZATION INFLUENCES

According to the Organisation for Economic Co-operation and Development (OECD Publishing, 2011), only around 40% of Americans finish some sort of collegiate-sponsored program. The United States can expect little to no collegiate enrollment growth, although it maintains the highest proportion of international students. About 25% more females graduate college than males (more males complete graduate-level programs (Macionis, 2010) and 34% of the world's Associate degrees originate in the United States. For American markets, the OECD findings clearly demonstrated market share availability for community colleges on a global scale. Over one-third of Associate degrees awarded originate in the United States, which captures more than one in twenty of all global academic degrees granted. In combination with IECC's endeavor to elevate academic standards and to increase IECC's probability of sustainability, the opportunities exist to grasp the gaps created by the downslide in global academic market shares from among American schools.

Currently, only one of IECC's four campuses provides incentives for international student enrollment, namely Wabash Valley College. Although Olney Central College also provides student housing, only WVC offers dedicated English as a Second Language (ESL) facilities for students not fluent in the English language. Both campuses offer athletic programs, but community involvement and support are minimal at best (Cutchin, 2012) with OCC strongly considering abandoning its athletic program. Unfortunately, the other two campuses, Frontier Community College and Lincoln Trail College, lack resources needed to accommodate foreign students seeking two-year programs. Capturing available global market shares in the academic industry obviously involves some level of organizational restructuring by the IECC district.

Attaining competitive advantage through strategic (long-term) planning by incorporating organizational design into the central strategy most often goes overlooked by organizational leaders. Bryan and Joyce's analogy (Bryan & Joyce, 2007) and holistic perspective summarizes precursors for globalized modernization and capitalization returns; "Executives may not be able to control the weather {market outcomes}, but they can design a ship {organization} and equip it ... [to] navigate the ocean {industry} under all-weather {market} conditions". IECC can competitively gain globalized market share (as a competitive advantage) through expansion and nurturing the ability to host international students throughout its multi-campus structure. Costs for an international student's attendance (books, tuition, medical insurance, housing, etc.) compare globally with Canada's lowest priced universities that accommodate foreign students. During 2011, Canada was the number two academic leader of the world, according to the OECD report, so IECC international pricing remains competitive with global leaders.

COMMUNITY AND INDUSTRIAL INFLUENCES

Vocational programs, such as many of those offered through IECC campuses, vary in scope of transformative change when politically tied to the size of influential organizations. For example, as firms collaborated program redesigns of the vocational skill systems, in alignment with personalized corporate needs, interests of large firms became more important to academic outcomes at German universities (Trampusch, 2010). In support of this transformation, German legislation altered two-year vocational training programs at all German universities to meet minimal standards that fail to end in vocational certifications for graduates; requiring instead, students complete apprenticeships beyond academic basics asserted as common within the particular industry, before degrees were awarded. This legislative change helps to explain why the OECD predicted German universities will continue to decline as academic leaders in future years – fewer academics and more industry-led on-the-job training.

Administrators of IECC gain two lessons from the German model. The first applies when designing vocational or academic programs. Tailoring these products to specific corporate influences can prove to undermine the academics system unless those influences generalize to the particular industry as a whole. Secondly, the potential of cannibalization to globalization attempts occurs within the district if administrators accept excessive corporate influence within the design and implementation of vocational or academic programs. In other words, industrial inputs should be sought in terms of program outcomes, but the colleges should draw the line when it comes to program curriculum to avoid academic decline. Economies need continuous skill enhancements and knowledge base adaptations in order to integrate into the global production process (Vos, 2010). To accomplish these ends, preparation of workers for future job markets involves strengthening skill development and active labor market policies, beginning with the training institution.

ORGANIZATIONAL DEVELOPMENT THEORIES

Evolution of Achievement theory perspectives drew focus upon approach/avoidance goals and their plausible combinations to explain effectiveness among attempts for modifying the motivation of students in educational settings (Senko, Hulleman, & Harackiewicz, 2011). Originally, researchers sought to determine the better conditions between mastery and performance goals in terms of student motivation. Table 6.2.1, *Motivation and Goals in Achievement Theory*, focuses upon the original theoretical background by summarizing current findings between motivation and goal setting, using performance and mastery goals, when set by students, instructors, and both working together.

The generalized definition of achievement goals as *"the purposes individuals describe for task engagement"*, gives differing impacts of the person's pursuit of achievement and varies the structure and processing of the relevant information (Harlow, DeBacker, & Crowson, 2011). Mastery goals indicate an individual's view toward developing new skills, retention of an understanding of their work, improving levels of personal competence, or finalizing their sense of mastery based upon self-imposed standards. Performance goals, on the other hand, occur when those individuals try to obtain favorable judgments (within themselves or from others) or to avoid negative judgments of their competence.

Students who pursued mastery goals when beginning courses demonstrated increases in motivation throughout their courses, whereas students endeavoring toward performance goals leaned with tendencies toward spurious motivation and ignoring task focus, demonstrated problems with collaborative learning, and revealed higher incidences of cheating. These students would "do what it takes" to get through the task or take avoidance steps from probability of failure rather than ask questions or practice in the direction of mastering concepts (Senko, Hulleman, & Harackiewicz, 2011).

Mixed results predominated findings when instructors established either performance or mastery goals within the classroom for their students. Motivation levels increased when set by the instructor using performance-oriented goals on behalf of students, even though lower academic performers demonstrated higher failure rates. For mastery goals, success of student attainment depended upon the instructor's ability to compensate for differing abilities of the students. Motivation levels decreased among struggling students; however, those learners with whom the instructor could adapt their teaching style showed higher levels of motivation toward mastering necessary skills.

Collaborating performance goals between teachers and students showed a display in higher levels of motivation throughout the courses than either group (students/instructors) leading goal obtainment individually. Motivation among performance goal students did not exceed beyond the classroom, unlike combinations that sought mastery goals. The indication here is when students and instructors work together at mastery goal attainment, motivation endures beyond the coursework and spills over into the student's lives – an indication of true learning (*learning* equals a change in behavior (Papalia, Olds, & Feldman, 2009)).

ORGANIZATIONAL RELATIONSHIP WITH ACHIEVEMENT

In 2009, Macneil, Prater, and Busch reported their study exploring the question if organizational culture made a difference by means of student achievement between "Acceptable" and "Exemplary" rated schools. Conclusions indicated that *Exemplary* schools outperformed *Acceptable* schools in nine of ten dimensions by 20% to 50% (Goal Focus, Communication, Power Equalization, Resource Utilization, Cohesiveness, Morale, Innovativeness, Adaptation, and Problem Solving). Smaller classrooms within community colleges, as expected, dominated at the smaller education institutions for the final dimension of *Autonomy*. The initial nine dimensions share as qualities found in students commonly expected to utilize critical thinking behaviors in their academic work, as well as meeting characteristics known for skill mastery (depending upon the required skill, of course).

Academic institutions known for mastery of academics, such as Harvard University, Stanford University, Massachusetts Institute of Technology (MIT), etc., typically enjoy reputations as exemplary schools with private Fortune 500 companies and government organizations actively seeking their graduates. Motivation combined with skillsets of goal-achievement strategy demonstrate how these personal assets translate to cultural influences, and in turn rely upon the organizational structure at micro and macro levels.

FACTORS AFFECTING THEORY EXTENSION

In terms that are clear and unlikely to change, *closure* includes the internalized desire for a firm answer to a question, the removal of ambiguity, and the extent to which people desire knowledge about the world in which they live (Harlow, DeBacker, & Crowson, 2011). The need for closure may cause persons to accept the first plausible response (immediacy) or to freeze upon or safeguard past knowledge. Students not engaged with mastery goal formations report difficulty in coursework required for foundational expertise in their programs of study since closure positively correlates with shallow processing. These students generate fewer hypotheses or perspectives when asked to solve practical problems than students (and employees) who grasp mastery within goal formation.

Internal motivation relates to an interior value of that individual to work of itself whereas *external motivation* represents an outward value based upon personal values and expectations not related to the work (Liu & Fang, 2010). The willingness to share information correlates to a person's practice of sharing that information, but only slightly (exact statistics unavailable). Seniority and position within the organizational hierarchy associate with levels of communication and mutual interaction, but do not exhibit direct influence upon sharing behaviors. These behaviors help to explain the differences between motivation levels in relation to goal-processing type.

Studies into power and political relationships generally reside within sociological readings, however, these studies contribute to Academic theory, especially when sharing knowledge or training other professionals. Members of individual professions may endure interference with their abilities to learn in a collaborative manner (Baker et.al., 2011) when they feel they need to protect their sense of identity. Consequently, the organization suffers and divisions remain intact concerning power structures. For example, if a physician feels he/she is a leader and therapists may only serve subordinately, then that physician may withhold interactive teaching experiences with therapists, therefore retaining his/her leadership status. Conversely, the same therapists who share information with nurses may describe collaborative team orientations for that relationship. Instructors who maintain this withdrawn philosophy may be more likely to refrain from enhancing mastery goal relationships with their students, preferring instead that students assume full responsibility for their learning.

TEAMING AT STUDENT AND ORGANIZATIONAL LEVELS

By definition, unless the group of individuals (as a unit) meets the following five benchmarks, that group is merely a workgroup and not a team (Katzenbach & Smith, 1993):

1. Shared leadership roles – a managerially controlled workgroup is indicated by any hierarchal structure of authority, such as having a clearly focused leader.

2. Individual and mutual accountability – nonexistence of cohesiveness within membership or shared responsibility indicates a lack of accountability as a group.

3. Collective work products – the presence of traditional workflows is indicated by reliance on the sum of each individual's work rather than a joint effort.

4. Performance measured by assessing collective work – team performance assessment fails when performance is measured by influence of outside influences, such as organizational financial ratios.

5. Discusses, decides, and performs work together – workgroups may discuss tasks and make decisions (same as a managerial meeting task), but they delegate work to others rather than perform in a collective manner toward task goals.

Individual workers do not meet competitive goals as well as work teams within organizations. Members of teams tend to display flexibility, self-discipline, and a wider array of skills in exchange for senses of empowerment, commitment, and increased job satisfaction (Sheng, Tian, & Chen, 2010). Other advantages include increased productivity and work quality; greater focus on task problems; reduced costs, turnover, and absenteeism; improved creativity and innovation; and fewer incidences of conflict. Proper implementation of the team concept precedes the surfacing of these benefits. For instance, the size of the team depends upon the goals or tasks under consideration by the organization. Groups find themselves susceptible to poor communication, social loafing, indecisiveness, hierarchies, and groupthink (Russell & Jacobs, 2008) when membership becomes too large. Although no specific formula exists to determine team size, research showed membership between five and eleven persons, with an odd-numbered enrollment, usually provided the greatest effectiveness.

Physicians at Heartland Women's Clinic of Mount Vernon, Illinois refuse to hire nursing graduates of FCC, claiming these persons generally demonstrate poor teamwork skills, questionable attendance ethics, and low integrity issues (Covlin, 2012). Lifting of the hiring freeze entails successful integration of teaming skills, strict attendance guidelines, and critical thinking concepts as core components of the nursing curriculum to the satisfaction of employer expectations. Such a change requires that all associated instructors collaborate with one another, the employers, and the students to design these values into the standard curriculum and implement them. In essence, utilize teams to train teaming concepts and skills.

JOB DESIGN CONSIDERATIONS

Job design within an organization is a complex process involving the goals of the institution, the people within it, and measurable outcomes. Whether jobs are individually focused or team-focused, the organization benefits most when jobs are designed collaboratively toward a unified end result. Although research has shown competency-based models outperform those models restricting themselves to Knowledge, Skills, Ability, and Other characteristics (KSAOs), competency models still require the KSAOs as "how-to" instructions for effective implementations of goal achievement.

Formal analysis of IECC's job design outcomes demonstrates the importance of collaboration, integration, and application of competency/KSAO fundamentals when designing jobs. With considerably more work and an emphasis on collaboration, IECC could reasonably develop an integrated approach toward meeting organizational goals through its job design process. Implementation of teaming requirements into jobs designs insures graduate outcomes meet or exceed employer expectations, such as in the case of teaming, as previously described.

CONCLUSIONS

Recommendations for IECC and its respective campuses begin with the resiliency dimensions concluded by McCann to assist the organization with development of an effective model for other organizational structures:

1) Absorbing shocks and surprises;
2) Creatively exploring alternatives;
3) Broadly assessing resources; and
4) Executing transformational change.

The organizational structure enables reciprocal development and persistence of the organization's goals and existence.

Development of IECC's International Student Program with emphasis on

1) enhancing international recruiting efforts;
2) facility development across all district campuses; and
3) curricular refinement that allows globalized application of academic and vocational offerings from perspectives of
    a) domestic students working international positions,
    b) foreign students returning abroad, and
    c) foreign and domestic students collaborating internationally.

Declines in American market shares in the globalized community, in conjunction with an overall acceleration of foreign universities as academic leaders, provides rare opportunity for IECC to turn the negative trends into competitive advantages. By transforming IECC's organizational design through globalized development, the college district can emerge as a world leader within its established primary academic markets.

Regardless of the goal approach utilized, instructors and professionals who share information with colleagues engage in application of academic theory. Although not comprehensive due to its infancy, academic theory helps with explanation of motivational understanding in relation to goal setting initiatives, as well as providing guidance for application. Theoretical extensions enable development into the realm of organizational culture and structural integrity by addressing when a perspective may or may not work and alternative approaches. With trends in globalization, collaborative relationships may find strength when cultural barriers preclude information sharing and teamwork requirements.

Even organizations that remain localized benefit from inducing global orientations. When implemented properly, teams outperform individuals so long as critical guidelines are maintained. Improbability reigns in the development of a team model oriented toward activating prepackaged team schemas, since not only are organizations unique, but also the goals and implementations driving demand for efficiency. The overall advantages of successful team formation orientations far outweigh the disadvantages, especially in light of ongoing research initiatives helping organizations to transform their negatives into positive assets. Therefore, IECC should incorporate teaming concepts within its organizational structure to ensure success between students and future employers.

* * *

PART SIX APPENDIX

Table 6.2.1

Motivation and Goals in Achievement Theory

Aspect	Goal Setting	
	Performance	Mastery
Motivational Responsibility		
Student lead	Researchers agree that when students pursue performance goals that motivation increases, but some cite more problems than successes.	Researchers agree that when students pursue mastery goals that motivation increases and maintains throughout the course.
Instructor lead	Researchers agree that when instructors set performance goals for students that students achieve higher motivation levels; however, some cite troubles for low performers. Mixed results during and beyond the course for continued motivation occur.	Researchers agree that when instructors set mastery goals for students, the skills of the instructor determine student motivation levels. Some cite that training and experience of instructors determine overall success during and beyond the course.
Combination of leaders	Researchers agree that when students and instructors work together in setting performance goals, motivation levels excel over either done alone, however, the degree of continued success remains disagreed upon by many.	Researchers agree that when students and instructors work together in setting mastery goals that motivation levels survive beyond the classroom.

Note: Compiled from the following sources: Baker, Egan-Lee, Martimianakis, & Reeves, 2011; Harlow, DeBacker, & Crowson, 2011; and Senko, Hulleman, & Harackiewicz, 2011.

Figures 6.1 to 6.3

Organizational Team Model

Step 1: Determine Structural Requirements

<u>Workgroup or team?</u>

1. Shared leadership roles?

2. Individual and mutual accountability?

3. Collective work products?

4. Performance measured by assessing collective work?

5. Discusses, decides, and performs work together?

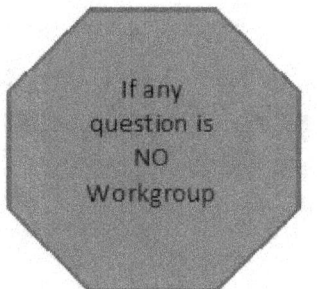

If any
question is
NO
Workgroup

If all questions are YES

Team: Proceed to Step 2

Continued next page…

Step 2: Determine Type of Team

Advice Team

Purpose:	Enhancement of managerial decisions through information.
Duration:	Temporary
Skills:	Low levels of technical specialization with equalized collaboration abilities.
Empowerment level:	Semiautonomous
Membership:	Appointed in interest of and by the creating organization.
Typical Usage:	Government agencies often create committees and advisory councils temporarily to address a particular set of questions and private companies utilize quality circles to quickly generate new ideas aimed at innovation.

Production Team

Purpose:	Responsibility for completing day-to-day operations.
Duration:	Permanent emphasis on adaptability.
Skills:	Do not require extensive technical skills for specialization but they do depend upon communication and collaboration between themselves and other work units in repeated continuity.
Empowerment level:	Semiautonomous
Membership:	Usually appointed by the creating organization, sometimes hired by team.
Typical Usage:	Serve purposes in assembly systems, manufacturing, mining, and aircraft crews.

Project Team

Purpose:	When highly specialized skillsets and coordination efforts find need through problem solving and specialized expertise.
Duration:	Temporary
Skills:	High technical specialization with enhanced collaboration abilities.
Empowerment level:	Autonomous
Membership:	Hired directly by the organized team..
Typical Usage:	Project engineers, task forces, and research groups.

Action Team

Purpose:	Similar to other types demanding brief and repeatable work cycles.
Duration:	Permanent with some flexibility.
Skills:	Highly technical specialization with extensive training.
Empowerment level:	Semiautonomous
Membership:	Appointed in interest of and by the creating organization, sometimes with team input.
Typical Usage:	Surgical teams, military squads, and sports teams.

Step 3: Establish Member Characteristics

Step 4: Review Measurable Feedback and Adapt as Necessary

Figure 6.1. The model depicts the process for effectively determining the organizational need for teams, how to decide upon a team format, and follow-through for implementation.

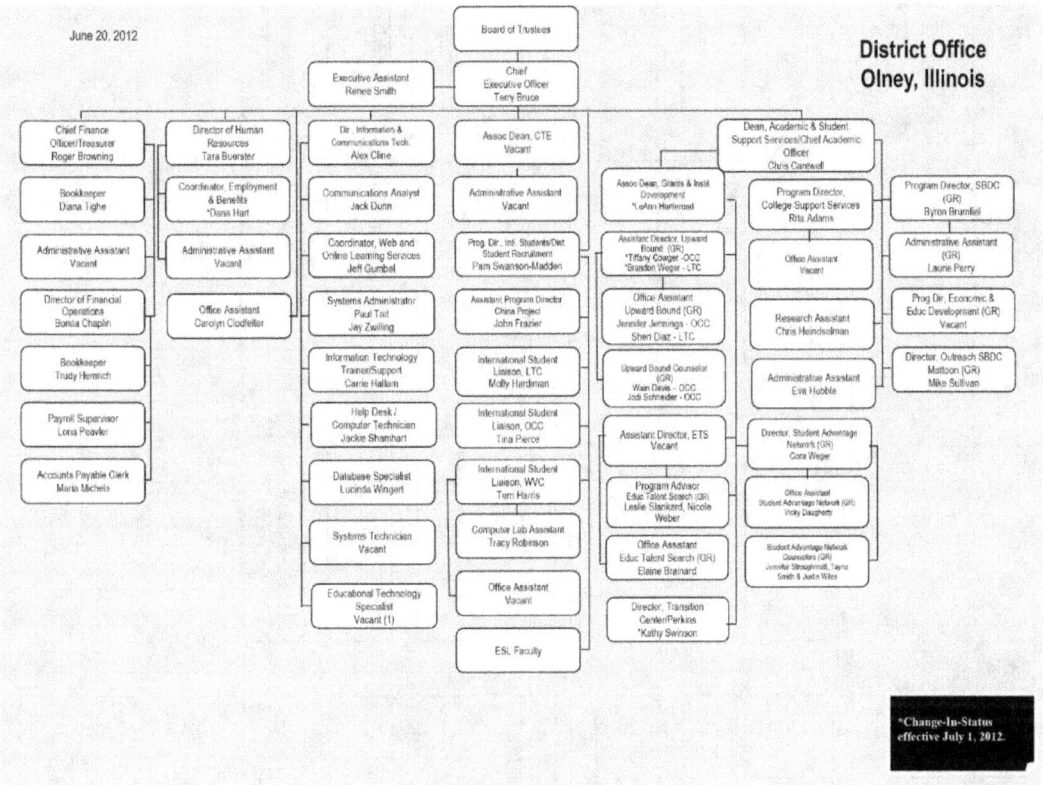

T. Nick Zinni

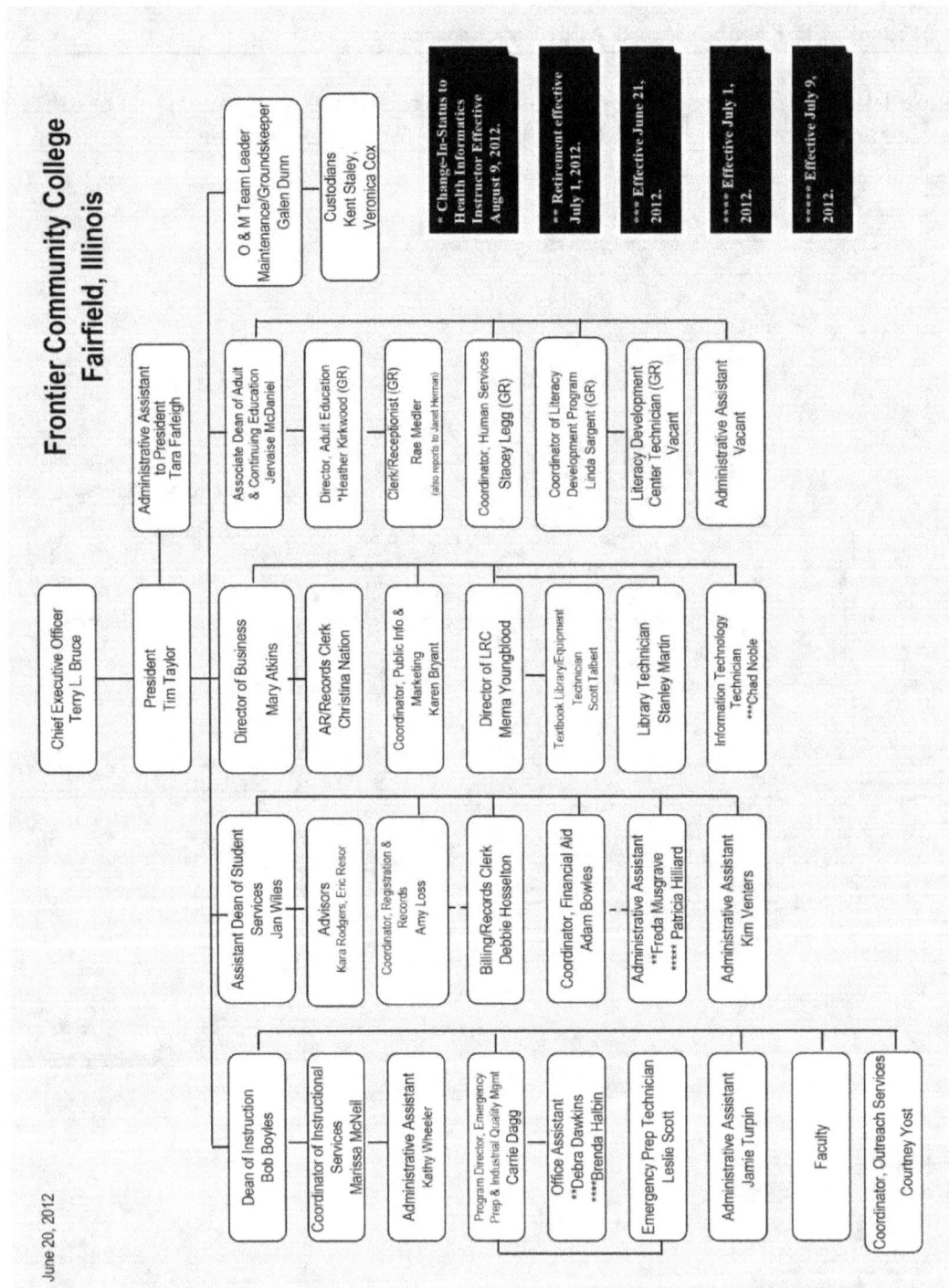

Figure 6.2 Organizational flowcharts of District 529 and Frontier Community College.

264

ILLINOIS EASTERN COMMUNITY COLLEGES

JOB DESCRIPTION

Position Title: Teaching Personnel   Effective Date: 10-29-04
Department: Various   Reports to: Dean of the College, Dean of Instruction, Associate Dean of Nursing & Allied Health

College:
- ☒ FCC
- ☒ LTC
- ☒ OCC
- ☒ WVC
- ☐ WED
- ☐ DO

Status:
- ☒ Full-time
- ☐ Full-time Modified
- ☐ Part-time
- ☐ Special Assignment

- ☒ Exempt
- ☐ Non-Exempt

Employment Classification:
- ☐ Administrative
- ☐ Professional/Non-Faculty
- ☒ Faculty
- ☐ Technical
- ☐ Clerical/Secretarial
- ☐ Maintenance/Custodial
- ☐ Student/Non-Work Study

Minimum Qualifications:

Job Duties:

Design and effectively use learning systems, which include the identification of:

a. Student characteristics
b. Knowledge essential to the subject being taught
c. Skills essential to the processes being taught
d. Attitudes required by individuals succeeding in the subject matter being taught
e. Instructional objectives and student learning outcomes
f. Technology required for effective teaching
g. Course content sequence schedules
h. Evaluation procedures
i. Assessment procedures at classroom, course, program, and institutional level

Cooperate with program coordinators, directors, deans, and appropriate administrative staff in monitoring curriculum, preparation of course outlines, selection of printed and non-printed instructional materials and development of grant proposals.

Assist students with the educational program by:

a. Advising students concerning degree or certificate program requirements
b. Maintaining accurate files on advisees as required by Student Services
c. Providing advisees with current information concerning educational and occupational opportunities
d. Referring students to sources of specialized services available in the college or from community agencies
e. Providing extra services to students with special needs
f. Sponsoring and attending authorized college activities

Maintain and further develop a high level of professional ethics and actions by contributing positively to the organizational environment and:

a. Participating in college staff development activities
b. Attending scheduled faculty meetings and serving on college committees as necessary
c. Supporting professional organizations associated with content specialty
d. Protecting the privacy of students and their records
e. Identifying the potential of each student and promoting their success
f. Observing scheduled office hours
g. Participating in community organizations to improve quality of community life
h. Keep course syllabi updated and current.

Provide administrative services by:

a. Assisting with pre-registration procedures
b. Submitting reports in an accurate and timely fashion
c. Observing and enforcing the regulations, policies, and programs of the college
d. Maintaining an inventory of assigned equipment and supplies
e. Assisting with the organization and meetings of advisory committees related to content specialty
f. Assisting with the supervision of part-time instructors assigned to teach courses in the content specialty of the instructor
g. Participating in student recruitment activities

Dir. of Human Resources   10/29/04
                                                             Date

Chief Executive Officer   11/2/04
                                                             Date

JOBDESCRIPFORM10-12-01

Figure 6.3 Instructor Job Description for Illinois Eastern Community Colleges (IECC)

PART SIX REFERENCES

Baker, L., Egan-Lee, E., Martimianakis, M. A., & Reeves, S. (2011). Relationships of Power: Implications for Interprofessional Education. Journal of Interprofessional Care, 25, 98-104. doi:10.3109/13561820.2010.505350.

Bate, P., Khan, R., & Pye, A. (2000). Towards a Culturally Sensitive Approach to Organizational Structuring: Where Organization Design Meets Organization Development. Organization Science, 11(2), 197-211.

Bovee, C. L., Thill, J. B., & Mescon, M. H. (2007). Excellence in Business (3rd ed.). Upper Saddle River, NJ: Pearson Prentice Hall.

Boyles, R. (2012, July). Personal Conversation. (T. Zinni, Interviewer).

Brewer, G. N. (2008). Organizational structure. Retrieved from McGraw-Hill Higher Education: http://highered.mcgraw-hill.com/sites/0073526703/student_view0/ebook/chapter1/chbody1/organizational_structure.html.

Bryan, L. L., & Joyce, C. I. (2007). Better Strategy Through Organizational Design. McKinsey Quarterly (2).

Cadotte, E. R. (2008). Market Opportunity Analysis for New Products. In E. R. Cadotte, H. J. Bruce, S. F. Gardial, D. Garval, K. C. Gilbert, J. D. Jacobs, . . . R. B. Woodruff, The Management of Strategy in the Marketplace (pp. 101-127). Knoxville, TN: Innovative Learning Solutions.

Chen, Y.-S., & Chen, C.-C. (2009). A Model of Factors Moderating the Relationship Between New Product Development and Company Performance. Social Behavior and Personality, 37(8), 1043-1050. doi:10.2224/sbp.2009.37.8.1043.

Covlin, M. A. (2012, May 16). Personal Discussion. (T. Zinni, Interviewer).

Cutchin, J. (2012, April). Personal Conversation. (T. Zinni, Interviewer).

Daniels, K., & de Jonge, J. (2010). Match Making and Match Breaking: The Nature of Match Within and Around Job Design. Journal of Occupational and Organizational Psychology, 83, 1-16. doi:10.1348/096317909x485144.

Dorenbosch, L., van Engen, M., & Verhagen, M. (2005). On-the-Job Innovation: The Impact of Job Design and Human Resource Management Through Production Ownership. Creativity and Innovation Management, 14(2), 129-141.

Drew, S. (1997). From knowledge to action: The Impact of Benchmarking on Organizational Performance. Long Range Planning, 30(3), 427-441.

Etzioni, A. (1964). Modern Organizations. Upper Saddle River, NJ: Prentice Hall.

Gauthier, J., Pettifor, J., & Ferrero, A. (2010). The Universal Declaration of Ethical Principles for Psychologists: A Culture-Sensitive Model for Creating and Reviewing a Code of Ethics. Ethics and Behavior, 20(3-4), 179-196. doi:10.1080/10508421003798885.

Gielens, K., Van De Gucht, L. M., Steenkamp, J.-B. E., & Dekimpe, M. G. (2008, October). Dancing with A Giant: The Effect of Wal-Mart's Entry into the United Kingdom on the Performance of European Retailers. Journal of Marketing Research, XLV, 519-534.

Harlow, L., DeBacker, T., & Crowson, H. M. (2011). Need for Closure, Achievement Goals, and Cognitive Engagement in High School Students. The Journal of Educational Research, 104, 110-119. doi:10.1080/00220670903567406.

Heneman III, H. G., & Judge, T. A. (2009). Staffing Organizations (6th ed.). Boston, MA: McGraw-Hill/Irwin.

Hult, G. T., Cavusgil, S. T., Deligonul, S., Kiyak, T., & Lagerstrom, K. (2007). What Drives Performance in Globally Focused Marketing Organizations? A Three-Country Study. Journal of International Marketing, 15(2), 58-85.

Ibata-Arens, K. (2008). The Kyoto Model of Innovation and Entrepreneurship: Regional Innovation Systems and Cluster Culture. Prometheus, 26(1), 89-109. doi:10.1080/08109020701846058.

Illinois Eastern Community Colleges. (2012). Mission and Values. Retrieved from Illinois Eastern Community Colleges: http://www.iecc.edu/catalog/PDF/03_Mission_Values_080811.pdf.

Jennings, M. M. (2006). Business: Its Legal, Ethical, And Global Environment (7th ed.). Mason, OH: Thomson Higher Learning.

Khan, A. M., & Manopichetwattana, V. (1989). Innovative and Noninnovative Small Firms: Types and Characteristics. Management Science, 35(5), 597-606.

Katzenbach, J. R., & Smith, D. K. (1993). The Wisdom of Teams: Creating the High-Performance Organization. Boston, MA: McKinsey & Company.

King, B. G., Felin, T., & Whetten, D. A. (2010). Finding the Organization in Organizational Theory: A Meta-Theory of the Organization as a Social Actor. Organization Science, 21(1), 290-305. doi:10.1287/orsc.1090.0443.

Kirkwood, W. G., & Ralston, S. M. (January 1999). Inviting Meaningful Applicant Performances in Employment Interviews. The Journal of Business Communication, 36(1), 55-76.

Kocev, E. N. (2002). Modern Concept of Power as a Social and Economic Category. Journal of International Research (2). Retrieved from http://www.ejournalnet.com/Contents/Issue_2/4/4_2002.htm.

Larco, N. (2009). Hybridizing place: Global and local identity in Puerto Madero, Buenos Aires. International Planning Studies, 14(3), 275-292. doi:10.1080/13563470903450614.

Liu, W.-C., & Fang, C.-L. (2010). The Effect of Different Motivation Factors on Knowledge-Sharing Willingness and Behavior. Social Behavior and Personality, 38(6), 753-758. doi:10.2224/sbp.2010.38.6.753.

Macionis, J. J. (2010). Sociology (13th ed.). Boston, MA: Prentice Hall.

Macneil, A. J., Prater, D. L., & Busch, S. (2009). The Effects of School Culture and Climate on Student Achievement. International Journal of Leadership in Education, 12(1), 73-84. doi:10.1080/13603120701576241.

McCann, J. (2004). Organizational Effectiveness: Changing Concepts for Changing Environments. Human Resource Planning, 27(1), 42-50.

McDonald's Corporation (a). (2012). Our company: Getting to know us. Retrieved from McDonald's: http://www.aboutmcdonalds.com/mcd/our_company.html#.

McDonald's Corporation (b). (2012). Inclusion and Diversity. Retrieved from McDonald's: http://www.aboutmcdonalds.com/mcd/our_company/inclusion_and_diversity.html.

McDonald's Corporation (c). (2012). Global Initiatives. Retrieved from McDonald's: http://www.aboutmcdonalds.com/mcd/our_company/inclusion_and_diversity/global_initiatives.html.

OECD Publishing. (2011). Education at a Glance 2011: OECD Indicators. Paris: OECD Publishing. Retrieved from http://dx.doi.org/10.1787/eag-2011-en.

Organization for Economic Co-operation and Development (OECD). (2012). About the Organization for Economic Co-operation and Development (OECD). Retrieved from OECD: Better Policies for Better Lives: http://www.oecd.org/pages/0,3417,en_36734052_36734103_1_1_1_1_1,00.html.

Papalia, D. E., Olds, S. W., & Feldman, R. D. (2009). Human Development (11th ed.). Boston, MA: McGraw-Hill.

Patterson, F., Ferguson, E., & Thomas, S. (2008). Using Job Analysis to Identify Core and Specific Competencies: Implications for Selection and Recruitment. Medical Education, 42, 1195-1204. doi:10.1111/j.1365-2923.2008.03174.x.

Ritti, R. R., & Levy, S. (2007). The Ropes to Skip and the Ropes to Know: Studies in Organizational Behavior (7th ed.). Hoboken, NJ: John Wiley and Sons.

Russell, J. E., & Jacobs, J. D. (2008). Group Dynamics, Processes, and Teamwork. In E. R. Cadotte, H. J. Bruce, S. F. Gardial, D. Garval, K. C. Gilbert, J. D. Jacobs, . . . R. B. Woodruff, The Management of Strategy in the Marketplace (pp. 49-75). Knoxville, TN: Innovative Learning Solutions.

Senko, C., Hulleman, C. S., & Harackiewicz, J. M. (2011). Achievement Goal Theory at the Crossroads: Old Controversies, Current Challenges, and New Directions. Educational Psychologist, 46(1), 26-47. doi:10.1080/00461520.2011.538646.

Sheng, C.-W., Tian, Y.-F., & Chen, M.-C. (2010). Relationships Among Teamwork Behavior, Trust, Perceived Team Support, and Team Commitment. Social Behavior and Personality, 38(10), 1297-1306. doi:10.2224/sbp.2010.38.10.1297.

Stromquist, N. P. (2007). Internationalization as a Response to Globalization: Radical Shifts in University Environments. Higher Education, 53, 81–105. doi:10.1007/s10734-005-1975-5.

Trampusch, C. (2010). Employers, the State and the Politics of Institutional Change: Vocational Education and Training in Austria, Germany and Switzerland. European Journal of Political Research, 49, 545-573. doi:10.1111/j.1475-6765.2009.01909.x.

van der Veen, M. (2010). Agricultural Innovation: Invention and Adoption or Change and Adaptation? World Archaeology, 42(1), 1-12. doi:10.1080/00438240903429649.

Vos, R. (2010, February). The Crisis of Globalization as an Opportunity to Create a Fairer World. Journal of Human Development and Capabilities, 11(1), 143-160. doi:10.1080/19452820903504599.

Wellins, R. S., Byham, W. C., & Wilson, J. M. (1991). Empowered Teams: Creating Self-Directed Work Groups that Improve Quality, Productivity, and Participation. San Francisco, CA: Jossey-Bass.

3M. (2012). Company Information: About Us: Who We Are. Retrieved from 3M: http://solutions.3m.com/wps/portal/3M/en_US/3M-Company/Information/AboutUs/WhoWeAre/.

PART SEVEN: CONSULTING IN BUSINESS, EDUCATION, AND HEALTH

7.1 KEY SKILLS AND ATTITUDES IN CONSULTING

Through self-examination of identified key skills and attitudes consultants utilize, one appreciates the scope, brevity, and direction of career choices made. By understanding how to turn weaknesses into strengths by everyday actions, performance and motivation efficiently increase the likelihood of prosperous practices. The purpose here is to identify the differential characteristics in consultation types, assess personal key character strengths, and then evaluate how to make them conjoin successfully.

DIFFERENTIAL CHARACTERISTICS IN CONSULTATION TYPES

Consultation types differ within three primary levels, general, mid-level, and specific processes/roles. Table 7.1.1 (Appendix) summarizes these differences at each level in areas such as skills required of the consultant to perform that function, the culture sensitivity needed for effectiveness, preventive and remediate measures often utilized by the consultant in each role, who is primarily affected by the consultant's work, common actions observed, and the level of directedness assumed toward the client or client system. The following sections discuss these differences by primary level.

Consultation v. Collaboration

Although closely related in the most generalized processes/roles of consulting, consultation and collaboration roles differ by the amount of dependence upon the consultant a client requires within interaction of that client's systems. For example, a consultant cooperates primarily with the client to solve a particular problem the client may have in a system (the client interacts directly with the system) while the collaborator works side-by-side with the client and shares responsibility for project completion (Dougherty, 2009). The majority of consultants inside private industry act within collaborative-type roles as salaried employees in positions like "account manager", "occupational health supervisor", and "solutions engagement supervisor" (United Parcel Service, 2011).

Table 7.1.1 (Appendix) demonstrates that collaborative roles require less directiveness as one moves farther away from consulting-like positions. Consultants provide skills the client lacks until that client acquires them, and conversely, collaborators enhance the client's existing knowledge, skills, and abilities. Specific skills required of the consultant depend upon the situation for which employed, such as cultural skills for diversified clients or self-awareness skills for accepting a challenge. Similarly, levels of needed cultural sensitivity dictate dependence upon the role taken by the consultant. Consultation roles provide ownership of change toward the client as well as the client's systems while collaborative roles direct ownership toward the client himself/herself. The results show that as the consultant moves farther away from collaborative roles, the more likely preventive and remediate measures become evident.

Supervision v. Mediation

Mid-level roles of consultants include supervision and mediation at opposite extremes by level of directedness involved. Supervisory roles, as expected, tend to direct processes (clients or client systems) while mediators purposely exclude themselves as referees between clients or clients and their systems. Likewise, supervisors act/react on behalf of the client. For example, attorneys represent clients during judicial proceedings and project managers plan and interact with process flows on behalf of their clients. Mediators on the other hand observe and limit action/reaction to the process of collaboration, such as between union representatives and employers (Pearson Learning Solutions, 2010).

Mediation uses no preventive measures and few remediate measures during the course of operations; these belong to the client or client system for resolution. Consultant skills and cultural sensitivity needed therefore significantly diminish in comparison to supervisory roles. This is not to say there exists no requirement for skills (communication, interpersonal, expert, etc.), but demonstrated levels may not seem as apparent due to the nature of the role. Supervisors demonstrate high levels of necessary skills and cultural sensitivity in successful, especially global, positions of authority (Jennings, 2006). See Table 7.1.1 for a graphical representation.

Specific Processes/Roles

Specific levels of process/roles among consultants include, in decreasing order of directedness, advocate, expert, trainer/educator, fact-finder, and process specialist (Nolan, 1998). Eight areas were initially identified in 1986 by Lippett and Lippett but expanded over the years through research (Dougherty, 2009). As Table 7.1.1 illustrates, actions taken by specific roles vary from defined and specific in the advocate position to analyzing the "how" across client system processes for specialists. Areas in between mix and match collaboration and consultation methods to achieve their desired goals for clients and client systems.

Advocate usage of preventative measures tend to align with the consultants individual knowledge, skills, and abilities (KSAs) while experts attempt to avoid the need for advocacy. Trainers and educators employ understanding of processes among clients to reduce dependence upon the consultant as a future prevention tactic, and fact-finders provide recommendations to clients after process evaluation. Process specialists occasionally struggle with prevention tactics as the analysis may cause unsolicited feedback among group members (Dougherty, 2009).

Remediate measures facilitate preventive measures to a large degree, however, comprise mostly of repetitive steps taken during prevention stages. For example, a trainer/educator may offer retraining or workshops and an expert will attempt to remove discrepancies discovered after initial feedback to the client.

Except for fact-finders, culture sensitivity always includes concerns with the regional, organizational, and specific group client systems under consideration. Depending upon the specialty, experts may also consider poverty, racism, and other value-related issues that affect outcomes of their efforts. Since fact-finders usually work behind the scenes, cultural sensitivity depends largely upon the problem imposed by the client and the interaction required of the consultant within the client system.

Skill requirements needed by the consultant, as identified by Dougherty, vary mostly by the process/role assumed, whether in consultation or collaborator mode. As previously noted, mediators outwardly display fewer skillsets than supervisors do, especially in expert positions. Overall experts may or may not utilize all the skills listed in Table 7.1.1. Fact-finders, inversely, may require the fewest number of skills when assumed they work as outside researchers and interact little with clients or client systems. Regardless of the process/role taken, consultants should exhibit good communication (written or oral), problem-solving, and cultural recognition skills.

VIA Survey of Character Strengths

Positive psychologist, Dr. Martin Seligman, developed the VIA Survey of Character Strengths (Table 7.1.2, Appendix) as a wellness initiative. Instead of focusing on the negative aspects of a person's character the purpose is to rank order 24 identified positive traits the person builds upon to enhance him or herself psychologically (Seligman, 2006). For example, rather than concentrate upon characteristics like "foolish", "angry", or "unsociable", the survey reports "judgment", "forgiveness", and "citizenship" in comparison to other positive traits. The hope is the individual initiates actions in their life to strengthen these characteristics.

In her presentation to Google employees, Carolyn Foster made two suggestions (Foster, 2008). First that managers identify their weakest characteristics from the Character Strengths survey then work to enhance those traits in order to balance their stronger points (opposed to Seligman's recommendation to focus upon the five strongest). Unfortunately, neither Foster nor Seligman offer details for survey-takers to "find ways to apply" characteristics without remuneration or purchase of additional materials, but others fortunately do.

Dr. Deborah Barnett posts multiple suggestions to her blog tackling the issue (Barnett, 2011). For instance, to enhance fairness, equity, and justice characteristics, Barnett imposes purposely listening to another's opinion without prejudice or judgment, or acting as a mediator in a dispute without personal involvement. Note that both suggestions serve as skills and roles of consultants (Table 7.1.1, Appendix).

The second suggestion from Foster involved discussion into five key strengths that "never fail once for any of us... to be satisfied and better performers" (Foster, 2008). By increasing awareness of these characteristics in oneself and working to enhance them, Foster professes increased performance results. The Values in Action (VIA) characteristics include:

1. Zest, enthusiasm, and energy
2. Curiosity and interest in the world
3. Hope, optimism, and future-mindedness
4. Gratitude
5. Appreciation of beauty and excellence

CONCLUSIONS

After completion of the VIA Survey of Character Strengths (Table 7.1.2, Appendix), results indicated the test-taker's personal top five character strengths include :

1) Judgment, critical thinking, and open-mindedness;
2) Citizenship, teamwork, and loyalty;
3) Fairness, equity, and justice;
4) Honesty, authenticity, and genuineness; and
5) Industry, diligence, and perseverance.

Essentially these mean the person is an independent thinker who works fairly and honestly with other people until the job is complete.

* * *

7.2 ENTRY STAGE OF CONSULTING

Military leadership courses teach that effective leaders tell subordinates how not to fall down, show subordinates how not to fall down, and then allow them to fall down. In this way, leadership strength increases once the subordinate gets back up through confidence in the leader's teaching. More often than not, the subordinate never falls down again for the same reason. Copying this format, the following sections discuss expectations from consultants when entering into consultation and shows what happens when they ignore these phases. By rewriting the Lindsey approach to comply with suggestions, the consultation likely endures success.

PHASES OF ENTRY INTO CONSULTATION

The entry level into consultation involves four related phases. Beginning with exploration of organizational needs and establishing a contract for services, the consultant moves toward physical entry, and the gradual acceptance within the organization of psychological entry. Attempts to diagnose problems at this point prove premature and relevant to the second step of the consultation process.

Phase 1: Exploring Organizational Needs

During the entry step of consulting, consultants should not plan implementation strategies to avoid misidentifying the real problems facing an organization (Dougherty, 2009). Before physical entry, consultants establish fitness between organizational need and their own expertise as well as the nature of the problem through a first contact meeting, preferably on-site for observation. Organizational commitment through resource allocation to change the problem draws as much attention in discussion as mutually understanding the expectations consultation brings to the organization. Learning the organization's history, mission, philosophy, and procedures align the task of familiarization with perceived problems and the client's attempts to solve them.

During this phase of entry, the consultant must not promise too much in terms of results or fail to recognize if the problem is beyond their competence level. By clarifying roles of the consultant, the client, and the system, the contact person better evaluates organizational need for consultation. After first contact establishes the relationship between organizational need and consultation, contracting occurs.

Phase 2: Contracting

Contracts explicitly formalize the parameters and character context of the consulting relationship while providing a form of self-protection for the consultant and the organization (Dougherty, 2009). The agreement covers expectations, obligations, frequency of meetings, client system access, data collection, program modifications, and payment arrangements for services. The Uniform Commercial Code of the United States requires that all valid and enforceable contracts contain the minimal elements of parties involved (consultant and client names), explicit promises of each party including delivery and performance of goods or services, price and payment terms, and the dates of execution and termination (Jennings, 2006). The psychological aspect of the contract enables a sense of partnership between the consultant and the client toward a common goal.

Phase 3: Physically Entering the System

Physical and psychological system entries by the consultant operate inseparably, yet distinctly. This phase begins when meeting with the client for the first time and provides the greatest impact when interacting with the client system (such as employees). First impressions grafted by the consultant include simple actions of minimizing interruptions to the client system and adjusting to client schedules (Dougherty, 2009). Employees should be aware of the consultant's expected arrival, purpose, and duration within the organization and confidentiality for information divulged to the consultant.

Phase 4: Psychologically Entering the System

Confidentiality also provides psychological advantages for the consultation process since persons who feel less threatened by administrative repercussion tend to interact more accurately when questioned (Coon & Mitterer, 2010). Administration of anonymous and interview-type surveys using identical questions easily demonstrate the differences between the *security versus fear* effect. Maintenance of confidence levels and trust toward the consultant result when client system interactions remain focused, relevant, and pertinent to the consultation process.

CRITIQUE OF THE LINDSEY APPROACH

Dr. Lindsey ignored the first step of consultation and dreamed up a diagnosis for the mental health center's turnover problem without any interaction with the client or the staff. Next, he repeated this action by assuming the organizational climate lacked a positive atmosphere and his prescription for dress-style would alleviate the problem. In fact, he may have inadvertently declined professional confidence by the staff in his abilities.

During initial contact, Dr. Lindsey chose to lecture about his imaginary burnout diagnosis rather than listen to the client or ask questions that discerned if the turnover problem actually lies within his field of expertise, let alone if burnout was involved. The client, Dr. Gonzalez, initiated questions Dr. Lindsey should have answered covering duration, resources, and results. These were part of the first phase and jeopardized the consultation relationship since his reply concluded, "these are things that will be worked out as the program develops".

By asking the staff to report an hour early and lecturing them as a group, Dr. Lindsey failed to adjust to the client schedule. A decrease among staff organizational cohesiveness likely further contributed to the turnover problem (Oketch, 2005) when Dr. Lindsey boasted how he expected staff members to change upon meeting them for the first time, and for assumed reasons. Human nature dictates that people naturally choose the path of least resistance (a tactic used for setting mine fields by the military) and resist changes not self-initiated (make it *their* idea – reverse psychology).

Dr. Lindsey failed each phase during the entry stage of consultation. He did not explore organizational needs of the client, effectively resolve contract issues, properly enter the system physically, or adhere to psychological system entrance considerations. Dr. Lindsey acted beyond his field of expertise.

SCENARIO REWRITE

The local mental health center has a high turnover of workers. The county Human Resources officer (Dr. Sara Gonzalez) contacted Dr. Lindsey of Mind Consulting to do a consultation at the mental health clinic. On hearing there was a large turnover of workers, Dr. Lindsey took note of the potential problem for future analysis, but refrained from diagnoses of cause at this stage in the consultation process. He scheduled a first contact meeting at the clinic to explore whether he would be a good fit for helping Dr. Gonzalez to resolve any discovered issues within his expertise.

Dr. Lindsey appeared on time for the first meeting. Dr. Gonzalez shared the organizational history, mission, philosophy, and procedures with Dr. Lindsey as well as the perceived problem. He asked her what activities proved successful at reducing the turnover and which failed in attempt to change the situation. Dr. Lindsey consulted Dr. Gonzalez with their respective roles during the consultation process, the goals consultation intended to achieve, resources needed for obtaining those goals, and the expected results.

After initial contact, Dr. Gonzalez approached her supervisors in the county office and recommended contracting with Mind Consulting for services. Dr. Lindsey drew up a contract outlining the work he will complete, expected results from that work, and the duration of time for services. Additionally, lines of authority and responsibility bring establishment in coherence with special agreements or contingency plans. Compensation and methods of payment to Dr. Lindsey also considered into the contract. If the county requires a form contract instead, Dr. Lindsey insures these items find inclusion.

Hoping to put the director and staff at ease, Dr. Lindsey dressed professionally to earn respect from the staff as a consultant when meeting them for the first time. Dr. Gonzalez already notified employees of the upcoming visit and why he was hired. Dr. Lindsey worked to establish his image by listening to his client and then approaching each staff member individually as he toured the facility. He allowed them to do most of the talking while reassuring staff members their replies remained confidential.

Dr. Lindsey, in hopes of gaining psychological acceptance within the organization, refrained from assuming roles that did not match his persona while considering the process and interaction levels of its members. Discussions remained pertinent to the consultation as possible as a demonstration of competence and attractive through identification with the client and staff.

* * *

7.3 THEORETICAL APPROACHED TO DIAGNOSIS

Before successful analysis and comparison of theoretical models, an understanding of what constitutes sound application is in order. Discussion of the phases involved during the process of appropriate diagnoses techniques within consultation allows for better understanding of models that work or fail to reach objectives. Evaluation of the Hanna Perkins Center model contrasted with socialization theory concepts and those outlined within the Structural Family Therapy model deliver appreciation for proper diagnosis techniques.

PHASES OF DIAGNOSIS WITHIN CONSULTATION

The diagnosis level of consultation involves four related phases. Beginning with the gathering of accurate information in order to conceptualize the problem, the consultant moves toward defining the problem based upon analysis of that data. Next setting goals toward outcomes allow the consultant to guide the client from where they are to where they want to be. The last phase involves generating possible interventions or strategies for reaching those goals. At this step of the consultation process identification of the real problem(s) reinforces tasks completed during the entry step by building upon the psychosocial atmosphere between the consultant, the client, and in some cases the client system (Dougherty, 2009). Discussion of these four phases follows for better understanding of their importance to the consultation process and precedent to the implementation step.

Phase 1: Gather Information

Although discovery of a generalized problem occurs during the entry step of the consultation process, this reason for needing the consultant may mask underlying problems or matters unobvious to the client. Depending upon the scope of consultation and the expertise of the stakeholders, including the consultant, methods vary for gathering information. For example, a child behavioral problem, employee negotiations, and curriculum development require different methods for gathering data in clinical, human resources, and educational settings, respectively. Scanning the related environment using the consultant's theories of description analysis, change, and dysfunction in combination with those of the client helps to eliminate biases and provides focus to gathering specific data (Dougherty, 2009).

Forms of data gathering consist of reviewing historical records, administering questionnaires and surveys, conducting interviews, observing the client system, combinations of techniques, or creating hybrid collection systems based upon valid and reliable methods. Whatever the choices made, data gathering should provide ethical treatment of stakeholders and cost efficient implementation (Carroll & Buchholtz, 2009; Luthans, 2008) as well as utility in purpose (Field, 2009).

Phase 2: Define the Problem

Data is worthless until analyzed for the intended necessity. Once analyzed, the task in question develops definition and affects the rest of the consultation process (Dougherty, 2009). Data analysis is deliberate, systematic, and planned to reduce unintended consequences. Working together, the consultant and client determine antecedents and consequences related to the situation and choose strategies for data analysis. Multiple problem discovery results in prioritizing finds by how they develop over time, how past events caused present problems, or how future expectations relate to one another.

Problems may then be framed using concise statements from multiple perspectives, e.g. administration, employee, and customer views of personal service quality. Definitions of framed problems should seem logical to the consultant and the client, practical in leading to new directions of action, and ensure willingness by the client to take action, taking limitations into account (Dougherty, 2009).

Phase 3: Set Goals

Goal setting occurs after data analysis provides a mechanism for defining the problem(s) under consideration and like other phases, goal setting is a process. Creating goals moves toward concrete and specific perspectives with resolutions as complex as the problem. The process involves seven steps (Dougherty, 2009) once goal possibilities emerge;

1) specify the task or objective,
2) specify the task measurement method,
3) specify the target to be reached,
4) allocate the timespan,
5) prioritize goal possibilities,
6) rate goals to difficulty and importance, and
7) determine coordination requirements.

Similar to problem statements, goals require clear and specific writing to regulate and evaluate the effectiveness of selected interventions. Methods of measurement allow verification of progress toward meeting goals which should be stated in terms of outcomes (hence, a goal), but may be either qualitative or quantitative (e.g. improved customer relations versus a 10% increase in sales per salesperson). Realistic goals in terms of resources available, control in meeting those goals, and obstacles that prevent outcome determine their possibility of success. Essentially goals help to focus attention and action and provide incentive toward their achievement from a behavioral perspective.

Phase 4: Generate Possible Interventions

After establishing goals, the last phase within the diagnosis step of the consultation process entails generating possible strategies toward accomplishment of those goals. Interventions detail the plan of "how" goals may reach fruition systematically. Consultants should encourage the client to generate implementations, with some assistance, to stimulate client creativity and to reduce future dependency upon the consultant. Utilization of other people within the organization or outsourcing ideas serve as effective prompts depending upon the need (Jennings, 2006). During the implementation step, consultants encourage effective practices by monitoring the implementation process and providing assistance to clients as needed for integrity (Dougherty, 2009).

CRITIQUE OF THE HANNA PERKINS CENTER MODEL USING SOCIALIZATION THEORY

While primarily explaining how consultants gain acceptance (or rejection) into a client system or consultation at entry level through interpersonal interactions, socialization theory also donates to explanation of how consultants contribute to the success of their clients during the diagnosis step. Barnes and Austin (2008) noted two primary responsibilities that advisors (consultants) owe toward their clients: help them be successful and develop as professionals. These are possible through the functions of collaboration, mentoring, chastising, and advocating.

Collaboration involves inclusion of the client within the diagnosis step. By guiding the client through analyzing data and setting goals, mentoring occurs. Chastising refers to correcting inappropriate behaviors of the client, unethical practices for example, and advocating relies upon the consultant performing tasks on behalf of the client when he or she lacks ability or expertise.

In addition, Barnes and Austin recognized five characteristics of the consultant/client relationship that determine success. A relationship that is strong and positive but has boundaries that both the advisor and client respect, denotes a professional/friendly quality. Collegial relationships dismantle, or at least blur, power structures so the client feels the relationship is balanced. Providing clients with the emotional and psychological encouragement they need for sustainment demonstrates support/care. "Accessible relationships" means the consultant remains available to meet with clients or responds to clients within a short/reasonable amount of time. Providing clients with candid and straightforward feedback builds relationships between the consultant and client described as honest. Culminating these characteristics show the consultant's role as multifaceted and somewhat complicated (Barnes & Austin, 2008) where the level of success depends significantly upon socialization throughout the diagnosis step.

The Hanna Perkins Center model of consultation (Barrett et. al., 2005) summarily fits the description supplied by socialization theory. The characteristics of professionalism, support/care, accessibility, and collegial readily translate into the model's processes of developing trusting relationships and elevating professionalism through its categorical divisions. However, findings of Barnes and Austin indicate the model needs improvement in the honesty characteristic by emphasizing candid and straightforward feedback.

At the functional level, collaboration emphasis is restricted to the consultant–client system mode (caregivers and parents, not the organization as defined in the model) rather than inclusive of the director. Repairing this defect strengthens the other functions that seem adequately implemented in practice at the Hanna Perkins Center. Unfortunately, the model requires the consultant to ignore the real client (director) and take on responsibility of the client system (caregivers and parents) directly.

Using the proven aspects of the model, the corrected consultant/client model prescribes the first phase involves working more closely with the director as the client to decide what information needs to be collected and how. This relationship is the primary contact between the consultant and the organization. Phase two involves working collaboratively with the director to analyze the data and define the underlying problems. Guiding the director with setting goals that alleviate the detected problems, then generating possible interventions alongside the director, strengthens professionalism within the director so that person may carry forth these skills to caregivers and parents.

CRITIQUE OF THE HANNA PERKINS CENTER MODEL USING THE STRUCTURAL FAMILY THERAPY MODEL

The structural family therapy model encompasses four stages that consultants use in practice (Parcover et. al., 2009). The initial stage, Joining and Accommodating, involves relationship building in ways that avoid conflict with resistance, namely avoiding silent or resistant clients. Obviously, this stage contradicts methods encouraged by the Hanna Perkins Center model as well as entry level recommendations for the consulting process (Dougherty, 2009).

Stage two, Assessing System Interactions, encounters a process of appraising the hierarchical organization, the ability of its subsystems to carry out their functions, permeability of boundaries, flexibility in meeting individual members' needs, and the capability of the system to resolve conflict. This process aligns with the Perkins model with similarities to gathering information and data analysis phases of the consultation process if one concludes that "appraisal of subsystems" meets the definition. However, many of the tasks converge steps and phases of the consultation process proving dysfunctional in purpose.

Structural consultants then work to modify system problems in stage three, Modifying System Dysfunctional Sets, as the core of the intervention process based upon problem assessment. This process does not include working with the client or client system members as the Perkins model requires and implies empirical assessment by the consultant. Setting goals and developing possible intervention techniques in a systematic, proven manner are nil concepts.

During stage four, Restructuring Transactional Patterns, efforts strategize to modify the system's rules, alter patterns that support undesirable behaviors, and change sequences of interaction. Consultants often use reframing to change the original meaning of an event or situation with the goal of providing a new context to provide a more constructive perspective than the one currently in use by members of the system (Parcover et.al., 2009). In other words, problems do not find resolution, but perspectives change to ignore them. Apparently, the structural family therapy model wastes time and resources and lacks beneficence for either the Perkins model or the consultation process outlined by Dougherty.

* * *

7.4 IMPLEMENTATION OF A CONSULTING PLAN

Total Quality Management (TQM) originated after WWII through efforts constructed by W. Edwards Deming in response to rebuilding war-torn Japan's industrial sector (Opara, 2010). Originally, TQM focused upon human and work processes with the primary goals of ensuring customer satisfaction and continuously improving organizational performance by focusing processes on customers. Today, the definition changes slightly with each application, especially as rendered within service industries, although basic principles remain intact (Anderson, 2010; Kezar et. al., 2008). The demonstration here attempts to show how TQM applies to higher education, healthcare, and Nigerian libraries as an intervention philosophy that perpetuates service applications across differing situations.

SETTING 1: HIGHER EDUCATION

Many researchers agree TQM generally fails as an intervention when applied to universities (Houston, 2007; Houston, Robertson, & Prebble, 2008; Kezar et. al., 2008) and summarily offer explanation due to complexity of diversity in subunit goals and processes. In simpler terms, everyone (departments) wants to do things their own way without interference from others. This behavior is understandable as human nature just as organizational psychologists clash with clinical specialists in their objective/subjective methods, or politicians take oppositional stances toward common ends (governance).

Houston alone, and together with Robertson and Prebble, explored the idea that TQM should adapt to the problem of non-convergence among complex client systems rather than changing the organization directly to fit the model. They suggested managing each subunit of the university using TQM components relative to those particular departments to achieve a balanced scorecard at the administrative level. In other words, turn that natural tendency toward self-direction into a tool for achieving the intervention goal.

Using the modified model of Total Systems Intervention (TSI), three phases emerge in the problem-solving mode which requires participants in the department to think about their organization and its issues within the creativity phase that may need management. Outcomes enrich understanding of the images of the organization and associated issues using alternative perspectives on the organization. Creativity is equal to the diagnosis stage of consultation (Dougherty, 2009) when combined with the choice phase where choosing appropriate systems-based methodologies and methods suit the organizational images and issues revealed in the creativity phase occur. The task during the implementation phase is to develop specific interventions for change in those aspects of the department seen as most critical to organization (Houston, Robertson, & Prebble, 2008) and apply them.

In essence, TQM fails when applied to university settings at the organizational level, but succeeds when appropriately modified and applied at the department level in conformance with Dougherty's stages of consultation and collaboration model.

SETTING 2: HEALTHCARE

Many consultants deliberated the feasibility of applying TQM principles to healthcare during the 1980s and 1990s (Anderson, 2010). Reasons for difficulty included: lack of standardized products in health care; absence of an assembly line in health care; differences in global cultural settings; physicians considered as consultants rather than team players; difficulties measuring or defining health care quality; and the belief that higher quality leads to higher costs.

The key to application required changing perspectives, just as in education. Studies discovered six keys for successfully applying TQM to healthcare when viewed as a service (Anderson, 2010):

1) recognizing the existence of long-term commitments in a supplier-customer dynamic;
2) clear communications and mutual trust;
3) acknowledging the importance of standardization while understanding the variability of processes;
4) perceiving that management of hand-offs between internal customers within a process reduced variation;
5) appreciating the importance of teamwork; and
6) development of methods for integrating the physician into the improvement process.

TQM principles succeed in healthcare when assessment is applied from the correct perspective; that as seeing healthcare as a service industry rather than a process-free assembly system. Through process identification, consultants can specify root problems and offer alternative interventions the client may implement (Dougherty, 2009). By including physicians as team members within the consultation process, commitment to organizational change results in higher implementation rates (Anderson, 2010; Dougherty, 2009).

SETTING 3: NIGERIAN LIBRARIES

Nigerian libraries lack understanding in purpose with residents, commensurate resources, and relevance with competing economic industries (Opara, 2010). High-quality library performance determines survivability within its parent institution and society because libraries "no longer enjoy monopoly of information provision in today's digital environment". Utilizing a service orientation helps sustain the confidence of the library's clientele by developing systems, philosophies, and strategies for managing and providing quality services.

Applied to the libraries' identified problems, TQM principles propose process interventions, that when implemented organization-wide, demonstrate effectiveness toward solutions. Opara suggested perceiving patrons as external customers who define the quality of library services while acknowledging departmental employees realize they are internal customers (everyone's performance affects the performance of everyone else). Increased literacy and education then perpetuate antecedents to increased demand for source funding and technological modernization. The interventions remain complex and inseparable suggesting parallel implementation requirements.

CONCLUSIONS

Total Quality Management as an intervention method seems confusing unless one realizes it does not encompass an overarching solution, rather a system of possibilities at the disposal of managers and consultants. Each situation (Dougherty, 2009) and individual organization (Alexopoulos & Konstantopoulos, 2007) provides unique opportunities for consultation initiatives. Interventions that work well for one organization or in a particular situation may require adaptation to successfully prevail in others.

Without a proper perspective of the problem, such as viewing the organization or process as a service, TQM generally fails as an intervention. The process orientation allows consultants to redefine problems within context to arrive at workable alternatives for their clients. Sometimes variations of the basic model inhibit disillusionment for applications needing complexity or simultaneous intervention efforts. After choosing interventions, the consultant may then formulate feasible plans for implementation and evaluate interventions once initiated for effectiveness (Dougherty, 2009), repeating the cycle if necessary.

* * *

7.5 PREPARING FOR DISENGAGEMENT

PHASES OF DISENGAGEMENT WITHIN CONSULTATION

The disengagement step of consultation and collaboration entails four phases: evaluation of the consultation process; planning post-consultation matters; reducing involvement and follow-up; and termination. Each phase requires consideration when disengaging from the implemented stress reduction program for nurses at the organ transplant center. The program included relaxation techniques, time management, and communication skill building. The purpose here outlines strategies for successful disengagement from the stress reduction program within the scope of these phases.

Phase 1: Evaluation of the Consultation Process

Evaluation involves looking at the overall consultation process and determining if established goals met satisfactory ends and whether the client potentially demonstrates adequate ability in effectively handling similar situations without the consultant in the future (Dougherty, 2009, p. 112). This definition relates to previous steps in the consultation and collaboration process by measuring the effectiveness of the program. Dougherty recommends evaluating perceived behavior by the client in addition to the consultation process itself to enhance consultant service performance. Inclusion of perceived benefits by the client helps to establish (or not) credibility of the consultant and potential for future consultation and collaboration (Coon & Mitterer, 2010; Dougherty, 2009).

In response, Cott et.al., (2006) developed a publicly available questionnaire for consultants to administer among clients with a high validity correlation of 0.78 ($p < .01$) between decision-making and goal setting, and the client's evaluation of outcomes. Similarly, equal correlations of 0.73 ($p < .01$) occurred for emotional support, and coordination and continuity, variables with decision-making and goal setting. Development and administration of a variation of this instrument to evaluate the effectiveness of consultation with the stress reduction program is in order inclusive of its subcomponents, relaxation techniques, time management, and communication skills.

Although evaluation of the means of consultation provides importance, measures taken throughout the program allow for adjustments when necessary, such as at the end of each phase (Dougherty, 2009). Qualitative research among college students showed that 54% of students felt their course improved after administration of midterm course/instructor evaluations although grades were not included in the study for quantitative review (Friedlander, 1978). Again, periodic evaluation of the program components allows for immediate adjustment while enhancing client perspectives.

Interviews with nursing staff and focus groups provide additional qualitative insight individually and collectively (Dougherty, 2009) as to the effectiveness of the stress reduction program. Since the program exists solely for the purpose of intervention, qualitative techniques infer greater efficiency for application purposes than research-based qualitative measures.

Phase 2: Planning Post-Consultation Matters

Post-consultation plans incur matters arising after departure of the consultant from the consulting and collaboration process, providing effectiveness especially when procedures used during the plan formulation phase of implementation carryover (Dougherty, 2009). The objective in this phase relies not upon creating plans to implement consultation efforts, but instead with assisting the client as needed in a helpful perspective after departure. Topics to consider when formulating post-consultation plans include assigning responsibilities the consultant no longer handles, cost effectiveness for program continuance, and the capabilities of the client and client system.

One method intended to assist the client with reducing stressors is the integration of self-reporting measures (Kamholz et.al., 2006) into the client's repertoire. As a planning initiative, self-reporting helps to decrease reliance upon the consultant post-consultation by providing the client a mechanism for regulating emotion and encouraging communication. In essence, this planning tool serves as an extension of the stress reduction program and carries over into the nursing client system at the organ transplant center.

Phase 3: Reducing Involvement and Following Up

The third phase begins after post-consultation planning meets to the satisfaction of the parties involved. Reducing involvement indicates gradual disconnection by the consultant from the consultation and collaboration effort rather than abrupt disengagement. Studies show that abrupt disengagement is nearly twice as likely to occur in consultations lasting less than a year (40%) than those enduring from one (26%) to five years (11%) (O'Brien, Fahmy, & Singh, 2009), further showing necessity for gradual disconnection.

In the case of the stress reduction program efforts to lower consultant contact, and hence transfer responsibilities to the client, some areas may require slower reduction than others may. For example, the client may have more difficulty implementing/enforcing relaxation techniques with nursing staff and less difficulty with time management challenges, requiring further assistance with the former. The object here then, is to allow the client to assume responsibilities in an independent format (Dougherty, 2009).

Dougherty contends that consultants often critically fail to conduct adequate follow-up and that doing so allows the consultant to review whether maintenance of gains made remain sustained. Follow-up demonstrates continued availability to the client, chances to close uncompleted plans, opportunities to prevent future problems, and reinforcement initiatives provided to the client.

Within the stress program, reduction and follow-up procedures include fading responsibilities to the client first in less critical areas by cutting meeting times when possible until periodic follow-up visits or calls deem appropriate. Follow-up entails reviewing successes of the program (with accolades), assisting with problem concerns of the client and working solutions, and providing guidance or feedback when needed.

Phase 4: Termination

Termination involves formally ending the consultation and collaboration relationship, mostly from psychological perspectives (Dougherty, 2009). Physical break-up occurs during fading and follow-up at a gradual pace, but psychologically, closure remains open. Mental aspects of closure comprise the sense of satisfaction of accomplishment. Successful termination may lead to repeat opportunities for consultation where failure to terminate indicates inadequate consideration emotionally.

Formalized meetings to mark termination of the consultation process allow for resolve of issues, review of the final report, debriefing of lessons learned, and establishment of a defined debarkation between the consultant and client. These meetings provide needed closure on behalf of the client and the organization (Dougherty, 2009).

Termination of consultation with the organ transplant center calls for holding a formal meeting with the client. Reviewing goals and accomplishments of the program to encourage independence and autonomy leads priority before discussion of unresolved discrepancies. Next, debriefing of lessons learned precedes literation and review of the final report. Opportunity to touch on future possibilities for consultation and/or collaboration closes the meeting prior to physically leaving the premises.

CONCLUSIONS

The disengagement step of consultation and collaboration is sensitive to proper handling. If improperly controlled, efforts achieved during previous steps may endure setbacks that prove disastrous to the program, or worse, future service opportunities. Attention to detail through planning and follow-up ensure smooth physical and psychological termination between the consultant and the client organization. Measurable outcomes provide evidential progress that allows for proper planning, reduced involvement from the consultant, and increased independence for the client. Follow-up increases autonomy within the client and the established program before formalization of the termination process. Once achieved, successful disengagement provides necessary closure.

* * *

7.6 RECOGNIZING AND MANAGING RESISTANCE

THE STANFORD COUNTY PRISON EXPERIMENT

Prison settings, in themselves, generate hostile and violent behaviors among prison guards and inmates alike (Macionis, 2010). In a study conducted by Phillip Zimbardo at Stanford University, recruits were selected into two groups; guards and prisoners, to role play in a mock prison setting for two weeks. Guards humiliated prisoners with tasks like cleaning toilets with their bare hands. After four days, five prisoners displayed extreme emotional depression, crying, rage, and acute anxiety. The experiment was cancelled at the end of the first week since conditions deteriorated to such extremes. Zimbardo concluded the social character of the jails, regardless of participant personality traits, roots the source of prison violence (Zimbardo, 2009).

These findings assist with recognition and understanding root causes of resistance among stakeholders within the prison scenario for the consultant. During the initial phase within the entry stage of the consultation, expectance for escalated resistance for changes within the client system than most organizations stands clear due to social roles of its members. The problem lies not in the mental health of either guards or prisoners, but certainly in the ways they interact. Increased actions through stronger penalties likely increase the risks of further retaliation.

AMERICAN PRISON REFORM

Originally, American prison design touted punishment and example-making of wrong-doers as the core philosophical purpose of operations without regards to rehabilitation (Depersis & Lewis, 2008). The four goals of incarceration include retribution, deterrence, rehabilitation, and incapacitation. Retribution refers to repayment of losses and fines imposed upon the criminal. Deterrence merely indicates the operant conditioning concept of causing the offender to refrain from repeating their crime in fear of returning to prison, where incapacitation limits their ability to freely interact with the outside world. The most evolved goal, rehabilitation, today involves training the offender to do other things that eliminate their need or willingness to commit those crimes in the future. In the time of America's first prison, rehabilitation was synonymous with punishment and involved seclusion tactics.

At the Walnut Street Prison in Philadelphia, relaxed harsh treatment of prisoners found replacement with leniency and immediate recognition of reduced violent tendencies among inmates. The exchange occurred with reconviction and promises of harsher treatment for repeat offenders. Caleb Lownes wrote, "Their good conduct was evident and many were [released], and before one year was expired, their behavior was, almost without exception, decent, orderly and respectful". Of course, staff behavior relevant to inmate interactions changed to precipitate acceptance of the reformation program.

CROWDING

Crowding within prison systems, especially inside cells, historically increases risks for disruptive behaviors within the community setting of the institution (Depersis & Lewis, 2008). This phenomenon tends to counteract previous improvements. Old adages like "Too many hens in the henhouse" and "There can be only one king of the castle" refer to territorial aggression due to overcrowding and illustrate this point. The answer as to why people become aggressive in crowded situations stems from the prison goal of incapacitation and the personal need of individuals to feel power in those situations (Macionis, 2010). These effects carry over among guards and staff according to contagion theory.

Sheer numbers decrease probabilities of success when designing programs with resistance reduction in mind. One option to overcome group dynamic tendencies toward self-reliant aggression and resistance requires development and implementation of inmate ranking systems. Using the military for example, soldiers assigned to units are grouped and quartered using an earned rank position. There is no question of who commands, of who follows instructions, or that a subordinate may become a superior's leader based upon merit and skill rather than coercion or brutality. Mob (gang) mentalities virtually never exist inside the unit's functional purpose. This suggestion adapts the successful Walnut Street Prison initiative previously discussed for application to crowded populations.

OPTIONS TO REDUCE RECIDIVISM

Success for piloted programs, such as the Sycamore Tree Project implemented in 42 prisons, depends upon the status of the inmate. For instance, "there were significant pre- and post-program improvements in prisoners' empathy with victims, their attitudes towards offending, and their perceptions of reoffending, although the results were not as positive for some prisons and for low security prisoners (who were mostly lifers reaching the end of their sentence)" (Dhami, Mantle, & Fox, 2009). In other words, "Short-timer's Disease" played a significant role with personal perceptions of the program. The chances for greatest effectiveness seemed to point to early initiation when incarcerated and those persons with significant amounts of time remaining in their sentences.

The Inside Out Trust program involves work projects within the local community and most staff report positive outcomes that fit within goals of the prison while establishing relationships within the community. Drawbacks occur with limited nature of work opportunities (Dhami, Mantle, & Fox, 2009). The Kentucky Correctional Institution for Women near Pewee Valley widely utilizes this rehabilitative framework as inmates dress in civilian clothing, catch the metro bus outside the prison gates to work, and are then trusted to return by a designated time (This writer witnessed the program in action).

Whatever program utilization takes place, concerns to eligibility include motivation, endorsement, reward structure, staffing levels, respect, and living conditions (Dhami, Mantle, & Fox, 2009). Inmates and staff should feel motivated to join in which increases the likelihood of program endorsement. Those persons participating solely for purposes of obtaining additional privileges usually slip into recidivism. Any program requires adequate staffing levels to implement correctly and consistently. Levels of respect between staff and inmates determine resistance while living conditions advance full-circle to induce motivation.

TIPS TO MINIMIZE RESISTANCE

Dougherty (2009) compiled a list of tips adaptable to prison systems. Topping the list resides "alleviate fear". This concept includes fear of punishment for failing to succeed or participate in a particular initiative as well as fear from personal harm or humiliation. By eliminating fear, motivation and endorsement levels increase as well as respect.

Collaboration entails working with stakeholders (inmates, staff, guards, and community) to develop programs that meet the needs of participants and to respond accordingly when concerns present themselves. Outcomes should appear worth the effort required. Providing choices, rather than setting brick-and-mortar sequences, trade senses of routineness for feelings of freedom and dignity through self-empowerment. Expectations from stakeholders should be clear and specific to avoid ambiguity and to intensify cohesiveness.

Time is a primary forethought in prison settings so learning new concepts or structures should be minimal and spread over time. Likewise, the skills necessary to carry out these new things need to be obtainable with the resources available and within ability of the learner. Recognizing and understanding referent power, especially between inmates and the staff structure, allows for prevention of resistance to begin with.

CONCLUSIONS

Nearly everyone knows change is inevitable and often encouraged, however, we still naturally resist it to some degree (Coon & Mitterer, 2010). Prisons provide extra challenges due to their socialization structures and confinement atmosphere. Regardless of mental states, prisoners and staff find themselves subject to role assumptions that can lead to aggressive tendencies they would not normally exhibit outside the scenario. Changes in definition of rehabilitation have led to initiatives that reduce resistance and enhance conformity, even after removal from the system. Increasing penalties leads to concurrent levels of resistance whereas implementing programs that foster dignity, cohesiveness, emotional stability, and skillsets needed within the community increase cooperation. Staff and inmates should work together in small steps without fear of humiliation or punishment and within their abilities for maximum effectiveness toward the goal of eliminating recidivism.

* * *

7.7 ORGANIZATIONAL CONSULTING SCENARIO

Dr. John Nichols of XYZ Consulting was contacted by Jane Patronne, fleet manager at Express Trucking, for consultation concerning extreme rates of turnover, frequent damage to equipment by drivers, consistently late deliveries, and higher than expected traffic ticket violations. Express Trucking has only been in business for two years and generally underbids competitors for loads, however, without much repeat business. Ms. Patronne iterated that she believed the problems root in the quality of the driver applicant pool and had engaged in hiring campaigns entailing what administration established as minimum qualifications of experience and quality. Unfortunately, no decreases in the underlying problems "seem evident" as a result of raising qualification standards.

Dr. Nichols had begun his career as a driver within the truckload industry and understood that "trucking industry" was a misnomer since driver types and companies remained as diversified as physicians did. For example, one would not realistically go to a podiatrist for heart problems; likewise, a tanker operator would not have the specialized skills necessary for refrigerated (reefer) operations, like those handled by Express Trucking. Dr. Nichols believes that his unique background assets the consultation concerns of Express Trucking and agrees to meet with Jane Patronne in her office.

STAGE 1: ENTRY

Dr. John Nichols, as a consultant, knows that diagnoses of the problems surrounding Express Trucking at this stage would prove premature (Dougherty, 2009) and personal past experiences could impose bias and misdiagnosis if he does not remain objective (Macionis, 2010) during his analysis of the organization's problems. For these reasons, Dr. Nichols defers diagnoses to the second stage and instead, concentrates upon gathering information, securing a contract for services, and entering the organizational system psychologically as well as physically.

Phase 1: Exploring Organizational Needs

Dr. Nichols meets with Jane Patronne at her office at the prearranged time. He prefers onsite initial meetings so he can gather observational data, including the general attitudinal and motivational atmosphere of the workplace, and to ensure mutual understanding of the expectations that consultation brings to the organization. He asks Ms. Patronne questions regarding the company's history, mission, philosophy, and procedures so he can align the tasks of familiarization with the problems previously reported and attempts at resolution.

Express Trucking formed after the previous employer of key administrators failed in bankruptcy and they realized demand for long-haul reefer transport services left by the previous employer left an unfilled competitive niche. None of the administrators ever drove trucks themselves, but they understood the need by transportation companies to acquire and maintain late-model equipment for overhead cost reduction, to provide on-time (expedient) services for repetitive referrals, and the importance of keeping trucks rolling for maximum income generation. This information provides perspective that Dr. Nichols can use later in identifying true root causes of the perceived problems already identified.

After evaluating the organizational situation, Dr. Nichols concludes that he can help Express Trucking toward resolution of the company's situation, reiterating to Jane Patronne his role as consultant, her role as the client and primary contact, and the role of the company as the client system in partnership toward goal fulfillment. He reinforces the concept that results are dependent upon participation and follow thru of the stakeholders and not the lone burden of any one member (Dougherty, 2009).

Phase 2: Contracting

Contracting is the process of explicitly formulating the parameters and nature of the consulting relationship that provides self-protection for the consultant and the client organization (Dougherty, 2009). The Uniform Commercial Code recommends that to be enforceable in case of default or dispute between the parties, contracts contain a minimum of explicit promises made by each party concerning performance, remuneration terms, and the proximal period the consultation service covers (Jennings, 2006). Contract securement reinforces psychological aspects of the consultation relationship on behalf of each party toward their common goal of assisting the organization in some way.

Given the volatile status of Express Trucking through information provided during the exploration of organizational needs phase, Dr. Nichols designs and writes a contract for Jane Patronne to submit to her administration for approval. He is sure to include the agreed upon payment amounts and schedule for his services, the fact he is a consultant and not an employee of Express Trucking (Milkovich & Newman, 2008), and a period not to exceed one year for the time period. Additionally, Dr. Nichols does not provide any written guarantees of consultation outcomes, but he does dictate the variable nature of scheduled meetings, obligations of each party during the consultation, needs for data collection, program modifications, and role expectations. After one week, he returns and collects the signed documents.

Phase 3: Physical System Entry

Physical and psychological entry occurs simultaneously with initial contact, yet separable in terms of impact upon the human perspectives of stakeholders. Interactions with truck drivers proves the most difficult for Dr. Nichols because they only return to the terminal (base of operations) approximately twice per month; usually near or on weekends, and never all at once due to the nature of the business. As a caveat, these personnel typically find themselves hurried to get home for time off while vehicle maintenance services are provided during their layover absence. Face-to-face interactions require Dr. Nichols to work with dispatchers to know when drivers return and to adjust his scheduling accordingly (Dougherty, 2009). Precipitating this process requires that Jane Patronne make dispatchers aware of his arrival, purpose, and duration within the organization to maximize cooperation. Upon introduction, Dr. Nichols explains his expectations and needs from the dispatchers.

Phase 4: Psychological System Entry

Understanding the differences between relevance, assumption, speculation, and the fear of administrative repercussion by participants helps Dr. Nichols psychologically sort fact from fiction during his inquiries. By ensuring confidentiality, he gains psychological advantages of trust, confidence, and honesty during interviews and other questioning (Coon & Mitterer, 2010). These qualities also enhance his persona of professionalism within the client system. Unfortunately, the uncertainty for interaction with drivers prohibits Dr. Nichols from seeking sufficient and timely direct contact with them, so he considers periodic development of anonymous surveys for inclusion with paystubs and an online option linked from (but not accessible by) the company website to maximize feedback opportunities. These alternative means allow interactions to remain focused, relevant, and pertinent to the consultation process with minimal disruption.

STAGE 2: DIAGNOSIS

The diagnostic stage of the consultation also entails four inter-related phases. Dr. Nichols and his client work together to gather accurate information to better conceptualize the root problems causing organizational problems and defining the real problems based upon that data. Once grounded, goal setting becomes plausible to help Dr. Nichols guide the organization toward their attainment. To do this, the consultant and client work together to generate strategies and interventions designed to get the organization where it desires to be.

Phase 1: Gather Information

Dr. Nichols knows the initial reason Express Trucking contacted him for consultation services may be masking underlying problems or matters unobvious to the organization (Dougherty, 2009). As discovered during the initial meeting, he understands the scope of expertise of administrators lies primarily within the perspective of business and customer outcomes, and not necessarily with the rarely seen drivers who carry out the main business function (transportation services).

To obtain their feedback, Dr. Nichols designs surveys with open-ended feedback mechanisms to catch information he may not perceive as concerns with truck drivers. These surveys are then included with driver paystubs and postage paid envelopes addressed to the consultant's office for anonymity and accuracy purposes. The encrypted online component enables savings and return time from those drivers who prefer internet submission. After compilation, Dr. Nichols meets with Jane Patronne to share and discuss results.

Phase 2: Problem Definition

Virtually no credible research exists over the last two decades concerning truck drivers of any kind. Many opinion pieces plague periodicals over legalities, but lack in credibility and research support. Many more appear as propaganda pieces geared toward recruiting efforts by human resource personnel. In short, data collected during the consultation process serves as the benchmark for comparison purposes. Fortunately, data analysis forces development and definition of the task in question to affect the rest of the consultation process (Dougherty, 2009) as Dr. Nichols and Ms. Patronne discovered from the open-ended components of the questionnaires.

More than 70% of Express Trucking drivers reported they were unhappy with their jobs. Roughly 34% reported having incurred a divorce since joining the company and approximately 45% claimed they did not receive adequate home time. Exactly 23% of drivers felt the company saw them as "expendable pawns", putting company goals over employee satisfaction. Similarly, dispatchers reported 12%, 1%, 1.5%, and 24%, respectively to the same questions. Reviewing benefits packages showed industry averages at first glance, however, closer analysis revealed that many benefits were unaffordable (health insurance), unusable (sick days), or unfair (vacation length dependent on number of days spent over the road – up to five days per year). No employee indicated any training sessions after hire for job enhancement or family services while the driver was away.

Together, Dr. Nichols and Ms. Patronne framed root problems as antecedents to the high turnover, low morale, and skill quality problems. First, overwork with little time for family obligations possibly contribute to high divorce rates and mental distraction from the job. Second, the benefits packages are inadequate and need reformulation to appeal to employees. Third employees feel underappreciated and possibly coerced through false pretenses by administration. Lastly, no training is provided to employees at the skill levels desired by the company. Jane commented resistance in that she could "not see administration implementing changes to these problems as it would surely be expensive". At this point Dr. Nichols reassured her the next steps set goals and generate possible solutions where many exist as free or low-cost alternatives. "The key here", he said, "is outsourcing ideas by asking employees what they want" (Jennings, 2006). "It may be less than anyone expects."

Phase 3: Goal Setting

Before selecting possibilities for interventions, the process of goal setting demands these interventions have end purposes. Some goals may be as complex as the problems intended for elimination, but all must be concrete and follow seven steps as outlined by Dougherty (2009):

1) specify the task or objective,
2) specify the task measurement method,
3) specify the target to be reached,
4) allocate the timespan,
5) prioritize goal possibilities,
6) rate goals to difficulty and importance, and
7) determine coordination requirements.

Dr. Nichols and Jane Patronne decide on four primary goals. The first goal is to recognize and encourage familial interaction. Measurement can be accomplished through the number of family-oriented complaints in comparison to satisfaction survey results administered to employees and their families. A target of zero is ideal, but not likely, so efforts to reduce these numbers as close to zero, while showing consistent improvement, is desirable. Coordination will primarily be the responsibility of dispatchers through coordination with drivers.

Benefit alternatives that provide value to employees need discovery and implementation. Quarterly survey of employees should near 100% ideally, however, significant improvement ratings should suffice. Coordination efforts between administration and employees with responsibility given to the human resources department for measurement and implementation are required.

Employees should feel appreciated and important to the organization, regardless of job title. This goal is the hardest to measure accurately, but may include empirical data from outside comments about organizational culture and morale. This task is the responsibility of administration (Luthans, 2008) through leadership initiatives in response to employee satisfaction levels.

Training programs at hire and post-hire should be developed and implemented that provide benefit to the organization and the individual employee. Although this task cannot be measured directly, outcomes of individual training initiatives can through profitability, reduced costs, and increased retention (Heneman III & Judge, 2009). Responsibility for development or outsourcing, implementation, and measurement is the responsibility human resources through coordination with employees, managers, and dispatchers. This goal also supplements the goal for increased appreciation.

Phase 4: Generate Intervention Possibilities

Interventions detail the systematic flow of goal attainment. Dr. Nichols encourages Ms. Patronne to generate as many possibilities as she can before their next meeting in order to stimulate creativity and to ease her future dependence upon him. Of course, he instructs her to ask others in the organization for ideas, especially truck drivers that may be passing through. This practice helps her to become successful and to develop as a professional (Barnes & Austin, 2008).

Over the next couple of sessions, Dr. Nichols reviews ideas presented by Ms. Patronne for feasibility, effectiveness in similar situations, costs of implementation and maintenance, ethical considerations, and ease of measurement. On occasion, he contributes ideas he knows to have validity, utility, and reliability through current research findings and practices within other organizations. Barnes and Austin iterate how by taking a supportive, rather than leadership, role the culmination of these characteristics show how Dr. Nichols' purpose is multifaceted and somewhat complicated. Selection begins the third stage: implementation.

STAGE 3: IMPLEMENTATION

Now the consultation team has generated possible interventions, the objective is to choose one or more with the highest probability of succeeding and implement them (Dougherty, 2009). This is essentially the stage where the greatest resistance from administration and employees is likely to be greatest since changes are put into action. For Dr. Nichols, and especially Jane Patronne, the difficulties of evaluation of plan initiatives compound their efforts.

Phase 1: Intervention Choices

The list of possible interventions generated by the consultation team varied in complexity, cost, and scope. They ranged from establishing daycare assistance for employees with working spouses, to development of an "At-a Boy"-type awards program, to establishing maximum allowable time on the road coupled with minimum time required off. At the individual level, consulting services for troubled marriages had been suggested for viability.

Dr. Nichols suggested adopting a Total Quality Management (TQM) philosophy within the organization to guide management of the singular initiatives. Many long-lived dry-bulk trucking companies have successfully adopted TQM in order to attain global certification under ISO 9000 series standards (Alexopoulos & Konstantopoulos, 2007). ISO certification also enables Express Trucking to begin the process of multicultural recognition and ethical differences.

Phase 2: Plan Formulation

Over the next few meetings, Dr. Nichols emphasizes the critical nature of collaboration with Jane Patronne by working with her and responsible personnel at developing alternative plans of action directed at prioritizing and implementing chosen interventions (Dougherty, 2009). For each plan, they determine its objectives, choose its procedures, and establish the time frame for action. Responsible persons are assigned while constantly scrutinizing components and making adjustments as necessary. Each step is check-listed as a sub-goal to measure progression.

Using force-field analysis, restraints for plans are weighed against their driving forces to help in determining the most feasible of choices (Egan, 2007). This way resistance and other identified pitfalls may be minimized when planned in advance at each step.

Phase 3: Plan Implementation

Dr. Nichols closely monitors how his client oversees implementation of the chosen plan in coordination with other collaborating personnel. Jane Patronne regularly contacts him with questions regarding technical assistance, as do administrators who found the TQM concept intriguing and worthwhile. Dr. Nichols provides training support on their behalf over the next few weeks that builds commitment to the overall consultation process (Egan, 2007). To help reduce the risk of failure and to increase social validity, he ensures that he provides feedback throughout the implementation process (Dougherty, 2009).

Phase 4: Plan Evaluation

At the end of each quarter, Dr. Nichols met with Jane Patronne to discuss and evaluate how well the overall plan was implemented. Agenda included items of measurement in comparison with original goal attainment and the levels of progress. Overall, turnover had reduced by 15% during the previous six months and satisfaction surveys indicated employees were 20% happier with Express Trucking as an employer. Damages to equipment, including abandonment of trucks, reduced significantly for an overall cost savings that more than paid for many program implementations. Although the consultation process was still in infancy, Dr. Nichols suggested that he disengage from aspects the organization seemed to have under control and concentrate his efforts more on delayed improvement areas.

STAGE 4: DISENGAGEMENT

Through feedback and plan evaluation, Dr. Nichols suggested he disengage from areas of the consultation process the company seemed to handle well without his interaction and assistance. Over time, his goal as consultant is to completely terminate the particular relationship in hopes of future consultation scenarios (Dougherty, 2009), but he knows gradual disengagement generally proves more successful than abrupt termination. The disengagement process works more in the background on his part, but has psychological and social implications that affect the client organization. He begins by evaluating the consultation process, continues to provide post-consultation remedies, reduces involvement, and finally terminates from the consultation.

Phase 1: Process Evaluation

Evaluation involves looking at the overall consultation process to determine if established goals meet satisfactory ends. Evaluation also looks at whether the client potentially demonstrates adequate ability in effectively handling similar situations in the future without the consultant. To accomplish this, Dr. Nichols must measure the overall effectiveness of the program by evaluating perceived behaviors of his client in addition to the consultation process itself. Inclusion of perceived benefits by the client helps to him to establish credibility and potential for future consultation and collaboration (Dougherty, 2009).

Dr. Nichols implements a questionnaire designed to assess aspects reporting the client's perceived abilities, effectiveness, and acceptability of his efforts adapted from one offered by Cott et.al., (2006) with a high validity correlation of 0.78 (p < .01). The evaluation also measured emotional support, coordination and continuity, and the link between goal setting and goal attainment.

Phase 2: Post-Consultation Planning

Dr. Nichols expected issues to occur after his departure and so made post-consultation plans to handle these matters effectively. The objective in this phase was to assist the client as needed in a helpful perspective after departure. Topics to consider when formulating post-consultation plans included assigning responsibilities he no longer handled, cost effectiveness for program continuance, and the capabilities of the client and client system.

By integrating methods of self-reporting measures into the client's routines, he decreased reliance upon him, increased confidence in the client and client system, and encouraged communication internally (Kamholz et.al., 2006).

Phase 3: Reduced Involvement and Follow-Up

The third phase begins after post-consultation planning meets to the satisfaction of everyone involved. Studies by O'Brien, Fahmy, and Singh (2009) showed that abrupt disengagement is nearly twice as likely to occur in consultations lasting less than a year (40%) than those enduring from one (26%) to five years (11%); further showing necessity for gradual disconnection.

Dr. Nichols began reducing involvement when feedback indicated successful implementation of certain program parts and his involvement was no longer necessary. This allowed his client to assume responsibilities in an independent manner while continuing availability to his client with reinforcement initiatives.

Phase 4: Termination

Termination involves formally ending the consultation and collaboration relationship, mostly from psychological perspectives (Dougherty, 2009). The physical break-up begins to occur during fading and follow-up at a gradual pace, but psychologically closure remains open. Successful termination provides mental aspects in a sense of satisfaction of accomplishment and may lead to repeat opportunities for consultation.

Accordingly, Dr. Nichols schedules final meetings that formally mark termination. During these interludes, he works with Jane Patronne, administrators, and other employees to resolve open issues, to review his final report, and to reiterate lessons learned. Dr. Nichols leaves with the comment that he would like to work with Express Transport again in the future, as he feels confident in the abilities of employees to prevail.

* * *

PART SEVEN APPENDIX

Table 7.1.1

Differential Characteristics in Consultation Types

Process /Role	Skills Required	Culture Sensitivity	Use of Preventative Measure	Use of Remediate Measures	Ownership of Change	Scope of Action	Level of Directedness
General:							Decreasing
Consultation			Usage	Usage	Client and Client's System	Provides knowledge, skills, and abilities the client lacks	
Collaboration	Depends upon specific role of consultant	Depends upon the problem in question			Client	Enhances client's existing KSAs	
Mid-Level:							Decreasing
Supervision	Usage	Usage	Depends upon specific role of consultant	Usage	Client	Take action with client's system on behalf of client	
Mediation			None		Client and Client's System	Referee between client and client's system	
Specific:							Decreasing
Advocate	Subject-knowledge; Interpersonal; Communication; Cultural-diversity; Problem-solving; Ethical skills	Regional; Organizational; Group	Recommendations based upon knowledge, skills, and abilities of consultant	Recommendations based upon knowledge, skills, and abilities of consultant	Client (e.g., tech advisor)	Specific goal or achievement	
Expert	Subject-knowledge; Interpersonal; Communication; Cultural-diversity; Problem-solving; Ethical skills	Regional; Organizational; Group; Poverty; Racism	Prevent needs of client system for advocacy	Discrepancy remediation	Varies – can be lose-lose if a client system focus	Professional obligation while eliminating avoidance	

Continued next page...

Process /Role	Skills Required	Culture Sensitivity	Use of Preventative Measure	Use of Remediate Measures	Ownership of Change	Scope of Action	Level of Directedness
Trainer /Educator	Subject-knowledge Interpersonal Communication Cultural-diversity Group skills	Regional Organizational Group	Stress importance of skills taught for active implementation by client	Retraining Workshops	Client even with client system interaction (trainer)	Client system through formal/informal training	
Fact Finder Process Specialist	Communication Cultural-diversity Problem-solving Research skills Some subject knowledge Interpersonal Communication Cultural-diversity Problem-solving Ethical skills Group skills	Depends upon the scope of the defined problem Regional Organizational Group	Recommendations to client after data analysis Risk of unsolicited interpersonal feedback	Recommendations to client after data analysis Use of guided group self-analysis	Client Client however their colleagues may be the client system	Find, analyze, and report information to client: no direct interaction with client system Analyze processes of client's systems: "How"	

Note: Composited from "Psychological Consultation and Collaboration in School and Community Settings, 5th edition," by A. Michael Dougherty, 2009, pp 22-35. The Level of Directedness column adapted from "Consulting-style Inventory: A Tool for Consultants and Others in Helping Roles," by Timothy M. Nolan, 1998, The Pfeiffer Library (2nd Ed., Vol.15, pp 1-3), 1998, Jossey-Bass/Pfeiffer.

Table 7.1.2

VIA Survey of Character Strengths

Strength	Title	Description
1	Judgment, critical thinking, and open-mindedness	Thinking things through and examining them from all sides are important aspects of who you are. You do not jump to conclusions, and you rely only on solid evidence to make your decisions. You are able to change your mind.
2	Citizenship, teamwork, and loyalty	You excel as a member of a group. You are a loyal and dedicated teammate, you always do your share, and you work hard for the success of your group.
3	Fairness, equity, and justice	Treating all people fairly is one of your abiding principles. You do not let your personal feelings bias your decisions about other people. You give everyone a chance.
4	Honesty, authenticity, and genuineness	You are an honest person, not only by speaking the truth but by living your life in a genuine and authentic way. You are down to earth and without pretense; you are a "real" person.
5	Industry, diligence, and perseverance	You work hard to finish what you start. No matter the project, you "get it out the door" in timely fashion. You do not get distracted when you work, and you take satisfaction in completing tasks.
6	Bravery and valor	You are a courageous person who does not shrink from threat, challenge, difficulty, or pain. You speak up for what is right even if there is opposition. You act on your convictions.
7	Hope, optimism, and future-mindedness	You expect the best in the future, and you work to achieve it. You believe that the future is something that you can control.
8	Creativity, ingenuity, and originality	Thinking of new ways to do things is a crucial part of who you are. You are never content with doing something the conventional way if a better way is possible.
9	Curiosity and interest in the world	You are curious about everything. You are always asking questions, and you find all subjects and topics fascinating. You like exploration and discovery.
10	Self-control and self-regulation	You self-consciously regulate what you feel and what you do. You are a disciplined person. You are in control of your appetites and your emotions, not vice versa.
11	Love of learning	You love learning new things, whether in a class or on your own. You have always loved school, reading, and museums--anywhere and everywhere there is an opportunity to learn.
12	Zest, enthusiasm, and energy	Regardless of what you do, you approach it with excitement and energy. You never do anything halfway or halfheartedly. For you, life is an adventure.
13	Forgiveness and mercy	You forgive those who have done you wrong. You always give people a second chance. Your guiding principle is mercy and not revenge.
14	Leadership	You excel at the tasks of leadership: encouraging a group to get things done and preserving harmony within the group by making everyone feel included. You do a good job organizing activities and seeing that they happen.
15	Social intelligence	You are aware of the motives and feelings of other people. You know what to do to fit in to different social situations and you know what to do to put others at ease.
16	Caution, prudence, and discretion	You are a careful person, and your choices are consistently prudent ones. You do not say or do things that you might later regret.

Strength	Title	Description
17	Gratitude	You are aware of the good things that happen to you, and you never take them for granted. Your friends and family members know that you are a grateful person because you always take the time to express your thanks.
18	Perspective (wisdom)	Although you may not think of yourself as wise, your friends hold this view of you. They value your perspective on matters and turn to you for advice. You have a way of looking at the world that makes sense to others and to yourself.
19	Humor and playfulness	You like to laugh and tease. Bringing smiles to other people is important to you. You try to see the light side of all situations.
20	Modesty and humility	You do not seek the spotlight, preferring to let your accomplishments speak for themselves. You do not regard yourself as special, and others recognize and value your modesty.
21	Capacity to love and be loved	You value close relations with others, in particular those in which sharing and caring reciprocate. The people to whom you feel most close are the same people who feel most close to you.
22	Kindness and generosity	You are kind and generous to others, and you are never too busy to do a favor. You enjoy doing good deeds for others, even if you do not know them well.
23	Spirituality, sense of purpose, and faith	You have strong and coherent beliefs about the higher purpose and meaning of the universe. You know where you fit in the larger scheme. Your beliefs shape your actions and are a source of comfort to you.
24	Appreciation of beauty and excellence	You notice and appreciate beauty, excellence, and/or skilled performance in all domains of life, from nature to art to mathematics to science to everyday experience.

Note: Results of the *VIA Survey of Character Strengths*, recorded October 2011. The first five translate into the strongest individual character strengths of those listed.

* * *

PART SEVEN REFERENCES

Alexopoulos, A. B., & Konstantopoulos, N. (2007). Total Quality Management in Dry-Bulk Shipping. In T. E. Simos, & G. Maroulis (Ed.), Computation in Modern Science and Engineering, Proceedings of the International Conference on Computational Methods in Science and Engineering 2007. 2, pp. 1110-1113. American Institute of Physics.

Anderson, J. A. (2010). Evolution of the Health Care Quality Journey: From cost reduction to facilitating patient safety. The Journal of Legal Medicine (31), 59-72. doi:10.1080/01947641003598252.

Barnes, B. J., & Austin, A. E. (2008, October 3). The Role of Doctoral Advisors: A Look at Advising from The Advisor's Perspective. Innovative Higher Education (33), 297-315. doi:10.1007/s10755-008-9084-x.

Barnett, D. (2011). Posts tagged 'VIA Survey of Character Strengths'. (WordPress) Retrieved from Dr. Deborah Barnett: Psychology in Asheville NC: http://deborahbarnett.com/blog/?tag=via-survey-of-character-strengths.

Barrett, T., Streeter, B., Lawson, P., Zraly, M., Longhofer, J., & Buchbinder, M. (2005). The Hanna Perkins Center Model for Consultation in Childcare: Meeting the Needs of Children and Their Caregivers. Hanna Perkins Center for Child Development.

Carroll, A. B., & Buchholtz, A. K. (2009). Business & Society: Ethics and Stakeholder Management (7th ed.). Mason, OH: South-Western Cengage Learning.

Coon, D., & Mitterer, J. O. (2010). Introduction to Psychology (12th ed.). Belmont, CA: Wadsworth.

Cott, C. A., Teare, G., McGilton, K. S., & Lineker, S. (2006, November). Reliability and Construct Validity of the Client-Centred Rehabilitation Questionnaire. Disability and Rehabilitation, 28(22), 1387-1397. doi:10.1080/09638280600638398.

Depersis, D. S., & Lewis, A. (2008, September). The Development of American Prisons and Punishment. The International Journal of Human Rights, 12(4), 637-651. doi:10.1080/13642980802204818.

Dhami, M. K., Mantle, G., & Fox, D. (2009, December). Restorative Justice in Prisons. Contemporary Justice Review, 12(4), 433-448. doi:DOI: 10.1080/10282580903343027.

Dougherty, A. M. (2009). Psychological Consultation and Collaboration in School and Community Settings (5th ed.). Belmont, CA: Brooks/Cole.

Egan, G. (2007). The Skilled Helper. In A. M. Dougherty, Psychological Consultation and Collaboration in School and Community Settings (5th ed., p. 99). Belmont, CA: Brooks/Cole.

Field, A. (2009). Discovering Statistics Using SPSS (3rd ed.). Thousand Oaks, CA: Sage Publishing, Inc.

Friedlander, J. (1978). Student Perceptions on the Effectiveness of Midterm Feedback to Modify College Instruction. Journal of Educational Research, 71(3), 140-143.

Foster, C. (2008, January 29). Coaching Series: Leading from Strength: Making a Difference as Only You Can.

Heneman III, H. G., & Judge, T. A. (2009). Staffing Organizations (6th ed.). Boston, MA: McGraw-Hill/Irwin.

Houston, D. (2007, April). TQM and Higher Education: A Critical Systems Perspective on Fitness for Purpose. Quality in Higher Education, 13(1), 3-17. doi:10.1080/13538320701272672.

Houston, D., Robertson, T., & Prebble, T. (2008, November). Exploring Quality in a University Department: Perspectives and Meanings. Quality in Higher Education, 14(3), 209-223. doi:10.1080/13538320802507463.

Jennings, M. M. (2006). Business: Its Legal, Ethical, and Global Environment (7th ed.). Mason, OH: Thomson Higher Learning.

Kamholz, B. W., Hayes, A. M., Carver, C. S., Gulliver, S. B., & Perlman, C. A. (2006, April). Identification and Evaluation of Cognitive Affect-Regulation Strategies: Development of a Self-Report Measure. Cognitive Therapy and Research, 30(2), 227-262. doi:10.1007/s10608-006-9013-1.

Kezar, A., Glenn, W. J., Lester, J., & Nakamoto, J. (2008, April). Examining Organizational Contextual Features That Affect Implementation of Equity Initiatives. The Journal of Higher Education, 79(2), 125-159.

Luthans, F. (2008). Organizational Behavior (11th ed.). Boston, MA: McGraw-Hill/Irwin.

Macionis, J. J. (2010). Sociology (13th ed.). Boston, MA: Prentice Hall.

Milkovich, G. T., & Newman, J. M. (2008). Compensation (9th ed.). New York, NY: McGraw-Hill/Irwin.

Nolan, T. M. (1998). Consulting-Style Inventory: A Tool for Consultants and Others in Helping Roles. In Jossey-Bass/Pfeiffer, The Pfeiffer Library (2nd ed., Vol. 15, pp. 1-3). USA: Jossey-Bass/Pfeiffer.

O'Brien, A., Fahmy, R., & Singh, S. P. (2009). Disengagement from Mental Health Services. Social Psychiatry, 44, 558-568. doi:10.1007/s00127-008-0476-0.

Oketch, M. O. (2005). The Corporate Stake in Social Cohesion. Peabody Journal of Education, 80(4), 30-52.

Opara, U. N. (2010). Shoert Communication: Toward Improving Library and Information Services Delivery in Nigeria Through Total Quality Management. African Journal of Library, Archives and Information Science, 20(1), 63-68.

Parcover, J. A., Mettrick, J., Parcover, C. A., & Griffin-Smith, P. (2009, Fall). University and College Counselors as Athletic Team Consultants: Using a Structural Family Therapy Model. Journal of College Counseling, 12, 149-161.

Pearson Learning Solutions. (2010). SKS7000 - Executive Concepts in Business Strategy. Boston, MA: Pearson Learning Solutions.

Seligman, M. (2006). Authentic Happiness. (The Trustees of the University of Pennsylvania) Retrieved from Authentic Happiness: http://www.authentichappiness.sas.upenn.edu/default.aspx.

United Parcel Service. (2011, October 30). United Parcel Service Jobs > Search results for 'consultant'. Retrieved from www.UPSjobs.com: http://jobs-ups.com/search/consultant.

Zimbardo, P. G. (2009). Pathology of Imprisonment. In J. J. Macionis, Sociology (13th ed., pp. 40-41). Boston, MA: Prentice Hall.

* * *

PART EIGHT: BUSINESS AND MANAGEMENT CONSULTING

8.1 MANAGEMENT CONSULTING IN CONTEXT

This paper examines the context of management consulting in brief overview. Discussion begins with a simplified description of the profession and moves into a comprehensive look at the roles in which consultants and collaborators serve (with summary table). Mention of many risks associated with consultation practices precedes how modern consultation models help to manage the processes involved for maximum benefit. The closing discussion provides personal preferences with consulting opportunities, lists recent encounters, and correlation with topics throughout the paper.

DESCRIPTION OF MANAGEMENT CONSULTANTS

Management consultants employ a variety of skills with support from as many management techniques. Skills are consolidated, rather than isolated, to particular tasks in a non-sequential fashion (Wickham & Wickham, 2008) as an activity. For some, management consulting is a demanding process found within organizations of all types with projects as mottled in scope and duration as the people employing them. Services provided add value to the organization (Cope, 2010) and facilitate change with (not on behalf of) the stakeholders involved (Dougherty, 2009), showing the relevance of relationships as the base construct. Examination of the roles, risks, and processes involved with consulting and collaboration enhances understanding of what the activity entails.

ROLES OF MANAGEMENT CONSULTANTS

Often the literature refers to recognition of five consulting roles established in the early 20th century: Planning, organizing, staffing, directing, and controlling (Wickham & Wickham, 2008). Planning includes deciding future courses of action within a project; a middle-tier task in more modern models (Dougherty, 2009; Cope, 2010). Organizing bonds as a sub-task with planning in these models through definition of relationships for individuals and sub-groups involved with the activities prescribed during the program. Similarly, and barely distinguishable, staffing serves with the actual dissemination of duties among project personnel, whether project administrators or members of the client system. Wickham and Wickham simplify modern interpretations of directing to involve the leadership skills needed to motivate individuals and teams within an organizational culture, and controlling as the management of resources. These latter roles from the older schema refer to skills necessary for the accomplishment of providing value to the consulting process in the newer conceptual models, not really roles as viewed from modern perspectives.

Consultants differ in the roles they undertake depending upon the situational nature of their client interactions. Dougherty (2009) identified at three levels of role types with emphases on skills required to perform their functions:

1) cultural sensitivity needed for effectiveness,
2) the degree of preventative or remediate measures utilized,
3) stakeholders affected by work results, and
4) for whom the consultant's actions are primarily directed.

The levels recognized included:

1) Consultation versus Collaboration,
2) Supervision versus Mediation, and
3) a catchall level formulated for specific roles that did not fully fit within the other two termed Specific Processes and Roles.

Table 1 (Appendix) demonstrates these correlations as described by Dougherty.

The first category differentiated from the others using variable levels of skills needed by the consultant and cultural sensitivity as dependent upon the role assumed and problem in question, respectively, while collaborators dealt less with preventive and remediate measures than persons operating in consultative roles. Insofar as their levels of directing the consultation process, the inverse was true. Among consultants fixated within the second category, Supervision versus Mediation, usage of remediate measures increased toward supervisory roles and decreased in levels of directedness within mediation services. It is important to note supervisory roles often required more skills and cultural sensitivity than mediators while the latter demonstrated no need for use of remediate measures in consultative practices.

Specific roles, as identified by Dougherty, ranked by lowering levels of directedness required in the consultation process: advocate, expert, trainer/educator, fact finder, and process specialist. Although many shared common skillsets (communication, problem solving, etc.), some skills were in greater demand for roles interfacing with people (e.g. group and interpersonal) in comparison to isolated practitioners (e.g. research skills). Conventions of remediate and preventative measures were defined for the client or client system with whom the consultant ultimately interacted.

Cope (2010) took more of a macro-perspective in noting "the process of consulting, where the goal is sustainable value within a diverse range of client situations [with a human touch]" (p. 1). Remembering the final goal of any consulting process, regardless of specific role, is to provide value to the people underwriting the consultation, stand firm as a key prerogative. The objective is not to employ the consultant, but to enable the client with definitive results that promote the client's interests. This is usually accomplished through a change process with which the client adheres after the consultant relieves himself/herself from the program. Cope failed to consider all consulting roles identified by Dougherty when he declared, "change is about people and people need it to be personal, and hence want social contact" (p. 4) as many fact finders and mediators work without direct contact with the client systems, taking positions of neutrality. Regardless of the primary model adopted, however, situations arise that require flexibility, adaptability, and compromise in the role(s) assumed by the consultant.

RISKS OF MANAGEMENT CONSULTING

Risks involved with consulting vary according to the roles assumed by the consultant. For example, external consultants endure the primary risk (or gain) of financial status. These persons depend upon project successes, marketing efforts, cash flows from organizations served, and consistency of work in order to survive in their specialties. On the other hand, internal consultants generally provide other services within an organization that allow for occasional project failures, little to no marketing, a steady paycheck, and little risk to overall reputation. The risks of commercial value reside with the organization rather than the individual consultant in most of these instances (Dougherty, 2009; Wickham & Wickham, 2008).

Cope (2010) argued that consultants fail if they lose sight of their purpose in servitude and model the project to their own best interests, risking the outcomes of the project. This did not mean the consultant should avoid internalizing the project to make it their own, but that he/she should remember the true social context of their involvement within the consultation as a temporary contract – "not a marriage" (p. 4). Additionally, Cope warned ignoring past failures condemns the consultant to repeat the same mistakes and thus hindering the development or change process.

In cooperation with culture sensitivity as depicted in Table 1, differences in social and cultural factors can prove detrimental to a consultation effort (Dougherty, 2009). For instance, attempting to help a religious organization develop anti-discriminatory practices can prove doomed from the outset if that particular religion outwardly supports some forms of discrimination, such as sexual preference selection. In these cases, the consultant must understand the underlying cultural values before engaging in the project or risk failure. Within the same line of thinking, personal biases from the consultant, when analyzing the data or recommending interventions, may deter collaborative efforts.

In short, the consultant should weigh the risks involved with each step of the consultation process and strive to balance those risks with expected outcomes. As each project is unique, so too are the risks involved. Obtaining as much information as possible at the initial meeting and striving for organizational support throughout the consultation process from the client and other stakeholders assists with (but rarely eliminates) risk minimization (Dougherty, 2009).

PROCESSES OF MANAGEMENT CONSULTING

Dougherty (2009) introduced a four-stage model for consulting and collaboration as a process. The first stage, Exploring Organizational Needs, involved assessing organizational needs, contracting, physically entering the system, and psychologically entering the system. The Diagnosis stage consisted of collaborating with the client to gather information before defining root problems and setting goals to generate possible solutions. After choosing an intervention in the third stage, plans were formulated and implemented with constant plan evaluations; hence the Implementation stage. Disengagement began by evaluating the consultation process as a whole and reducing consultant involvement until the clients handled implementations on their own. Once satisfied, the consultant could then terminate the process.

Cope (2010) followed a seven-stage process similar to Dougherty with only one distinctive change; Dougherty's Implementation stage was broken down into four separate stages, although these resemble the individual phases (sub parts) of Implementation. Cope's stages included Client (exploring), Clarify (diagnosis), Create (implement), Change (implement), Confirm (implement), Continue (implement), and Close (disengage). Following either model should yield similar outcomes.

CONCLUSIONS

Personally, I have no desire to work as an external consultant and dependent upon economic conditions for income. I prefer internalized projects in addition to my regular duties as a reward for recognition of my skills. I currently work as a social science instructor for a small college with two ongoing consultation projects. The first began in September to develop, recruit, and begin competition with an academic bowl team (similar to Jeopardy!) within 30 days representing the college throughout southern Illinois. Successful with completion of a uniformed and partial-scholarship team finishing their fourth match at the 60-day mark. I was then asked to advance the team to state-level competition and assigned a second project.

I gained the microbiology program after teaching one course over the summer and recommending update and makeover of the lab to the college Dean. The new assignment is to research, locate, and recommend necessary equipment that meets curriculum requirements in addition to potential student-employer expectations. Both projects provide no direct additional compensation, but do advance opportunity for tenure (a sevenfold base salary increase).

These projects demonstrate the diversity of consultation through skills needed by the consultant and the nature/scope of the projects themselves. Rewards for success can be high, even if delayed, especially when following an adaptive consultation model. Roles taken may alter outcomes to the positive when properly assessed and implemented. The greatest challenge is weighing the risks of all identified stakeholders for a balance in relational support.

* * *

8.2 BUILDING A CLIENT RELATIONSHIP

This paper examines trust as it relates to the five human elements identified in the TRUST model and expands these concepts through evaluation of the Change Ladder model at the organizational level. Recommendations for effective consultants follow based upon the principles of application gleamed from those examinations.

DEFINING TRUST

Trust between the consultant and the client serves as the basis for higher levels of rapport (Wickham & Wickham, 2008). Rapport is the skill of building cooperative relationships that enable persons to put each other at ease and, in turn, improves trust. These mutually exclusive concepts may appear cyclic, but actually serve as complementary forces. For example, if a client distrusts the consultant then rapport levels minimize and likely carry forward in the reputation of the consultant seeking future work. However, the consultant experiencing high levels of trust with clients may not only enjoy rapport with the current client through repeat business, but also find an excellent reputation precedes higher workloads. Together rapport and trust increase through effective communication at every point of interaction in a similar relational fashion.

The TRUST acronym developed by Cope (2010) reinforced these relationships in that consultants should remain truthful, responsive, uniform, safe, and trained. Just as a married couple expects unyielding *truthful*ness from one another to keep the bonds of the relationship strong, so too does a consultant/client affiliation. This business requisite extends to disclosure of full truths without predicating what the client may want to hear. Dishonesty at any level destroys trust. Likewise, a marriage partner who fails to be *responsive* to the needs of the other often finds the partnership irrevocably broken. "I can't trust you to be there for me when I need you" and "We just don't talk anymore" similarly echo into failed consultations where either the consultant or the client does not fully engage.

Uniformity extends throughout the consultation through consistency of ideas and attitudes (Wickham & Wickham, 2008). Frequent mind changing indulges confusion among clients and enhances doubt in the consultant's abilities that erode trust. Dialog that reassures the client's emotional context helps them to feel *safe* in the working relationship, further stabilizing trust issues. Finally, Cope insisted clients who feel competent in the consultant's expertise through *training* and experience find deeper confidence with offered skills. Additionally, prior reputation sets the stage for future trust levels. The TRUST elements, when combined, assist with understanding how rapport and communication work intertwined with trust within the consulting relationship.

CHANGE LADDER AND TRUST

The Change Ladder model describes five elements (Asset, Blueprint, Capability, Desire, and Ethos) related to trust building. This framework allows for assessment of the issues under consideration and the extent to which sustainable change is delivered within a consultation project. Although tangible and intangible factors weigh in under the Change Ladder model, only the latter provides concern in relation to trust. Examination of individual elements follows.

Assets

Sustainable benefit of tangible assets requires understanding the associated symbolic meaning tied to them (Cope, 2010). This is a fundamental concept found in religious dogma and rituals (Macionis, 2010) that spills over into other human activities. For instance, just as the cross implies connotations of belief in Christians beyond Judaism or Mecca symbolizes a sense of fulfillment in Muslims, something as simple as location of a manager's office denotes differentiation of leadership levels. All of these intangible concepts denote meaning throughout the organization and respecting them instills greater trust in the consultant by the client.

Blueprint

Blueprinting covers the methods by which systems are managed. These methods range from complex tactical and strategic plans in larger organizations to the written script that produces a play or movie. Usually, canned (prepackaged) solutions provide limited value over the short term for the organization (Cope, 2010) and hence, little in terms of reputation creation (trust) for the consultant. Molding these methods to the client situation, rather than the other way around, creates challenges for the consultant in providing sustainable change that provides value over the long-term.

Assessing the organizational environment as tight (structured) or loose (flexible) allows the consultant to find a middle ground approach for application of the change process that benefits the greatest number of stakeholders. The primary goal is to encourage the client to generate implementations (with assistance, of course) that stimulate creativity and reduce future dependence upon the consultant (Dougherty, 2009). Inclusion of other persons affected by the change project serve as effective prompts (Jennings, 2006), depending upon the nature of the venture. Just as a child bonds tighter to a parent who interacts with them (Papalia, Olds, & Feldman, 2009), stakeholders learn to trust implementers who include those persons affected.

Capability

Training previously described by the TRUST model not only entails the explicit (overt) skills required by consultants in building the trust relationship, but also the incorporation and application of skillsets within the client system. At a deeper level, the covert skills demonstrated by the consultant, the organizational culture, and the scope of the change project provide insight to the level of competitive advantage desired by the client. These implicit capabilities tend to be difficult to describe yet provide a competitive advantage to those organizations and individuals that possess it (Cope, 2010).

Possessing insight due to experience within a particular project provides the implicit skills sought by the client from a consultant. This ability is non-transferrable in the short-term and allows the organization to gain advantages over competitors. The trust in the consultant to deliver added value to the organization, beyond tangible skillsets, transfers to the quality of outcomes. The responsibility of the consultant is to deliver success and development as professionals to their clients through implicit and explicit learning (Barnes & Austin, 2008).

Desire

Desire most often finds oversimplification as the amount of motivation found within change characters. During many projects, stakeholders display high levels of motivation (Cope, 2010) until the dopamine subsides and the romance fades (Coon & Mitterer, 2010). This then leads to a decline of membership cohesiveness that contributes to withdrawal from participation (Oketch, 2005). Cope argued desire consisted of the primary (motivation) component and the secondary component that often contradicted or negated the primary desire. We often describe the opposing force with terms like "hidden agenda", "hidden desires", and "personal ambitions". As an example, clients may outwardly support a change program, but take actions that minimize effects that alter them personally... like pressing for management bonuses although the assignment calls for reduction of subordinate positions. Mismanagement of desire can destroy trust in clients and consultants alike.

Ethos

The last rung of the Change Ladder model describes the ethos (Greek for "ethic"). Ethos resembles secondary desire and covert capability in that it distinguishes *want* from *need*. Espoused ethos encompasses the understanding of what should be done from an ethical standpoint, whereas actual ethos is the extent to which those ethics are actually implemented (Cope, 2010). Although a formal list of organizational values (espoused) may be framed nicely at the business entrance, punishment for violations may be non-existent (actual). A consultant who says one thing and does another drops weight rapidly on the trust scale.

CONCLUSIONS

Cope's TRUST provided the consultant with personal behaviors to maximize the attainment and teaching of skills that enable trusting relationships lasting beyond the consultation period. Although truthfulness, responsiveness, uniformity, safety, and training pertain to the human element, they fail to encompass the gravity of factors involved in building and maintaining trust. The Change Ladder model expands (albeit not a whole lot) understanding of these relationships beyond the personal level. The following recommendations for consultants demonstrate principles extruded from the TRUST and Change Ladder models:

1. Disclose full truths without predicting what the client may want to hear.
2. Keep the client informed through regular and open communication by responding in a timely manner.
3. Be consistent with ideas and actions throughout the consultation process.
4. Regularly reassure the client with confident language for emotional safety.
5. Continually seek training to enhance professional skills and reputation.
6. Seek to identify and incorporate connotative symbolism in every aspect of the consultation process owned by the stakeholders of the project.
7. Mold new processes and changes into the organization rather try to change the people to match the project.
8. Include as many of the stakeholders as possible throughout the project and encourage maximum participation.
9. Strive to exhibit insightful skills that add value to the organization.
10. Remember that motivation is sometimes temporary and that covert agendas prevail after the consultant has left the project so design systems to minimize this effect.
11. Always, but always follow through.

8.3 THE WORK SCOPE

Although no two consulting projects ever execute identically, all engagements include standardized aspects and relationships between the consultant and the client. The activity of developing projects requires an accurate approach that eliminates confusion and misunderstanding. This perception often misleadingly simplifies the scope of the consultation process as "what should and should not be included" (Wickham & Wickham, 2008, p. 120) without acknowledgement of the factors and elements working behind the scenes that bring the relationship into harmonious completion. As discussed in the following sections, Cope's (2010) *Clarify* stage of consulting shows internal and external forces of human behavior need consideration to bring structure to the consulting process.

CLARIFYING THE SCOPE

By the time the clients seek assistance from the consultant, procrastination has nearly often reached its breaking point with the reality that a problem requires outside help "yesterday". The display of the client's intensity of urgency may manifest into pseudo-transference of personal thoughts and emotional attachment of the problem upon the consultant (Coon & Mitterer, 2010). In simpler terms, the client assumes the consultant should feel the same emotional need to solve the situation quickly, often with an overarching and incorrect self-diagnosis (Cope, 2010).

For instance, consider the patient with unexplained pain in their abdomen who enters the emergency room. Because the patient is limited in their understanding of the physiology of the human body, they may self-diagnose themselves with appendicitis and expect the attending physician to concur the problem by rushing the patient into surgery. If the examiner failed to use appropriate knowledge, skills, and experience to first run tests, the surgeon may incorrectly perform the surgery realizing the patient suffered from constipation; hence requiring only a laxative to solve the problem. Each problem shows the same symptoms, but the root causes necessitate drastically different solutions.

Just as the physician endures legal and ethical responsibilities toward the patient to provide the correct diagnosis and treatment, so too does the consultant owe the client the same consideration. It is this understanding that provides the framework for establishing the scope of the consultation process. Factors such as situational blindness, the diagnosis, phase mapping, shadow dancing, culture, decision makers, system construction, stakeholders, and the risks involved in the project life cycle require appropriate consideration.

Situational Blindness

The patients who incorrectly diagnosed themselves with appendicitis and expected the physician to treat the ailment without confirmation demonstrated situational blindness. Until the pain subsided after the correct treatment was administered, a patient would naturally have doubt in the new diagnosis. The task of a consultant in a similar situation is to deal with the client that is distorting reality by presenting the situation in a way that eases the person in the short term (Cope, 2010). Only then can the project proceed toward the intended goal. Dougherty (2009) warned, however, that planning implementation strategies at this point in the consultation leads to misidentification of the real problems facing the organization on the part of the consultant, reaffirming the need to avoid haste.

Diagnosis

After stepping back to look at the bigger picture, the consultant gathers information that assists in compiling the correct diagnosis of the problem at hand, similar to the physician running diagnostic tests. The objective is to accumulate data in a timely manner that is robust and, above all, accurate (Cope, 2010). By minimizing interruptions to the client system and adjusting to the client's schedules, the consultant influences the greatest impact on the consultation process (Dougherty, 2009) at this stage.

Following the inside-out model provides the consultant with the most flexibility through the content of the data rather than a rigid set of guidelines dictated by an outside-in model. Analyses of the natural settings, the particular people affected, intuition, and qualitative information not available with preset methods enable the widest accumulation of data specific to the organization. Just as every patient undergoing specific tests returns varying results, the plasticity provided by this concept enables the consultant to diagnose the root problem faced by the organization correctly.

Phase Mapping

Phase mapping involves the determination of the extent that known and unknown factors within the change process affect the potential for project success. Continuing with the medical scenario, the constipation diagnoses may not be the actual root cause of the patient's problem, but instead a midlevel symptom. If the physician notices the patient has a recurring frequent history of constipation, then it should trigger a deeper analysis. By running more specialized testing, the revelation of the presence of a tumor or other constriction in the bowel may be causing the constipation that lead to the pain similar to appendicitis. The new treatment plan could involve surgery after all, just not the kind initially anticipated by the patient.

A physician cannot complete the above procedure without the assistance of other people. Lab technicians, nurses, and sometimes the patient's family provide collaboration toward diagnosis. Phase mapping contributes to healthcare (Anderson, 2010) much the way consultants should seek assistance (inputs) from as many people as possible with association to the outcomes of the project (Cope, 2010).

Shadow Dancing

Shadow dancing stands as a precursor to "beating around the bush" or "hiding skeletons in the closet", as the adages go. On occasion, clients may retain information pertinent to the project that could potentially affect its outcome. These can be revealed through phase mapping and attainment of trust in the consultant. The *security versus fear* hypothesis states that confidentiality provides psychological advantages because persons who feel less threatened by repercussions tend to interact with the consultant more openly and accurately (Coon & Mitterer, 2010). Similarly, a patient will not reveal taboo violations to a physician they feel will not retain the information in confidence, although it could make a difference in their diagnosis and treatment. These fears can then be seen through inconsistencies of information, innuendo, withdrawal, and other disconnected behaviors. Utilizing a shadow map process, the consultant can identify these bottlenecks and approaches to overcoming them.

Culture

Physicians typically acknowledge that differences in religious cultures provide the greatest challenge to their professions (Macionis, 2010). The Jehovah's Witness patient will refuse blood from other people during surgery; the Muslim patient cannot be fed pork products and may refuse assistance from the opposite sex; and the Catholic patient down the hall may request divination consultation before making a life-changing decision. All the while, the physician seeks to balance personal religious views that may contradict with those of the patients. Each cultural difference must be honored or the system fails.

For the consultant entering a project it is equally important to learn not only the cultural differences of the individual persons involved (such as stakeholders), but also the culture of the organization as a whole. No two organizations are alike, even within the same industry. Conscious effort should be made to learn cultural barriers of the project's success and to provide adjustments or alternatives as necessary.

Decision Makers

Knowing who is actually making the decisions during a consulting project is not always easy to identify (Cope, 2010). It may be the client, the client's superiors, a joint committee, or someone in the background. Sometimes at funerals, the directors have to isolate the person with decision-making authority when the family members cannot agree on burial arrangements. Most of the time, legal hierarchies make the solution easy, but occasionally, relationships blur and add confusion to the turmoil. Consultants should quickly identify the decision-making authority to reduce wasted time and resources expended on the project.

System Construction

The *Two Percent Rule of Common Sense*, often quoted by maintenance workers, states "you must be at least 2% smarter than the equipment you're working with [in order to succeed]". This adage also applies to consultants in they should know the client system they are attempting to change (Muchinsky, 2006). The consultant needs to understand how the change process affects (and is affected by) external forces, people within the organization, and the resources utilized by the organization. By mapping these relationships, clarity follows and responses to obstacles planned accordingly (Cope, 2010). Think of the physician that prescribes antibiotics after a surgery in anticipation of *possible* infection.

Stakeholders

Stakeholders include everyone who is affected, or will potentially be affected, by actions taken for a given scenario (Gardial, 2007). Whether customers, employees, stockholders, or the community served, one or more (usually more) persons tend to react, positively or negatively, to every action of change implemented by the organization. Using the Change Ladder model for building trust, the consultant should map the stakeholders to better understand each group and how proposed changes might be affected (Cope, 2010). The physician seeks out the family of the surgical patient and the funeral director identifies the family hierarchy for similar reasons: to ease the stakeholders, to build trust, and to reduce turmoil during the changes taking place.

Risk

The balance of risks and rewards associated with a consulting project needs to coincide with the desires of the client organization. Smaller organizations tend to avoid high risk while larger organizations yielding more resources lean toward the higher rewards obtained after obtaining success. In either case, the stakeholders and system construction dictate the process of risk management. The goal is to determine the problems that can be tolerated without damaging the change process (Cope, 2010) rather than total elimination. Testing changes in a controlled environment before full implementation and provision of contingency plans serve as the most recommended methods for assessing risk (Cadotte, et al., 2008; Cope, 2010). As an example, before new medical procedures or medications may be rolled out to the respective markets, the Food and Drug Administration requires stringent sample testing to evaluate the risk potential against the proposed benefits.

CONCLUSIONS

The medical profession serves as an exquisite example for demonstration of consulting techniques at the level of clarification. The nine concepts work together in provision of answering the call to standardization of the consulting process. Even though no one has yet found a "how to" model for application in all scenarios, similarities provide a framework that enables smoother change project development and implementation over a wide range of possibilities. Cope's *Clarify* stage in his *Seven C's of Consulting* model works to meet this need, although the concept is not new (called *triage* in the medical industry and "evaluate the situation before action" in police and military units).

Regardless of the professional service, the scope of consulting involves, in no particular order):

1) Removing situational blindness where possible,
2) Accumulating relevant data for an accurate diagnosis,
3) Paying attention to every source of information,
4) Alleviating fears and building trust,
5) Identifying and integrating cultural concerns into the project,
6) Knowing who the real decision makers is,
7) Understanding the client system from a broad perspective beyond the limits of the project,
8) Identifying and utilizing potential stakeholders, and
9) Balancing and managing potential risks.

8.4 MANAGE CONSULTANT AND CLIENT TENSION

Upon agreement of the work scope, and after the contract for consultation is signed, the management consultant is challenged with generating specific ideas to resolve the client's problem. Management of interactions and skill development in client expertise base the outcomes of the project. To do this, the consultant has to reduce tension and effectively address the client's real needs. This paper discusses how these objectives are met through possible solution generation and the criteria for identifying solutions at the organizational level.

CRITERIA FOR AN EFFECTIVE SOLUTION

Many researchers agree (Cope, 2010; Dougherty, 2009; Wickham & Wickham, 2008) creativity (also called *innovation* or *invention*) bridges the consulting problem with its practical solution(s). Competitive and market advantages occur in relationship to the organization's ability to leverage creativity through careful management of ideas. This primary skillset conveys what the consultant actually brings to the change project (Cope, 2010). Offering slight variations to previous offerings yields marginal contributions at best. People naturally rely on the tendencies of experiences, beliefs, and viewpoints into their interpretations of safety, practicality, and appropriateness, essentially failing to consider alternative approaches when solving problems.

For example, organizations often lack understanding in purpose with communities, commensurate resources, and relevance with competing industries (Opara, 2010). Standing as a central objective for the consultant, an effective solution requires relieving the tunnel vision and assisting management with the deliverance of a solution that breaks the paradigm. The following sections supplement Cope's *Create* stage (Challenge, Randomize, Explore, Appraise, Test, and Evaluate) of consultation to help define the effective solution through discussion of stakeholders, methods of generating possible solutions, and evaluation of what seems the obvious solution.

GENERATING POSSIBLE SOLUTIONS

After goal establishment, the process of generating possible interventions begins. The purpose is to detail the "how to" plans for reaching the recognized goals. Consultants serve their clients best as mentors who encourage the client to generate implementations, using the consultant's assistance and guidance, so that future dependence upon outside help is reduced by stimulating internal creativity (Dougherty, 2009). This internalization demands stakeholders' input serve as prompts for effective collaboration (Jennings, 2006). Establishment of these relationship objectives provide effective means for choosing appropriate methods of generating possible solutions.

STAKEHOLDERS

For any given scenario, stakeholders include everyone who is affected, or will be potentially affected, by actions/inactions taken because of the consultation. This definition implies stakeholders comprise the customers, the employees, the stockholders, and the communities ultimately touched by the engagements taken. These persons and groups tend to react (positively or negatively) to every exploit of change implemented by the organization.

Depending upon on the situation, consultants and clients benefit from remembrance of the words of the popular Rush song, "When you fail to choose, you still have made a choice" (Peart & Talbot, 1977). In other words, when forgetting or ignoring the stakeholders (similar to consequences), those decisions still resonate with the people holding a stake in the success/failure of the project. For example, unionized employees may strike and managers may choose not to enforce new policies they do not understand or support, thus causing bottlenecks and failure of the change project. It is imperative stakeholders feel they have a consistent and directed sense of ownership in the change process throughout the program (Dougherty, 2009). The elongated term for this personalization process is *internalization of responsibility* (Cope, 2010): a personal passion or hunger to see the project succeed.

SOLUTION METHODS

Rarely does any singular (as in only one) solution exist for a given consulting scenario as each project is unique in its scope (Cope, 2010), allowing variation within the possibilities. For instance, general arguments proclaim Total Quality Management (TQM) fails when applied to universities as an intervention solution (Houston, Robertson, & Prebble, 2008). By adapting TQM principles to specific departments and processes within collegiate institutions, opposed to adapting organizations as whole units, balanced scorecards at the administrative level saw realization (Kezar et.al., 2008). Creativity improved by requiring departmental participants to consider how issues might affect the university beyond respective departments.

Other common techniques for generating ideas and stimulating creativity (Wickham & Wickham, 2008) include mind mapping, brainstorming, features analysis, and Delphi auditing. These methods share communication at the individual and group levels as the fundamental core behind maximum results for creative idea generation. Mind mapping allows the individual, particularly the consultant, to visualize thought processes and relationships in an organized manner. Rather than simply taking notes, relationships are drawn between concepts in a non-linear fashion. It can be debated that outlining performs similar categorical functions, however, outlining loses the networked semantic relationships of ideas displayed by mind mapping. The map provides the additional benefit of communicating ideas more clearly to the stakeholders, reducing confusion and ambiguity.

Brainstorming operates at the small group level to generate ideas while refraining from member criticism (Wickham & Wickham, 2008). All ideas are recorded and collaborated towards relevance in concept before discussion. The discussion focuses upon positive aspects of ideas without discouraging further input from session members. Consultants should adhere to caution by not allowing the brainstorming session to self-defeat its constructive purpose. Brainstorming differs from quality circle sessions when concentrating efforts solely on idea generation, as the latter has been shown to be ineffective (Cadotte, et al., 2008) for this purpose.

Features analysis builds upon brainstorming and mind mapping by gaining insights into manipulated features of a topic of interest. One feature is mind-mapped or brainstormed at a time rather than the entire topic under consideration. The process begins with asking questions into the importance of features to users, tradeoffs of features versus cost, and willingness to utilize particular aspects in order to prioritize discussions. Features are then modified or removed and the results analyzed. Lastly, results call comparisons when combined with other features. The intention, aside from a more thorough analysis of the project considerations, lies with the improvement of communication between stakeholders and further reduction of dependence upon the consultant.

Delphi auditing mimics market research in practice and cost (Wickham & Wickham, 2008). This method polls experts outside the organization with experience in similar topics as considered by the consulting project. Questions asked can generalize issues or drill down to specific features. Subsequent polling compounds results and clarifies issues that may seem vague. Usage of Delphi auditing obviously bypasses internal communication objectives, so should merely supplement other methods, rather than replace them when possible.

OBVIOUS SOLUTIONS

Data is worthless until analyzed for the intended necessity. Afterwards, the task in question affects the rest of the consultation process by developing definition (Dougherty, 2009). Data analysis works in deliberate, systematic, and planned steps to reduce unintended consequences. The consultant and client work together to determine antecedents and consequences related to the situation and choose strategies for data analysis (discussed previously). Multiple problem discovery leads to prioritizing finds by how they develop over time, how past events caused present problems, or how future expectations relate to one another. Problem framing results from using concise statements from multiple perspectives, e.g. administration, employee, and customer views of personal service quality. These definitions should seem logical to the consultant and the client, practical in leading to new directions of action, and ensure willingness by the client to take action. Early solutions that seem obvious before data analysis may prove presumptuous (Cope, 2010) and disastrous to project outcomes.

CONCLUSIONS

Albert Einstein famously stated, "The measure of intelligence is the ability to change". This realization metaphorically refers to the consultant who broadens the vision of the organization that desires to solve a problem. Like Einstein, the consultant helps the people within the organization to find their own genius by teaching them how to gather the correct data and to analyze it from perspectives outside what they already know. Albeit the consultant likely does not have a solution when the project begins, but the toolkit of skills brought allows the process to flourish.

Identification and implementation of stakeholders provides the greatest quantity of feedback that in turn builds communication infrastructures. This foundational structure then provides senses of ownership for the stakeholders who develop a passion to see the change process succeed... like a funnel leading to a singular outcome... together. When ingredients (people) are left out, the resulting solution is not homogenous (organizational).

Breaking the problem down and systematically analyzing the components individually assists with understanding how once disregarded possible solutions may work. Whichever method(s) is chosen, it should stimulate creativity within the stakeholders and reduce dependence upon outsiders, eventually enhancing the probability of the organization creating competitive advantage on its own in the future.

* * *

8.5 LEAD AND MANAGE CHANGE

L eadership and management provide challenges for the consultant when implementing solutions to problems or issues within an organization. Anticipated changes require buy-in of the people involved. Management of resistance, understanding team models, and leadership qualities play important roles in the early stages of the project, that when properly accounted for, ease the transition process of desired change.

MANAGING RESISTANCE

The most common element encountered by consultants in change projects, as mentioned in the literature, is resistance to that change. Many factors including the size of the organization, the scope of the project, resources consumed by the project, and the level of change required in the routine activities of the stakeholders determine the amount of difficulty the consultant may expect (Cope, 2010). How these issues are planned for and handled, in turn, reflects upon the consultant's abilities and reputation. As a manufacturing segment example, the fears of job loss, wage reductions, and skill absolution in preference of the newer technologies resulted with in unions tending to strike when organizations announced planned conversions to automated processes (Pearson Learning Solutions, 2010). The result could lead to unintended consequences, such as plant closure, if improperly managed.

Frequent reactions observed with behavioral resistance consist of lack of conviction, dislike, fear, reluctance, poor performance, and lack of respect (Cope, 2010). Through understanding the natural tendencies behind these behaviors, consultants can minimize their occurrences and cause feelings of engagement instead. Openly communicating the change process and its worth to stakeholders often causes those affected to take ownership within the project and to sustain that change (Dougherty, 2009).

For instance, the adage "if you want to get the boss's attention, explain how [your proposal] affects the company in dollars", demonstrates the concept. Simply stating a truck needs tires is not as effective at getting the parts as noting that refusal can result in the vehicle placed out of service with expensive fines by state officials during a frequent inspection... sometimes on the side of the highway. The manager then makes tire replacement a priority to avoid losses from fines, inflated service costs, unproductive wages, and customer detention time or total customer loss.

One of the earliest observable indicators of resistance is the organizational setting. The social character of organizations, regardless of individual member personality traits, sets the stage for behaviors within the organization. In his mock prison experiment, Zimbardo (2009) demonstrated the jail setting caused persons pretending as guards to assume the roles beyond the instructions given. These guards humiliated prisoners and resorted to mild violence that forced Zimbardo to end the experiment after only seven days. The organizational setting serves as a predictor of the anticipated level of fear existing among its members, such as phobia of managers by subordinates (e.g. military) or fear of punishment for noncompliance (e.g. humiliation or loss of special privileges). Elimination of fears increases motivation, endorsement, and respect.

Other indicators of resistance include performance measures and back talking. Slowdowns and similar outcome differences may show participants fail to understand the importance of their efforts and that more buy-in initiatives are required (Dougherty, 2009) on the parts of the consultation leaders. Comments along the lines of "I just don't understand why…", "Why can't they just leave things alone?", and "I don't care – I'm not…" exacerbate the situation with uncertainty. In the case of the old timer that proclaims, "This is the way I have always done it and it still works for me", the consultant's challenge is to convince the worker to adopt a new method so that contagion theory provides assistance with their peers. In any case, the expectations from stakeholders need clarity and specificity to avoid ambiguity in order to intensify cohesiveness and to reduce resistance.

TEAMWORK

The work performed by teams requires that members interact through exchange of information, sharing of resources, and coordination of efforts resulting in some degree of interdependence among themselves and other groups (Muchinsky, 2006). More often than not, team members decide for themselves (collectively) who does what, where, when, and how the work is done. Multi-team scenarios provide as many layers of difficulty for consultants when implementing change projects due to variance in variety of individual team cultures.

Five principles of teamwork were identified (McIntyre & Salas, 1995) as relevant to organizations and the change process:

Teamwork implies that members provide feedback and accept it from one another. Open communication, climate, and power (hierarchy) should not block feedback, as teams need to be aware of strengths and weaknesses (collective and individual) for effectiveness. Therefore, consultants should work with all members of teams implementing change projects.

Teamwork implies that willingness, preparedness, and proclivity to back fellow members up during operations. Competence should be displayed in individual areas and those of other members without fear of retaliation. When training teams, consultants should ensure the team trains as a unit without identifying specific individuals as weak or incompetent.

Teamwork involves group members collectively viewing themselves as a group whose success depends on their interactions. Teams view themselves as a group rather than a collection of individuals whose success remains dependent on that mentality. Building upon the previous principle, consultants should be aware that if one team member fails, the effectiveness of the entire team fails as well, and so efforts at change affect every team member.

Teamwork means fostering within-team interdependence. Interdependence is seen as a virtue essential to performance of the team, regardless of what goes on within the rest of the organization. Failure to recognize this aspect means certain failure of the consultant to implement a change project. Therefore, changes at the organizational level should not be expected to trickle down to all lower levels in every situation.

Team leadership makes a difference with respect to the performance of the team. Team leaders who openly engage in teamwork and who serve as models for the other team members strongly persuade those members to conformity. Consultants who embrace this principle may see timesaving with implementation and reduced resistance.

CONSULTANT LEADERSHIP

Dozens of leadership styles have been described with no singular preference applicable in every situation (Luthans, 2008). As roles change with organizational contexts, the general agreement is that leadership increases in difficulty with the severity of the situation. For the consultant, this effort magnifies as an outsider (Cope, 2010) and is perceived as threatening. The skill and ability to shift roles requires innovative techniques and understanding of leadership styles, activities, and effectiveness.

Avoidance of project shock, or unplanned errors outside the consultant's control, requires planning with flexibility to respond to unexpected events (Wickham & Wickham, 2008). Changes in client interests, business situations, losses of resource allocations, and key people movements occur without warning. These variances demand contingency through leadership adaptability by preparing for the unexpected, avoiding panic, careful evaluation of resources, the ability to modify plans as needed, and above all, communication. Consultants are managers that lead change through example and guidance (Cope, 2010).

CONCLUSIONS

The general expected persona of the consultant by clients is one of a guru with the magic pill that cures everything. Although this attitude strays far from truth, the consultant must demonstrate the highest levels of professionalism. Flexibility to adapt to the client's situation is the key to adapting the client's situation to the solution desired. This chief skill enables competencies to excel for both parties. The role assumed by the consultant demands an understanding of the client's characteristics: Are teams the base framework within the organization, and if so, are they similar or complementary?

Simultaneous management of resistance at individual, group, and organizational levels can prove difficult even for the most seasoned of consultants. Through careful leadership, the consultant can ensure timely success of the change project by applying necessary leadership styles, exercising appropriate management activities, and encouragement of effectiveness that complements the situation.

* * *

8.6 MEASUREMENTS

The management consultant and client are charged with the responsibility of assuring expected outcomes are delivered because of the change project. Confirmation of successful progress begins with benchmarking before the project actually begins with techniques of measurement developed by the consultant. Similarly, as the work continues, measurements of progress periodically must be taken to ensure intermediate goals reach attainment through to project completion (Dougherty, 2009). Initiatives often seem slow-to-start during the early phases of the project, creating tensions between the client and consultant (Cope, 2010). The sections that follow address this tension and discuss when measurements are taken, how confirmation strengthens project outcomes, and provides a working measurement sample for explanatory application.

CLIENT – CONSULTANT TENSION

The role of the consultant is to help the client analyze emotions within the organization from an objective perspective (Cope, 2010). Understanding the differences between relevance, assumption, speculation, and the fear of administrative repercussion by participants helps with sorting fact from fiction during inquiry (Dougherty, 2009). More simply applied, respondents tend to respond to questions with answers they feel the interrogator expects to hear, rather than those truths the respondent believes is accurate and personalized. Assurance of confidentiality gains psychological advantages through trust, confidence, and honesty during interviews (Coon & Mitterer, 2010) while enhancing the persona of professionalism within the client system.

Utilization of alternative measurement means allows interactions to remain focused, relevant, and pertinent to the consultation process with minimal disruption. This last statement infers delivery of a measurement objective through alternative means for accuracy and validity, such as internet, intranet, email, etcetera, rather than utilizing devices that could potentially yield conflicting or unrelated results (e.g. questionnaire versus naturalistic observation).

During the initial phases of the consultation, when perceived problems succumb to realized root causes, measurement occurs as the mechanism of discovery. Ownership to these realities often defers to emotional responses of denial and scapegoating behaviors by the client. For instance, the client may feel the benefits package offered to employees is generous, whereas high turnover rates remain unchanged. Polling (measuring) the employee's perspective may reveal the package as inadequate, uncompetitive within the industry, or maybe even somewhat insulting.

The role of the consultant becomes that of mediator between the client and system at the lower levels in order to attain the higher goal of retention. However, the difficulty lies in recognizing and accepting respective responsibilities on behalf of the client before resolutions may retain permanence. By taking a supportive role, rather than one of leader (Barnes & Austin, 2008), the consultant's purpose is somewhat complicated and multifaceted as these characteristics culminate.

Ideas generated require measurement for feasibility, effectiveness in similar situations, costs of implementation and maintenance, ethical considerations, and their ease of measurement. The consultant contributes ideas known to provide validity, utility, and reliability found in current research and practices within other organizations. Only those ideas showing the highest probability of success within acceptable cost-budget ranges and time constraints rate possibility for implementation.

WHEN TO TAKE MEASUREMENTS

Previously noted, measurement begins as a process at the beginning of the project and flows until after implementation when the consultant leaves and the client assumes control. Although responsibility for measurement may be assumed by any member of the change process, such as administrators, team members, or the consultant (Cope, 2010), results are dependent upon participation and follow-thru of the stakeholders as a unit, rather than the burden of any one person (Dougherty, 2009). The consulting contract reflects this relationship to include the variable nature of possible outcomes and measurement systems (Milkovich & Newman, 2008).

Adjusting to the schedule of the client's system takes priority for the consultant, especially when designing and utilizing measurement instruments. For example, a transportation company whose drivers only return to the terminal once or twice per month will not logically force the drivers in to the office to complete a survey. Going home to their families supersedes the desires of drivers to conform to the consultant's needs. Almost never are all drivers at the same location at the same time, or at uniform hours of the day, or consistently with a given schedule due to the nature of the industry. Obviously, it would be impractical and costly for the consultant to attempt interviews on a large scale or to arrange meetings with select drivers. By providing other options with kiosk surveys, pay stub enclosures, and other similar methods, the consultant could reach a larger sample in less time. The probability of success is not dependent on just having access to information, but also the ability to create new insights and find new opportunities (Wickham & Wickham, 2008).

Always and *continuously* appear to be the best times to take measurements, depending upon the tasked situation. Some events, such as financial ratio analyses and behavioral modification programs prove fruitless if conducted too soon, while mechanical adaptation results may require constant observation to detect effectiveness. Regardless of the situation, the measurement cycle exists throughout the lifetime of the project. The primary concern is that results are immediately communicated and shared with stakeholders (Kamholz et.al., 2006).

CONFIRMING CHANGE

Confirming prescribed changes have taken place wraps the consultant's participation in the project. The final report reiterates measurements in a fashion that is understandable to the stakeholders by use of a number of techniques that facilitate individual and group creativity, including ad hoc visuals. These methods reveal patterns and relationships in data using visual forms (diagrams, flow charts, graphs, grids, etc.) that match the cognitive styles of the respective clients. When people can identify with the information, process it, and then use it to wrestle problems, then communication improves (Wickham & Wickham, 2008). Confidence builds within the client system participants when they can visualize the accomplishment.

MEASUREMENT EXAMPLE

Process evaluation involves viewing the overall consultation process for determination of meeting established goals toward satisfactory ends. Assessment also includes whether the client potentially demonstrates effective ability in handling comparable future situations without consultant assistance (Dougherty, 2009). Accomplishment through measuring the overall effectiveness of the program by evaluation of perceived behaviors of the client stakeholders jointly, with project assessments, establishes credibility and potentially increased chances for other consultation engagements.

A questionnaire designed to assess aspects reporting the client's perceived abilities, effectiveness, and acceptability of the consultant's efforts was developed by Cott, Teare, McGilton, and Lineker in 2006 with high validity correlation of 0.78 ($p < .01$). Additionally, the evaluation measured emotional support, coordination and continuity, and the link between goal setting and goal attainment. Adaptation and implementation of this instrument to the consulting scenario provides invaluable feedback from not only the consultation process, but also the consultant's abilities.

CONCLUSIONS

Successful outcomes to consultation projects determine not only the future sustainability of the consultant's career, but also the growth of the client's organization. Without measurement techniques that verify expected conclusions, the project loses definition and scope. Comparative benchmarking serves as the reference point for successive measurements that determine periodic progress until the change is confirmed at the end of the program.

Tensions excel between the consultant and client with expectancy of success as the consultant moves the client to self-sufficiency. Understanding the emotional conflicts tied to the change process enables the consultant to manage these difficulties. Through research into industry practices and measurement developments, the consultant increases effectiveness, acceptability, and emotional support from the client's stakeholders.

* * *

8.7 FOLLOW-UP PLAN: SUPPLEMENTAL TEXT FOR ACCOMPANYING PRESENTATION

During the follow-up, the consultant serves in a post-project troubleshooting role to the client (Dougherty, 2009). This phase begins after post-consultation planning meets to the satisfaction of the stakeholders and the gradual disconnection by the consultant from the consultation effort. Abrupt disengagement occurs more frequently in projects lasting less than a year; 40% versus 26% for projects lasting one to five years (O'Brien, Fahmy, & Singh, 2009).

Help is provided to the organization on an as-needed basis. Follow-up demonstrates continued availability to the client, complete closure of plans, opportunities to prevent future problems, and provides reinforcement to the client. However, it is important to avoid a dependency relationship so closure may occur.

EXPECTATIONS OF FOLLOW-UP

Follow-up expectations exist from two perspectives: those of the client or organization, and those of the consultant. System feedback triggers the frequency of follow-up contact meetings. For instance, in a new stress reduction program, indicators may show the client demonstrates difficulty implementing or enforcing relaxation techniques although staff members have mastered time management challenges. The objective of the consultant in this case is to allow the client to assume responsibilities in an independent format (Dougherty, 2009). In other words, time and experience on the client's behalf appear necessary with minor guidance from the consultant.

Consultants often fail to conduct thorough follow-up when doing so as part of the process plan, which allows the consultant to review whether maintenance gains achieved remain sustained by the client. With each meeting, the consultant should review successes of the program and assist with problematic concerns of the client, including workable solutions, and guidance or assistance as needed.

CONSULTANT EXPECTATIONS

Consultants expect particular skills and behaviors from the clients because of the consulting relationship. The sections that follow discuss how persistence with the consultation efforts should endure after the project has ended, how clients should change their behaviors, why self-reporting measures are important, and why it is important for the client to learn how to solve their own problems. Each of these follow-up plan tasks incorporates these initiatives with emphasis on the value, ownership, and duration of the derived principles (follow-through, non-dependency, self-reporting measures, and rooting) and provides a heuristic for application.

Task One: Follow-Through

The consultant expects the client to utilize the knowledge and skills provided beyond the consultation period. Almost no one likes to perform hours of tedious planning and work only to have the final project placed upon a shelf and forgotten about. The same concept applies to consultants and their desires from the client. Essentially then, if the project outcomes are not placed into service, then the project holds no value to either the consultant or the client stakeholders. This is also true of projects only requesting recommendations that seem to go ignored. Therefore, the consultant should instill the value of the project within the client so the client adopts the outcomes as necessary and purposeful (O'Brien, Fahmy, & Singh, 2009). For example, a physician who treats an obese patient for heart problems and does not instill the value of a controlled diet is not likely to see that patient lose weight for the sake of their heart. Follow-up consultations similarly demand that project value be reassured in the client's mind as long as the outcomes are desirable and necessary.

Task Two: Non-Dependency

The consultant expects the client to learn from the consultation and to adopt the methods used as their own in similar situations. In studies where individuals demonstrated a high dependence on caregivers, the psychosocial bond contributed to longer periods of treatment (Carpenter, Luce, & Wooff, 2011). Since organizations are comprised of individuals, this behavior justifiably carries over to the group level. Think of the number of projects that are abandoned because key personnel move out of the organization, including lateral shifts and complete termination (Wickham & Wickham, 2008).

If the client can utilize the skills and knowledge provided beyond the consultation without further assistance, then the true purpose of the project has been achieved. The consultant is therefore responsible for seeing the client organization (as a whole) learns to handle the project outcomes without dependence on outsiders or certain key individuals. The change should survive indefinitely beyond the consultation period.

Task Three: Self-Reporting Measures

Consultants expect clients to utilize the self-reporting measures provided to gain valuable feedback. Integration of these tools reduce stressors with the client (Kamholz et.al., 2006) and serve as a planning mechanism for regulating emotion and further encouraging communication, internally and with the consultant. The measures allow the client to check their own progress and to provide insightful feedback to the consultant if needed. The purpose relies not upon creating extra work for the client after consultant departure, but with assisting the client in a helpful manner without future reliance upon the consultant. The consultant is then responsible for ensuring the self-reporting measures are implemented and accurately utilized well beyond project closure.

Task Four: Rooting

The consultant expects clients will understand the process of identifying the root cause of future problems. With this skill, the organization will increase its ability to solve problems faster and with lower costs of maintenance. Although many consultants would argue that repeat business lies in the ability of the consultant to provide value to the organization (Cope, 2010; Wickham & Wickham, 2008), the reality of worth derives from the consultant that can provide an organization with the skills necessary to solve its own problems. This very concept survives within the well-known Code of Ethics for psychological practitioners.

The consultant is responsible for walking the client through the problem identification process and seeking alternative solutions applicable to the root problem, abilities that could lengthen the lifetime of the organization if understood and appreciated. The famous mantra, "Teach a man to fish and you feed him for a lifetime", applies to the consultant's expectation of the organization as "Learn to fish and you survive a lifetime".

CLIENT AND ORGANIZATIONAL EXPECTATIONS

Clients expect certain services and behaviors from the consultant when the contract begins winding down. The sections that follow discuss how communication practices should be effective and in place throughout the project hierarchy; why clients need to understand their strengths to overcome their weaknesses; how consistency of personnel impacts the outcomes of the project and organization; and why knowing when to act is as important as how to perform. Each of these follow-up plan tasks incorporates these initiatives with emphasis on the value, ownership, and duration of the derived principles (communication, task focus, follow-up ownership, and immediacy) and provides a heuristic for application.

Task One: Communication

The client expects the consultant to maintain communications beyond the formal exiting date of the project. The method of communication serves as the most important characteristic of follow-up to client stakeholders (Kimman et.al., 2010). Sometimes, a simple telephone call is sufficient, whereas other times may require a formal visit for efficiency and trust building (Cope, 2010). Generally, the consultant is responsible for initiating follow-up contact with the client as well as responding to client inquiries in a timely manner.

Effective communication enhances the consultant's brand (Cope, 2010), provides strength to the project by contributing closure to unanswered questions (Dougherty, 2009), and ingrains a sense a dependability about the consultant with the client (Wickham & Wickham, 2008). The duration of follow-up communications lasts until the client no longer needs the consultant's assistance and occurs as often as necessary.

Task Two: Task Focus

The consultant should periodically reiterate the accomplishments achieved by the client with focus on the most difficult activities. By focusing on the most troublesome aspects of the project, the client demonstrates higher degrees of collaboration and responsiveness to the consultant. Psychiatric patients who realize their accomplishments within their treatment programs tend to endure fewer sessions and readmissions than patients without supportive reaffirmations (Carpenter, Luce, & Wooff, 2011). This reaction shows clients who understand and visualize their progress lead to greater self-reliance. The consultant is responsible for instilling a sense of competence within the client with reminders of past victories, as often as necessary, until project closure.

Task Three: Follow-Up Ownership

The client expects the same consultant(s) who worked on the project to conduct the follow-up. In a post-treatment study of women undergoing follow-up procedures for breast cancer (Kew, Galaal, & Manderville, 2009), most women (82/92, 89%) preferred to see the attending physician to a review by a specialist nurse or general practitioner (p <.001). Women thought the examination was the most important part of the visit (p < .0001). Women viewed the other persons as filling secondary roles, rather than detecting recurrence (p < .0001). In other consultancy scenarios, this study would translate to clients feeling that primarily the consultant was the only qualified person to evaluate their follow-up.

Taking ownership of the follow-up reaffirms the consultant's loyalty to the client and increases the brand. It is the responsibility of the participating consultant to conduct follow-up procedures without passing tasks to other persons until project completion.

Task Four: Immediacy

Clients expect the consultant to make immediate adjustments that enhance client perspectives. Qualitative research showed (Friedlander, 1978) that more than half (54%) of college students felt their course improved after administration of midterm course/instructor evaluations, although grades were not included in the study for quantitative review. Essentially, these students felt they were listened to during the course rather than after the course ended, boosting their senses of cohesion with the material and the instructor. Follow-up is a continual process within the consultation project that strengthens the consultant/client relationship rather than a mundane and finite task. Clients feel that the consultant adds value to their organization when adjustments are provided on a timely basis, leaving the consultant responsible for making frequent periodic adjustments that conform as needed to the client's expectations.

CONCLUSIONS

The points to remember for effective follow-up include:

1) Do not lose sight of the purpose(s) of the follow-up plan... Stay on track.
2) Remain aware of the client and organizational expectations from the consultant while communicating/enforcing expectations of the client.
3) Instill and reinforce the value of the project within the client.
4) Ensure the client learns from the consultation and adopts the methods used as their own in similar situations.

5) Implement accurate self-reporting measures and ensure they are utilized.
6) Verify the organization learned how to discover its root problems and identify alternative solutions.
7) Maintain communications with the client beyond the formal exiting date of the project.
8) Reiterate the accomplishments achieved with focus on the most difficult activities.
9) The consultant who conducts the change project should also perform follow-up activities.
10) Make frequent periodic adjustments that conform as needed to the client's expectations.

The common attribute shared by every expectation lies in the matter of responsibility. The result clearly indicates the consultant assumes sole ownership in preparing, initiating, and completing the follow-up plan. Although the client and consultant delineate with prescribed expectations within their roles of one another, none realize successful application without the conscious efforts of the consultant making them happen.

* * *

8.8 THE PROPOSAL

Ken Philipe of Premium Transportation and Logistics (PTL) approached Mr. Nichols, an internal employee of the company, with a project consideration to help reduce turnover at one of the organization's client sites, Maximum Distribution (MD). Currently, PTL services MD by providing logistical services at its facility. These services include management of yard operations, where PTL supplies staffed spotter trucks that move loaded trailers into receiving docks, tracks empty trailers, and then works in partnership for utilization of the empties through shipping docks and final pickup by outside companies. The benefit to MD is controlled operations that reduce losses through accidents and yard congestion.

Unfortunately, PTL realized that average turnover for spotter drivers ranged from three to six months, drastically increasing its costs due to recruitment and training of a skilled and dependable onsite workforce, higher accident rates resulting in excessive repair costs, and threat of losses from contract negation by MD.

CLIENT NEEDS

Mr. Nichols is a trained spotter driver who understands the needs of PTL, as well as those of Maximum Distribution from a macro orientation. He agrees to work within the client system to identify and resolve the root causes of the initial perceived problems (Cope, 2010). The goals of working alongside the current crew members enable confidence and trust with Mr. Nichols (Sheng, Tian, & Chen, 2010) while preventing the Hawthorne Effect from distorting data collection efforts (Roethlisberger & Dickson, 1939), and eventual outcomes for recommendations of remediation. For maximum effectiveness, Mr. Nichols suggests he spend time working with each shift (day shift and night shift) to observe differences in input from crew members and working conditions. Initial data serves as qualitative benchmarking in areas of behavior, attitude, performance through quality service to MD, and procedural conformity of operations.

OBJECTIVES

Since crew members had not ever met Mr. Nichols, he was able to present himself as a new employee at the worksite, with minimal experience, operating a spotter truck. This tactic allowed Mr. Nichols to experience orientation, training, and specific operating procedures at the customer site without bias to his purpose from the crew members. Orientation included the viewing of a ten-minute video covering accidental mishaps and procurement of a new employee handbook at an offsite location conducted by a recruiter. The next step consisted of a backing test as evaluated by the onsite day-shift supervisor, lasting 15 minutes.

Training, as it turned out, was minimal. Intentional interaction on the part of the supervisor with Mr. Nichols included a tour of the customer facility (windshield view) and the passing of cheat sheets for computer communication codes before releasing Mr. Nichols to begin work. Unfortunately, Mr. Nichols did not receive computer logon credentials until his second week performing the job after complaints from the customer administration that real-time updates to his work were needed. Meanwhile, Mr. Nichols interviewed crew members for common attributes, using open-ended questions, seeking patterns of job traits, and concerns that would cause individuals to leave the job.

Night shift began in the second week and did not have an appointed supervisor. Crew members cooperated using a democratic process of work division with little conflict, in opposition to the day shift, whose supervisor utilized a strict authoritarian leadership style. The following three primary responses were identified from among eight crew members across both shifts:

1. Each spotter backs between 30 and 70 trailers each shift, varying with customer demand.
2. Lighting is poor in a few locations and painted guide lines are difficult to see or nonexistent, increasing the chance of an accident while backing.
3. The current PTL policy requires the immediate termination of any spotter driver involved in an accident causing property damage to any degree.

As confirmed by formal research (Southeastern Institute of Research, 2008), the primary worry of spotter drivers is unexpected job loss: a dominant stressor.

Spotter drivers have no available facilities, such as a break area, for utilization to heat or store foods and beverages. Policy dictates spotters have no defined break or meal times and should avoid such rest periods if customer demand is high, although the customer workforce is unionized. Additionally, 30 minutes is deducted each day from paid time, regardless if a lunch is taken or not, to meet state legal requirements.

Spotter drivers lack respect for the day-shift supervisor. Most often, demands from the supervisor are placated, but a few employees meet the supervisor's demands with avoidance or rebellion. The supervisor is extremely disliked and the object of countless jokes as a consensus among all shift workers. At one point, the person indicated the belief the position was administrative by scope of responsibility and power in lieu of reality.

Mr. Nichols met with Ken Philipe after a month to discuss concerns and they agreed upon the following objectives toward improving turnover based upon identified root causes:

1. Work with MD to improve lighting conditions and guide line repainting. This safety measure will reduce accidents and unexpected turnover.
2. Meet with PTL administration to seek adjustment to the automatic termination policy to a case-by-case basis grounded upon severity of the accident and cost of reparations.
3. Work with MD to establish a break area, shared or unshared with MD workers, for spotter drivers.
4. Establish at least one defined break period for spotter drivers to rest and consume meals that coincide with customer demand.
5. Establish a peer review system for administration to detect conflict with personnel and supervisors.
6. Design and implement a defined checklist to ensure new personnel complete orientation and training tasks.
7. Design and implement a training program that orients new spotter drivers with the specific customer worksite.

SCOPE

Without actively participating as a spotter driver, Mr. Nichols may not have identified the perceived root causes of the turnover problem. Most administrators do not possess the necessary skills and required licensure to perform the work, allowing feedback to remain biased and incomplete because of social apathy (Macionis, 2010). In other words, employees often refrain from full disclosure to their bosses for various reasons, telling only minimal information they believe the administrator really wants to hear, especially in groups and similar to the Hawthorne Effect. This phenomenon results in outcomes persuaded by situational blindness at the administrative level (Cope, 2010).

By integrating with the client system and adjusting to client schedules (Dougherty, 2009), Mr. Nichols gained the trust of the spotter drivers more quickly and obtained reliable data relevant to the root causes (Cope, 2010) of the turnover problem. By knowing the client system under investigation, he was able to comprehend the system construction at the proper level and appropriately map the relationships between external forces, people within the organization, and available resources for clarity.

APPROACH AND IMPLEMENTATION WITH COST CONSIDERATIONS

The approach for resolving the needs of PTL and turnover begin with prioritizing the identified objectives to reach maximum effectiveness, while providing "added value" (Wickham, 2008; Cope, 2010; Dougherty, 2009) to PTL and MD. Items requiring minimal cost while allowing speed of execution seem appropriate for the highest priority. Not only does implementation provide immediate recognition by the stakeholders most affected, but also this observation builds rapport and trust with the spotter drivers for changes that may take more time to implement. Specifically, the objectives of changing the automatic termination policy and adding the provision of a defined break period meet this goal. Communicating these changes directly to the spotter drivers should provide immediate stress relief to the drivers, increase motivation, and improve job satisfaction with immediate noticeable reduction in turnover, even in the short term (Liu, Liu, & Hu, 2010).

Items needing action, coordination, and effort on behalf of the customer (MD) take the next priority as these may take longer to accomplish and require customer expense. Improving lighting conditions increases visibility, reduces accidents, and decreases costs to PTL that ultimately are passed to MD in the form of service costs. In a few cases, lights may simply require maintenance or repair, but in other locations, the addition of new lighting is appropriate. PTL should provide MD administrators with cost reports for damages occurring in these poorly lit areas to justify the claim and recommend comparison to costs for the lighting project. The second task, provision of an accessible break area, can require little to no cost to MD or PTL by allowing the spotter drivers to utilize facilities available to MD employees. Currently, spotters believe they are barred from sharing customer facilities as communicated by the day-shift PTL supervisor.

No budget is necessary in resolving the above objectives. However, the final three items may require financial insertion by PTL for implementation. Establishing the peer-review feedback system requires the lowest development cost, although coordination with human resource personnel processes for integration is essential (Jackson & LePine, 2003). Exact costs are beyond the scope of this discussion and in need of further review. Creation of a comprehensive site-specific training program indulges the highest up-front expense with coordination of all drivers and supervisors providing input for maximum coverage and effectiveness.

A combination of hands-on training (Trampusch, 2010) with safety orientation to vehicle operation, site hazards, customer expectations, and productivity tips provides new employees with confidence and higher job satisfaction (Liu, Liu, & Hu, 2010). The final objective of designing and implementing the orientation checklist remains dependent upon successful integration of the other tasks and serves as a guide for insuring topic coverage.

BEHAVIORAL ISSUES

Providing the consultant with personal behaviors to maximize the attainment and teaching of skills that enable trusting relationships lasting beyond the consultation period, Cope (2010) offered his TRUST model. The components of truthfulness, responsiveness, uniformity, safety, and training pertain to the human element, but fail to conglomerate the magnitude of factors involved in building and maintaining trust. The encompassing Change Ladder model did expand understanding of these relationships beyond the personal level. The following recommendations reveal principles extruded from the TRUST model that Mr. Nichols will integrate into the change process:

1. Disclose full truths without predicting what stakeholders may want to hear. This helps to eliminate occurrences of social apathy among stakeholders.
2. Keep the client informed through regular and open communication by responding in a timely manner. As the primary observer, Mr. Nichols should report progress and potential problems as they occur.
3. Seek to identify and incorporate connotative symbolism in every aspect of the consultation process owned by the stakeholders of the project. In other words, Mr. Nichols should help the stakeholders own the changes.
4. Mold new processes and changes into the organization rather try to change the people to match the project.
5. Include as many of the stakeholders as possible throughout the project and encourage maximum participation.

RISK MANAGEMENT

Some risk is involved with the change program. Either PTL or MD could refuse to perform respective tasks, in which Mr. Nichols will have to reiterate the benefits of completing the program, especially the cost savings. Although some countries have banned genetically modified foods, consumers in the United States still promote their production due to the cost savings (Traill, et al., 2006). This finding stresses the importance of remaining cost-conscious when recommending and implementing the proposed changes.

To reduce risks further, Mr. Nichols will periodically poll the spotter drivers with questions regarding their satisfaction towards the implemented changes and compare these data with the original feedback. This qualitative benchmarking procedure will allow reporting of measured outcomes against expected task results and provide for additional correlation to turnover rates. Deconstructing the problem and systematically analyzing the components individually, assists with understanding of how the combined solutions work, eventually enhancing the probability of the organizations creating competitive advantage. For PTL, testing changes in the controlled environment before full implementation at other potential customer sites and provision of contingency plans serve as the most recommended methods for assessing risk at the organizational level.

COMMUNICATION PLAN

The role of Mr. Nichols is to help the stakeholders with analyzing emotions within the organizational setting from an objective perspective (Cope, 2010). When the persons involved recognize differences between relevance, assumption, speculation, and the fear of administrative repercussion, sorting fact from fiction during inquiry occurs (Dougherty, 2009). People naturally tend to answer questions with replies they personally feel the interrogator expects to hear, rather than truths the respondent believes are accurate and personalized. With trust and assurance of confidentiality with the participative role Mr. Nichols assumes with the spotter drivers, psychological advantages through trust, confidence, and honesty during interviews are gained (Coon & Mitterer, 2010). This tactic allows interactions to remain focused, relevant, and pertinent to the change process with minimal disruption.

Communication between Mr. Nichols, PTL, MD, and the spotter drivers will remain open, frequent, concise, and focused for maximum effectiveness within the group project (Opara, 2010). The intent is for members to learn to trust and communicate with one another after Mr. Nichols has left the customer site in hopes of avoiding future problems and tensions of a similar nature.

SCOPE AND QUALITY VERIFICATION

The scope of this consulting project involves, in no particular order:

1) Removing situational blindness (social apathy) where possible,
2) Accumulating relevant data for an accurate diagnosis,
3) Paying attention to every source of information,
4) Alleviating fears and building trust,
5) Identifying and integrating organizational culture concerns into the project,
6) Knowing who the real decision makers are,
7) Understanding the client system from a broad perspective beyond the limits of the project,
8) Identifying and utilizing potential stakeholders, and
9) Balancing and managing potential risks.

Verifying the scope of this project involves measurement of feedback through communication and analysis of feedback as previously discussed. Additionally, improved turnover rates of spotter drivers, reduced costs from incidences of accidents and damage, and smoother productivity outcomes verify the quality of the project through financial analyses.

DELIVERABLES

The estimated total completion time for this project is six months, mostly dependent upon actions taken for lighting conditions and guide line repainting. Once completed, spotter drivers can be expected to produce lower turnover, higher productivity, increased job satisfaction, lowered stress from fears of sudden job loss, scheduled breaks with facilities, respect for supervisors, better orientation and training procedures, and fewer accidents. Maximum Distribution will enjoy reduced service costs relative to these changes and improved facilities. Premium Trucking and Logistics will learn to communicate more effectively with its employees and customers in terms of needs versus expected outcomes while reaping the benefits sponsored by its stakeholders. Working together, this group will increase competitive advantages and operative cohesion.

* * *

PART EIGHT APPENDIX

Table 8.1.1

Differential Characteristics in Consultation Types

Process /Role	Skills Required	Culture Sensitivity	Use of Preventative Measure	Use of Remediate Measures	Ownership of Change	Scope of Action	Level of Directedness
General:							Decreasing
Consultation			Usage ↑	Usage ↑	Client and Client's System	Provides knowledge, skills, and abilities the client lacks	
Collaboration	Depends upon specific role of consultant	Depends upon the problem in question			Client	Enhances client's existing KSAs	
Mid-Level: Supervision	Usage ↑	Usage ↑	Depends upon specific role of consultant	Usage ↑	Client	Take action with client's system on behalf of client	Decreasing
Mediation			None		Client and Client's System	Referee between client and client's system	
Specific: Advocate	Subject-knowledge, Interpersonal, Communication, Cultural-diversity, Problem-solving, Ethical skills	Regional, Organizational, Group	Recommendations based upon knowledge, skills, and abilities of consultant	Recommendations based upon knowledge, skills, and abilities of consultant	Client (e.g., tech advisor)	Specific goal or achievement	Decreasing
Expert	Subject-knowledge, Interpersonal, Communication, Cultural-diversity, Problem-solving, Ethical skills	Regional, Organizational, Group, Poverty, Racism	Prevent needs of client system for advocacy	Discrepancy remediation	Varies – can be lose-lose if a client system focus	Professional obligation while eliminating avoidance	

Continued

next page...

Process /Role	Skills Required	Culture Sensitivity	Use of Preventative Measure	Use of Remediate Measures	Ownership of Change	Scope of Action	Level of Directedness
Trainer /Educator	Subject-knowledge	Regional	Stress importance of skills taught for active implementation by client	Retraining Workshops	Client even with client system interaction (trainer)	Client system through formal/informal training	
	Interpersonal	Organizational					
	Communication	Group					
	Cultural-diversity						
	Group skills						
Fact Finder	Communication	Depends upon the scope of the defined problem	Recommendations to client after data analysis	Recommendations to client after data analysis	Client	Find, analyze, and report information to client: no direct interaction with client system	
	Cultural-diversity	Regional		Use of guided group self-analysis			
Process Specialist	Problem-solving	Organizational	Risk of unsolicited interpersonal feedback		Client however their colleagues may be the client system	Analyze processes of client's systems: "How"	
	Research skills Some subject knowledge	Group					
	Interpersonal						
	Communication						
	Cultural-diversity						
	Problem-solving						
	Ethical skills						
	Group skills						

Composited from "Psychological Consultation and Collaboration in School and Community Settings, 5th edition," by A. Michael Dougherty, 2009, pp 22-35. The Level of Directedness column adapted from "Consulting-style Inventory: A Tool for Consultants and Others in Helping Roles," by Timothy M. Nolan, 1998, The Pfeiffer Library (2nd Ed., Vol.15, pp 1-3), 1998, Jossey-Bass/Pfeiffer. Arrows indicate direction of increasing/decreasing usage of the skillset in the particular role set.

PART EIGHT REFERENCES

Anderson, J. A. (2010). Evolution of the Health Care Quality Journey: From Cost Reduction to Facilitating Patient Safety. The Journal of Legal Medicine (31), 59-72. doi:10.1080/01947641003598252.

Barnes, B. J., & Austin, A. E. (2008, October 3). The Role of Doctoral Advisors: A Look at Advising from the Advisor's Perspective. Innovative Higher Education (33), 297-315. doi:10.1007/s10755-008-9084-x.

Cadotte, E. R., Bruce, H. J., Gardial, S. F., Garval, D., Gilbert, K. C., Jacobs, J. D., . . . Woodruff, R. B. (2008). The Management of Strategy in the Marketplace. Knoxville, TN: Innovative Learning Solutions.

Carpenter, J., Luce, A., & Wooff, D. (2011). Predictors of Outcomes of Assertive Outreach Teams: A 3-Year Follow-Up Study in North East England. Soc Psychiatry Epidemiol, 46, 463-471. doi:DOI 10.1007/s00127-010-0211-5.

Coon, D., & Mitterer, J. O. (2010). Introduction to Psychology (12th ed.). Belmont, CA: Wadsworth.

Cope, M. (2010). The Seven Cs of Consulting: The Definitive Guide to the Consulting Process (3rd ed.). Harlow, England: Prentice Hall.

Dougherty, A. M. (2009). Psychological Consultation and Collaboration in School and Community Settings (5th ed.). Belmont, CA: Cole.

Friedlander, J. (1978). Student Perceptions on the Effectiveness of Midterm Feedback to Modify College Instruction. Journal of Educational Research, 71(3), 140-143.

Gardial, S. F. (2007). Understanding Customer Value. In H. J. Bruce, The Management of Strategy (pp. 128-146). Knoxville, TN: Innovative Learning Solutions.

Houston, D., Robertson, T., & Prebble, T. (2008, November). Exploring Quality in a University Department: Perspectives and Meanings. Quality in Higher Education, 14(3), 209-223. doi:10.1080/13538320802507463.

Jackson, C. L., & LePine, J. A. (2003). Peer Responses to a Team's Weakest Link: A Test and Extension of Lepine and Van Dyn's Model. Journal of Applied Psychology (88), pp. 459-475.

Jennings, M. M. (2006). Business: Its Legal, Ethical, and Global Environment (7th ed.). Mason, OH: Thomson Higher Learning.

Kamholz, B. W., Hayes, A. M., Carver, C. S., Gulliver, S. B., & Perlman, C. A. (2006, April). Identification and Evaluation of Cognitive Affect-Regulation Strategies: Development of a Self-Report Measure. Cognitive Therapy and Research, 30(2), 227-262. doi:10.1007/s10608-006-9013-1.

Kew, F. M., Galaal, K., & Manderville, H. (2009). Patients' Views of Follow-Up After Treatment for Gynecological Cancer. Journal of Obstetrics and Gynecology, 29(2), 135-142. doi:DOI: 10.1080/01443610802646801.

Kezar, A., Glenn, W. J., Lester, J., & Nakamoto, J. (2008, April). Examining Organizational Contextual Features That Affect Implementation of Equity Initiatives. The Journal of Higher Education, 79(2), 125-159.

Kimman, M. L., Dellaert, B. G., Boersma, L. J., Lambin, P., & Dirksen, C. D. (2010). Follow-up after treatment for breast cancer: One strategy fits all? An investigation of patient preferences using a discrete choice experiment. Acta Oncologica, 49, 328-337. doi:10.3109/02841860903536002.

Liu, B., Liu, J., & Hu, J. (2010). Person-Organization Fit, Job Satisfaction, and Turnover Intention: An Empirical Study in the Chinese Public Sector. Social Behavior and Personality, 38(5), 615-626. doi:10.2224/sbp.2010.38.5.615.

Luthans, F. (2008). Organizational Behavior (11th ed.). Boston, MA: McGraw-Hill/Irwin.

Macionis, J. J. (2010). Sociology (13th ed.). Boston, MA: Prentice Hall.

McIntyre, R. M., & Salas, E. (1995). Managing and Measuring for Team Performance: Lessons from Complex Environments. In R. A. Guzzo, & E. Salas, Team Effectiveness and Decision Making in Organizations (pp. 9-45). San Francisco, CA: Jossey-Bass.

Milkovich, G. T., & Newman, J. M. (2008). Compensation (9th ed.). New York, NY: McGraw-Hill/Irwin.

Muchinsky, P. M. (2006). Psychology Applied to Work (8th ed.). Belmont, CA: Thomson Wadsworth.

O'Brien, A., Fahmy, R., & Singh, S. P. (2009). Disengagement from Mental Health Services. Social Psychiatry, 44, 558-568. doi:10.1007/s00127-008-0476-0.

Oketch, M. O. (2005). The Corporate Stake in Social Cohesion. Peabody Journal of Education, 80(4), 30-52.

Opara, U. N. (2010). Short Communication: Toward Improving Library and Information Services Delivery in Nigeria Through Total Quality Management. African Journal of Library, Archives and Information Science, 20(1), 63-68.

Papalia, D. E., Olds, S. W., & Feldman, R. D. (2009). Human Development (11th ed.). Boston, MA: McGraw-Hill.

Pearson Learning Solutions. (2010). SKS7000 - Executive Concepts in Business Strategy. Boston, MA: Pearson Learning Solutions.

Peart, N., & Talbot, P. (Composers). (1977). Closer to the Heart. [Rush, Performer] Toronto, ON, Canada.

Roethlisberger, F. J., & Dickson, W. J. (1939). Management and the Worker. Cambridge, MA: Harvard University Press.

Sheng, C.-W., Tian, Y.-F., & Chen, M.-C. (2010). Relationships Among Teamwork Behavior, Trust, Perceived Team Support, and Team Commitment. Social Behavior and Personality, 38(10), 1297-1306. doi:10.2224/sbp.2010.38.10.1297.

Southeastern Institute of Research. (2008). The Change Report. New York: The First 30 Days.

Traill, W. B., Yee, W. M., Lusk, J. L., Jaeger, S. R., House, L. O., Morrow Jr., J. L., . . . Moore, M. (2006). Perceptions of the Risks and Benefits of Genetically-Modified Foods and Their Influence on Willingness to Consume. Food Economics Acta Agricult Scand C (3), 12-19.

Trampusch, C. (2010). Employers, the State and The Politics of Institutional Change: Vocational Education and Training in Austria, Germany and Switzerland. European Journal of Political Research, 49, 545-573. doi:10.1111/j.1475-6765.2009.01909.x.

Wickham, P. A., & Wickham, L. (2008). Management Consulting: Delivering an Effective Project (3rd ed.). Harlow, England: Prentice Hall.

Zimbardo, P. G. (2009). Pathology of Imprisonment. In J. J. Macionis, Sociology (13th ed., pp. 40-41). Boston, MA: Prentice Hall.

* * *

PART NINE:
BUSINESS STATISTICS

9.1 RELATIONSHIPS IN EDUCATION WITH GENDER, PARENTAL INTERACTIONS, AGE, AND MARITAL STATUS

This study is divided into four parts: gender, parents, age, and marital status. The attempt is to look at how each of these influences effect one's educational outcomes if a relationship exists, and then to evaluate what these relationships mean, depending upon statistical measures. Data was analyzed using the education pre-compiled dataset (Northcentral University, 2009).

GENDER AND EDUCATION

Studies into questions of (in)equality within educational opportunities between males and, particularly, females have been a hot topic in the United States for many years. Rooting from historical context, females were discouraged from attending college and those who did attend were counseled away from science and mathematically-based occupational choices, such as engineering or stock brokering. As attitudes and social controls have gradually changed, the need to understand these changes has evolved accordingly. This study begins by evaluating the relationships between males and females and how educational achievement levels (degrees) and time in school are related.

The null and alternative hypotheses under scrutiny for this statistical analysis have been determined as:

H_0 = Gender (sex) has no relationship with educational level outcomes.

H_A = Gender is related to educational level outcomes.

LITERATURE REVIEW

Commonly, the terms *gender* and *sex* are mistakenly used interchangeably, although each has different connotations. Sex refers to the biological makeup of males and females, whereas gender infers socially defined roles and characteristics associated with those respective sexes (Papalia, Olds, & Feldman, 2009; Macionis, 2010). For example, during the American 1960s, females who attended college generally received their degrees in home economics and supportive fields rather than occupational areas, a gender expectation of the American society at that time. In fear for claims of violating Title VII of the Civil Rights Act (as amended), many employers who understand these differences have revised employment applications to remove gender related questions when it is the applicant's sex (male or female) that was originally inquired of for identification and statistical purposes. For this analysis of educational achievement, the term *gender* refers only to the physical differences, or sex, of males and females unless otherwise noted.

According to studies completed by Eccles, Wigfield, and Byrnes (2003), males are more likely to be underachievers than females, more likely to drop out of school, and most likely to take remedial courses, but they also tend to complete more honors courses, apply to more top colleges, and undertake more challenging careers than females. This flanking trend is corroborated in that males achieve higher scores for standardized college admissions tests than females even though females (as a group) have the tendency to score higher in math and science coursework (Halpern et.al., 2007). In other words, males either tend to perform either very poorly, or exceptionally well, while females grouped together somewhere in the middle.

Explanations given for these differences range from biological, to social, to quality (and bias) in educational curriculum. For instance, the biological perspective claims the females have more gray matter in their brains and the corpus callosum is larger in contrast to males, yielding more myelin for neuronal interconnections. These findings indicate males may have more active brains when learning, but girls use more of a balance between the hemispheres (Halpern et.al., 2007). Still, other environmental effects influence educational outcomes; home, peers, socioeconomic status, cultural traditions, and gender roles established by the encompassing society (Macionis, 2010).

Understanding these covariates exist, the focus of this analysis is limited solely to testing for relationships between educational achievement levels and gender (sex) without implication of cause or covariate interdependence.

EXPLORATORY DATA ANALYSIS

The educational degree (Degree) obtained by the respondent was ranked in ascending order from zero (less than high school), to one (high school), to two (associates degree), to three (bachelor's degree), to four (graduate degree). Using Table 9.1.1 for a summation of descriptives, Year represents the number of years of schooling, regardless if a degree level was obtained. Although 21.5% more females responded than males, each group had enough sample data to provide an acceptable effect size. Males, on average, had completed about half a year more of schooling than females and are reflected by the slightly higher average degree level, which equates to some college, but no degree for both sexes. The standard deviations explain that education levels for males and females average from high school dropout to junior in college although the ranges explain this spread can be 25% more for females.

This is where the importance of skewness is revealed. The high positive skewness for female education levels versus their time in school indicates that most women congregate around the lower end of the range for the nearly average time in school. Conversely, the skewness for males indicates that more men obtain the higher education level within their range, also for about the average time in school for males. Kurtosis among education levels (Degree) is negative for females, albeit somewhat negligible, and positive for males collaborating the skewness effect.

With time in school (Year), the opposite is again true with tentative explanation from the higher range dispersion for females. See Figures 9.1 and 9.2 in the Appendix for graphical representations.

P-P plots were prepared in Figure 9.3 for education level and time in school. These graphs extend explanations of the descriptives provided while adding comparability into the probable trend of more people going to school than was obtaining a degree level.

The relationships between gender and the highest degree level obtained with years of schooling show that males may go to college than females, both on average, and in general. However, the higher range in years indicates that some females tend to go further in school.

TESTING AND RESULTS

Although a fairly large sample was collected, the skews and kurtosis of the data prove to be problematic with normality; therefore, the non-parametric Wilcoxon signed-rank and Mann-Whitney tests were selected over the independent t-test for this analysis. This decision makes further sense in that the variables in themselves are ranked providing greater cohesion with the testing procedures. Figure 9.4 (Appendix) displays the output tables for these tests.

Education levels (Degree) were equally significant for males and females (Mdn = 1.00), z = -2.31, ρ < .05, r = -.06. However, the time spent in school (Year) was more significant for males (Mdn = 13.00) than females (Mdn = 12.00), z = -3.33, ρ < .001, r = -.09. These effects were small but show that, especially for males, the more time invested in going to school the more likely the probability a higher educational level may be achieved. No causation is implied; however, these small effects do show that other covariates likely better explain these relationships and the null hypothesis should be rejected as there was a significant influence detected. This confirms previous research, such as that conducted by Halpern et.al. (2007), but contradicts studies by Eccles, Wigfield, and Byrnes (2003) that males are more likely to drop out of school and more likely to be underachievers than females. Obviously then, further research into these relationships is necessary.

* * *

9.2 PARENTAL EDUCATION EFFECTS

It has often been rumored through social stereotyping that behavioral characteristics of parents can be attributed to their children. Sociological behaviorists argue that environment and self-will cause us to make our own decisions in spite of what our parents have done. It turns out that both are correct, yet incorrect, as subjective variables determine when we listen and act in accordance with others, and when we stray to our own desires. For example, twins that are raised separately have been shown to develop physically in similar fashions, but may differ in attitudes, personalities, and aptitudes depending upon the conditions in which they were raised and experiences that shape cognitive understanding (Papalia, Olds, & Feldman, 2009).

Keeping with this theme of parental influences, the null and alternative hypotheses under scrutiny for this statistical analysis have been determined as:

H_0 = Parental education level has no relationship with educational level outcomes.
H_A = Parental education level is related to educational level outcomes.
H_0 = the father's education level has no relationship with educational level outcomes.
H_A = the father's education level is related to educational level outcomes.
H_0 = the mother's education level has no relationship with educational level outcomes.
H_A = the mother's education level is related to educational level outcomes.

LITERATURE REVIEW

The values of parents influence the values and occupational goals of their children in regards to academic achievement (Jodl et.al., 2001). If parents do not value education, then their children most likely will have disregard for its value as well and vice versa. Of course, parental influence is not the only determinant as self-efficacy, financial barriers, minority status, the academic experience, and peer influences have also been shown to stimulate educational persistence (Papalia, Olds, & Feldman, 2009). Amanda Ripley (2008) reported that children today are less likely to complete high school than their parents were, although John Macionis (2010) claims that high school dropout rates are lower than any time in history (the first is more likely compared with the 25% local dropout rate for 2010 in the hometown of this author coupled with the record high enrollment in GED courses).

The purpose of this study is to test the claims of Jodl, Michael, Malanchuk, Eccles, and Sameroff by looking for relationships between parents' education and that of their children at the individual level (mother, father).

EXPLORATORY DATA ANALYSIS

The amount of education over time was compared to that of the mother and father of the respondent from zero to twenty years and descriptive statistics are listed in Table 9.2.1. The varying directions and amounts of skew and kurtosis verify the non-normality of the data, however the data appears to normalize near transition grades (8, 12, 16) when the respondent is most likely to transfer to a higher level institution, such as from junior high (8) to high school or high school (12) to college. At the grade level, this non-normality can be expected due to the very low numbers of respondents in each grouping, although overall some normality could become apparent, as these numbers are lower towards the extremes (0, 20) and higher in the center (12).

Some trending appears, mostly on the father's side, where as the father's education increases, so does that of the respondent. The exception is in the junior high years for reasons unknown. The mother's influence on the respondent seems to have less influence and is more sporadic, except for respondents who attend graduate school. This could be attributed to other factors that affect the home environment as discussed in the Gender and Education section.

Deviations and ranges appear fairly consistent for fathers except at the beginning of the educational period. Extremity for mothers around eighth and ninth grade deviates from surrounding patterns although averages remain consistent.

The relationships between respondent's education and those of the parents show variation mostly with the mother. Although there appears to be a closer tie with father's education, the data appears to normalize when viewed from an overall perspective.

TESTING AND RESULTS

The Kruskal-Wallis test was selected by father and mother against the educational outcome of the respondent. Trend reporting was unavailable through the Jonckheere-Terpstra test as the variables were not categorized for this purpose. The Kruskal-Wallis test indicates that both the father's education level $H(17) = 173.80$, $p < .001$, and mother's education level $H(19) = 218.89$, $p < .001$, were highly significant with the respondent's educational outcome. Unfortunately, post hoc testing proved improbable.

Realizing that all samples were based upon the same participants and that separate tests needed to be conducted for the Respondent/Father and Respondent/Mother combinations respectively, the Wilcoxon signed-rank test was employed. Once again, the educational level of each parent was highly significant with that of the respondent. The Wilcoxon signed-ranked test indicated the father's education level was significant (Mdn = 12.00), $z = -16.89$, $p < .001$, $r = -0.54$. For the mother's education level, the significance (Mdn = 12.00), $z = -19.36$, $p < .001$, $r = -0.56$, effect was slightly greater indicating that although both parents education level may affect their child's education level, the mother has a little more influence (but not much). Figure 9.5 (Appendix) displays test results.

For the three hypotheses provided, we must reject all of the nulls and propose a new hypothesis that:

H_0 = Mother's education level effect on respondent's educational outcomes > Father's education level effect on respondent's educational outcomes.

Research into covariate relationships is necessary before attempting to determine the reasons why these results exist.

* * *

9.3 AGE AND EDUCATION

Who is more likely to go to school longer, older generations or their descendants? This analysis attempts to answer this question, but albeit, is limited in scope. Many colleges and universities compile simple statistics as to the ages of their student bodies and reasons for going to school, but even fewer attempt comparative studies into representative analyses of the communities they serve. Often, middle-aged parents are heard saying something to their children like, "I wish I could go back to school. I would go as far as I could". The elderly often extends this rational to "If I could do it all over again, I never would have left school". With this theme in mind, this analysis looks to see if any of those aging persons have done anything to back up their claims.

LITERATURE REVIEW

Students during 2005 seeking a degree totaled 39% in composition of the student body and ranged in age between the mid-twenties through the seventies (Macionis, 2010). In 2010, the average student at Frontier Community College was 36 years old (Illinois Eastern Community Colleges, 2010), in stark contrast to the 4% illiteracy rate for the region. Many are the first in their extended families to attend college and some alongside their children. When surveyed as to the purpose of attendance, older students most commonly replied they are returning to school for "self-improvement" over financial, job skill enhancement, and other economic reasons.

Within the last century, people in the United States have become more educated per capita than any other time in the country's history, although some argument is given for the quality of education as compared to other high-income nations. With this trend it could be expected that as comparisons are made between educational level and age that the oldest persons, on average, would have less time in the classroom than the newest generations. As older students return to school these proportions may be changing rapidly in response to various factors; such as the availability of free high school equivalency certification programs, the creation of Pell Grant programs administered by the U.S. Department of Education, sponsorship by many employers for tuition reimbursement and flex-time scheduling, and the willingness of parents to provide modeling actions for their children.

Given these assumptions, it would be unfair to draw any conclusions from age-to-education relationships without realizing these results are nothing more than snapshots in time that could be used for comparisons to other studies of a historical nature. From a predictive standpoint then, these studies could be utilized in a multiple regression analysis in discovery of trending models, but should not be used alone for accuracy.

DESCRIPTIVES AND TESTING

Descriptive statistics were calculated for the number of years of education and the age of each respondent (Table 9.3.1) before performing a simple regression analysis to test for any significance in correlation. Although neither variable appeared to contain normalized relationships due to their high kurtosis and skewness results, age appeared to be nearly four times more likely to be skewed than the education level and each was inversely proportioned (see Figure 9.6, Appendix), indicating that younger people tended to have more time in school than older persons. The standard deviation of age reveals that any age represented could reflect nearly any other age within two decades, drawing doubt about collinear relationships and possible rejection of the null hypothesis where

H_0 = Age has no relationship with educational level outcomes.
H_A = Age is related to educational level outcomes.

The relationships between years of education and age show that age is not normally distributed. The opposing directions of skewness indicate that younger people tend to be more educated (by length of time in school, not degree level) than older persons. Simple regression analysis reveals that a linear relationship does indeed exist between age and education level. Using the equation (calculated from Table 9.3.2):

Education$_{Years}$ = 14.50 − (0.03)Age

It can be understood that to predict the education level of a person, we multiply their age by 0.03 and then subtract this result from 14.50 (the mean education level of persons age 18 through age 89). So, for example, if we want to know the probable education level a person aged 65 may have, multiplying 65 by 0.03 = 1.95; then subtracting, 14.50 − 1.95 = 12.55 years. In this study then, a 65 year old can be expected to have had at least a half-year of college.

It is important to note this estimate is based upon an average of all persons (included in this sample) in the age range reflected and does not consider particular ages for which certain educational levels may occur. Since correlations between gender (sex) and parental educational levels have been established in previous sections, it can also be assumed that other covariates that may affect the expected education level of a person are excluded and further study is needed. Using the scatterplot depicted in Figure 9.8

(Appendix), the data demonstrates a possible covariate is the common degree levels expected at particular ages through banding of the data points, in a declining linear fashion.

Although highly significant, Pearson's Correlation (R^2) verifies that this relationship between age and education is extremely small (about three percent) and is more likely due to covariate factors. See Figure 9.6 in the Appendix for a more detailed calculation. In essence, we must reject the null hypothesis that age is not related to the number of years of education that a person has, but must accept that it is a very small relationship. This finding causes an adjustment for new null hypotheses:

H_0 = Age is slightly related to educational outcomes, and/or

H_0 = Age is related to other variables when testing for relationships with educational outcomes.

* * *

9.4 MARITAL STATUS AND EDUCATION

Many questions arise when correlating marital status with education level: Who is more likely to have a higher education level – husbands or wives? Is there any correlation between marital status and education level? If one spouse holds an advanced degree, is the other likely to return to school and for how long? How is the divorce rate affected with differing education levels compared to those persons with equalized education levels? Although most of these questions are beyond the scope of this examination, the first was selected as a basic starting point for statistical analysis. Respondents were asked their marital status, and if married, to provide the educational level of their spouse. Unfortunately, data for divorced, widowed, and separated respondents were not collected for comparative analyses that would have allowed testing of additional hypotheses (such as divorce rate v. spousal education).

The null and alternative hypotheses under scrutiny for this statistical analysis therefore have been reduced to:

H_0 = Education levels for respondents are not related to educational levels of their spouses.
H_A = Education levels for respondents are related to education levels of their spouses.

These hypothetical tests may seem somewhat vague, but they allow for contextual design variance in that assumption into the sexes of respondents and their spouses can be ignored, e.g., both spouses in the marriage are male or both female. Even though data was analyzed using the *husband* and *wife* labels, no assumption in these cases was made into the sex of the respondent for fear of biasing results based upon gender (sex).

LITERATURE REVIEW

John Macionis reported through meta-analysis that spouses with successful careers are more likely to divorce than spouses in other career combinations (Macionis, 2010). This attribute cannot be attributed to educational outcomes of either spouse since Macionis failed to elaborate any such correlation or to signify what exactly determines a successful career. In a study conducted at Rutgers University, the declining divorce rate for the United States since 1970 was correlated with increasing educational levels and the tendency of Americans to marry the first time at later ages than previous generations (National Marriage Project, 2004), which would cause some assumption that educational levels indeed affect divorce rates. "Some assumption" is key to this interpretation as other factors like increased cohabitation tendencies, family violence causes, and religiosity were also considered in the Rutgers University study.

It is interesting that although enrollments for females are higher than males in collegiate institutions (see discussion of Sex and Education) that more males tend to pursue doctoral academic goals. This find then begs the questions of how many of these students are married, what are the educational outcomes of their spouses, and at what age do they typically marry? Of course, race and ethnicity provide barriers to education for minority peoples, including majority minority affiliations in some geographic arenas (Adams & Strother-Adams, 2001), but cannot be precluded from educational outcome relationships with their spouses. For this reason, race and ethnicity were not considered as factors in this generalized study.

Given this body of knowledge, it therefore conclusive to reverse the initial null and alternative hypotheses to test the composite assumptions created by prior studies:

H_0 = Education levels for respondents are related to education levels of their spouses.

H_A = Education levels for respondents are not related to educational levels of their spouses.

EXPLORATORY DATA ANALYSIS

Of the 1218 married respondents, exactly half (609) had husbands and the other half had wives at the time intake was conducted. Descriptive statistical analyses were performed for each group separately to determine how educational outcomes of the respondent may be related to that of their spouses. Only married respondents were included in the study so three variables were used: Respondent education level with husband education level, and respondent education level with wife education level.

In each group, spouses averaged around a year and a half of college (Table 9.4.1) with the median at exactly 13 years (one year of college) for both groups. Table 9.4.2 breaks down these summaries at the grade level. Husbands deviated from this mean by nearly three years while wives deviated by only about two and a half years, indicating that a respondent's wife is probably closer to educational outcomes of a respondent than a husband is. It is not until reviewing the skewness, kurtosis, and ranges of these groups that an understanding of the data can be fully appreciated. In contrast to average outcomes, wives educational level actually slightly exceeded husband's educational level by one year (range) across the spectrum with more wives being less educated than the respondent (negative skewness), but yet the high positive kurtosis indicates that wives may either be either more educated or less educated than the respondent. This is also slightly true for husbands, however the values approaching zero show that husband's education is nearly the same as the respondent.

Therefore, when considering the null hypothesis that spousal educational outcomes are related to the respondent's educational outcomes, precedential analysis predicts the determination depends upon if the spouse is a husband or a wife as to the degree of the relationship.

The relationships between the educational level of respondents and their husbands was nearly normal while that of respondents and their wives showed a slightly greater range of disparity with those scores clustering in the tails of that range (kurtosis). This preliminary descriptive indicates husband's education level was more closely related to that of the respondent while the education level of wives tended to be higher or lower than that of the respondent, still generating nearly matching averages (means).

TESTING AND RESULTS

Comparative analysis from the data could not be reasonably conducted with the information collected to determine relationships between educational levels of single versus married respondents even though educational levels of 201 respondents were available because it is unknown if these respondents failed to report a previous positive marital status (divorced, widowed, separated, never married) or were not requested to provide information if not currently married. Of the 1419 total respondents then, only the 85.8% (1218) who reported they were married at the time of the study were utilized, instead, to test the relationship of the respondent's educational outcomes with that of their respective spouse (husband or wife).

Using partial linear multiple regression to distinguish relationships of husband's and wives' education levels those of married respondents, the scatterplots in Figure 9.9 (Appendix) show that linear relationships do exist for each spousal type. For husbands, this relationship is closer to that of the respondent than for a wife as demonstrated by the coefficients (B) listed in Table 9.4.3. Overall, these relationships correlate with high significance to account for 78% of a married person's education level.

No causation is implied; however, these effects do show that other covariates likely also explain these relationships and the null hypothesis should be accepted as there was a significant influence detected. Previous research discussed in the literature review is strengthened by these findings although further research is necessary to test covariate possibilities. Additionally, new null hypotheses are mandated by the difference in spousal relationships of husbands and wives:

H_0 = Education levels for husbands >= Education levels for wives.

H_0 = Education levels for respondents are more closely related to education levels of husbands than education levels of wives.

PART NINE APPENDIX

Table 9.1.1

Descriptive Statistics for Gender (sex), Degree Level, and Highest Year Completed

Variable	n	M	Mdn	SD	Range	Skew	Kurtosis
Female							
Degree	789	1.38	1.00	1.10	4	0.84	-0.20
Year	789	13.00	12.00	2.84	20	-0.02	1.26
Male							
Degree	619	1.56	1.00	1.25	4	-0.70	0.70
Year	619	13.54	13.00	2.95	16	-0.13	-0.02

Table 9.3.1

Descriptive Statistics for Education (years) and Age

Variable	n	M	Mdn	SD	Range	Skew	Kurtosis
Education	1413	13.23	13.00	2.90	20	-0.126	0.725
Age	1413	46.56	44.00	17.33	71	0.486	-0.589

Table 9.3.2

Correlation of Coefficients

Variable	B	SE B	β
Age (constant)	14.50	0.22	
Education (Years)	-0.03	0.00	-0.16

$R^2 = .03, \rho < .001$

Table 9.4.1

Descriptive Statistics for Highest Year Completed of Respondents and their Spouses

Variable	n	M	Mdn	D	Range	Skew	Kurtosis
Husband	609	13.58	13.00	2.93	17	-.031	.264
Wife	609	13.29	13.00	2.64	18	-.119	1.53

Table 9.4.3

Correlation of Coefficients

Variable	B	SE B	β
Education Level (constant)	-0.19	0.30	
Education (Husband)	0.49	0.02	0.50
Education (Wife)	0.53	0.02	0.50

$R^2 = .78, \rho < .001$

Table 9.2.1

Descriptive Statistics for Parents and Respondent Highest Year Completed

Variable	n	M	Mdn	SD	Range	Skew	Kurtosis
Mother							
0	9	10.89	11.00	3.37	12	0.17	1.07
1	0						
2	11	10.55	12.00	3.45	10	- 1.02	- 0.06
3	13	12.38	12.00	2.63	11	- 0.04	1.80
4	12	12.67	12.00	2.67	9	1.66	2.35
5	9	11.22	12.00	3.42	10	- 0.82	- 0.56
6	19	12.53	13.00	2.65	8	- 0.22	- 0.94
7	15	13.00	12.00	3.57	6	1.17	0.18
8	85	12.14	12.00	8.98	17	- 0.31	1.70
9	28	12.57	13.00	10.85	16	- 0.29	0.88
10	50	13.38	12.00	2.67	10	1.06	0.59
11	31	13.81	12.00	2.56	11	0.59	- 0.39
12	367	14.02	14.00	2.41	13	0.42	- 0.09
13	29	14.66	16.00	4.52	8	- 0.47	- 0.91
14	85	15.12	16.00	2.20	9	0.28	- 0.29
15	16	14.25	13.50	2.24	8	1.16	1.40
16	91	15.52	16.00	2.03	8	0.22	- 0.18
17	6	15.17	15.50	2.79	7	- 0.01	- 1.27
18	17	16.06	16.00	2.41	8	0.04	- 0.63
19	2	17.50	17.50	2.12	3	0	0
20	9	15.67	16.00	2.35	8	0.44	0.55
Father							
0	13	10.92	11.00	4.61	16	0.37	- 0.09
1	2	11.50	11.50	.71	1	0	0
2	7	11.71	13.00	5.56	14	- 0.49	- 1.58
3	17	12.24	12.00	2.71	12	0.84	2.31
4	14	13.00	12.00	2.80	11	0.81	1.30
5	16	13.19	13.50	2.83	10	- 0.28	- 0.07
6	47	13.00	12.00	1.96	8	0.53	- 0.29
7	18	12.39	12.00	3.22	14	- 0.52	2.26
8	116	13.00	12.00	3.15	18	- 0.11	0.85
9	26	13.50	13.50	2.32	9	- 0.21	- 0.34
10	47	13.43	13.00	2.82	10	0.14	- 0.37
11	26	13.88	13.50	2.85	12	0.40	- 0.07
12	275	13.72	13.00	2.34	12	0.65	0.37
13	34	14.85	15.00	2.23	9	0.21	- 0.64
14	64	14.91	16.00	2.59	13	- 0.16	0.26
15	12	15.50	16.00	2.78	11	- 0.81	2.27
16	98	15.12	16.00	2.12	8	0.29	- 0.18
17	8	15.50	16.00	2.51	7	- 0.33	- 0.65
18	30	15.70	16.00	2.09	8	0.14	- 0.05
19	6	16.33	16.00	2.34	6	0.67	- 0.45
20	28	16.11	16.00	1.81	8	- 0.01	0.29

Table 9.4.2

Descriptive Statistics for Spouses and Respondents Highest Year Completed (by Years)

Variable	n	M	Mdn	SD	Range	Skew	Kurtosis
Husband							
5	3	8.00	9.00	2.65	5	-1.46	0
7	3	8.00	7.00	1.43	3	1.73	0
8	24	9.17	8.00	2.06	7	1.23	-0.06
9	7	10.43	11.00	1.13	3	-0.24	-1.23
10	22	10.50	10.00	1.66	7	2.36	5.75
11	28	11.21	11.00	2.50	15	-1.43	7.02
12	183	12.48	12.00	2.78	12	1.73	5.78
13	46	13.07	13.00	0.98	6	0.77	4.48
14	80	13.60	14.00	1.36	10	-1.33	6.41
15	28	14.18	15.00	1.47	6	-1.39	1.02
16	95	15.41	16.00	1.53	9	-0.76	1.37
17	22	16.18	17.00	1.62	6	-1.79	2.52
18	27	16.85	18.00	1.51	5	-1.10	0.28
19	20	17.17	19.00	2.06	7	-1.53	1.79
20	17	18.12	20.00	4.48	17	-2.85	8.48
Wife							
2	3	7.33	8.00	5.03	10	-0.59	0
8	16	9.25	8.00	2.21	7	1.64	1.72
9	16	9.88	9.00	1.86	7	1.92	3.19
10	24	10.58	10.00	1.53	8	-0.33	3.32
11	18	10.56	11.00	1.65	7	-2.62	7.72
12	220	12.39	12.00	1.75	15	0.41	5.24
13	53	13.23	13.00	1.68	14	-0.05	10.91
14	81	14.26	14.00	2.03	12	1.02	2.90
15	30	14.87	15.00	1.20	7	- .81	2.27
16	89	15.12	16.00	2.12	8	0.40	5.86
17	16	15.92	16.00	1.49	13	-2.69	15.75
18	22	17.23	18.00	1.88	7	-0.84	0.11
19	7	18.71	19.00	0.49	1	-1.23	-0.84
20	11	18.73	20.00	2.28	7	-1.99	3.58

Early (grade school) reports of spousal education are nearly non-existent. These data represent grade-level breakdowns of the categorical relationships summarized in Table 9.4.5.

Figure 9.1 through Figure 9.9

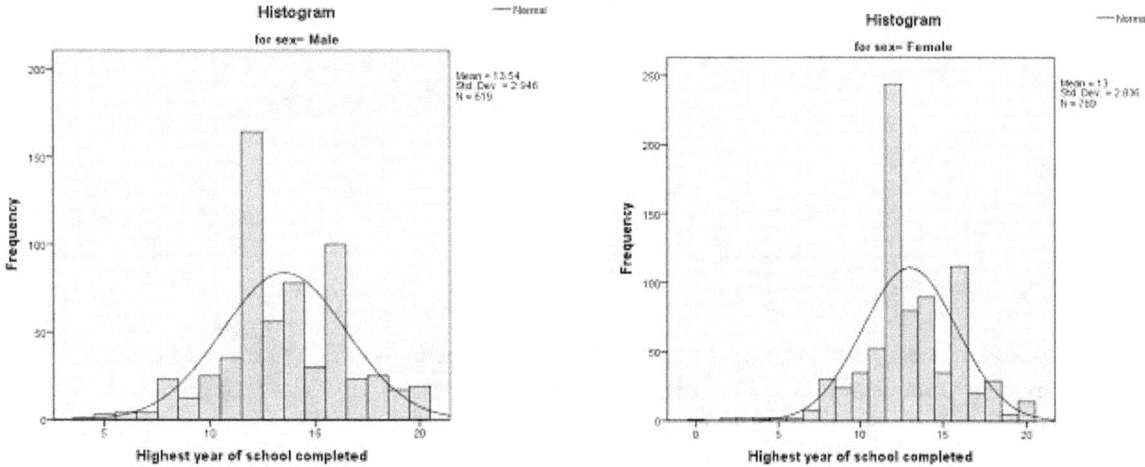

Figure 9.1. Frequency distribution histograms for highest year of school completed for males and females. Looking at the normality curves, it becomes apparent that data for males appears nearly normal while positive kurtosis is evident for females.

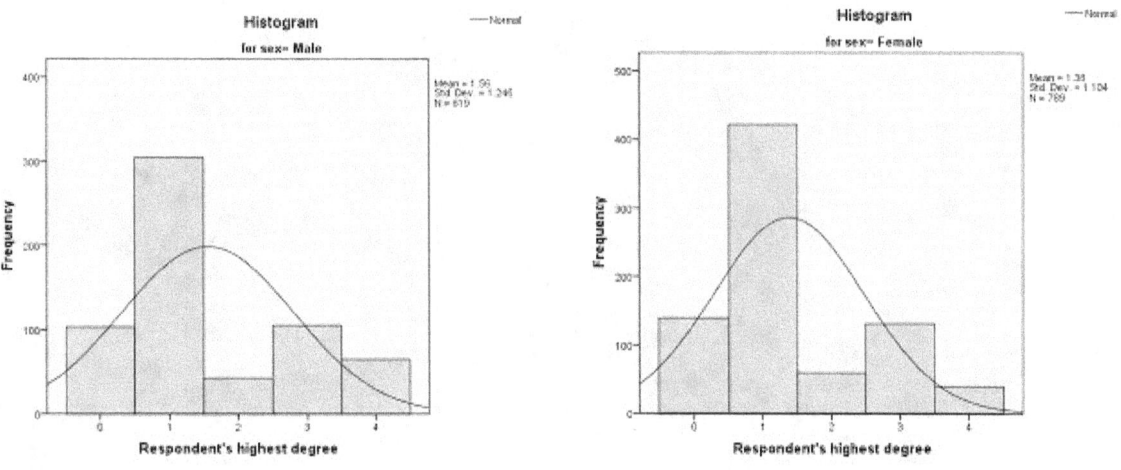

Figure 9.2. Frequency distribution histograms for education level for males and females. The male distribution appears flatter than the female distribution, indicating a higher positive kurtosis within the female data.

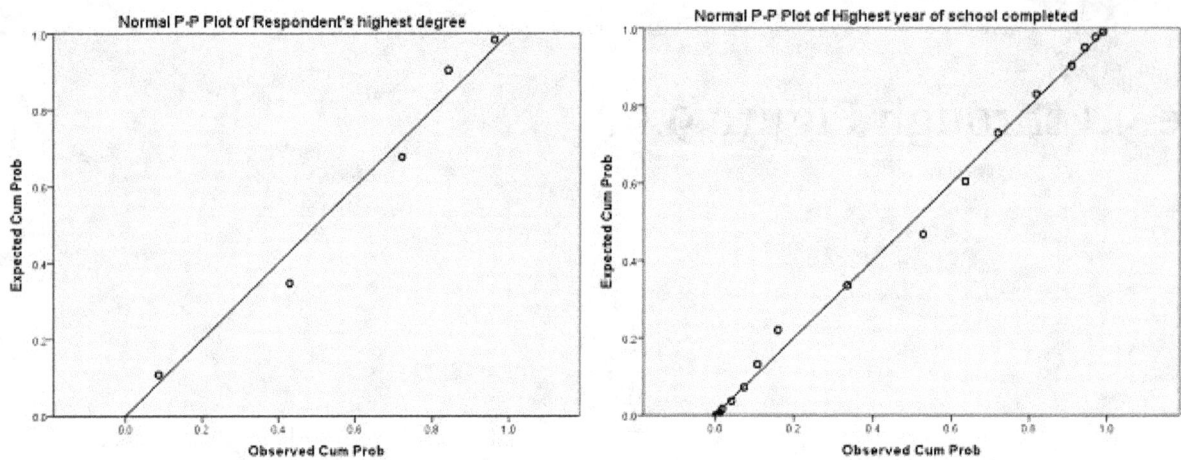

Figure 9.3. P-P plots for education level and time in school. The variance in data points on each side of the lines indicates multiple modes and skewness of the data. The lag of plots for highest degree in comparison with year in school may be explained by more people going to school than was finishing at determined levels.

Descriptive Statistics

	N	Mean	Std. Deviation	Minimum	Maximum
Respondent's highest degree	1411	1.46	1.174	0	4
Highest year of school completed	1415	13.23	2.895	0	20
Respondent's sex	1419	1.56	.496	1	2

Ranks

	Respondent's sex	N	Mean Rank	Sum of Ranks
Respondent's highest degree	Male	620	732.16	453936.50
	Female	791	685.50	542229.50
	Total	1411		
Highest year of school completed	Male	621	748.21	464640.00
	Female	794	676.55	537180.00
	Total	1415		

Test Statistics[a]

	Respondent's highest degree	Highest year of school completed
Mann-Whitney U	228993.500	221565.000
Wilcoxon W	542229.500	537180.000
Z	-2.310	-3.325
Asymp. Sig. (2-tailed)	.021	.001

a. Grouping Variable: Respondent's sex

Figure 4. Output tables for the Wilcoxon signed-rank and Mann-Whitney tests showing relationships between educational level and time in school by gender (sex).

Ranks

		N	Mean Rank	Sum of Ranks
HIGHEST YEAR SCHOOL COMPLETED, MOTHER - Highest year of school completed	Negative Ranks	737[a]	498.50	367396.50
	Positive Ranks	183[b]	307.45	56263.50
	Ties	269[c]		
	Total	1189		
HIGHEST YEAR SCHOOL COMPLETED, FATHER - Highest year of school completed	Negative Ranks	621[d]	439.21	272752.50
	Positive Ranks	183[e]	277.91	50857.50
	Ties	170[f]		
	Total	974		

a. HIGHEST YEAR SCHOOL COMPLETED, MOTHER < Highest year of school completed

b. HIGHEST YEAR SCHOOL COMPLETED, MOTHER > Highest year of school completed

c. HIGHEST YEAR SCHOOL COMPLETED, MOTHER = Highest year of school completed

d. HIGHEST YEAR SCHOOL COMPLETED, FATHER < Highest year of school completed

e. HIGHEST YEAR SCHOOL COMPLETED, FATHER > Highest year of school completed

f. HIGHEST YEAR SCHOOL COMPLETED, FATHER = Highest year of school completed

Figure 9.5 (above). Tables indicating test statistics for the respondent/parent education levels. Median and z-score statistics are provided in the upper tables while the ranks table breaks down comparisons by mother and father.

Model Summary[b]

Model	R	R Square	Adjusted R Square	Std. Error of the Estimate	Change Statistics					Durbin-Watson
					R Square Change	F Change	df1	df2	Sig. F Change	
1	.163[a]	.027	.026	2.859	.027	38.679	1	1411	.000	1.628

a. Predictors: (Constant), Age of respondent

b. Dependent Variable: Highest year of school completed

Figure 9.6. Model Summary for the Education to Age correlation. This model explains less than 3% of the relationship in the correlation, indicating the need for further study.

Normal P-P Plot of Regression Standardized Residual

Dependent Variable: Highest year of school completed

Figure 7. P-P plot for Age and Education. The variability in the data points demonstrates the differences in skewness and kurtosis.

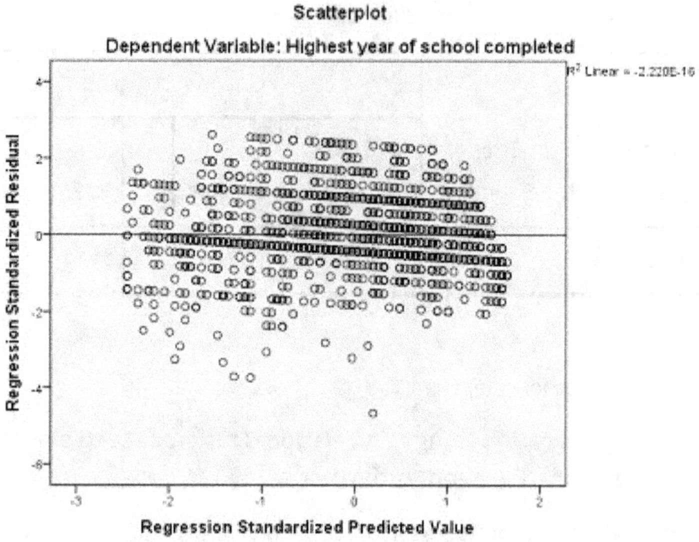

Scatterplot
Dependent Variable: Highest year of school completed

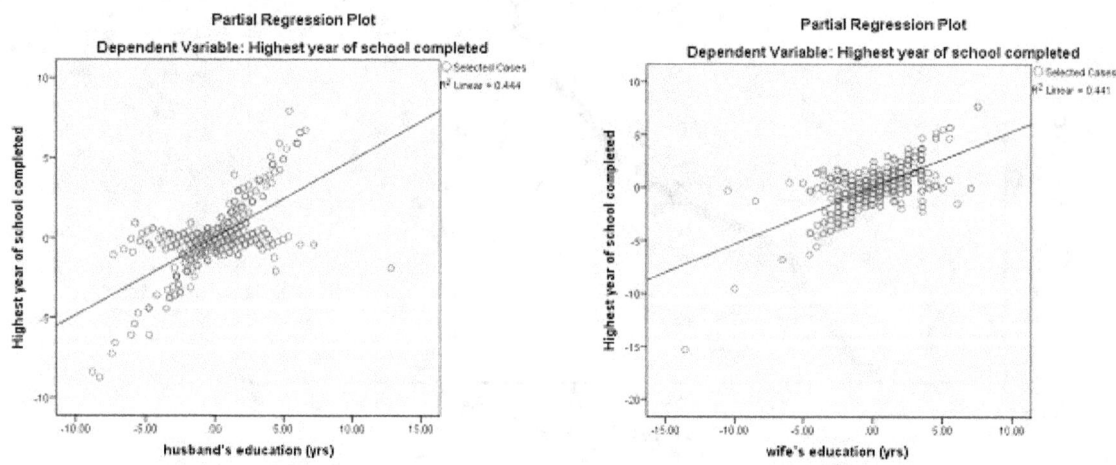

Figure 9.8. Scatterplot of Age and Education. Notice the banding effect of the data points. This can be explained by the more common educational levels typically expected across age groups (high school, community college, undergraduate, and graduate).

Figure 9.9. Partial Regression Scatterplots for Husband/Wife and Respondent Education Levels. The difference in slope of the regression lines support the hypothesis that as the education level of the respondent increases, the education level of the husband also increases faster than that of the wife of the respondent.

PART NINE REFERENCES

Adams, J. Q., & Strother-Adams, P. (2001). Dealing with Diversity: The Anthology. Dubuque, IA: Kendall/Hunt.

Eccles, J. S., Wigfield, A., & Byrnes, J. (2003). Cognitive Development in Adolescence. In I. B. Weiner, R. M. Lerner, M. A. Easterbrooks, & J. Mistry, Handbook of Psychology (Vol. 6). New York, NY: Wiley.

Field, A. (2009). Discovering Statistics Using SPSS (3rd ed.). Thousand Oaks, CA: Sage Publishing, Inc.

Halpern, D. F., Benbow, C. P., Geary, D. C., Gur, R. C., Hyde, J. S., & Gernsbacher, M. A. (2007). The Science of Sex Differences in Science and Mathematics. Psychological Science in the Public Interest (8), 1-51.

Illinois Eastern Community Colleges. (2010). Fact Book. Olney: Illinois Eastern Community Colleges.

Jodl, K. M., Michael, A., Malanchuk, O., Eccles, J. S., & Sameroff, A. (2001). Parents' Roles in Shaping Early Adolescents' Occupational Aspirations. Child Development, 72(4), 1247-1265.

Macionis, J. J. (2010). Sociology (13th ed.). Boston, MA: Prentice Hall.

National Marriage Project. (2004). The State of Our Unions 2004: The Social Health of Marriage in America. (D. Popenoe, & B. D. Whitehead, Eds.) Piscataway, NJ: Rutgers University.

Northcentral University. (2009). Education [Data file]. Retrieved from http://learners.ncu.edu/syllabus/download_file.asp?syllabus_rr_id=146587.

Papalia, D. E., Olds, S. W., & Feldman, R. D. (2009). Human Development (11th ed.). Boston, MA: McGraw-Hill.

Ripley, A. (2008, December 8). Can She Save Our Schools? Time, pp. 36-44.

* * *

ABOUT THE AUTHOR

Nick Zinni holds four degrees in interdisciplinary studies and business, including a Master's in Business Administration from Bellevue University. After serving in the U.S. Army, he followed the next two decades working the logistics industry. Nick taught psychology and sociology courses at a nearby community college for five years to aspiring nursing students before settling on a small fruit farm with his companion, Gloria.

Other Works by T. Nick Zinni

My Undergraduate Essays (eBook and Paperback available)

Coming Soon:

The Craftmaker's Ghosts

Connect with T. Nick Zinni

See my website at TNickZinni.WordPress.com

Follow on Twitter: @NzinniT

www.ingramcontent.com/pod-product-compliance
Lightning Source LLC
Chambersburg PA
CBHW081553220526
45468CB00010B/2651